MENTAL HEALTH
AND THE ECONOMY

PAPERS PRESENTED AT A
CONFERENCE CO-SPONSORED
BY
THE INSTITUTE OF LABOR AND
INDUSTRIAL RELATIONS,
THE UNIVERSITY OF MICHIGAN-
WAYNE STATE UNIVERSITY
AND
THE CENTER FOR STUDIES
OF METROPOLITAN PROBLEMS,
NATIONAL INSTITUTE OF MENTAL HEALTH

Louis A. Ferman
Jeanne P. Gordus
Editors

December 1979

The W. E. Upjohn Institute for Employment Research

D1500273

Library of Congress Cataloging in Publication Data

Conference on Mental Health and the Economy, Hunt Valley,
    Md., 1978.
    Mental health and the economy.

    1. Social psychiatry—Congresses. 2. Psychology,
Pathological—Social aspects—Congresses. 3. Psychology,
Pathological—Economic aspects—Congresses. 4. Stress
(Psychology)—Congresses. I. Ferman, Louis A.
II. Gordus, Jeanne P. III. Institute of Labor and
Industrial Relations (University of Michigan-Wayne State
University) IV. United States. National Institute of
Mental Health. Center for Studies of Metropolitan
Problems. V. Title.
RC455.C625 1978   616.8'9'071   79-25809
ISBN 0-911558-69-1

THE INSTITUTE, a nonprofit research organization, was established
on July 1, 1945. It is an activity of the W. E. Upjohn Unemployment
Trustee Corporation, which was formed in 1932 to administer a fund set
aside by the late Dr. W. E. Upjohn for the purpose of carrying on
"research into the causes and effects of unemployment and measures for
the alleviation of unemployment."

This study is for sale by the Institute at $8.50 per copy for hardcover and
$6.25 per copy for paperback. For quantity order of this publication or
any combination of Institute publications, price reductions are as
follows: 10-25 copies, 10 percent; 26-50, 15; 51-100, 20; over 100,25.

iii

FOREWORD

Social scientists from a number of disciplines have long explored the relationship between the state of the economy and the physical and mental well-being of people. During the past decade, there has been a sharp increase in attempts to identify, measure, and assess the implications of the process by which economic change and unemployment affect individual and collective mental health.

The Hunt Valley Conference provided a forum for the exchange of theories and research findings among scholars in sociology, psychology, economics, and other specific areas of applied social research. The conference papers are published by the Institute with the expectation that the publication will contribute to a clarification of the issues, a definition of new research directions, and to an informed discussion of public policy options.

The facts presented in this study and the observations and viewpoints expressed are the sole responsibility of the authors. They do not necessarily represent positions of the W. E. Upjohn Institute for Employment Research.

E. Earl Wright
Director

Kalamazoo, Michigan
December 1979

iv

PREFACE

The idea of a working conference at which those scholars whose research efforts were directed toward understanding the relationships between large-scale economic change and individual and collective mental and physical well-being would gather to share ideas, information, and insight in order to develop new research directions and policy options was first discussed in 1975. By summer 1976, planning had begun and a series of meetings was held to develop the conference agenda. Many of the authors of articles in this volume, Professors Berg, Fried, Ferman, and Kahn participated in this process. A firm commitment to the value of directed discussion suggested that those presenting formal papers should prepare these papers for distribution to all conference participants well before the meeting, which was held June 1-3, 1978 in Hunt Valley, Maryland. Meeting time would be devoted to discussion, response, and comments upon these papers. Professors Brenner, Kahn, and House took responsibility for extensive commentary upon papers presented, while Dr. Miller and Dr. Alperovitz provided summaries and new research and policy suggestions for the entire conference. The three days of intense discussion produced masses of transcribed materials and the discussion also provided impetus for the authors to revise their initial versions of the papers presented.

While, in some sense, this volume contains final versions, it is itself only an interim report on the conference at Hunt Valley. The final outcome of that conference, will, we are certain, be found in books and articles not yet completed, policies and legislation still under discussion, and research now begun as a result of the discussion and exchange at the Hunt Valley Conference.

ACKNOWLEDGEMENTS

This volume is a collection of papers and comments originally presented at the Conference on Mental Health and the Economy at Hunt Valley, Maryland in June 1978 which was co-sponsored by the Center for Studies of Metropolitan Problems of the National Institute of Mental Health and the Research Division of the Institute of Labor and Industrial Relations, The University of Michigan-Wayne State University. The editors wish to thank the authors of the papers and all participants in the conference, as well as their colleagues at the Center and the Institute. Special thanks are due Elliot Liebow, Director of the Center for Studies of Metropolitan Problems, not only for financial support for the conference but for his leadership in the planning and publication of this volume. The W. E. Upjohn Institute for Employment Research agreed to publish these proceedings and the assistance provided the editors by Dr. E. Earl Wright, Director of the Upjohn Institute, and Ms. Judith Brawer, the Institute editor, has been invaluable. Ms. Alice K. Gibson provided editorial assistance during the preparation of the manuscripts for which we thank her. To Barbara A. Zvirblis for her work particularly during the conference itself and to Gregory S. Langworthy for his assistance in the final stages of the publication process, we extend our special appreciation.

CONTENTS

1
ENRICHING THE COMPLEXITIES: PAPERS FROM THE HUNT VALLEY CONFERENCE

LOUIS A. FERMAN
JEANNE PRIAL GORDUS

The relationships between major economic change and individual distress, deviant behavior, and other symptoms of underlying pathology have long been a matter of debate and concern. Emotional illness in individuals and disorder in collective life have been associated with economic instability for centuries. Yet despite the antiquity of these perceptions and concerns, the collection, correlations, and interpretation of evidence of these connections in a scientific manner is a relatively recent development.

These modern studies have clustered chronologically during periods of economic disjunction from the foundation laid by Durkheim in 1897 through the work of Angell, Bakke, and Komarovsky during the great depression. If, in fact, the appearance of major studies in this area could be considered an indicator of widespread economic change, yet another era began with the publication of *Mental Illness and the Economy* by M. Harvey Brenner in 1973. In this study, Brenner demonstrated and described the inverse relationship between the state of the economy and mental illness by relating the fluctuations in the mental hospitalization levels and rates and fluctuations of the employment index in New York State from about 1914 to 1960. The complex processes whereby individuals are stressed to an intolerable degree by macroeconomic change and thus become visible are not amenable to such clear exposition as the major relationship that Brenner so firmly established. Those processes, how they should be conceptualized for research purposes, how they should be explored methodologically, and how these research findings can best and most efficaciously be brought into the policy development and decision making levels of government, were the central concern of The Hunt Valley Conference and of the papers in this volume.

In fact, these processes eluded precise description to the point where a shorthand term for them came into use and will appear in this collection several times: Harvey Brenner's "black box." In one sense, the black box is the space in which the connections between the macro and micro levels in economic and social large-scale change could be made. What that imaginary black box conceals from view is not only the variety of paths followed by individuals from initial economic stress to visible mental illness, but also the points along these paths where intervention could or should occur. In an effort to circumscribe the subject area and to introduce some unifying themes, one specific phenomenon among the several comprising macroeconomic change received more attention than some others: unemployment. But no sooner had that focus been established and recent research of several authors been considered than it became very clear that unemployment was too narrow an area for the development of a realistic research strategy. A more longitudinal dimension, still firmly associated with employment, was sought to parallel Brenner's work and to reflect other research, and the resulting change in emphasis is apparent as the discussion addresses the consequences of work transitions.

Although the organizers of the conference wished to assure maximum participation by all who attended and considered that a rigid structure for the conference might inhibit discussion, a general outline was gradually developed. The interchange of ideas, the gradual clarification of viewpoints, and the productive disagreements did take place, and every paper in this volume reflects the feedback from both formal and informal discussion. However, this flexibility did not obscure completely the initial guidelines and categories which were discussed, refined, and distributed to authors, and the structure of the conference is still clearly discernible in this volume.

First, it was necessary to know where research on the consequences of work transitions is at present and to use that knowledge to develop an overall framework both for the conference and for future study. It was also considered crucial that key variables in the process be identified very early in the proceedings. Although there are a variety of conceptual approaches to research on the relationship between the macroeconomy and social and psychological outcomes, three different kinds of concepts were selected for presentation, with the expectation that the papers would contain reviews of relevant literature and the results of current research within the field and outside it as well. Because of current research interests, certain variables were selected for presentation which permitted a review of work in progress across a broad spectrum of disciplines, a breadth consistently characteristic of work-transition research. Intervening variables, particularly those of current interest, were also selected, not for their timeliness alone but because they were useful in focusing on the broad issues raised by the overview, the conceptual approaches outlined earlier, as well as the conceptual and methodological issues raised by the discussion of key variables. Throughout the papers, the responses, and the discussion, emphasis was constantly placed upon the utility of certain approaches and variables in constructing research design for future study and the all-important relationship between concept formation and research methodology. The work of the conference should then be summarized from both a research and a policy perspective.

The major subdivisions in this volume reflect the structure of the conference. Ivar Berg and Michael Hughes present an overview of the concerns and issues basic to the consideration of work transitions and the respondent to this paper, M. Harvey Brenner, develops his own thesis at some length to amplify their presentation.

The second major section consists of three papers, each of which presents a possible conceptual framework in which these concerns have been or should be studied. These approaches differ in some respects one from the other, but they complement rather than contradict each other. While Caplan emphasizes person-environment fit, Fried relies heavily on role theory, and Ferman and Gardner underline the importance of economic deprivation in adjustment or maladjustment to work transitions, these explanatory schemes reinforce each other at certain points, as Robert Kahn indicates in his summary in which he underlines the concerns of these authors and relates them to the larger questions raised earlier.

Current emphasis on stress as a major conceptual and methodological tool suggested that this important variable be given broad coverage. The third section of this volume considers stress in the physiological, psychological, and social spheres in the papers by Curtis, Kasl and Cobb, and Marris. The task of relating these very different studies, undertaken by James House, was undoubtedly difficult, but the identification of common themes across such disciplinary chasms is most provocative.

In the fourth section of this volume, Catalano and Dooley report research results which support Brenner's findings that behavioral disorders are associated with prior macroeconomic change, while the Liems present a study in which social support is considered as an important personal and social intervening variable which can influence significantly the psychological and social distress associated with such economic change.

In the final section of this book, three commentators return to the broad concerns which provide the rationale for this conference. Joseph Blasi reviews recent legislative initiatives concerned with preventing catastrophic unemployment and provides a dramatic illustration of how research and policy are related. What issues need further investigations, how such questions might be framed, and how the answers might best be sought by researchers is set forth by S. M. Miller. In a companion piece, Gar Alperovitz discusses in detail the policy options and strategies now under consideration and what the future may hold. Throughout the papers, and particularly in the discussion and comment papers of Brenner, Kahn, and House, it will be obvious that the participants in the conference other than those presenting papers contributed significantly to the development of new formulations and insights. Unfortunately, even a drastically edited transcript amounts to several hundred pages. It is hoped that most of the important points discussed are covered by the papers, the comments and summaries, and the introduction.

The first selection places the social and psychological dimensions of work transitions in a broad context, with the result that some of the fundamental assumptions underlying current research are identified explicitly and questioned. Ivar Berg and Michael Hughes note that the approach they call "sociogenic," is only one way in which these questions can be phrased and these problems understood. This focus promotes a research design in which the mental health consequences of economic and employment experience are traced, providing policy directions in which the emphasis is upon actions taken to stabilize or reform some portion of the economy in order to improve health and well-being. Indeed, another entire genre of research understands the physical and mental conditions of populations to be studied, not as consequences of economic experiences, but as one, or one of a number of "causes" of unfortunate labor market experiences or unpleasant working conditions. In fact, this division between the notion of "social causation" on the one side and "social selection" on the other has been much argued and seems nearly as far from resolution as ever. Berg and Hughes favor a conceptual approach which combines these two in a compromise conceptualization which they call an "interactive" approach, admittedly more difficult, more complex, but ultimately more likely to reveal new and important understanding of the processes and variables between macroeconomic change and individual outcomes. In an exemplary attempt to address the whole range of research concerns, Berg and Hughes review a broad spectrum of research efforts, not only to support their proposed "interactive" conceptualization, but to suggest strategies whereby the utility of data already gathered might be optimized through secondary analysis. Such research might well supplement and clarify Brenner's work which is based upon archival evidence, a type of evidence which has limited value for analyzing processes.

6

The response to this overview given by M. Harvey Brenner became more than a simple comment as it moved from conceptual problems in these sorts of studies to methodological difficulties. While Dr. Brenner agreed that it would indeed be desirable if a model could be developed as a result of these discussions, he points out that, given the complexity of the problem, such hopes are probably doomed to disappointment. No one discipline is equipped methodologically or conceptually to probe more than a specific area of the relationship between the macroeconomy and individual and collective well-being. Moreover, the several approaches taken by each of the disciplines involved in these investigations are, because of the nature of the inquiry, different and therefore difficult, if not impossible, to reconcile to the point where a single model or a framework can be constructed. In fact, as Brenner points out, the fact that the social and psychological consequences of one macroeconomic change may very well provide a set of microeconomic decisions which subsequently have a secondary and important impact upon the economy, complicates the problem further. While this point is made by Brenner for reasons other than those stated by Berg and Hughes, it is clear that some sort of interactive system, rather than a simple social causation or social selection explanation, is desirable. What Brenner cites as particularly difficult conceptually and method-ologically is the fact that virtually none of the terms used—"health" for example—is a unitary concept and that the terms may be misused or misconstrued so as to obscure a situation where social selection prevails rather than social causation. Indeed, an important ingredient in refining our understanding of the American economy and American mental health and the interactions between them, should be studies in other societies, for we do not now clearly see what phenomena may be only American. While Brenner suggests new and significant directions which should be taken in the broad area of social systems research, he also makes a strong case for specific work dealing with short term downturns and a series of different kinds of studies on the consequences of economic development in specific areas. This suggestion anticipates a number of points to be made by later authors and throughout the discussion. For individuals and groups, is it change and mobility, whether positive or negative, which is critical? If individuals can adapt to the change readily—and as Kasl and Cobb as well as Ferman and Gardner indicate, some do—is it only individuals at risk who suffer? If that is the case, what reduces risk for individuals or groups? What approaches to these problems are available?

The second section of the conference was devoted to three possible conceptual approaches to the problems presented by all those intervening variables between economic change and mental illness.

Robert Caplan, responding to the conference organizers' interest in how individuals cope with economic change, has developed in his study a conceptual framework in which social support is defined as a result of an extensive review and evaluation of the definitions already available in a broad range of scholarly literature. Caplan then hypothesizes how social support relates to individuals' perceptions of their environment as well as their own capacities and abilities, the motivations of individuals, their physical and mental health and well-being, and the objective environmental resources available. This conceptualization is rich and relatively elaborate, and clearly has the capacity for explaining a great deal about the processes intervening between large-scale economic change and individual coping and adaptation. Further, it seems that some of Caplan's untested hypotheses could be validated or reformulated through some of the secondary analyses suggested by Berg and Hughes.

Marc Fried emphasizes individual responses to economic change also, but from a very different perspective. The initial impact of job loss, for example, occurs at the level of role activities and job loss may mean not only a loss of role functions but a loss of role completely. This formulation has the virtue of providing an orderly analysis of how work role changes for one person impinge on family and community through role change and role loss, while attaching considerable importance to changes in individual's financial resources. Moreover, since Fried's use of role theory relies heavily upon the concept of equilibrium among individuals' roles, the problem of short term versus long term unemployment is underlined in this conceptualization.

This theme is picked up and amplified in the paper presented by Ferman and Gardner in which they present a simple schematic understanding of the "black box" and then proceed to people this unknown territory with types of work careers and mental health outcomes. Drawing upon theoretical and empirical studies, Ferman and Gardner propose a conceptualization in which different types of employment experiences and different strategies for coping with upward or downward mobility are combined to produce a series of typical work histories with associated typical mental health outcomes. Some of the concerns expressed by both Fried and Caplan are contained in this formulation, but the emphasis is more economic, more closely associated with labor market experience, than either of the other theoretical approaches offered.

These three major formulations do more than simply point to strategies for further research. They do more than simply complement and supplement each other. They elaborate the fundamental questions raised earlier about whether change itself—the rapidity with which it occurs, the resources available to those who must cope with it, the specific way in which it strikes different groups, and how long it continues—may not be the culprit whether or not the specific macroeconomic change is, in itself, positive or negative. In many respects, as Robert Kahn indicates, these papers respond to the issues raised by Berg and Hughes as well as Brenner, not by simplifying for the sake of tidy research design, but by enriching the complexities for the sake of capturing the intricate realities of the psychological and social consequences of economic change.

Perhaps one of the most significant aspects of the Hunt Valley Conference and of this volume is the emphasis placed upon stress as a crucial factor in explaining how individuals respond to stimuli, physiologically and psychologically, and how both individuals and institutions respond and thereby interact with each other under stressful circumstances. The three major papers which concentrate upon stress, Dr. George Curtis on the psychophysiology of stress, Professors Kasl and Cobb on the stress-related mental health consequences of job loss, and Peter Marris on the relationships of stress to several deeply ambivalent currents in the American belief system, are strikingly dissimilar in style, approach, and conclusions. No more dramatic way of demonstrating the vast array of overlapping definitions of stress commonly used could have been devised, although no such McLuhanish intention occurred to anyone. Dr. Curtis' paper serves notice that no organism on any level is exempt from stress and its consequences. At the same time, the dangers of moving too simply, too quickly, and too carelessly from a biological system to a social system in the case of stress-related research are clearly and simply stated while it is also made plain that stress must be regarded as something more than simple stimulus. In concluding his paper, Dr. Curtis suggests that, at the very least, stress, to be a useful concept, must be redefined in a more realistic manner which includes change, both positive and negative, and permits the concept of stress to include a feedback system. At this basic biological level, Dr. Curtis suggests something which echoes the remarks of Berg and Hughes as they presented their case for an "interactive" rather than either a "social causation" or "social selection" approach.

The second paper in this section is based upon a longitudinal research study which can already, without exaggeration, be called a classic study of the consequences of unemployment, whether short term or prolonged, re-employment and other work transitions. Once again, common themes are elaborated as Kasl and Cobb attempt to analyze how individuals were affected by job loss. Although significant variation occurred between rural and urban workers and their responses to work transitions, the outcomes were also influenced significantly by the levels of social support these unemployed men experienced. The importance of relative economic deprivation, identified by Ferman not only in his paper at this conference but also in his work on plant closings over a decade ago, is emphasized by Kasl and Cobb. At the same time, they also underline an important point which did not receive much attention at the conference. Their findings, that middle-aged blue collar workers experienced less distress at loss of the work role than might have been expected, suggest that results which show that negative mental health outcomes related to unfulfilling work should always be considered in any studies analyzing the responses to work transitions.

Extracting and communicating the meaning of significant human experience is the theme of Peter Marris' paper in which the endemic stressful relationships between individuals and societies are considered. The importance of the constant interactions between persons and institutions and how stresses are generated and transformed in these processes is the central issue for Marris just as, in a very different disciplinary perspective, it is for Berg and Hughes. How to communicate the meaning of these interactive processes is a crucial point for Marris because only through effective communication of this meaning can appropriate intervention and policy change be accomplished, a point of view echoed later by Gar Alperovitz.

David Dooley and Ralph Catalano's paper with which the fourth section of this volume begins, focuses once more on the correlation between macroeconomic phenomena and individual mental health outcomes as measured by admissions to treatment facilities. In general, this research confirms Brenner's work which had been questioned in several respects. Dooley and Catalano do suggest that those same economic changes which may correctly, in many instances, be associated with admissions to hospitals, might also complicate problems faced by those who wish to study such relationships more closely. For example, in a community with a shrinking economy, persons might be labeled deviant and denied roles and resources which would be available to them in an expanding and "undermanned" economy. For Dooley and Catalano, the black box, the site of all these intervening variables, is the area still requiring explanation. Their study was not designed to identify many of these variables, nor especially to discriminate between two theses. Does economic change provoke behavioral disorder? Or does economic change uncover behavioral disorder? Where and how intervention is targeted depends on which of these hypotheses is correct, and it is clear that a study designed to discriminate between them is needed. But, once again, this distinction is not completely new to us because it is a specification of those two separate schools of thought described by Berg and Hughes, "social causation" or "social selection."

Joan and Ramsay Liem, returning to two important elements of the conference agenda, stress and social support, relate them to one another and demonstrate the dangers of simplicity. Just as Catalano and Dooley show that the economy can, through other actions, complicate the problems of discovering one consequence of economic change, so social support, considered as a buffer between economic distress and individual health, can carry with it costs which are expressed in terms of increased stress. But their emphasis, that social support is not only an individual resource but a distributed social commodity, points toward intervention and policy development by noting that where individual social support resources are sparse and structured inequities fall hardest, there socially distributed support is most needed.

The concluding section of this book begins with a brief paper by Joseph Blasi in which he details the legislative developments in one area of strategy aimed at reducing the incidence of economic disjunction, the federal support of employee-owned business and industry. Here too complexities are apparent as proposed bills traverse the thickets of committees, subcommittees, House-Senate conferences, and federal agencies. But connections are clear here too, especially between research and policy formation. Indeed, such close productive interactions are probably rare but they are a pattern available for emulation.

Professor Miller, charged with the responsibility of summarizing the conference, might well have chosen to adopt a valedictory tone and approach. Instead, he viewed The Hunt Valley Conference as an appropriate place to stop briefly, review the past, and assess present efforts while pushing toward future research and action. Once again, the angle of approach reveals not just another side of the issue, but perhaps an entirely new set of issues. Which of two possible paths will ultimately be chosen for the American economy during the remainder of this century and perhaps well beyond it? Will contraction and concern for quality rather than growth and the need for quantity dominate decision making? Or will the thrust of the future be toward what Miller has called "the recapitalization of capitalism," an era in which new and massive investment is made to increase American productivity and to achieve a favorable balance of trade once more? With some misgivings, Miller sees the emergence of this new era of capitalism and in that context the human and social costs of these economic development strategies are considered. The prospect of a future such as this makes the development of new ideas and research even more urgent, but Miller makes a special point of emphasizing that the meaning of stress and change, in human terms as Peter Marris has discussed it, will become more and more critical in the future.

Gar Alperovitz sees the immediate future in similar terms, and his vision is a dark one. There is little chance that industrial capitalism can be renewed, even if that were desirable, Alperovitz asserts. Undoubtedly, attempts to do again what Americans have been so successful at doing before will be made, because of the function of history in social and economic processes. We remember the future, and remembering the future has worked, at least for some in the past. But at this time when America is faced for the first time with real scarcity, such repetition of inappropriate responses will not work at all. In an argument which seems based upon an implicit notion that human gratification is conserved just as energy is in thermodynamic formulations, Alperovitz sees that psychological satisfaction may substitute for consumer goods in a new balance where workers have more responsibility in their jobs and citizens more decision-making power over their economy.

In some sense, this collection of papers reflects not only the structure of the conference but its process as well. No participant came away satisfied. Those whose work is methodologically most sophisticated concerned themselves, some for the first time, with major assumptions underlying research efforts. Others emphasizing at first the appropriate forms of research and presentation styles most likely to appeal to public policy makers, came to consider the ambiguities within the many seemingly simple terms used in research as subjects of serious concern in themselves. One or another key variable or intervening variable receded in the discussion from its previous place of importance, while others emerged as more crucial to future understanding. The contextual variables, particularly the new and poorly understood American "economies," assumed new dimensions.

The work undertaken by all the participants in The Hunt Valley Conference is evident in the papers and discussions presented here. But this volume is simply an interim report. Future research, future policy, and a future which, at least in the area of mental health and the economy, is invented and not just remembered will be the final report from Hunt Valley.

2
ECONOMIC CIRCUMSTANCES
AND THE ENTANGLING WEB
OF PATHOLOGIES: AN ESQUISSE

IVAR BERG[1]
MICHAEL HUGHES

The central theme of this paper, a slightly more elaborate version of that presented originally at the symposium covered by this volume, derives its inspiration from two articles appearing in the first and second sections, respectively, of the *Detroit Free Press* for August 26, 1976. In the first article the newspaper's labor editor reported relevant social science findings under the descriptive headline: "Job Layoffs Can Make Workers Sick." In the second, the science editor presented the first of a series of articles on social scientists' studies of the mental health of employed Americans. His equally descriptive headline was: "Work is the Most Common Cause of Tension Today." At the end of this article there appears, in boxed boldface type, a bit of cynical advice to readers afflicted with the disorders related to joblessness that had been itemized in the first article: "Tuesday:" it reads, "Learn to Love Leisure."

These two popular news items, while not nearly so well footnoted or rigorously reasoned as were the critical studies from which the journalists borrowed, offer a sort of paradigmatic summary of the state of present scientific efforts and the critical differences among them which our symposium's contributors must take into account. Consider that most of this work may, with only a slight simplification, be divided into nearly separated sciences.

First, scientists have sought to trace the implications for mental and physical well-being of economic circumstances—social

15

economic background, income, employment experience—as applied to people of different demographic and personal characteristics. A considerable literature has thus grown up around one dimension of what may be called a sociogenic version of the problem before the symposium. Many of the contributors to this literature hope that the lessons to be learned from their investigations may ultimately be taught to those policy makers concerned with reliable estimates of the benefits and costs either of preserving the economic status quo or of introducing sundry public and private reforms, targeted on the economy, to improve health, generate productivity, and make society more equitable. A title by Brenner, cited later, is revealing: "Estimating the Social Costs of Economic Policy: Implications for Mental and Physical Health, and Criminal Aggression."

Investigators in a second stream of research efforts subscribe to one or another version of what is commonly called the drift hypothesis. They generally bypass the concerns and efforts of the first group in favor of research designs in which the mental and physical circumstances of their subjects or population groups are taken to be essentially given; or else to be among the critical "first causes" of observed variations among respondents who drift, therefore, into their labor market experiences, their incomes or social status, and, in a few instances, their working conditions. Rarely do the two streams of research, amounting to separate schools of thought, run together. With few exceptions,[2] investigators in one school either omit references in their reports to the others' works, or they praise such work with faint damns.

It is our purpose here to review a few of the vexing issues in the subject area of the conference. We will urge that an effective effort to join these issues demands research designs whose dimensions are delineated with an eye to the limitations as well as to the strengths of the impressive empirical efforts made by investigators of each school, and to their differing findings as well. It will become clear that we are more disposed to an interaction model than to the linear models generally employed by these schools, as we understand them. As we shall see, we also agree with Rushing that there is abundant room for further incorporation of sociomedical materials into model-building efforts. These materials bear in particularly relevant ways on the accesses of different socioeconomic groups to quality health care. The incorporation of these materials will help, in ways sociopsychiatric materials cannot, to clarify the role of economic conditions and circumstances in both inter- and intragenerational studies of health and illness.

In Part I of this paper, we identify several conceptual axes of loci along which a sample of our illustrative investigations has been organized. The reader should bear these axes in mind, because they cut across what we later identify as several distinguishable research modalities; we turn to the identification of these in Part II. We have been led to construct a preliminary matrix-like schema which may be useful in helping to organize and distill the materials presented by the symposium's contributors. We see this matrix as a general ordering device as well, useful in helping us to recognize the difficulties that are involved in making informed evaluations of the policy implications either of reforms or of programmatic meliorations targeted upon the structure and functioning of the economy. Finally, in Part III, we commend systematic studies of a contrived age cohort, born between the Second World War and the late years of the great depression, through secondary analyses of a mass of survey and survey-like data. Studies conducted in accord with such a schematic outline would, we suggest, aid in a clearer perception of the interaction among the social, psychological, and perhaps genetic "causes" operating in the rows and columns of data in others' discrete studies, differentiated in accord with the horizontal and vertical headings and subheadings of the matrix described in Part II.

PART I: CONCEPTUAL AXES

Social Causation Versus "Drift"

A basic difference in the conceptualizations employed in the broad area of our concern involves, as we have already suggested, a choice between the studying economic factors essentially as independent or as dependent variables.

For some researchers, employment experiences, job exposures, social status, and income receipts (the most typical of the economic factors under examination) are independent variables impacting upon health; for others the causal process is deemed to operate in quite the reverse order. Among those sociologists who pursue research in this realm, the intellectual perspectives underlying investigative choice borrow from one side or the other of a theoretical controversy over "social causation" and "social selection."

That the theoretical and therefore the conceptual and methodological issues involved are both lively and controversial is evident in a recent issue of the *American Sociological Review,* in which the authors of successive articles reach diametrically opposite conclusions about causes and effects. In the first one, Turner and Gartrell[3] conclude from their studies that their lower "social competence" combines with or reinforces psychopathological tendencies in certain individuals, such that citizens of lower social competence are disproportionally likely to occupy low or undesirable social statuses. Social competence is defined as the individuals' level of psychosocial development, which they capture in mensurational terms in an index based on the marital status, occupational level, educational achievement, and work performance of certain subjects and respondents. Their conclusion is that social selection processes are quite evidently involved in shaping the paths of many of those who ultimately suffer adverse economic circumstances, as well as psychological illnesses and distresses. In the very next article, Wheaton[4] concludes, from an analysis constructed around panel data on each of two separate populations, that the statistical relationships between socioeconomic circumstances and mental disorders are stronger, *over time,* than those obtaining between mental disorder and socioeconomic circumstances. It should also be noted that, with the exception of Rushing, in studies cited later, investigators given to the drift model gloss over differences between *inter*generational and *intra*generational mobility processes in their search for causes of illness.

The prospects are dim that a scientific resolution of the issue of cause and effect, as between social cause and selection, is soon likely to materialize. Indeed, although no less than fifteen commendable efforts have been made to review and sort out the relevant evidence regarding sociogenic and selection models in the period between 1940 and 1975, the verdict is clearly the Scottish one of no verdict. Rushing argues from persuasive evidence, however, that *both* arguments are valid "but [that] the *significance* of processes stipulated in each hypothesis may vary depending on the mental disorder. In particular, drift processes may be more important for serious disorders than for less serious disorders. Unfortunately, most studies are based on measures of single disorders . . . or else include a variety of disorders in a single measure. In addition [each of the several] different measures of socioeconomic status [used by different investigators] are not equally good indices for [conducting] tests of the two hypotheses."[5]

Eugenic and Genetic Predispositions

A second basic conceptual locus may be plotted about points in the research literature concerning the factors that predispose subjects and respondents, technically speaking, to psychological disorders or difficulties. On the one hand, such predispositions are conceived to be eugenic; on the other, they are conceived to be genetic in character.

Thus in the neo-Freudian view there are predispositions of a eugenic variety among adults who have not effectively worked through "nuclear-neurotic processes." These processes are triggered by critical experiences and by exposures in early childhood, especially during one or more of what are termed the psychosexual stages of development. These predispositions will persist; they will become more or less disabling to the extent that defense mechanisms employed by the potential victims of otherwise receding psychological backgrounds are inappropriately or "dysfunctionally" matched, over extended time periods, to interpersonal, familial, occupational, and social obligations. Room is made, at the edges of this etiological construction, for the possibility that an objectively neurotic tendency, against which a given individual's defense mechanisms are insufficiently mobilized, may have fewer untoward consequences in some occupations than in others. For example, an obsessive preoccupation with cleanliness is less likely to impede the occupational prospects and frustrate aspirations for upward social mobility among surgeons than among coke sackers in collieries or cork soakers in distilleries.

A competing modern version of an age-old, if long-neglected, view holds that predisposing factors of a more basically genetic type are significantly involved in the genesis of serious mental disorders, schizophrenia, and manic depressive psychosis in particular. This genetic view is gaining considerable ground in a number of scholarly circles, and the empirical evidence in its support is by no means unimpressive.[6] There is evidence, furthermore, that even some variations observable in the data on a few of the more clearly conceptualized neuroses may be attributable to genetic factors.[7]

Though Kringlen[8] has shown that monozygotic twins, even when reared apart, are almost always concordantly schizophrenic, the genetic argument is rarely made in strictly causal terms. Rather, proponents in this emerging literature postulate that genetic predispositions interact with social and psychological exposures and experiences in ways that generate a higher rate of mental disorders and difficulties among the "predisposed" than among others. It is perfectly reasonable to suppose that much more research will soon be undertaken in pursuit of genetic "fixes," both in direct and indirect terms, the indirect efforts involving a number of studies essentially psycho-pharmacological and neurological in character.[9] At the same time, informed studies of the correlates of psycho-therapeutic interventions are becoming more scientifically rigorous than in the past. These studies should serve to strengthen or weaken one's sense of the validities of the central axioms in respect to nuclear-neurotic processes favored in the orthodox psychoanalytical and "revisionist" versions of the eugenic model.[10] Indeed, physical-chemical, genetic, and sociobiological factors in health and illnesses either mediate or are mediated by economic and socioeconomic circumstances in research studies when their research designs are constructed in ways that provide realistic opportunities for identifying these more complex interactions, as reported in Rushing's work (in footnotes 4 and 8).

"Tis But T'aint"

A third axis of research focuses upon the part played by institutions charged with operational responsibilities for the maintenance of control in society. Indeed a school of sorts has grown up around the assertion that mental illness, as such, does not exist at all. These "labelling theorists," in company with some radical psychiatrists, thus assert that what most social scientists conventionally understand to be mental illnesses are more objectively described as "problems in living" or as "residual deviance."[11] Thus, Scheff suggests that the most important causes of "careers of social deviance" among "residual-rule breakers"[12] are the actions and reactions of the managers of institutions charged by their legislative fathers with responsibilities for maintaining social control. These careers do not result, in the first instance, from the terribly twisted intrapsychic processes of those whose behavior provokes the public and its institutionalized control agencies. According to the proponents of labelling theory, institutions charged implicitly or explicitly with the responsibility for maintaining social control react to a variety of particular behavior patterns, especially the behavior of the powerless poor, in highly normative ways, and thereby are the actors labelled. The "careers of social deviance" among "residual-rule breakers" are thus *not* the careers of those who, by some objective measure, *are* sick; rather they are the careers of those who are *defined* by institutional decision makers, holding conventional ideas about normality, as being mentally ill. These investigators may be said, with apologies to Daniel Bell, to believe in "the end of etiology." This highly relativistic view has been attacked energetically and, in the eyes of many, quite convincingly, by Walter Gove.[13]

While many are prepared to give way to Gove's highly critical assessment of labelling theorists, there are not a few scientists who still wonder about a more circumscribed but pertinent question. This question pertains to whether or not the differential resources of individuals and the differential accesses to the resources on which the social statuses of individuals are based, may not lead to differential exposures to social sanctions, quite apart from the severity of their "real" illnesses and quite apart from the labelling question. Surely, these skeptics say, there are differences in the vulnerability to social control agents between the accesses of the parents, sons, daughters, husbands and wives of the well-endowed and well-connected to physicians, attorneys, and public officials, on the one side, and those who have access only to aggressive pimps, shysters, sympathetic social workers, ward-heelers, inner-city scout leaders, or to the ministers, deacons, and Sunday school teachers in low-income parishes, on the other. Issues associated with involuntary hospitalization, for example, are thus not entirely resolved in the minds even of those who are prepared to acknowledge that many Americans are as sick by objective technical standards as by highly normative standards and definitions. Rushing, meantime, presents impressive empirical evidence in support of the proposition that those who possess few "status resources"—little education, problematical family circumstances, and marginal occupational claims—are indeed more likely than their peers with more solid status to suffer more severe social reactions. Thus, in Rushing's data, marginally situated Americans are more likely to be hospitalized, for example, if they are identified as mentally ill—which is to say, labelled as mentally ill—than others who are thus labelled but who are otherwise more favorably situated in society. As Rushing points out, the social reactions to those labelled as sick-deviant are not "universalistic," a fact that suggests a more promising line of inquiry than that suggested by the "tis but t'aint" formulation.[14] Gove and Howell,[15] and Fain[16] argue, from empirically informed exercises, that Americans suffering from psychological distresses are more likely to be treated in sensitive and supportive ways if they enjoy the economic and other resources associated with higher socioeconomic status than they otherwise would be; those who are committed to mental hospitals are likely to be suffering from more severe disorders. One is reminded, in reviewing the disputes between the more cautious labelling theorists and the most thoughtful among their antagonists, of the three baseball umpires who were discussing their guiding philosophies with a *New York Times* sports writer. "Some are balls and some are strikes," said the first umpire, "and I call them as they are. I am an objectivist." "Indeed," said the second, "some are balls and some are strikes; I call them as I see them. I am," he said with some confidence, "a subjectivist." The third umpire, an Ivy League dropout with his own highly developed sense of complexity but with the *angst* befitting his tortured academic exposures, shook his head, as Paul Tillich or Soren Kiergaard might have shaken theirs in similar circumstances, and said, "Yes, to be sure, some are strikes and some are balls; but, you see, until I call them, they are nothing, for I am an existentialist." The prospects that labelers and anti-labelers, like the conflicting umpires, will find common meeting grounds are not great. In fairness to the antagonists, it may be said that they tend to live loyally by their basically conflicting views about either the prepotent or the marginal effects of what labelers take to be the maldistribution of power in society. For the antilabelling school, psychopathology is a thing-in-itself; it is not an epiphenomenon or an artifactual by-product of the imputations and attributions of those who simply behold others' "difficulties in living." These imputations and attributions are institutionalized, as labelers see it, through the formal means and mechanisms by which social majorities induce and enforce conformity to laws, regulations, and norms. For investigators like Rushing there are important questions, as well, about the differential accesses to medical care, and to medical care of differential quality, among persons of different socioeconomic groups who, as we noted, may *also* be differentially labeled for reasons linked to socioeconomic circumstances.

Etiological Subsets of the Sociogenic Approach

There are of course a number of investigators who are prepared to allow that selection, predisposition, and the labelling inclinations of social agents be systematically taken into account in efforts to explain variations in the rates of different mental illnesses, but that sociogenic analysis are by no means thereby rendered meaningless. After all, the data presented in sociogenic accounts of mental disorders may not simply be gainsaid, nor may the questions to which these accounts point simply be begged. Once one admits that there is room for sociogenic considerations, however, one confronts the fact that etiological questions need also to be joined; indeed, the sociogenic literatures does go in several different etiological directions.

Consider that those given to sociogenic explanations often emphasize observable correlates and consequences of disruptive or "disintegrating" developments within social systems: families, neighborhoods, and especially communities. As some investigators see them, these developments combine, contrive, or conspire to produce the forms of estrangement associated with the condition first captured so vividly in Emile Durkheim's classical analyses of anomie and suicide.[17] The most celebrated modern work in this genre was published in 1938 by Faris and Dunham,[18] in which the rates for schizophrenia were reported to be highest in the disorganized center of a large city characterized by high orders of alienation, isolation, and deterioration. Myerson, and Dunham himself, have subsequently suggested that selection factors may have been confounded with sociogenic factors in the data on which this classic study was based.[19] The breakdown of social groupings has also been linked empirically to the psychological responses of American POWs in China during the Korean War,[20] of workers in Marienthal, Austria, during the great depression,[21] of Berlin Jews in German concentration camps as discussed by Bruno Bettelheim in his autobiographical writings,[22] and of a host of victims of disasters and radically uprooting experiences in studies performed by, among others, students of Alexander Leighton.[23] Some of these studies give attention to the contributing role of predisposition, mentioned above, in accounting for differences in the health of persons who shared what were, quite literally, taken to be disintegrating experiences.

A variation of this social-systemic theme is reported in studies conducted at the microlevel of analysis, though the mechanisms seen as operative are rather different. Thus, Faris has suggested that the communications of abnormal children, especially, appear incomprehensible to others because many of these children have endured relatively greater isolation; isolation, it is argued, prevents the victims from learning conventional modes of communication and conceptualization. The isolates are thereafter frozen out of meaningful interpersonal relations, a process that reinforces their isolation; the cumulative effects, Faris suggests, are thereafter embodied in the schizophrenic's psychopathological makeup.[24]

Bateson,[25] and Laing and Esterton[26] suggest that if one studies the content of the productions of schizophrenic patients, while being especially attentive to the logic they employ in them, and while informing one's analysis by detailed knowledge of the ways in which these patients have been treated by family members, the once incomprehensible content of their communications will become intelligible. Family members, then, for various reasons of their own, may literally drive certain persons mad. This fascinating idea has apparently not been an organizing one in the design of most investigations of schizophrenia, perhaps because so few persons who have been exposed to the contradictory environments contemplated by Laing and Esterton have actually become mentally ill.[27]

A somewhat more general version of this "family process" model of etiology, though it does not derive from the foregoing model, is currently attracting attention. Gove,[28] Gove and Tudor,[29] and Gove and Geerken[30] are led by empirical studies to suggest that the stresses endured in a variety of roles in modern society may contribute to their incumbents' particularly high rates of mental illnesses. Thus, while married persons are better off in this regard than single ones, women are less frequently the beneficiaries of marriage because the roles of many women as spouses *and* laborforce participants are more stressful. The more demands women confront as parents and workers, for example, the higher are their rates of mental illnesses, however these illnesses are measured. Rushing, however, in the articles cited in footnotes 4 and 8, shows that the regularly observed inverse relationship between socioeconomic status and mental health may well be due to *socio-medical* factors (e.g., class differences in accesses to quality medical care, including prenatal care) rather than to *socio-psychiatric* factors (e.g., class differences in "stress").

The Role of Precipitating Events

Another etiological conception emphasizes the impact of crises, events of life changes that become sudden psychologically threatening experiences that can bend many minds sufficiently to leave them disabled in respect to one or more vital areas of daily living. Such events may include the illnesses of others, especially in a victim's kinship group, but they can also include the paralyzing effects of guilt among the survivors of a calamity, as Eric Lindemann discovered after the tragic Coconut Grove fire in Boston,[31] or of a casualty-ridden bombing mission, a front-line combat firefight,[32] or an industrial accident. Psychopathological deterioration of persons has also been linked to their survival of a frightening and dangerous personal experience, as reported in Eli Ginzberg's massive study of *The Ineffective Soldier,*[33] and in studies of retirement.[34] Finally, catalytic events may involve a devastated victim's loss—for example, of a job, a lover, a fetus, a reputation for heterosexuality or integrity, or of a significant amount of money in a stock market crash. The possibilities encompassed by this domain are stupefyingly large. Fortunately, the quest for a defensible model that will impart theoretical order to these possibilities has been well begun; the prospects for effective research in this potentially fruitful line of inquiry appear to be promising, a judgment we base on a perusal of a well-edited volume by Dohrenwend and Dohrenwend.[35] The empirical works of Melick, Micklen and Lean, and of Eaton, further support the view that an approach to mental illness that views it as being engendered, triggered, or forced by events and crises may be valuable in pursuit of the etiological courses (and causes) of psychological disorders.[36] The vast number of potentially disabling events that can take place in any person's life and the difficulties inherent in the measurement of their different impacts on different persons point, of course, to methodological debates that have also been set in motion.[37] We may note finally that crisis cases occur too among the persons in the rows and cells of tables descriptive of those who "fall" precipitously into poverty, as opposed to those whose impoverishments are classified under the "intergenerational" rubric.[38]

We are not unimpressed by the quality of the efforts undertaken by investigators as outlined in the foregoing pages; each etiological conception appears to have been applicable to the relevant data considered. But if indeed each etiological model is applicable at least to certain readily identifiable cases, then it would be more useful to seek a theory that leaves room for these differentiated sets of findings as special cases. As matters now stand, the differentiated sets of findings, to the extent they are attended to at all, are treated by competing investigators as being contradictory or anomalous, or, in exchanges that are often heated, as being artifacts of flawed methods.

Methodological Axes

Methodological and related issues to which we have so far only alluded, meantime, merit the same considerations, for these too are among the research "axes" that concern us in this first part of our overview.

Consider that some studies, as those by Luft[39] and Brenner,[40] are organized around putatively causal factors derived from a variety of sets of aggregated data. Others, as the study of soldiers by Ginzberg[41] or of social class and mental illness by Hollingshead and Redlich,[42] are based on data that link specific physical and psychological reactions to their subjects' own background and experiences. These two approaches are not often followed simultaneously, the better to analyze aggregated data with high-order specifications of non-economic variables, whether economic circumstances are postulated as being situated at the independent or dependent ends of a causal chain.[43] One concern about even responsible aggregate analyses based on individual observations is that the exceedingly high R^2s reported by Brenner, for example, may be so high because a number of variables observed in individual data are obscured in the more parsimoniously conceived but underspecified and more comprehensive variables. Brenner, in a series of major and methodologically responsible studies of the linkages between business conditions and mental illnesses, based on aggregated data, thus admits that there is a need for further specifications of his very parsimonious model of business cycles and illnesses, especially in the face of the near-anomalies present among his findings in the extraordinarily prepotent effects of the economy on health.[44] The risks that ecological fallacies will creep into analyses of aggregated data are appreciably reduced, obviously, if the health attributes of individuals can be linked directly to their own individual experiences and to their own personal attributes.

Closely paralleling the conceptual split between aggregated and individual data-based analyses is the split between longitudinal and cross-sectional approaches. Once again, it would apparently be desirable to augment available studies by cohort and panel-type analyses. The word "apparently" is used here advisedly; such analyses help to avoid the hazards of ecological fallacies while providing grist for inter-temporal and institutional-type analyses that take account of external events and the additive (or other) effects, for example, of aging, as analytically distinguishable variables. The collection of longitudinal data is both difficult and expensive, and it has recently been argued by Davis that panel designs are not necessarily so valuable in scientific terms as they have generally been made out to be.[45] The closest we can come to addressing this problem, in view of the facts about the literature as we know them from our brief encounter, is to commend the work of Kohn and Schooler,[46] Rushing, and Luft, together with the projected results of what, in Part III, we will call a contrived cohort analysis; these studies have employed methods relevant to the disentanglement of causes from effects in longitudinal terms.[47]

Finally, there are the implications to consider for our understanding of the different conceptions of health, illness, and disability that go with the use by investigators of (1) self-reports, (2) diagnostic studies or hospital admissions, and (3) sundry paper-and-pencil scales used to obtain measures of physical and psychological well-being. We cannot reproduce here the long list of complications that accompany the use of any one of these measures. Those of us who work in universities are especially aware of the inventiveness of students and colleagues when they seek to explain why their papers are late or shoddy, and we well know that there are probably not enough hospitals to handle the spouses, siblings, parents, or grandparents whose health problems cause these students and colleagues to be absent from classes and other academic obligations. The hospitals, experience suggests, in Ft. Lauderdale, Aspen, the Bahamas, and in other popular resort centers, must be especially overburdened.

We have no reason to doubt that some Americans will meretriciously report themselves disabled, while others will report nonexistent symptoms to professional diagnosticians and therapeutic agents in proportion to the personal difficulties they have in truthfully acknowledging their circumstances—when, for example, they are out of work. Still others may defer much needed treatment for real disorders, so that major discomforts go unattended when labor markets are promisingly tight and may be brought to the psychiatrist or the proctologist only when the opportunity costs of doing so are appreciably reduced. The results, for example, of the Public Health Service's "Health Examination Survey" (in which diagnosticians perform examinations of subjects) and its "Health Interview Survey" (wherein subjects themselves are asked about the state of their health) are not encouragingly consistent across a variety of demographic categories.

The fact is that, lunar theories of mental health and seasonal theories of ulcers and suicides aside, we have only a few glimmerings of the periodicities in different forms of health status that might be plotted were we to have respondent reports uncontaminated by self-serving, defensive, income-maximizing, or other egocentric impulses. Similarly, we are able to interpret data on "disability"—self-reported or otherwise—only with considerable difficulty. One person's debilitating indisposition is another's marginally irritating inconvenience. Many supervisors and employers have marginally irritating inconveniences. And many supervisors and employers have protected drug addicts, alcoholics, and seriously disturbed staff members, the heavy-handed disposition of whose lives, for a variety of reasons, is not undertaken lightly. The problems of dealing with alcoholism, as perusal of the *Quarterly Journal of Alcohol Studies* will show, are far more serious than their neglect in scholarly explorations of mental health and the economy suggest. The senior author indeed has never, in twenty years of research, met employers faced with periodic obligations to lay off employees who do not, in the event, avail themselves of the opportunity to get ride of the problem drinkers and others with intrusive problems, in both blue- and white-collar ranks, who cannot otherwise be so readily discharged and who are not later rehired.

Whether data on disability or indisposition is self-reported or diagnosed by others, there are further problems in (1) avoiding "labelling," about which, as we noted earlier, there is now a very large body of literature; (2) identifying the objective severity of indispositions, distortions aside; (3) taking account of the precise roles of income differences in the acquisition of different types of treatment for different maladies, disorders, and afflictions (and at different stages within them). Dooley and Catalano inform the symposium's participants about this with great expertise.[48] The last of these problems is an especially interesting one because there are significant divergences in the health service consumption patterns of various groups, patterns that are increasingly influenced moreover by differential accesses to and differential uses made of third-party payment plans by persons with different "fringe" programs in occupations differentially sheltered in the primary and secondary labor markets of our so-called dual economy.

Next, studies vary in terms of sites, which is to say, in terms of whether research populations and the units of analysis derive from national probability samples, The National Health Surveys, a series of residents in different SMSAs, a community,[49] an urban neighborhood,[50] a city block,[51] a housing project, or within crowded apartments and other single dwellings.[52] It is notable that some of these studies bear upon questions of cultural impact and social control mechanisms and not just of aggregate versus individual and other methodological issues. Finally, the former questions also emerge in connection with studies that differ in their conceptualizations of relevant populations. These differences in conceptualization lead to research results that theoretically constrain their applicability, because they do not readily permit truly comparative analyses of incidence or etiology among different age groups or social classes, and so on. Cultural or "subcultural" factors, furthermore, may influence the ways in which the members of particular groups are influenced by the social environment. These issues are explored by Dohrenwend and Dohrenwend in discussions of blacks and persons of Puerto Rican background, and of urban and rural persons,[53] though the directions of cause and effect can be disputed.[54]

The conceptual and methodological issues touched upon in the first section of our paper are joined differently in different studies. Assuming that most of the results are valid as far as they go, the results, if stitched together, would reveal a series of very complex pictures. A reasonably definitive characterization of these pictures must necessarily be derived from a large number of simultaneous equations, while the stitching together would involve skills that are beyond the scope of our mandate and beyond our ken as well. In the next section we do attempt to draw a simplified version of such a picture.

PART II: SEVEN RESEARCH MODALITIES

Keeping in mind the distinctions discussed in Part I, we may move to the construction of a device that will help us to order a number of representative studies of mental health and mental illness, with special reference to the relative importance of the roles of economic conditions and economic experiences on particular research populations. We may note at the outset that we have given a good deal less attention to studies that emphasize physical-chemical, genetic, and the newer wave of sociobiological factors in health and illness than these studies, as we noted earlier, really deserve. And we have drawn very selectively from studies otherwise, for illustrative purposes only.

Though few investigators limit themselves to single conceptualizations of etiology, many have focused on one or more of the following: (A) The socioeconomic backgrounds of subjects, respondents, or sample populations, including exposures that contribute in some instances to what we earlier called eugenic predispositions; (B) The *personal economic* experiences of research populations; (C) The *personal non-economic* circumstances of research populations. These three foci are combined in a number of studies under the additional headings (A) *and* (B); (A) *and* (C); and of course, (A) *and* (B) *and* (C). In the remainder of Part II we shall present outlines of some prototypic materials reported in the literature that fall under these seven general rubrics.

A. Background and Predisposing Factors in Health

In a number of well-informed discussions, the status of adult health is traced back in ecological-demographic terms or linked empirically to personal youthful experiences, especially to family backgrounds.

Thus, Morgan has shown that many impoverished adults with disabling conditions are victims of processes that are intergenerational in character. Their illnesses can be linked statistically to their own poverty—as in cases studied under the next rubric—but the poverty and illness of a statistically disproportionate number of persons of very low income in America are strongly related to their parents' and even to their grandparents' economic miseries. Reared in families without stable economic shelters such as health benefits, unemployment insurance, educational accesses and the rest, they grow up (and age!) with highly developed vulnerabilities to health problems of all types. Working-age nonwhites, and persons with incomes under $10,000 for example,[55] have consistently higher rates of work loss due to disability than whites and persons with incomes over $10,000.[56] As late as 1972, the last year for which data are currently available, employed Americans not covered by private retirement and group health insurance plans were disproportionally nonwhite, employed in service and farm workers' jobs, and earned under $10,000.[57] Additional retrospective statistics would undoubtedly show, as Morgan's do, that disproportionally large numbers of disabled Americans who are forty-five or older were reared in families with very marginal economic resources.

Stinchcombe, Coleman, and Matza, in separate studies,[58] have linked the difficulties of young workers with childhood experiences and peer exposures that left them lacking adult role models. Merton, Ohlin and Cloward, and Parsons, again in separate discussions,[59] have posited linkages between deviant behavior and the frustrations that accompany a subject's commitment to legitimate economic ends while having only limited access to the means that best serve those ends—the so-called deviance paradigm. E. Wight Bakke, on the basis of research on the great depression, and David Potter, on the basis of a thoughtful review of others' studies, have theorized that many Americans experience psychologically crippling guilt feelings about economic reverses in their adult fortunes because their childhood experiences have left them literally unable to blame the flaws and failures in the operation of the "system" that may have contributed to their pitiable circumstances.[60] Consistent with this assessment are findings by the junior author and his collaborator, based on a preliminary analysis of survey data, that black Americans who report they have experienced discrimination have better mental health than those who do not, a finding that bears upon the possible differential effects on health of self-blame versus system blame and of feelings of self-efficacy.[61] This may conceivably be coupled with the findings of Gurin and Gurin that "People with a greater sense of personal efficacy feel *more* often that periodic inflations and recessions are inevitable . . . people who have strong feelings of personal control are more often sensitive to external systemic constraints."[62] The demographic characteristics of respondents to the Gurins' survey who are characterized as having a high sense of "personal efficacy" and of "economic control idealogy" suggest, though they do not prove, that differential background experience helps to explain the differential scores on these investigators' measures. Again, it needs to be added that demographic characteristics are also related to physical-chemical and to sociobiological factors, and that the mediating linkages are interpretable in terms that take account of socioeconomic differences (1) in societal reactions to deviance/illness, (2) in accesses to medical care, and (3) in social labelling practices.

Caplovitz has recently examined the social-psychological impacts on the essentially helpless youths of the mid-1970s whose families have been substantially victimized by "stagflation." One may reasonably anticipate that at least some of the young household members of Caplovitz's survey sample will appear similar, when they are in their mid-forties, to the members of the cohort born between 1916 and 1930, examined by Elder in 1974.[63] It is both relevant and remarkable that the first born in Elder's sample whose families were most conspicuously victimized were *better* able to cope with life overall than those whose families' wellbeing was unaffected by the great depression.

Erikson, in widely applauded clinical and nomothetic assessments that borrow only in indistinct ways from systematic findings, linked what he terms the identity crises of older adolescents in the late 1950s to a complex of circumstances that they had confronted, which were in most particulars independent of their families' economic circumstances.[64] And Knupfer correlated what she called American underdogs' psychological prospects with differences in type of punishment—physical beatings, as contrasted with the withdrawal of love by middle-class parents—accorded them in lower-income "ethnic" families.[65] Obverse observations are reported by Seeley and his colleagues in a study of an upper-middle-class community in Tornoto, where coaxing tactics and the withholding of affection are regularly employed in efforts to correct childrens' misbehavior.[66]

For Gans and Whyte, economically relevant middle-class aspirations and activities were repressed and avoided by young

Italian-Americans in Boston's old West End, in favor of attitudes and behavior patterns that their close-knit community did not regard as disloyal and threatening to norms that were highly critical of social mobility.[67] Compliance with these norms produced better health in the subjects through a communal sense of integration with their neighbors. Finally, Ginzberg reported that the psychological adaptations of U.S. soldiers to induction, garrison duty, and to either noncombat or combat exposures overseas could be readily attributed to differences in their educational achievements. Ginzberg, with his massive data file, linked these achievements, in turn, to differences in soldiers' backgrounds, regardless of whether or not the afflicted soldiers had bad preinduction encounters with psychological disorders. Preinduction encounters with psychological problems, meanwhile, accounted for slightly more than half the variance in wartime breakdowns.[68]

A thoughtful reading of the sample of representative studies cited in these passages supports the following chain of inferences: background factors are associated, in causal and predisposing (though not necessarily in wholly determinate) ways, both with classical psychological disorders as well as with an array of familiar psychosomatic ones, but by no means all those who have been similarly exposed to poverty or to job-and-marital pressures, for example—are similarly affected. Instead, those who are the most likely, in purely statistical terms, to be affected by a variety of potentially pathogenic experiences are among the healthiest and most productive members of a given cohort of a sample population, as is shown in studies by Hollingshead and Redlich of a New Haven, Connecticut sample[69] by Ginzberg and by Elder, as cited above. Gove and Brocki report, from a study in progress, that those in their sample with the worst mental health are more apt than their apparently healthy peers to report that they had unhappy childhoods, parents with drinking problems, and siblings or parents who had been treated, while the respondents lived at home, in mental hospitals.[70]

B. Personal Economic Experience and Health

In contrast with studies in which early background exposures are found to contribute to poor mental health in some persons and to predispose others to it, a second group of studies emphasizes the personal economic experience of their subjects. Much is made in these studies of "life changes," "crises" or critical events, and in general of the etiological concept of disintegration discussed in Part I. Ferman, Cobb, Slote, Sennet, and Kasl have offered vivid descriptions and detailed statistical data on the psychiatric and physiologic states of men and women cast adrift when their employers shut down the plants in which they worked.[71] Bales, in an imaginative study has described the whiskey-drenched experiences of unemployed Irish-American fathers in the 1930s, after migration and their subsequent displacement as bread-winners by the very sons—"boys" until they inherited land as mature middle-aged men—over whom they had reigned in the old country, as land-owning patriarchs.[72] And the senior author remembers reading, while a member of this symposium sponsor's Research Review Panel, an intriguing proposal, submitted by a New England scholar who had completed initial studies of the psychological malaise of those scientists and engineers who had been discharged from the Boston "Rt. 128, [the circumferential road encircling Boston] science industries" in the wake of cutbacks in space and defense-related public investments. Gove reports that similar professionals, formerly fully employed household heads, were either unhappy or happy doing house chores after their job losses, and did, or did not, have mental health problems, depending on whether they were or were not looking for new jobs.[73] Rogler and Hollingshead claim to have shown that poverty multiplied the vulnerabilities of a sample of Puerto Rican families and contributed to stressful situations that, for some, led to schizophrenia, a claim questioned on methodological grounds by Rushing (footnote 8).

Kohn and Schooler, meanwhile, in the study cited in Part I, have inventively, and in seemingly clear causal terms, documented the effect of specific, highly proximal working conditions on the degree of workers' "alienation."[74] The studies by Bakke,

Ginzberg and Elder, to which we alluded in Part I, could also be listed under this second rubric because they considered their subjects' own economic circumstances as well as those of their families of orientation and uncovered patterns like those adumbrated here.

Again, in these studies, by *no* means all those who face these hypothesized threats to health are reduced by them to mere vestiges of healthy people, or to twitching ganglia. This fact makes the visitor to this, as to other investigative areas, wonder why researchers seek so much more often to explain only the "minority phenomena"—illness, work discontent, suicide, unemployment, social mobility, and so on—when the ranges of variations to be explained are so narrow that they leave little for the independent variables (also with restricted ranges) to explain. We social scientists, one supposes, have our own version of misgivings about silent majorities in America. It needs to be added, too, that bad *conditions,* in respect to one end of a possible continuum, are so frequently associated with enough good rather than bad *outcomes* that one is left highly skeptical of linear models. Nor, incidentally, do conditions that are postulated to be good or favorable always link up with good outcomes! Thus, in a four-nation worker study by Tannenbaum and his colleagues, worker participation—a consummation devoutly wished for by many these days—was *not* linked to reduced alienation or reductions in ulcer symptoms.[75]

Findings about the basically satisfactory condition of many who have suffered from one or more economic trauma or from long term economic deprivation leads one either to be skeptical of one or another detail in a given study or to move straightaway to a modified version of Marx's "false consciousness" as an explanatory factor operative in "feigned" health reports.

C. Health and Non-Economic Experiences

A third body of literature, with the same persuasive and problematical qualities as the first two, has been built around studies of subjects' non-economic experiences. Here data on social systems' "disintegration," traumas, and crises, are juxtaposed with data on subjects' psychological and psychosomatic disorders, as in the previous body of investigations. The precipitating circumstances, long term or short term, are reported in these studies to be essentially uncorrelated with economic events, although the *resulting* health conditions are often enumerated among those that *thereafter* reduce earning capacities, undermine work-relevant skills or habits, and reduce subjects' tolerances for the obligations facing them in their workplaces.

Though this literature is heavy with neo-Freudian formulations, it is well populated by Lewinian field theorists and ego psychologists who are disinclined to see traumas in adult life only as triggering or precipitating mechanisms for the putatively more important repressed, complex-generating experiences of the first seven to ten years of life. Thus, enlisted POWs in the Korean War who collaborated with the enemy by engaging in what the POWs called "making out" behavior had difficulty in keeping faith with the patriotic fervor relished in the preachments of *The Readers Digest* because their captors systematically disrupted those POW groups that might otherwise have helped the soldiers to mobilize their fragile psychological-patriotic resources.[76] A number of Ginzberg's World War II soldiers, who otherwise exhibited statistically reassuring traits, had breakdowns that were actually specific to differing military assignments.[77] And Stouffer and associates' World War II soldiers were found to be better off if they could fall back on psychological resources significantly strengthened by well-developed linkages to primary groups, in contrast to soldiers with fewer primary group ties.[78] Stouffer's findings were essentially replicated, in more or less clinical terms, by General S.L.A. Marshall and, in Vietnam, in a Russell Sage study.[79]

Erikson and D.J. Levinson have argued and demonstrated, respectively, that identity crises among the young (Erikson) and what we may call "non-entity crises" among adults (D.J. Levinson, with references to crises at several stages of what he calls "Middlessence") can have longer or shorter term crippling effects; neither investigation makes much of economic circumstances per se. D.J. Levinson (and H. Levinson, elsewhere)[80] emphasize the effects of career plateauing, loss of parents, siblings and spouses, the departure of children, a certain boredom with spouses, and a frightening reduction in sexual appetites, as among the crucial noneconomic experiences in middlessence, a term with a clear biological ring. These experiences often produce reactions marked by the almost compulsive assertion of "ego strength," by the dissolution of super-egos in alcohol, by madcap love affairs and other irrepressible urges to engage in physical exercise beyond safe limits, and in other activities that have been the subjects of films, TV dramas, and family-section newspaper columns. In more ideologically slanted efforts, righteous investigators blame the unacceptably "sick" behavior they observe among socially critical and radical young adults upon the indulgent ways of too-liberal parents, as in Midge Decter's assaults on affluent middle-class protestors whose behavior has sorely offended her and many others.[81] The fact that the subjects of Erikson's, Levinson's, and Decter's analyses are typically neither physically disabled nor psychotic merely highlights the width of the range of conditions considered in the vast literature that concerns us. One of the problems we face in our symposium is that this range is so wide that it leaves us in doubt as to what it is exactly about health that needs to be measured and whether, as we have already noted, the health variable that emerges is conceived to be an independent, intervening, or dependent one. The same may be said, by the way, of economic and non-economic variables; the terms, as we hope we have made clear, cover a great variety of exposures and experiences. The senior author has, parenthetically, always advised his students that they can work fairly promisingly with loosely conceived independent *or* dependent variables, but that major problems confront the scientist who works with loosely conceived independent *and* dependent variables. In the research problems that concern us here the advice needs modification in part because the dependent variables are likely to be heterogeneous with respect to the independent variables; as Rushing warns, different types of mental illness/deviance, as dependent variables, are likely to be related in different ways to different aspects of a variety of the components of the independent "economic" variables (see footnotes 4 and 8).

D. Health and the "Residual" Research Modalities

There is a need, but neither the space and time nor the resources available, to conduct a detailed review of the studies in which the approaches, A, B, and C, outlined in the three foregoing sections, are combined, though a few suggestive ones may be mentioned in passing.[82]

Liebow has provided us with a penetrating case study of a small but archetypical sample of low-income American blacks[83] whose participation in everyday strife is colored by both their background experience and their own current economic circumstances (A and B). A number of Elder's cases of "depression children," Merton's "deviants," Sorbin's "working poor,"[84] Goodwin's frustrated, unemployed poor-who-want-to-work,[85] Wilensky and Edwards' "skidders,"[86] and Morgan's downwardly mobile and disabled household heads also fit, unhappily one expects, under this heading.[87]

Catalano, Ginzberg (in studies of talented women, this time),[88] and Glass are among those who have written of subjects whose background experiences and current non-economic conditions (A and C) have conspired to produce varying orders of disability. Glass, a military psychologist, has shown that the psychological breakdowns, and even the combat injuries, that occurred among U.S. troops in Korea had a distinctly temporal dimension:[89] the "number of combat days which can be endured" in World War II and in the Korean War were different, and this was statistically dependent in the aggregate upon what individuals in each war came to believe was expected of them. The length of combat assignments was shortened during the Korean War by general order, and the breakdowns and combat injuries occurred earlier and earlier as time passed, in accordance with what Glass (and some of the rest of us, in those horrible days) called the "short-timer's syndrome."

The reader may be assured, finally, that studies could also be cited of some subjects whose own economic *and* non-economic experiences, independent of background (B and C), and others whose backgrounds, economic and non-economic experiences together (A and B and C) combined to contribute to sundry types of disorders; limitations of space compel us to skip over these permutations.

The findings discussed in Part II cannot readily be gainsaid; they are, after all, part of a large and accumulating body of evidence of special cases for which an adequate theory of health would have to suggest a satisfactory accounting. Such a theory would also have to be constructed with one eye to the problems inherent in each of the conceptual issues rehearsed in Part I, and with the other eye to methodological issues.

Before we proceed to the remaining segments of our preliminary overview, it is useful to remember that there is a fairly substantial literature targeted upon the empirical correlates of what may broadly be called interventions. Under this heading we would include studies in which investigators have considered how both public and private economic and non-economic programs aimed to serve them have actually helped a variety of subjects; the causes of ill health may apparently thus be tempered in ways that are not made clear in gross, i.e., "underspecified," models.

Among the studies are: Goodwin's assessment of manpower programs (which delayed but ultimately did not forever forestall the psychological despair of unemployed youths and their parents);[90] Ferman's study, currently in progress in Ann Arbor, of support systems in neighborhoods and communities; studies of union leaders' efforts in Chester, Pennsylvania, to help the hapless victims of the relocation of a manufacturing plant; Matza's current study of the long term impact on longshoremen of the novel "Mechanization and Modernization Agreement" of 1965, an agreement designed to help ease the effects of technological change on the West Coast docks; studies of the roles and efficacies of different types of transfer payments; and, finally, studies by Strumpel and others, including the Gurins, of factors associated with subjects' differential capacities to mobilize their senses of personal efficacy and to order their expectations in workably realistic ways, in a world in which "opportunity structures" are more than a little problematical.[91] Above and beyond the stresses, frustrations, and disappointments noted in these studies are also the differences in accesses of different groups' members to preventive or remedial medical and psychiatric care that may be implicated in statistics on illness and deviance.

Additional studies—of the effectiveness of credit counseling, of community mental health programs, of flood relief agencies, of visiting nurse programs, of child-care programs, of relief and welfare agencies, and of community action programs aimed at providing care, money, treatment, advice, or hope—need also to be considered if we are to construct the axiomatic elements of a purposeful theory that will place economic and non-economic factors in health in proper perspective. Critical sample questions would be under what conditions are either therapeutic or institutional-economic interventions of different types most successful in giving hope to self-blamers versus system-blamers in a society in which so incredibly much has been made of ethical imperatives, personal pride, and so on? And, anyway, does better health care reduce the apparent differences in the well-being of *both* self-blamers and system-blamers?

E. A "First Order Synthesis"

The following matrix is descriptive of the studies (non-sociobiological, non-generic, and non-physical/chemical) sampled in the foregoing discussion.

The Economy, Non-Economic Factors and Health: In Quest of Specifications

Type A:

I. Background Factors and Predispositions:

For example:
1. Poverty at home
2. Unstable income, job loss, etc. (including "skidding")
3. Disintegration of family (including divorce)
4. Community disintegration
5. Child-rearing practices
6. Migration, etc.
N. Etc.

II. Effects/Correlates Using:

1. Employment data
2. Income data
3. Working experience data
4. Mental illness
   a. Low severity %
   n. High severity %

Type B:

I. Subjects' Own Economic Experiences:

For example:
1. Poverty
2. Status loss
3. Periodic unemployment
4. Job loss and readjustment
5. Nisei experiences
6. Depression breadwinner
7. Legal problems (including bankruptcy, liability suits)
N. Etc.

II. Effects/Correlates Using:

1. Employment data
2. Income data
3. Working experience data
4. Mental illness
   a. Low severity %
   n. High severity %

Type C:

I. Subjects' Own Non-Economic Experiences:

For example:
1. Illness, including family members
2. Disability
3. Spouse abuse (including desertion)
4. Military service
5. Weakened coping mechanisms
6. Life-cycle adjustments
7. "Drift"
N. Etc.

II. Effects/Correlates Using:

1. Employment data
2. Income data
3. Working experience data

Type A:

5. Physical illness
   a. Low severity %
   n. High severity %
6. Mental Health
   a. Low severity %
   n. High severity %

III. Effects of Interventions and Support Systems:

1. Family
2. Neighborhood
3. Therapists
4. Welfare, etc.
N. Etc.

Type B:

5. Physical illness
   a. Low severity %
   n. High severity %
6. Mental Health
   a. Low severity %
   n. High severity %

III. Effects of Interventions and Support Systems:

1. Family
2. Neighborhood
3. Therapists
4. Welfare, etc.
N. Etc.

Type C:

4. Mental illness
   a. Low severity %
   n. High severity %
5. Physical illness
   a. Low severity %
   n. High severity %
6. Mental Health
   a. Low severity %
   n. High severity %

III. Effects of Interventions and Support Systems:

1. Family
2. Neighborhood
3. Therapists
4. Welfare, etc.
N. Etc.

Type A & B

I. Background factors/predispositions *and* subjects' own economic experiences:

1. Poverty in youth *and* job loss in own career.

2. Unstable family in youth and alienating work.

Etc.

[See Col. A and B]

Type A & B & C

(Types A, B, & C *combined*)

1. Child abuse *and* unemployment *and* divorce.

2. Disintegrated community in youth *and* military trauma *and* job loss.

Etc.

[See Col. A and B and C]

Type A & C

I. Background factors/predispositions *and* subjects' own economic experiences:

1. Disintegrated family life *and* divorce in adult life.

2. Child-rearing terrors and spouse abuse.

Etc.

[See Col. A and C]

Type B & C

I. Subjects' own economic experiences *and* subjects' own non-economic experiences:

1. Job loss and divorce.

2. Status loss and military service trauma.

Etc.

[See Col. B and C]

PART III: TOWARD COHORT-PANEL ANALYSES

Having considered studies of health in conceptual terms and in terms of what might be construed as an interaction approach, we suggest, in this third, final (and mercifully brief) part of our discussion, that it would be worthwhile to examine the health reports by and about the age cohort now 45 to 55 years of age, a cohort that includes a fair number of our symposium's principals. Such an examination, we suggest, would be persuasive of the need for (and provide some hints concerning) a more elaborate set of specifications than were built, for example, into Brenner's admirable path-breaking, but underspecified, efforts. We may describe the task as a "contrived cohort" analysis; it requires that all relevant information on health, backgrounds, and experiences be extracted from all reasonably rigorous studies of this age group, in its different age steps.

One might begin by looking at this cohort's childhood experiences through the eyes of E. Wight Bakke; then through those of the interviewers who provided the raw (Berkeley) data for Elder's work on depression children; then through the eyes of the Chicago sociologists who did field studies in the 1930s, and so on, while controlling for class, ethnic and other attributes, as the data on these attributes are available. Next, one might look at the studies by the Lynds and others of adolescents and young adults in the 1930s, when our contrived cohort's members entered the labor market. Third, one might examine the wartime experiences of this cohort in the comprehensive studies reported by Ginzberg, cited earlier, and by Stouffer and his associates in the now classic study of the *American Soldier.*

Fourth, one might like to consider systematic survey data, from 1945 to 1975, on the attitudes, the reactions to work, the employment experiences, and the mental health scale scores for our age cohort. Such an effort could proceed along the lines staked out by Quinn and his colleagues in their fine distillation of so-called marginals from a dozen work-satisfaction studies conducted between 1945 and 1973 and presented in a report for the Department of Labor.[92] These surveys—Roper, Gallup, Harris,

NORC and ISR—are now sufficiently numerous to enable an investigator (with a staff the size of Stouffer's in the Second World War!) to plot concomitant variations among many of the critical variables discussed in these pages, on what would be fairly close to an annual basis—close enough, therefore, to make crude estimates of the putative effects of the major economic and non-economic events covered by this long period. The latest studies to which we have been exposed—for example, Gurin's Pre- and Post-1972 Election Surveys, the Quality of American Life Survey (1973), and the 1977 Quality of Employment Survey—are simply loaded with relevant data.[93] One specific advantage of such an effort would be that we could move, if only crudely, from exclusive trend data to data on individuals, while controlling for individual traits and attributes. We would thus avoid what Brenner, for example, well recognizes as one of the major studies of the symposium's subject: the vexing problems inherent in straightforward time series analyses. While not every survey of the type we have in mind touches *all* the interesting and relevant issues, there are sufficient overlaps to make inventive estimates possible as to the concomitants among some economic, some non-economic, and some health measures.[94] The senior author has always been more taken with efforts to examine the cumulative weight of many "social facts" than with what he willingly concedes are more respectable, rigorously intensive studies of a few variables, most of which are necessarily studied by indirect means, through the use of surrogate measures, and so on.

Next, one might wish to look at the data files of D.J. Levinson and others on the 45- to 55-year-olds, involving the "middle-aging" phenomenon, and the problems attached to job changes, immobility, and shifts in social relationships during "middlessence."

Given that many of the studies we have in mind are based on national probability samples and contain data on health, the analyses proposed here would augment the studies based upon aggregated time series data. While self-reports on mental states are not necessarily accurate, as we noted earlier, intergroup and intertemporal comparisons of respondents can be undertaken with allowances and discounts (computed on the basis of earlier studies from which important clues may be derived about both validity and reliability) that can be readily introduced.

It is clear that a comprehensive study of health and economic conditions could be designed but that the efforts involved would be costly. Much could be done in anticipation of such a study, however, to order our thinking more carefully about causes and effects and the differential weights that could be hypothesized to attach to a variety of "intervening variables." Hopefully, our observations herein will serve to direct attention to a number of basic sets of conceptual and methodological problems.

Coda

While questions of validity and reliability can well be raised concerning a number of the studies we have used to illustrate the points in our discussion, these studies do suggest issues that deserve attention and that one ought to be prepared to join. One of us thus recalls the glib but not altogether thoughtless observation of one of our European grandmothers when she was asked about a dear but highly eccentric old friend: "Everybody" she said, "has a right to go crazy in their own way." While the diagnostic category would not be widely used among sophisticates, the fundamental judgment is, in a manner of speaking, supported in goodly measure by the investigators upon whose work we have drawn; researchers offer us copious quantities of information about the bewildering variety of ways in which these "rights" are exercised by the rich and the poor, the attended and the unattended, the loved and the unloved, the ambitious, the complacent and the passive, the optimists and the pessimists, the hapless young, the dependent aged, the hardworking ones, the disreputable ones, the lumpen proletariat, the power elite, and many other populations whose experiences and problems have been favored with the attentions of social and health scientists.

It is our own judgment that great care should be exercised by those who are inclined to overlook the exceedingly large number of complexities to which our overview points in their urges for their favorite specific economic reforms. While one may admire good intentions, it is clear from our survey that opponents of reforms which have been justified by well-intentioned scientists on grounds that illnesses would be reduced, can readily find competently executed research that points in *other* directions! As Max Weber put it in a discussion of biases, one ought not to trip over "inconvenient facts . . . and for every partisan opinion there are facts that are extremely inconvenient." To put it another way, good causes deserve to be well, not badly served; problematic research findings by a heterogeneous scientific community of investigators do not greatly help to resolve moral and political issues, however useful they may be in pushing forward against "scientific" frontiers.

NOTES

1. The senior author's main interests are in manpower problems and policies, employment and human resource problems, and in labor-management relations; he does not normally deal with mental health and mental illness. The planners of the Symposium asked for this paper on the assumption that introductory remarks can sometimes usefully be made by one with the negative virtue first identified by the economist Thorstein Veblen: as a non-expert, the senior author may possess fewer of what Veblen termed "trained incapacities" than do those from the well-populated ranks of able and accomplished scholars whose works we have sampled. We are grateful for comments on an earlier draft by Walter R. Gove, William A. Rushing, and John Harkey.

2. M. L. Kohn, "Class, Family and Schizophrenia," *Social Forces,* 1972, 50 (March), 295-304.

3. R. J. Turner and J. W. Gartrell, "Social Factors in Psychiatric Outcome: Toward the Resolution of Interpretative Controversies," *American Sociological Review,* 1978, 43 (June), 368-382.

4. Blair Wheaton, "The Sociogenesis of Psychological Disorder: Reexamining the Causal Issues with Longitudinal Data," *American Sociological Review,* 1978, 43 (June), 383-404.

5. See W. A. Rushing, "Interpretation of the Relationship between Socioeconomic Status and Mental Disorder: A Question of the Measure of Mental Disorder and a Question of the Measure of SES," 1978, Vanderbilt University, mimeo (emphasis added). For reviews, see A. Myerson, "Review of Mental Disorders in Urban Areas," *American Journal of Psychiatry,* 1940, 96, 995-999; M. H. Lystad, "Social Mobility Among Selected Groups of Schizophrenic Patients," *American Sociological Review,* 1957, 22, 288-292; W. H. Dunham, *Community and Schizophrenia: An Epidemiological Analysis* (Detroit: Wayne State University Press, 1965); W. H. Dunham, Patricia Phillips, and Barbara Srinivasan, "A Research Note on Diagnosed Mental Illness and Social Class," *American Sociological Review,* 1966, 31, 223-237; E. M. Goldberg and S. L. Morrison, "Schizophrenia and Social Class," *British Journal of Psychiatry,* 1963, 109 (November), 785-802; R. J. Turner and M. O. Wagenfeld, "Occupational Mobility and Schizophrenia: An Assessment of the Social Causation and Social Selection Hypothesis," *American Sociological Review,* 1967, 32 (February), 104-113; M. L.

Kohn, "Social Class and Schizophrenia: A Critical Review," pp. 155-173 in David Rosenthal and S. S. Kety, eds., *The Transmission of Schizophrenia* (London: Pergamon Press, 1968); B. P. Dohrenwend and B. S. Dohrenwend, *Social Status and Psychological Disorder* (New York: John Wiley, 1969); B. P. Dohrenwend, "Sociocultural and Social-Psychological Factors in the Genesis of Mental Disorders," *Journal of Health and Social Behavior,* 1975, 16 (December), 365-392; Marc Fried, "Social Differences in Mental Health," pp. 135-192 in John Kosa and I. K. Zola, eds., *Poverty and Health: A Sociological Analysis,* rev. ed. (Cambridge, MA: Harvard University Press, 1975); M. L. Kohn, 1972, op. cit.; L. N. Robins, *Deviant Children Grown Up: A Sociological and Psychiatric Study of Sociopathic Personalities* (Baltimore: Williams and Wilkins, 1966); David Mechanic, "Social Class and Schizophrenia: Some Requirements for a Plausible Theory of Social Influence," *Social Forces,* 1972, 50 (March), 305-309; B. P. Dohrenwend, "Social Status and Psychological Disorders: An Issue of Substance and an Issue of Method," *American Sociological Review,* 1966, 31 (February), 14-34; E. M. Gruenberg, "Comments on 'Social Structures and Mental Disorders: Competing Hypotheses of Explanation' by H. W. Dunham," pp. 265-270 in *Causes of Mental Disorders: A Review of Epidemiological Knowledge* (New York: Milbank Memorial Fund, 1959).

6. Leonard Heston, "Psychiatric Disorders in Foster-Home-Reared Children of Schizophrenic Mothers," *British Journal of Psychiatry.* 1966, 112 (August), 819-825; Leonard Heston and Donald Denny, "Interaction Between Early Life Experience and Biological Factors in Schizophrenia," pp. 363-376 in David Rosenthal and S. S. Kety, eds., *The Transmission of Schizophrenia;* David Rosenthal, P. Wender, S. S. Kety, F. Schulsinger, J. A. Welner, and L. Ostergaard, "Schizophrenics' Offspring Reared in Adoptive Homes," pp. 337-391 in *The Transmission of Schizophrenia;* I. I. Gottesman and James Shields, *Schizophrenia and Genetics: A Twin Study Vantage Point* (New York: Academic Press, 1972); Elnar Kringlen, "An Epidemiological-Clinical Twin Study on Schizophrenia," pp. 49-63in *The Transmission of Schizophrenia;* C. Perris, "Genetic Transmission of Depressive Psychoses," *Acta Psychiatrica Scandinavica Supplementum,* 1968, 203 (November), 45-52; Jules Angst and G. Perric, "Zur Nosologie endogener Depressionen: Vergleich der Ergebnisse zweier Untersuchungen," *Archiv fur Psychiatric und Zeitschrift f.d. ges Neurobgic,* 1968, 210, 373-386.

7. Gary D. Minor, "The Evidence for Genetic Components in the Neuroses," *Archives of General Psychiatry,* 1973, 29 (July), 111-118.

For an epigenetic approach to the similarities of the mental development of monozygotic twins and differences between dizygotic twins, see R. S. Wilson, "Synchronies in Mental Development: An Epigenetic Perspective," *Science*, 202 (1 December 1978), pp. 939-948.

8. Kringlen, *op. cit.*

9. H. I. Kaplan, B. J. Sadlock, and A. M. Freedman, "Neurochemistry of Behavior: Recent Advances," pp. 132-143, in A. M. Freedman, H. I. Kaplan and B. J. Sadlock, eds., *Comprehensive Textbook of Psychiatry—II*, 2nd ed. (Baltimore: Williams and Wilkins Co., 1975). For a detailed, empirically based and highly inventive discussion of medical, socioeconomic, and genetic factors, in juxtaposition with "stress," psychiatric and socioeconomic factors in mental illness, see W. A. Rushing and S. T. Ortega, "Socioeconomic Status and Mental Disorders: New Evidence and a Socio-Medical Formulation," *American Journal of Sociology*, forthcoming in 1979.

10. H. H. Strupp and G. Blackwood, "Recent Methods of Psychotherapy," pp. 1909-1920 in A. M. Freedman, H. I. Kaplan, and B. J. Sadlock, eds., *Comprehensive Textbook of Psychiatry—II*. See also H. H. Strupp, "Psychotherapy Research and Practice: An Overview," in S. L. Garfield and A. E. Bergin, eds., *Handbook of Psychotherapy and Behavior Change*, 2nd ed. (New York: Wiley, 1978).

11. T. S. Szasz, *Ideology and Insanity: Essays on the Psychiatric Dehumanization of Man* (Garden City, NY: Anchor Books-Doubleday and Co., Inc., 1970), pp. 20-27, 80-89.

12. T. J. Scheff, *Being Mentally Ill: A Sociological Theory* (Chicago: Aldine, 1966).

13. W. R. Gove, "Societal Reaction as an Explanation of Mental Illness: An Evaluation," *American Sociological Review*, 1970, 35 (October), 873-884; W. R. Gove, "Who is Hospitalized: A Critical Review of Some Sociological Studies of Mental Illness," *Journal of Health and Social Behavior*, 1970, 11 (December), 294-303; W. R. Gove, "Labelling and Mental Illness: A Critique," pp. 35-81 in W. R. Gove, ed., *The Labelling of Deviance: Evaluating a Perspective* (New York: Halsted Press, 1975).

14. W. A. Rushing, "Individual Resources, Societal Reaction and Hospital Commitment," *American Journal of Sociology*, 1971, 77, 511-526; W. A. Rushing and J. Esco, "The Status Resource Hypothesis

and Length of Hospitalization," pp. 445-455 in W. A. Rushing, eds., *Deviant Behavior and Social Process* (Chicago: Rand McNally, 1975); W. A. Rushing, "Status Resources and Behavioral Deviance as Contingencies of Societal Reaction," *Social Forces,* 1977, 56, 132-147; W. A. Rushing, "Status Resources, Societal Reactions and Type of Mental Hospital Admission," *American Sociological Review,* 1978, 43 (August), 521-533.

15. W. R. Gove and Patric Howell, "Individual Resources and Mental Hospitalization: A Comparison and Evaluation of the Societal Reaction and Psychiatric Perspectives," *American Sociological Review,* 1974, 39, 86-100.

16. W. R. Gove and T. Fain, "A Comparison of Voluntary and Committed Psychiatric Patients," *Archives of General Psychiatry,* 1977, 34, 669-676.

17. Emile Durkheim, *Suicide: A Study in Sociology,* J. A. Spaulding and G. Simpson, trans. (New York: The Free Press, 1951).

18. R. E. L. Faris and H. W. Dunham, *Mental Disorders in Urban Areas* (Chicago: The University of Chicago Press, 1939).

19. Myerson, 1940, *op. cit.;* Dunham, 1965, *op. cit.* See also W. A. Rushing and S. T. Ortega, *op. cit.*

20. E. H. Schein, "The Indoctrination Program for Prisoners of War," *Psychiatry,* 1956, 19, 49-172.

21. *Die Arbeitslosen von Marienthal* (Leipzig: *Psychologische Monographien,* 1933).

22. Bruno Bettelheim, *The Informed Heart: Autonomy in a Mass Age* (Glencoe, IL: Free Press, 1960).

23. B. H. Kaplan, ed., *Psychiatric Disorder and the Urban Environment* (New York: Behavioral Publication, 1971), *passim.*

24. R. E. L. Faris, *Social Psychology* (New York: The Ronald Press Co., 1952).

25. Gregory Bateson, "Minimal Requirements for a Theory of Schizophrenia," *Archives of General Psychiatry,* 1960, 2, 477-491.

26. R. D. Laing and A. L. Esterton, *Sanity, Madness and the Family* (Middlesex, England: Pelican Books, 1964).

27. W. R. Gove, personal communication.

28. W. R. Gove, "The Relationship Between Sex Roles, Mental Illness and Marital Status," *Social Forces,* 1972, 51, 34-44; W. R. Gove, "Sex Differences in Mental Illness Among Adult Men and Women: An Evaluation of Four Questions Raised Regarding the Evidence on the Higher Rates of Women," *Social Science and Medicine,* 1977, 12B, 187-198; W. R. Gove, "Sex, Marital Status and Psychiatric Treatment: A Research Note," *Social Forces* (forthcoming).

29. W. R. Gove and Jeannette Tudor, "Adult Sex Roles and Mental Illness," *American Journal of Sociology,* 1973, 78 (January), 812-835; W. R. Gove and Jeannette Tudor, "Sex Differences in Mental Illness: A Comment on Dohrenwend and Dohrenwend," *American Journal of Sociology,* 1977, 82 (May), 1327-1336.

30. W. R. Gove and M. R. Geerken, "The Effect of Children and Employment on the Mental Health of Married Men and Women," *Social Forces,* 1977, 56, 66-77. See also M. Komarovsky, *Blue Collar Marriage* (New York: Random House, 1967), chapters 3, 7, and 13.

31. Erich Lindemann, "Symptomatology and Management of Acute Grief," *American Journal of Psychiatry,* 1944, 101, 141ff. See also J. S. Tyhurst, "Displacement and Migration: A Study in Social Psychiatry," *American Journal of Psychiatry,* 1951, 107, 561ff; and J. S. Tyhurst, "The Role of Transition States—Including Disasters—in Mental Illness," *Symposium on Preventive and Social Psychiatry,* Walter Reed Army Institute of Research (Washington, DC: U.S. Government Printing Office, 1957), pp. 149-169.

32. See the contributions of Lt. Col. Fred G. Harris, Capt. Roger W. Little and Col. Albert J. Glass, all of the Army Medical Corps, to the *Symposium* cited in footnote 31.

33. Eli Ginzberg, *The Ineffective Soldier* (New York: Columbia University Press, 1959), three volumes.

34. See J. S. Tyhurst's comments on the neurologic and psychiatric aspects of the disorders of aging in *Symposium, op. cit.*

35. B. S. Dohrenwend and B. P. Dohrenwend, eds., *Stressful Life Events: Their Nature and Effects* (New York: John Wiley and Sons, 1974).

36. M. E. Melick, "Life Change and Illness: Illness Behavior of Males in the Recovery Period of a National Disaster," *Journal of Health and Social Behavior,* 1978, 19, 335-343; Michael Micklin and C. A. Lean,

"Life Change and Psychiatric Disturbance in a South American City: The Effects of Geographic and Social Mobility," *Journal of Health and Social Behavior,* 1978, 19, 92-107; W. W. Eaton, "Life Events, Social Supports and Psychiatric Symptoms: A Reanalysis of the New Haven Data," *Journal of Health and Social Behavior,* 1978, 19, 230-234.

37. T. H. Holmes and R. H. Rahe, "The Social Readjustment Rating Scale," *Journal of Psychosomatic Research,* 1967, 11, 213-218; T. H. Holmes and M. Masuda, "Life Changes and Illness Susceptibility," in B. S. Dohrenwend and B. P. Dohrenwend, eds., 1974, *op. cit.,* pp. 9-44; G. W. Brown, "Meaning, Measurement, and Stress of Life Events," in B. S. Dohrenwend and B. P. Dohrenwend, eds., 1974, *op. cit.,* pp. 217-243; L. E. Kinkle, Jr., "The Effect of Exposure to Culture Change, Social Change, and Change in Interpersonal Relationships on Health," in B. S. Dohrenwend and B. P. Dohrenwend, eds., 1974, *op. cit.,* pp. 9-44; R. W. Hudgens, "Personal Catastrophe and Depression: A Consideration of the Subject with Respect to Medically Ill Adolescents and A Requiem for Retrospective Life Event Studies;" B. S. Dohrenwend, Larry Krasnoff, A. R. Askenasy, and B. P. Dohrenwend, "Exemplification of a Method for Scaling Life Events: The PERI Life Events Scale," *Journal of Health and Social Behavior,* 1978, 19 (June), 205-229.

38. James N. Morgan, et al., *Income and Welfare in the United States* (New York: McGraw-Hill, 1962).

39. H. S. Luft, "The Impact of Poor Health on Earnings," *The Review of Economics and Statistics,* 57, 43.

40. M. H. Brenner, "Estimating the Social Costs of Economic Policy: Implications for Mental and Physical Health, and Criminal Aggression,"Report to the Congressional Research Service of the Library of Congress and the Joint Economic Committee of Congress (Washington, DC: U.S. Government Printing Office, 1976).

41. *Op. cit.,* Vol. 1, *passim.*

42. A. B. Hollingshead and F. C. Redlich, *Social Class and Mental Illness* (New York: Wiley, 1958).

43. It should be noted of course that individual and aggregated analyses may be targeted on what are generally seen by epidemiologists and sociologists to be different issues: in individual-based studies the investigator may be in search of individual etiological factors associated

with certain health problems, while aggregate data analysts may seek to identify what, since Durkheim, have been termed "social facts." For discussions of the possibilities of using aggregated data while drawing conclusions about individuals, see Gove and Hughes, "Reexamining the Ecological Fallacy: A Study Where Ecological Data Play a Critical Role in Investigating the Pathological Effects of Living Alone," 1978, Vanderbilt University, mimeo; and E. A. Hanushek, et al., "Model Specification, Use of Aggregate Data and the Ecological Correlation Fallacy," *Political Methodology,* 1, 89-107.

44. See M. H. Brenner, *Mental Illness and the Economy* (Cambridge: Harvard University Press, 1973); *Estimating the Social Costs of Economic Policy: Implications for Mental and Physical Health, and Criminal Aggression,* Report to the Congressional Research Service and the Library of Congress and the Joint Economic Committee of Congress (Washington, DC: U.S. Government Printing Office, 1976); and "Personal Stability and Economic Security," *Social Policy,* 1977, 8, 2-5.

45. J. A. Davis, "Studying Categorical Data Over Time," *Social Science Research,* 1978, 7 (June), 151-179.

46. M. L. Kohn and Carmi Schooler, "Occupational Experience and Psychological Functioning: An Assessment of Reciprocal Effects," *American Sociological Review,* 1973, 38 (February), 97-118.

47. For a brief but lucid discussion of the longitudinal/cross-sectional and the aggregated individual issues, see David Dooley and Ralph Catalano, *Economic Change as a Cause of Behavioral Disorder* (Irvine, CA: University of California, 1978), mimeo; and Glenn Firebaugh, "A Rule for Inferring Individual-Level Relationships from Aggregate Data," *American Sociological Review,* 1978, 43 (August), 557-572.

48. See David Dooley and Ralph Catalano, "Money and Mental Disorder: Toward Behavioral Cost Accounting for Primary Prevention," *American Journal of Community Psychiatry,* 1977, 5, 217-227, and these authors' contribution to the present symposium.

49. B. Kaplan, *op. cit.*

50. Leo Srole, T. S. Langues, S. T. Michael, M. K. Opler, and T. A. C. Rennie, *Mental Health in the Metropolis: The Midtown Manhattan Study* (New York: McGraw-Hill, 1962).

51. W. F. Whyte, *Street Corner Society* (Chicago: University of Chicago Press, 1943); Herbert Gans, *Boston West End Study, The*

58

Urban Villagers (New York: Free Press, 1962); E. Liebow, *Talley's Corner: A Study of Negro Streetcorner Men* (Boston: Little Brown, 1967).

52. Mark Baldassare, *Residential Crowding in Urban American* (Berkeley: University of California Press, 1978); Alan Booth, *Urban Crowding and Its Consequences* (New York: Praeger, 1976); O. R. Galle, W. R. Gove, and M. McPherson, "Population Density and Social Pathology: What are the Relationships for Man?", *Science,* 1972 (April), 23-30; W. R. Gove, M. Hughes, and O. R. Galle, "Overcrowding in the Home: An Empirical Investigation of its Possible Pathological Consequences," *American Sociological Review,* 1979 (forthcoming).

53. Dohrenwend and Dohrenwend, 1969, *op. cit.*

54. Leo Srole, "Urbanization and Mental Health: Some Reformulation," *American Scientist,* 60 (5), 576-583.

55. See for example, *Medical Care, Health Status, and Family Income: United States* (Washington, DC: U. S. Department of Health, Education and Welfare, Public Health Service, National Center for Health Statistics, 1964), Series 10, No. 9, p. 9ff.

56. *Statistical Indicators 1976: Selected Data on Social Conditions and Trends in the United States, Department of Commerce* (Washington, DC: U. S. Government Printing Office, 1977), pp. 157-158.

57. *Ibid,* p. 137.

58. A. L. Stinchcombe, *Rebellion in High School* (Chicago: Quadrangle Books, 1964); James Coleman, *The Adolescent Society* (New York: Free Press, 1961); David Matza, *Delinquency and Drift* (New York: John Wiley, 1964).

59. R. K. Merton, *Social Theory and Social Structuring,* 2nd ed. (Glencoe, IL: The Free Press, 1957), pp. 131-194; R. H. Cloward and L. E. Ohlin, *Delinquency and Opportunity* (Glencoe, IL: The Free Press, 1960); Talcott Parsons, *The Social System* (Glencoe, IL: The Free Press, 1951), Chapter 7; Emile Durkheim, 1951, *op. cit.*

60. E. Wight Bakke, *The Unemployed Man* (New York: Dutton, 1934) and *Citizens Without Work* (New Haven: Yale University Press, 1940); David Potter, *People of Plenty* (Chicago: University of Chicago Press, 1965).

61. W. R. Gove and Michael Hughes, Vanderbilt University, unpublished data.

62. See Gerald Gurin and Patricia Gurin, "Personal Efficacy and the Ideology of Individual Responsibility," in Burkhard Strumpel, *Economic Means for Human Needs* (Ann Arbor, MI: Survey Research Center, 1976), pp. 139, 150. Emphasis added.

63. G. H. Elder, *Children of the Great Depression: Social Change in Life Experience* (Chicago: University of Chicago Press, 1974).

64. E. H. Erikson, *Childhood and Society* (New York: W. W. Norton Co., 1950).

65. Genevieve Knupfer, "Portrait of the Underdog," in Reinhard Bendex and S. M. Lipset, eds., *Class, Status and Power, A Reader in Social Stratification* (Glencoe, IL: The Free Press, 1953), pp. 255-262.

66. J. R. Seeley, R. A. Sim, and E. W. Loosley, *Crestwood Heights: A Study of the Culture of Suburban Life* (New York: Basic Books, Inc., 1956).

67. Gans, *op. cit., passim;* Whyte, *op. cit., passim.*

68. Ginzberg, *op. cit.,* Vol. II, *passim.*

69. Hollingshead and Redlich, *op. cit., Social Class and Mental Illness* (New York: Wilson, 1958).

70. S. Brocki and W. R. Gove, in progress, Vanderbilt University, Department of Sociology and Anthropology.

71. For a comprehensive study in which these investigators' and others' work are discussed, see Sidney Cobb and S. V. Kasl, *Termination: The Consequences of Job Loss* (Cincinnati: U.S. Department of Health, Education and Welfare, Public Health Service, Center for Disease Control, National Institute for Occupational Safety and Health, 1977), mimeo.

72. R. F. Bales, "Cultural Differences in Rates of Alcoholism," *Quarterly Journal of Studies on Alcohol,* 1946, 6, 480-499.

73. Personal communication.

74. M. L. Kohn and Carmi Schooler, *op. cit.* An earlier study by A. Kornhauser, of auto workers, is also an interesting one, but it is not nearly as rich in either theory or method: A. Kornhauser, *Mental Health of Industrial Workers* (New York: Wiley, 1965).

60

75. Arnold Tannenbaum, et al., *Hierarchy in Organizations: An International Comparison* (San Francisco: Jossey-Bass, 1974), Chapter 5. For an extended and pessimistic treatment of worker participation schemes and other widely discussed workplace innovations, see Ivar Berg, et al., *Managers and Work Reform: A Limited Engagement* (New York: Free Press, 1978).

76. E. H. Schein, *op. cit.*

77. E. Ginzberg, *op. cit.*

78. R. K. Merton and Paul F. Lazarsfeld, eds., *Studies in the Scope and Method of "The American Soldier"* (Glencoe, IL: The Free Press, 1950).

79. S. L. A. Marshall, *Men Against Fire* (New York: William Marrow Co., Inc., 1947).

80. Charles Moscos, "Why Men Fight," *Transaction,* 1969 (November); E. H. Erickson, 1950, *op. cit.;* D. J. Levinson, *The Seasons of a Man's Life* (New York: Knopf, 1978); H. Levinson, *Emotional Health and the World of Work* (Cambridge: Harvard University Press, 1971); S. L. Baker, "Military Psychiatry," in A. M. Freedman, et al., eds., 1975, *op. cit.,* pp. 2355-2367; R. F. Grinker and S. P. Spiegel, *Men Under Stress* (Philadelphia: Blakiston, McGraw-Hill, 1945); M. D. Nefzger, "Followup Studies of World War II and Korean War Prisoners: Study Plan and Mortality Findings," *American Journal of Epidemiology,* 1970, 91, 123.

81. Midge Decter, *Liberal Parents, Radical Children* (E. Rutherford, NJ: Cowart, McCann and Geoghegan, Inc., 1975).

82. G. L. Engle, "The Need for a New Medical Model: A Challenge for Bio-Medicine," *Science,* 1977, 196, 129-136. In this article the author has sought to construct a bio-psycho-social model for studying health, a model that encompasses all three of our approaches and more, including the biological-genetic approaches we have deliberately neglected.

83. Liebow, *op. cit.*

84. P. P. Sorbin, *The Working Poor: Minority Workers in Low-Wage, Low-Skill Jobs* (Port Washington, NY: Kennikat, 1973).

85. Leonard Goodwin, *Do the Poor Want to Work? A Social-Psychological Study of Work Orientations* (Washington,DC: Brookings, 1972).

86. H. L. Wilensky and Hugh Edwards, "The Skidder: Ideological Adjustments of Downward Mobile Workers," *American Sociological Review,* 1959, 24, 2 (April), 215-231.

87. A. J. Morgan, *op. cit.*

88. E. Ginzberg, et al., *Talented Women* (New York: Columbia University Press, 1963).

89. *Symposium on Preventive and Social Psychiatry, op. cit.*

90. Goodwin, *op. cit.*

91. B. Strumpel, ed., *op. cit., passim.*

92. R. P. Quinn, et al., *Job Satisfaction: Is There a Trend?,* Manpower Research Monograph, No. 30 (Washington, DC: U.S. Government Printing Office, 1974).

93. For citations see I. Berg, et al., *op. cit., passim.*

94. For an inventive analysis of the type we are suggesting, see H. H. Hyman, et al., *The Enduring Effects of Education* (Chicago: University of Chicago Press, 1975), in which the responses of four age cohorts on the relevant "knowledge" items in two hundred different surveys were used to study the effects on different persons and groups of differential educational experiences.

3
HEALTH AND THE NATIONAL ECONOMY: COMMENTARY AND GENERAL PRINCIPLES

M. HARVEY BRENNER

The scope of Dr. Berg's rich, scholarly, and multifaceted material provides a difficult task for the reviewer. His paper focuses on the multivariate causal nature of any one problem suspected of being due to, or of being a consequence of, economic change. Furthermore, serious ideological issues are involved in attempting to properly isolate the variables that one believes are crucial to the research hypothesis, whether for theoretical or policy reasons. What I intend to do is elaborate on the core issues presented by Dr. Berg, with the optimistic intention of leading the discussion toward something like a research agenda.

A possibility exists, as Dr. Berg indicated, for solving the "problem" of specification of *the* models, or the specification of *a* model, for explaining the relationship between the economy and health. However, at the present time, it may not be the most appropriate strategy. Some very profound research issues remain in the field because of the interdisciplinary character of the work. Research conducted over the past thirty or forty years has touched on economic and health matters, but the concepts of economy and health may be too large for the purposes of arriving at a *singular, parsimonious* theory or set of general relations. I would like to argue, instead, that there are quite specific ways in which a generalized set of relations can be broken down into intermediate stages based on theoretical approaches developed within the social and behavioral sciences.

63

64

The first part of the story must focus on the definitional nature of the major variables and their functions in the conceptual reconstruction of reality. Thus, the independent variable(s), which for the sake of discussion are understood to represent the "economy," are described so differently, depending on the level of analysis, that it has not been possible to have anything like a singular definition. Some of the obvious issues are as follows. On the most general level, are we concerned with the *rate* of behavior in a population—e.g., the rate of unemployment—or its occurrence in the individual? If we are interested in unemployment on the individual level only, then we might concentrate on an individual's reaction to his or her own state of unemployment. However, if we consider the individual's—as dependent on a general population group's—relation to unemployment, then we must take into account the implications of unemployment for the rest of society.

What, for example, is the implication of a relatively high rate of unemployment for the individual's family? On a macro level, a high unemployment rate, and hence an economic downturn, will mean that while many persons are losing or have lost jobs, many others maintain their jobs but will have lost income or are losing income. It is also possible that even where a loss of job or income has not occurred, there will nevertheless have been a state of anxiety created, or states of conflict created within the family, or within the work organization, where individuals compete with one another under threat of losing jobs or losing income. This is typical of the firm in the midst of economic disaster or of impending disaster, where the management and employees gradually observe that the firm's ability to do business is gradually curtailed. In these times, incidentally, this picture is accurate for many of our academic institutions, where funding for research projects is diminished and where educational institutions have generally been experiencing some decline in enrollment due to the discontinuity of the favorable demography that has made it possible for massive numbers of people to attend educational institutions over the last twenty years or so.

A general rate of decline, consequently, can be characterized by an unemployment rate while *not* necessarily by the state of unemployment of specific individuals. Thus, a focus on individual unemployment will give a very different picture of the "effects of unemployment" than when the societal rate of unemployment is examined. This concept, was, of course, pointed out a long time ago by Durkheim, with the distinction of suicide as an individual phenomenon versus that of a rate among nations or other social aggregates. In the selection of the level of analysis as the nation, special issues present themselves; for instance, in an analysis of suicide, one can deliberately study the effects of differing cultural nationalities. Hollingshead and Rogler conducted their study of schizophrenia in Puerto Rico using this method, because they knew full well that there was an inverse relationship between the prevalence of schizophrenia and socio-economic status. Such a powerful determinant of prevalence as the socio-economic status meant that they wanted to rigorously control for it by creating a sample of only low socio-economic persons. Very frequently, as we focus individually within the United States, we unknowingly eliminate consideration of what it is particularly about the U.S. that may be of critical significance, particularly with regard to matters affecting the economy and health. In what way is the U.S. comparable, for instance, to Northwestern Europe, or specifically to Spain or Sweden, where the meaning and implications of unemployment, may be quite different? All in all then, the interpretation of the independent variable is a general problem and will change depending on the level of analysis.

We can usually characterize levels of analysis by the traditional disciplines, with psychology claiming that it deals with something called "individuals," which by and large we can believe until we get to the discipline of social psychology. To some, social psychology refers to small groups, while for others it signifies the relationships between individual behavior and a large-scale macroscopic societal level. The discipline of sociology, on the other hand, concerns itself with so many levels that it is quite difficult to characterize conceptually. It has a nation-state level, at which a substantial number of the people in our profession work; it has a cultural level, which is often not treated in sociology per se, but more particularly in anthropology; it has an urban level, an organizational level, and several others.

Each level of focus will involve different implications for the independent variable. If, as sociologists, we focus on the small group, the study is not quite the same as if we were psychologists. Given the conceptual variety of disciplines, we will have different variables to contend with, a different meaning for the independent variable, and we haven't even begun to talk about the dependent variable, which also varies with the level of focus. As Dr. Berg points out, the higher the level of analysis, the more parsimonious we can be; and that is true up to a point. We can also be parsimonious within a particular discipline; for example, we can be quite parsimonious within psychology of learning theory, where we have some well developed principles. We can be parsimonious at the macroscopic level within economics or sociology, in which, again, there is a reasonably well developed set of principles, but we have difficulty moving from one level to another in the same analysis. When we try to do that, we need to incorporate within the framework of theory at least two different disciplinary levels. Such maneuvers have occasionally been accomplished in the social sciences; i.e., the creation of a social psychology. It is a very difficult area of work, but not impossible. Many examples, moreover, exist in the natural sciences; e.g., physical chemistry is not physics, and not chemistry, but a unique theoretical integration of the two.

The higher the analytic level of the variable, the greater the number of people who are affected (an obvious reference would be to the comparison of unemployment rate among nations as distinguished from regions or cities). If we are talking about a world-wide depression, the implication for "individual behavior" is going to be quite different than if we are talking simply about the unemployment rate in a city, much less the unemployment of only a single individual. The significance is that where very large numbers of persons are unemployed, the implications for any individual are going to be different from those in the case of a small number of persons being unemployed. The "unemployment" variables in each of these cases are altogether different in their impact on the same individual.

Let me demonstrate this point by a single example. One might think that it would be quite an easy matter to establish a causal connection between a plant closing and subsequent health through a comparison of the health of (1) persons laid off with (2) persons not laid off or (3) persons in the community not attached to the plant. The first problem in a comparison of those laid off and those not laid off *in the same firm* is that the anxiety levels of those not laid off can be raised to a pitch that is similar to those who are laid off, such that the health consequences for both groups might indeed be very similar. The second problem involves the assumption that only the plant itself is in difficulty, rather than the economy of the general community. This assumption will be false if the plant in question is important to the economy of the community. Thus, in the same community, many of the people who are not laid off are still losing income, and if one is a loser of income, he may well be in a quite similar position to the loser of a job. Therefore, this semi-microscopic kind of "layoff"-comparison study, where distinction is not made as to the precise character of the independent variable, may result in little scientific yield. What *is* required in such a study is a comparison of what goes on at various levels—the macroscopic, the organizational, the small group, and the microscopic. In addition, Dr. Berg begins his discussion with the focus on possible interdependencies in the general relation between the economy and health. Now, for any particular economic or health problem we may ask: Is there a one way series of causation affecting the health problem, or a one way series of causation affected by the health problem, or a one way series of causation affecting the health problem which in turn is affecting another economic problem, with simultaneous sequence of causation? It is clear that a comparatively small sample analysis of the type ordinarily used in epidemiological studies does not provide the statistical basis for answering these extremely common questions.

Putting this crucial matter another way, Dr. Berg refers to the "drift hypothesis" of illness where, in focusing on the individual level of analysis, we find it virtually impossible to discriminate which occurs first—a theoretically classic chicken-egg issue. Does the economic situation lead to the illness, or the illness lead to the economic situation? Indeed, this problem puts in doubt the entire history of epidemiological research into psychiatric disorder, and economic status, because of the inability to discriminate the dependent from the independent variable. As Dr. Berg ends his discussion, we are left with the question: is it that people who have the illnesses, or have the predispositions toward the illnesses, are less competent, and therefore do poorer in their work lives, or is it that the people who are affected by the economic situation are subsequently in poorer health?

In an entirely cross-sectional mode of analysis, or on an entirely individual level, it is absolutely impossible to make this discrimination. Furthermore, there is some doubt as to whether it would be possible, even in the situation of a plant closing involving a general situation of unemployment or economic deterioration of a region. The economic deterioration of a region may be the overriding inclusive variable. The crucial variables that are missing are contextual ones. Also, without a control for what is generally going on in a region, we cannot isolate the particular kinds of unemployment problems that are occurring for an individual, an organization, a city, a county, a neighborhood, or a census tract. Only if one can hold constant what is generally going on at related levels is it possible to discriminate in a reasonable way the effect of a specific attribute of the employment situation on the individual.

To take these methodological considerations a step further, we also have a problem with timing. How long shall we observe the independent variable, if indeed the economic problems bring about a variety of other stresses or make a variety of other stresses more stressful? We shall have to wait long enough to observe the "totality" of the effect before we can get an assessment of what the impact is. How long shall this wait be? The answer to this question at least partly depends on the duration of the particular dependent variable selected. Dr. Berg also refers to the need to look at intergenerational factors, as evidenced from the great depression study. We also need to look at stages of life, because what happens at one stage of life presumably has implications for subsequent stages. One may not see within a period of months, weeks, or even a couple of years what we would expect to see, given our most reasonable hypotheses, simply because the measured effect requires a longer period for observation. For example, the Holmes and Rahe material on life stresses indicates that something approaching a two-year lag period is necessary in order to observe changes in illnesses with respect to "epidemic-like" movements of stress in the lives of individuals.

In my own research, two to three years is reasonably accurate for looking at the most serious consequences of employment loss for the majority of the population who die of a major chronic disease. Two to three years is the minimum, and probably closer to five years captures the larger phenomenon, if we wish to express only the initial effects without respect to later life stages or the intergenerational impact, which Dr. Berg is especially concerned about.

The next research issue that Dr. Berg mentions has to do with the severity of the economic trauma. In this instance we are talking *not* about the dependent variable, which is quite another issue, but the independent variable. What is the threshold at which we have a "problem"? How large must it be? The results of our analysis will again vary depending on the level of analysis we choose, i.e., the individual, city, region, or nation. Quite different consequences for severity of the economic trauma evolve from the selection of the analytic level, since (1) specific stresses typically ignite others at neighboring levels and, (2) policy "solutions" to employment problems also depend on specific geopolitical levels.

The dependent variable presents even more serious problems for analysis. Health is by no means a unitary concept. If one is truly to isolate the impact of a phenomenon like unemployment on, say, the cardio-vascular health status of a population, one obviously needs to focus on those special illnesses that are "cardio-vascular." Focusing on total health won't do in this case, because the more general measure may be different from, and/or affected by, other diseases which behave differently. It is necessary in this example to focus on the epidemiology of cardio-vascular disease, ideally in a manner of the Framingham cohort studies over long periods of time, in which one can observe changes in the study population based on changes in the variety of risk factors which ordinarily influence cardio-vascular problems. It is only through identification of the "ordinary" risk factors that one can possibly isolate additional factors (such as economic stress) that would influence the probability of cardio-vascular disturbance. The usual risk factors must, of course, be held constant either by including them in the sampling design or in the analysis itself.

Additionally, we have a variety of predisposing factors, and Dr. Berg mentions two very important types of particular interest. One, we might call sensitivity to economic stress. Here the issue of the subject's own non-economic experiences is important. However, what was not mentioned was sensitivity to the particular *illness*, which represents the dependent variable. For example, does more smoking emerge under periods of stress associated with economic decline? In order to understand whether an increase in smoking for a given period occurs, one would have to know under what conditions people would *ordinarily* be smoking. What are the usual risk factors? If one holds these constant as predisposing or risk factors, one can then, and only then, test the additional independent variable as to the potential as additional predispositional factors that might influence the risk of smoking (or of any other pathological behavior for that matter).

It is not reasonable to entirely segregate predisposing and precipitating problems. Very often one simply will not be able to observe the effect of the precipitant on individuals unless the background variables—the usual risk factors pertaining to those individuals—are taken into account. These risk factors include genetic factors, interuterine life, and family upbringing to the extent that these factors are pertinent. We must enter these factors into our general equations, because if we fail to do so, they might well overwhelm the equations. The only reason that we can be parsimonious in our theoretical interpretation is that we have methodologically held at bay other variables which typically affect the phenomenon under study.

With the preceding in mind, let me define, if I may, a distinction between predisposing and precipitating factors. Predisposing factors, altogether, are those that influence *which* people will react to a given phenomenon; i.e., who among the population will react with a *specific* pathology (such that differentiation can be made, for example, as to who will suicide rather than who will homicide, or who will develop cardio-vascular illness). Predispositional phenomena , then, are (1) those which account for the sensitivity of the population to a stress or (2) those which are particular risk factors in a patterned reaction, such as a disease syndrome, where we are interested in predicting the likelihood of one disease versus another.

Therefore, the three questions for the student of predispositional factors are: (1) will any member(s) of the population react, and (2) who will react, and (3) what will be the reaction? If we are interested in stress responses, we may be able to use as models the Mertonian anomie schema in order to differentiate typologies of reaction. We can also use those put forward by students of psychophysiology, which list many different types of psychosomatically-oriented illnesses. We can list a series of aggressive behaviors or criminal behaviors, which are also associated with the same kinds of phenomena. The choice is ours. If we pick any *one* of these behaviors, for instance suicide, we shall have to have a good deal of background about suicide. If we pick a composite of these behaviors, we shall have to know a lot more in order to be able to control for what ordinarily influences these composite phenomena.

Now, the researcher working at the predispositional issue, who is interested, for example, in the impact of early home life on a situation that typically occurs later in life, has a special problem. The researcher must now control for factors which affect the individual's life *after* he left home, otherwise it will not be possible to attribute subsequent behavior to the early home life. This problem of controls is very much the same in each of the social sciences.

Dr. Berg makes reference to the parsimoniousness of the models one is able to use in sociological-econometric studies, especially with respect to the very high R^2s observed. Why are these R^2s so very high? Is it that any specific one of the independent variables is extraordinarily powerful? Not necessarily; they may in fact be relatively weak. The R^2s are high only because we control, in a general model, for nearly all of what usually influences the dependent phenomenon. If we are looking at suicide rates, we may need to consider five or six variables at the national level which are influential, only one of which will be unemployment, and where the unemployment has a comparatively minimal effect. The total R^2 is going to be large, because it is the equation as a whole that is explaining the dependent phenomenon, not any one variable.

Indeed, it is only possible to ascertain the statistical significance of any one of the variables by controlling for those which are ordinarily of influence. If we are not able to do that, our general equation systems are not workable, and our critic has the perfect right to say to us, "Look, you have not included 'variable A.' If you had included 'variable A,' you would find that your basic hypothesized variable can be dismissed." Indeed, we had better include 'variable A' and not leave ourselves open to that scientifically appropriate kind of critique.

The implications for the researcher are, once again, that he must be thoroughly knowledgeable about the usual risk factors associated with the dependent variable; i.e., familiar with all that can be gleaned from all the sciences—medical, biological, epidemiological, and social—which tell us what usually plays a part in the behavior of that variable.

We will need, therefore, to discriminate different types of health problems. It is difficult, under those conditions, to think about a general health scale. It may not mean very much to think about a health scale, quite simply because one is compounding the errors of a lack of understanding of each of several sub-scales. What does it mean to arithmetically add a cardio-vascular problem to a mental health problem? What would such a sum mean? The problem arises because different risk factors are associated with each of the sub-behaviors. What we shall need to do is discriminate carefully and precisely what our dependent variable is. Moreover, as Dr. Berg indicates, we shall have to discriminate carefully its severity, because a mild form of the same problem will probably be more common, and its epidemiology will take one form, while a severe form will have yet another set of risk factors associated with it. The normal use of alcohol is perhaps quite different from alcohol abuse problems, for example. The factors associated with alcohol problems are different epidemiologically from general alcohol use.

All of this leads to the issue of reporting, or self-reporting, which is stressed by Dr. Berg as a very serious problem. I agree; however, my opinion is that we should not disregard them as simply not capable of reflecting the essence of a "pure" illness pattern. They do convey a state of being, about which a person may feel good or bad, and which is therefore worthy of study in its own right—regardless of whether, when the person feels bad, his blood pressure is not in fact elevated. The elevation of blood pressure is a subject on its own, with its own peculiar epidemiology. There is a related problem of taking reports from institutions, for example, as measures of the occurrence of more "essential" illness phenomena, when the hospitalization measure itself may be the more severe indicator of the actual dependent variable.

Estimates of morbidity, in turn, create problems that mortality measures can often resolve, simply because with mortality we know at least that the individual has died. There is no question as to what the dependent variable means. If one uses hospitalization, for example, there is a question as to whether one can infer only use of service or actual signs and symptoms of illness, or both. However, the use of mortality as a dependent variable avoids the very profound set of problems that Catalano and Dooley discuss later.

The dependent variable itself and the definitional and level problems don't stop at this point in the discussion. Indeed, some of them begin here. Just as we have the problem of focusing on the magnitude of the independent variable, the economy, we have exactly the same problem with the dependent variable. For example, let's look at the individual who loses a job and measure his or her response over as long a period as we care to. We know that we shall be able to see very quickly and very easily that with an increase in the unemployment rate, there is reverberation among all of the age groups, and in both sexes. Mortality among infants, 5-10 year olds, and age groupings all the way through 85 and above are involved. Since most of those affected probably did not themselves suffer a job loss, how is it that the high unemployment rate, *as a variable,* is going to be affecting children and the elderly, as well as non-working women?

We can very easily write that scenario in terms of family dynamics, in terms of extended kin dynamics, in terms of relations between organizations and individual family members. It is not at all necessary that the individual breadwinner theoretically or actually absorb all the stress associated with a specific economic downturn *or* with his own unemployment. How does one appropriately measure the dependent variable in such a situation? Shall we measure the cardio-vascular response of the person who loses a job? Or, shall we involve each of the family members, including the children who don't themselves suffer from cardiovascular disease? Also, the variation in response pattern can mean for youth, for instance, that they may get violent, or use alcohol, or kill themselves or someone else while driving. And what about the elderly? They might not kill someone on the highway, but they may suicide. What can we look at? And whom shall we look at? It makes a very large difference to the analysis. The research issue, in general, is concerned with determining what the magnitude of the dependent variable is in terms of the target population and types of pathology or response pattern one believes is associated with the independent variable.

I would now like to focus on the entire question that Dr. Berg raises as to the ecological nature of relationships between the economy and health, and their solubility or lack thereof. One can solve, for example, the problem of the relationship between socio-economic status and the prevalence of some illness, but probably not on the individual level. It becomes almost impossible on the individual level because of the chicken-egg question. One can do it at the macroscopic level. How can this be done? How can one establish with relative certainty what the direction of causation is when macro and micro levels are simultaneously involved? If one is looking at the relation between the unemployment rate and the suicide rate, one simply cannot argue that the individual or his/her condition of suicide has a significant effect on the national unemployment rate. That solves the directional problem completely.

Selecting the variables at a level of aggregation which eliminates the individualized response pattern as an exogenous factor ordinarily will remove the variables from a backward, or a simultaneous, sequence of causation. This is possible at the macroscopic level alone. At lower levels of analysis one gets into the same problem of the plant closings, where the ecological problem of causal interpretation is extremely difficult, to the extent that one has highly individualized data on employment, as an independent variable. This may be surprising and perhaps even amusing: the closer to the individual one gets, the harder it is to determine a causal connection. The major reason for this is that it becomes more and more difficult to take appropriate contextual variables into consideration. For example, in exploring the relationship between marital status and ill health, however it is measured, we find that married persons have better health. As has usually been the case, we can argue theoretically that the state of being married is protective to one's health. This is a very reasonable idea, except of course when one comes to the question of why certain people are getting married and others are not. Is it that those who get married have better health to start with and are more desirable as mates? This problem occurs in all of our disciplines at the individual level. In order to interpret the relationships, one must use very elaborate causal sequences with multiple independent variables to tease out other possible explanations of the relationship as well as the likelihood of backward causation. The problem is much easier to handle on the macro level, since it occurs less frequently.

This is not, however, an argument for a methodological imperialism on the macroscopic level, but rather an argument for research on multiple levels. There are no perfect studies. There are problems on the macro level such that one cannot take into consideration individual psychodynamics. It is also true there are problems of a very serious ecological sort at the individual level. It seems to me that we learn most from an exploration of these problems at many levels of analysis. I think that Dr. Berg already gives us his considered opinion that cumulative information and experience from different levels is the only way that we are going to get closer to anything approximating a model which bridges the gap between economic and health phenomena.

To focus on the link between the economy and health, let me address a fundamental problem in psychology and in social psychology that Dr. Berg refers to but does not discuss in detail. There is a major problem with the life stress studies in that they typically do not explain whether it is absolute change (or change per se) that is difficult, i.e., whether things which are understood to be inherently bad or good are indeed equally stressful. Is the "good" occasionally "bad?" We should understand that these issues are quite critical to the stress literature currently. The theoretical problem is that what is good or bad for one as an individual will depend on the context of the social relationship in which the life change occurs.

Marriage, ordinarily, is thought to be a good thing—divorce a bad thing. That, of course, depends upon the specific marriage. Getting involved in a bad marriage is not good; leaving a bad marriage is perhaps better. It depends on the relational system. A promotion, ordinarily, is a good thing, but if the promotion is to a position in which the individual is not capable of functioning or if it is an inappropriate promotion, it will be bad. Now, if we take any single phenomenon and talk about a population at risk, and try to define it in these life stress terms as good or bad, we shall find necessarily that the more marriages we take into consideration, the more it is likely we shall have bad marriages. The more promotions we take into consideration, the more likely it is that we shall find some inappropriate promotions. This is a problem that has yet to be faced within the life change literature. It is the absolute number in those scales that is the basis for the ultimate test of the presence of stress.

The relational system, then, is the social context in which the observations occur, which is usually not taken into consideration.

These contexts, however, may be the key factors through which the *statistical* relationships make sense. Our problem, then, is not to remove the ecological issue, but to bring it in. It is the social ecology that will specify whether or not there is a meaningful problem. It is that third piece, in addition to the factors of predisposition and precipitation, that Dr. Berg mentions, the social systems element, which rarely is taken into consideration. The point is that the precipitation factor will only make interpretive sense in the light of some social-ecological system. The final point, then, is again to try to bring in the macroscopic level because it is the social context of the economy, as a whole, that is central to Dr. Berg's discussion and to much of the analysis in this field.

Lately, a number of people have been looking at the phenomenon of rapid economic growth as a potential source of stress. We are finding that economic growth itself, despite the upward mobility related to it, acts as a source of risk to health. There are a number of theoretical sources of this problem: one is that economic growth itself, under all conditions and in all types of societies, brings about changes in values and norms and the reordering of social organization. There are new priorities in firms; there are new priorities in informal organizations. If the new is accepted, the old is devalued. To the extent that new ideas take over, old ideas are degraded, and those persons who held those ideas, and have held the positions based on those ideas, are also hurt. There is no way around that problem. Social change always involves injury. It involves benefits for many, but injury to a minority. In order to understand the impact of an economic downturn, then, on the general epidemiology of a health problem—let us say suicide—one also has to take into consideration other features of the economic system which may be doing damage, such as rapid economic growth. We need equations, for instance, that would include both economic growth phenomena and unemployment. Such equations have been developed for the United States and it can be shown that without those, it is a very tricky business to achieve a parsimonious solution to the health problems of unemployment alone for a relatively short period, such as 1940 through the 1970s. If one does not take into account the economic growth issue as well as the downturn issue, one is leaving out a very crucial set of factors.

Lack of accounting for the rapid economic growth issue leaves one open to the problem of whether it is change per se, beneficial movements in the economy, deleterious movements in the economy, or economic transitions altogether that are really causing the health damage. It is a central concern of our fields, and one that Catalano and Dooley deal with in their paper. The issue is not soluble without a distinction between the different kinds of trauma that will necessarily be associated with economic growth and those that have to do with loss of employment.

Indeed, very typically, the long lag between unemployment and severe morbidity or mortality, similar to the two years that Holmes and Rahe find in the relation between life stress and morbidity, persists not because the unemployment situation is doing damage three or four years later. Rather the unemployment problem results in several problems—often involving adjustment to the new work situation. The recent work of Ferman, if I'm describing his position accurately, demonstrates that this can be as much of a problem as those related to the initial, or even the later, stages of the unemployment itself. What do we mean by that? Let us take a person in his or her thirties or forties, who has developed some seniority on the job, becomes unemployed for awhile, and subsequently moves to a new job, let us say in the same industry. That individual, who once had seniority, will now probably find himself junior to people younger and less skilled than himself. He may find himself of considerably lower status, indeed, than he was when unemployed. This is the central feature of downward mobility, which is associated with loss of employment for many people.

That might be the situation if the individual goes into the same industry. Suppose that he or she does not go into the same industry. Suppose there was a general decline in the industry of original employment; then the situation of downward mobility would be even more extreme. This is typical of long term economic growth patterns that, paradoxically, produce considerable downward mobility. How does that happen?

The great depression, in many of our minds, was simply an aberrant cyclical phenomenon that exhibited its potential for nastiness over a period of three or four years and perhaps into a second generation, but not as part of a more general trend. If we look at the situation of agriculture during the great depression, however, we shall find that for people in the agricultural sector, it was a last gasp. This was the last time that a major migration of farm workers took place. It marked the loss of much of the remainder of what had been the great agricultural employment sector of the United States. This did not happen because of the unproductive character of American agriculture. Exactly the reverse; because agriculture was so productive, far fewer workers were required. Exactly the same thing is happening now in manufacturing industries. It is not only that many firms are relocating. Instead, it appears that, as a nation, we simply do not need so many people in the manufacturing sector. We are losing many manufacturing jobs and will be losing many more. We are moving into a world of industries that are service-oriented, thought-oriented, and communication-oriented, and many people will move from the lower rungs of the manufacturing industry to lower rungs of the service industry. This has been our history, generally, for a substantial segment of the labor force. It is downward mobility for specific minorities associated with the general economic development of society.

The relational system, once again, is key. It is difficult to understand the individual's "absolute" position in the society without reference to other people. An individual may have received a promotion, for example, but if many others in the same firm were simultaneously promoted, then the promotion may not signify significant relative advancement. All of these types of questions require relative resolutions, and the entire relational context must be taken into account.

Another general point I wish to make, very much along the lines of Dr. Berg's comments, is that it is necessary to have an overall, multivariate strategy of research which takes into account the other variables that normally influence the individual type of pathology, whether it's a suicide, a mental health problem such as schizophrenia, a cardiovascular problem, or any specific reaction. Our world, in terms of the technology of the sciences we deal with, is now far too sophisticated for us to rely any longer upon single variable models. The models that Dr. Berg proposed represent a large part of the picture that, of necessity, have to be taken into account in all cases, and even then, these models are not complete.

Q. (Catalano): Harvey, based upon your regression equations, I've heard people say that had we avoided those one percent increases in unemployment, we would have . . . saved 51,000 lives. I'm not sure if I heard you state that but I've heard people say that, based on your research. Your model, however, specifies (and I guess I'm wondering if you agree with me because I'm afraid your model does say that there are other important variables) that to avoid that one percent increase in unemployment might have changed the other variables which may have produced the same or greater loss of life. Isn't that possible?

A. (Brenner): It is possible; it depends on whether the policy change you are speaking of influences the other variables in the system and on *how* the policy change influences the other variables in the system. Now, more specifically, we must take into account the other three dispositional phenomena so that a number of people will certainly succumb to cardiovascular mortality, if the risk factors for that illness are present. But we don't know when that mortality will happen. This kind of equation is of a temporal nature. It is the kind of equation which specifies what will happen *now* instead of in two years or five years or ten years. The model I would like you to focus on is, indeed, an integrated model. Supposing (and I give this example frequently) we had an individual who was at a "perfect" risk, let's say, of dying of cardiovascular disease. Let us compare that situation with a Russian roulette model in which all six chambers of the revolver are loaded. If an individual is in an absolutely perfect risk situation, all he needs to do is pull the trigger and he will surely die—but he needs to pull the trigger. Depending upon when the trigger is pulled, he will die. If it is not pulled, he will not die, certainly, within the limited time frame that we are speaking about.

So there is a great variety of predisposing factors that are also acting on each of the diseases in question, or sources of pathology, whether its suicide or homicide, or cirrhosis mortality, or whatever else. But those predisposing factors do not enter this particular equation because we are controlling for them by using *temporal* equations. Another attack on the same problem would be, as again Dr. Berg specifies, to work with risk factors of either a genetic or lifestyle sort, which decrease the risk potential of cardiovascular disease. Altogether, the society does have trade-off choices to make among risk factors to health; such a position, however, does not detract in the least from the argument that a particular increase in unemployment may also have speeded up the mortality process.

Q. (Berg): Arthur Burns would argue that the kinds of trade-offs that might reduce the unemployment by X-number of public interventions might very well induce the heart attacks that the enemies of inflation are so preoccupied with.

A. (Brenner): Just to deal with that one matter of inflation, incidentally, it appears we will have to remove it from the predictive equations. In this particular study for the Joint Economic Committee, partially funded under the NIMH Metro Center, we found that the inflation measure is an extremely unstable *predictor.* In our most recent equations, we have eliminated it almost entirely. It has not been a necessary variable in that we can now demonstrate that inflation does not have a unique damaging effect in terms of the social costs we have been discussing.

Q. (Eliot Sclar): What I hear going on in terms of the methodology is not just a question of a single variable kind of model versus a multiple regression. Instead, I think we really have to start thinking methodologically about moving from single equation models to simultaneous equation models, which start to get at these points that if you pull one thing out, something else is going to be happening. Because what you really have on the screen is a reduced form of some kind of simultaneous equation system. And by not knowing what's what, you don't know what kind of simultaneous equation biases are creeping into the model. I think one of the things we ought to start thinking about is "How do we begin to build that more elaborate model?"

Q. (Berg): I think that's the question we were both addressing indirectly, or certainly, implicitly.

A. (Brenner): Let's be a little careful, if you will, with the terminology. In a simultaneous model, a simultaneous system, what happens is that the dependent variable—say suicide, in this case—also affects the economic variables. This is probably false. Probably the suicide rate does not affect the unemployment rate; probably it does not affect the rate of inflation or the rate of economic growth.

Q. (Sclar): I'm not sure I'm willing to . . . I understand in a large sense why . . . you've made the case very eloquently on a number of occasions. You can't simply say that if a few people go into a mental hospital or kill themselves that that's going to cause a downturn in the economy. But to the extent you are dealing with aggregated phenomena, it may very well be that things like a big increase in suicide that cause certain kinds of stresses can have very real effects on productivity or social relationships. It seems to me that there are a number of ways in which one would resound back upon the other. I agree it's not simple, but one would have to look at that.

A. (Brenner): I won't argue with that; I'll simply say that it is an empirical issue. Either it does or it doesn't. In my own opinion, it is inconceivable that the state of suicide or the state of homicide would have an effect on the national economy. Our economist friends do not seem to require it to explain movements in unemployment or economic growth or economic decline, for that matter. It is an empirical question, I agree, and there are simultaneous methods for attempting that. They are very straightforward. They can be used very easily with data much like these. We've just been engaged in a project to look at the relationship between crime indicators and drug abuse indicators. In a simultaneous model, we find that the alleged relationship between drug abuse and crime, with drug abuse producing crime, does not work. Nor is it the case that crime produces drug abuse. The relationship between the two of them is spurious. They simply co-exist. The drug abuse and the crime in the same population are subject to the same economic and demographic forces. These are important questions and I agree that we should look at them, one at a time, as they arise.

Q. (Sclar): I think there's more to it than that. With the exception of things like death, as you pointed out, the variables that you use for dependent variables are compounds of both demand factors, such as stresses, and supply factors such as availability of hospital beds or doctors who are looking for patients. I'm always amazed when physicians record reviews. If they are cardiologists, they find so much undetected heart disease, and if they are psychiatrists, they find neuroses. So part of the simultaneous effect is things get substituted one way or another, as a result of the policy, "We're going to emphasize this versus that this year."

A. (Brenner): Yes, in the case of the intermediate variables, in the case of institutions like mental hospitals, prisons, and hospitals generally, I certainly think that's true.

Q. (Sally Bould): This is a question that you suggested in your talk about the whole area of economic growth and bad effects and, also, the effects you are looking at here with suicide as one indicator and economic growth as, essentially, another indicator. That part of pathology that you attributed to instability (but which your last figure clearly shows to be a very small proportion of the total, in terms of the contextual) raises the question of whether some contextual constants are associated with the economy with a major part of mortality, which isn't affected by the instability?

A. (Brenner): Again, this is a temporal equation. It is a time series equation; it only deals with changes over time. A constant, in this sense, is that which is invariant over time. Most of the chronic disease phenomena are relatively invariant over time; that is, that which is over and above what is fairly stable. That additional variance in mortality is what we explain by the variant parts of the equation. Even in a cross-sectional equation, however, one may not be able to understand the constant. For example, if we look at cities in the United States at a specific time, say 1970, and set up a cross-sectional equation, we will not be able to account for what is average or constant among them, but we can try to explain what varies. We will not understand why rates for the United States as a whole are so high, however, unless we compare them with Swedish rates, rates for India, rates for China, and so on. We will know nothing about those constants unless we make the kinds of population comparisons that allow us to focus on them. So, for example, we won't know why our figures are so stable at the national level in these temporal equations unless we examine similar kinds of equations for different countries. Several countries are now replicating this kind of work; the Canadian government has recently informed us that it has replicated this set of equations for the nation of Canada and for each of its provinces. There is some interest in doing this for all OECD countries, which include all European, and neighboring countries that have substantial relationships with us. That kind of comparison would begin to look at what is behind the different constants involved.

As to the economic growth component of the question, there are general types. The long term trend in economic growth of all populations we examined is a beneficial one—that is, economic growth beyond approximately ten years. But economic growth does not occur only in long-term trends; it occurs in staccato movements. The economy moves up in a rush and then pauses, then moves up again and pauses. In the strict economic terminology, the pause is called contraction. When we add the short-term economic growth component to the equation, we find that type of economic growth to be deleterious; it does damage. The long-term trend in the economy is also part of the same equation and is a beneficial economic growth variable. But all of these stem from the same overall movements in the economy and are, thus, all loosely related to one another.

Q. (Mike Miller): I would like to see if I can get greater clarity on what you were saying with regard to what Dr. Berg was saying. You seem to be using three terms here: independent variable, dependent variables, and contextual analysis. In the independent variable you have unemployment and other things you talked about; I take it that you use Dr. Berg's emphasis upon predisposition variables as one of the controls you would put on the use of independent variables. There might be times that you want to use predisposition as an important variable as a control to see whether certain persons have great stress when reacting with a more concentrated or particular population; but in general, you talk about using that as a control on the independent variable.

I take it that the contextual variable that you are talking about is related to the dependent variables—that is, the various ways of trying to understand the operation of the independent variable on the dependent variable by looking at the contexts in which the dependent variable is rooted. So there you talked at one point about relational things—how you can't understand the impact of the emotional factor without understanding what's happened to other people. I think I took it that that entered into the analysis of dependent variables. You mentioned that an unemployment problem may lead to a new problem, that is, a new work situation, and that difficulties may come from this new experience rather than from unemployment. I wasn't clear where that fitted in, whether that was the contextual variable, whether that was leading you to look at intervening variables of various kinds, and so on. I'm not sure Dr. Berg's emphasis upon events and disintegration fit into the way you classify the influence upon events and disintegration and the consequences of these influences.

A. (Brenner): Well, let me take it again, backward. The events of disintegration fit in precisely as I think Dr. Berg intended them in the sense that the "events" refer entirely to independent variables. Those are really the precipitating phenomena, like unemployment, that we've been talking about. The disintegration phenomena are related to what I have called contextual or relational. They more specifically refer, as Dr. Berg was talking about them, to the general situation described by Durkheim as anomie, or its inverse, integration. It is the issue of integration, or lack of it in a society, generally, that is the context in which both the independent and dependent variables naturally occur. But insofar as our emphasis is in explaining the dependent variables, more of our concentration in this case would be on the network of social relations within which the dependent variable situation occurred.

If we're looking at divorce, for example, the question is what, altogether, as in Lazarsfeld's studies in the 1930s was the situation prior to the divorce and to what extent was that context influenced by the economic situation. So the independent variable there has an influence on the context itself. In that sense, it comes back to the intermediate part of your question—what are the intervening variables and how are they related to the potential problem of rehiring or of moving into a new job-adjustment situation. That's a little difficult. The question "What is an intervening variable?" has to do with the statement of the research problem, rather than anything empirical, I think.

The independent variables tend to be very long lasting in their effects. One can attribute, for example, the . . . effects on health that are associated with a new job adjustment to the original unemployment because, without the initial unemployment, the individual would not have been required to adjust to a new work situation. One may do this if one wishes, or one may as I think Dr. Ferman does and I am currently a little more inclined to do, look at the rehiring situation as a separate problem with its own effects. The rehiring problem will not occur without the prior issue of unemployment but, again, it's a question of emphasis in research strategy.

What is intervening as compared with what is "independent" is an analytical question, which will also be a function of the definition of predispositional problems. For example, whether an intervening factor between, for instance, the unemployment or the suicide, will be family separation is also a function of those kinds of problems that are contingent on separation; i.e., the independent variables which usually influence separation. Here then, separation as the dependent variable is consequent upon the independent variable (unemployment), but doesn't come into being unless other variables which ordinarily bring about separation are also active. So the unemployment will stimulate separation in those people who are "ready" or who are otherwise at high risk for it. Once the separation is set in motion, the separation itself may have other consequences as one stress leads to a series of other stresses. This is the particularly pernicious thing about stresses; they tend to be related to one another, and the occurrence of any one puts two persons at greater risk for the occurrence of the next. So you have an entire interrelational system among the stresses. A complete analysis, then, is one that makes use of the intervening and contextual variables, and takes into account the kinds of new situations which in turn might be produced by the independent variables themselves.

4
SOCIAL SUPPORT, PERSON-ENVIRONMENT FIT, AND COPING

ROBERT D. CAPLAN

"Perhaps the strangest thing of all is this: in a city of two millions of people there are no hotels! That means, of course, that there are no visitors."

Walter Besant, *East London,* 1901, p. 9.

When there is a lack of fit between people and their environments, what determines how well they cope? This chapter presents a framework for examining this question. The framework is based on the premise that coping is probably a function of characteristics of both the person and the environment. Social support plays an important role in this framework because it is viewed as an aid (or hindrance) in helping people cope effectively.

The first section of this paper presents the major categories of human response to misfit and the ways in which motivation determines which of those responses to misfit are manifested. Then we turn to the topic of social support. The first task involves defining social support. To do this, a number of definitions from the literature are reviewed and evaluated. This evaluation provides the basis for the definitions of support that are used throughout the paper.

The framework presents social support as a hypothesized determinant of (a) people's perceptions of their environments and of their own abilities and needs, (b) motivation to respond by coping and by defensive processes, (c) mental and physical

90

well-being, and (d) objective environmental resources available to the person.

Although the framework is based on previous theory and research, it is largely untested. Consequently, the reader should consider the hypotheses that follow in a critical manner by considering how the model should be further elaborated and tested. Although methods for measuring the constructs are not discussed at length, the framework should suggest the types of variables that need to be measured.

The model should also suggest the intermediate goals of social technologies that attempt to increase social support, coping, and environmental mastery. It should be able to suggest the variables that need to be altered to enhance mastery and the points of intervention for producing such enhancement. Only a brief discussion of the actual technologies for inducing such changes is attempted here.

HUMAN ADJUSTMENT AS A FUNCTION OF PERSON-ENVIRONMENT
FIT AND SOCIAL SUPPORT

Responses to an Undesirable Human Condition

Figure 1 lists a number of basic categories of responses that people may show when faced with a challenge or condition they would like to change. Throughout, this paper will attempt to describe the social-psychological variables that determine such responses.[1] First there will be a brief review of what is included under each category of response in figure 1.

Affective responses refer to emotions such as anxiety, depression, satisfaction, resentment, anger, and happiness. *Physiological responses* refer to those emotions hypothesized to be related to psychological challenge or stress. They include: risk factors in coronary heart disease such as serum cholesterol, blood

---

1. A discussion of the influence of genetic heredity, diet, exercise, and exposure to toxic substances is beyond the scope of this paper. These influences may, in part, determine some of the responses, particularly the physiological ones. The joint study of such variables and of social-psychological ones would be required to assess the relative role of each set of influences.

Figure 1
Person-Environment Fit, Social Support and Responses to Misfit

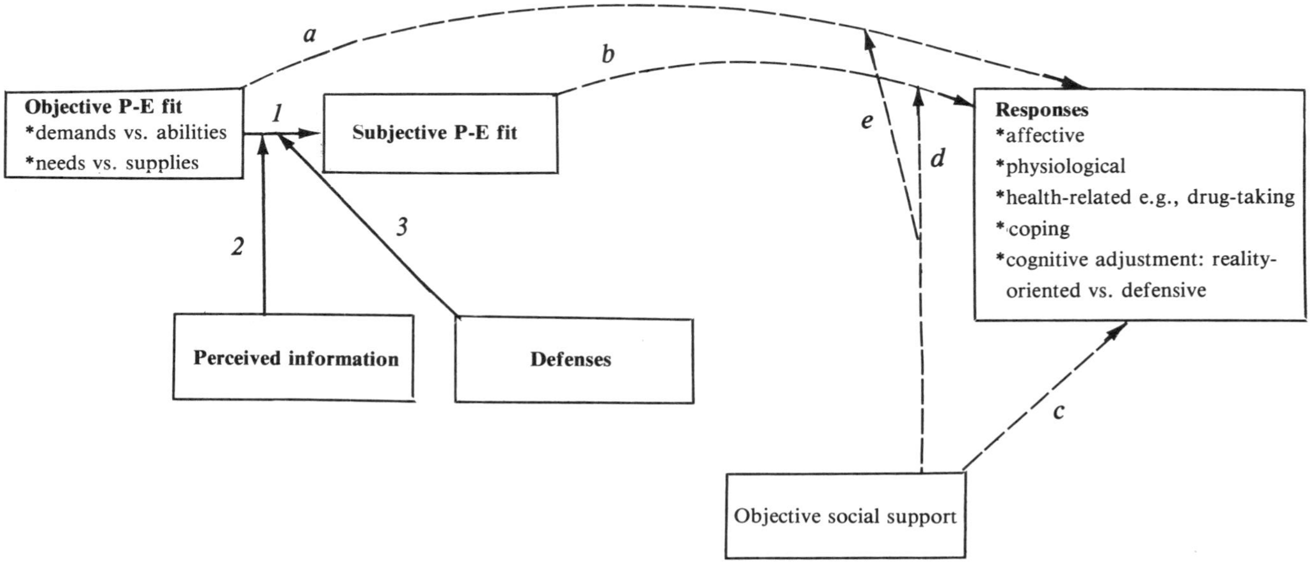

Objective P-E fit
*demands vs. abilities
*needs vs. supplies

Subjective P-E fit

Perceived information

Defenses

Objective social support

Responses
*affective
*physiological
*health-related e.g., drug-taking
*coping
*cognitive adjustment: reality-
 oriented vs. defensive

Note: Solid arrows represent hypothesized relationships. Dotted arrows represent relationships observed in other studies which are believed to have their effects through intervening variables. Those intervening variables will be considered in the figures that follow. Interactions are represented by the intersection of one arrow upon another.

pressure, and serum glucose (e.g., Rosenman and Friedman, 1963; Glass, 1977); secretions of the adrenal cortex, brought to prominence by Selye's (1956) theory of the general adaptation syndrome; changes in the electrical conductivity of the skin; and changes in the antibodies that protect against colds and influenza (Palmblad, Cantell, Strander, Froberg, Karlsson, and Levi, 1974).

Some studies have tried to predict the physiological antecedents of illness rather than illness itself. Studies of risk factors of illness and disease have sought, in some cases, to determine the social and psychological predictors of the antecedents. Social-psychological studies seeking to predict states of illness rather than their risk factors have been relatively rare because of the large samples required and the fact that considerable research support is required for the multiyear longitudinal designs. Theories that integrate findings from the social-psychological literature on risk factors and from the literature of related diseases have been even more rare. One outstanding example is the study of coronary behavior patterns by Glass (1977).

Coping responses refer to attempts to reduce objective stress by altering the objective self (e.g., seeking training in relevant job skills) or the objective environment (e.g., changing to a job that makes better use of one's skills (Doehrman, 1978). These attempts illustrate behavioral coping. Coping also refers to attempts to improve one's awareness of one's abilities and needs and one's awareness of the demands and resources of the environment (e.g., through counseling, introspection) where such knowledge is hypothesized to improve the person's objective fit with the environment. These attempts illustrate cognitive coping. Cognitive coping can also involve changes in attitude, such as a conscious effort to suppress anger or frustration because one believes that the result will be detrimental to future performance. If the person involved were to engage in preventive and secondary health care, this would represent coping by a behavioral response that is health-related (e.g., Becker, Maiman, Kirscht, Haefner, and Drachman, 1977; Caplan, Robinson, French, Caldwell, and Shinn, 1976).

Defensive responses refer to attempts to delay or avoid the perception of misfit although objective misfit exists (Doehrman, 1978). These responses may be directed toward the objective environment (e.g., a verbal or physical attack in anger against another person) or toward the objective person as in the case of suicide. Defensive responses may also be directed to the subjective environment, as with the use of classical defenses such as projection, or towards the subjective person, as with denial of affect. Such defensive cognitive alterations may be seen as efforts to distort perceptions of reality so that the demands of the environment are more in line with a person's abilities, or so that the needs of the person may *fit* the environmental resources. The concept of person-environment fit will be explained below in greater detail. Defensive responses may also involve the use of psychotropic drugs (e.g., Beckman, 1975) or smoking (e.g., Caplan, Cobb, and French, 1975), habits that seem to alter perceptions both of the self and the environment.

Predictors of Responses

Figure 1 presents a beginning framework for finding the determinants of these responses, and it provides the basis for a later, more detailed framework. Arrows with solid lines represent hypothesized paths between panels of variables. Those arrows with dotted lines represent observed relationships believed to be the result of a set of intervening processes described below.

Person-environment fit (misfit). On the left of figure 1 are boxes dealing with person-environment fit. Fit refers to the relationship between characteristics of the person (needs and abilities) and characteristics of the environment (resources and demands) measured along commensurate dimensions (such as the need for autonomy in the work setting and the availability of jobs that can provide it). The concept of person-environment (P-E) fit comes from a number of theories of human behavior (Murray, 1938; Lewin, 1951; Pervin, 1968; French, Rodgers, and Cobb, 1974) which state that human response is a function of the person and the environment. These theories may be contrasted with others that seek to explain behavior solely in terms of personality traits or environmental characteristics (such as physical space, norms, or information).

In many instances, behavior is determined largely by the environment alone (for example, most of us drive on the safe side of the road and not on the sidewalk). It is also likely that personal attributes explain individual differences in behavior. (Two people drive similar cars. One driver will accelerate rapidly after each stop, braking hard on turns and stopping suddenly; another will drive as if there were a raw egg between the gas pedal and the driver's foot.)

In some cases personality and environment may interact. For example, in a study of white-collar and blue-collar workers, Harrison (1978) and Caplan, Cobb, French, Harrison, and Pinneau (1975) found that person-environment fit explained additional variance in mental well-being not accounted for by measures either of the person's needs and abilities or the environment's supplies and demands. On the other hand, Kulka, Mann, and Klingle (1977) found that, although person-environment fit did predict variance in high school students' well-being and performance, it did not account for any variance beyond that already accounted for by measures of the person's needs and abilities alone or the school environment alone.

In any event, if one takes the position of the person-environment fit theorists, then one is likely to measure all the variables necessary to determine whether a given population responds as a function of person, environment, or of the interaction between the two.

Although the concepts of fit and dissatisfaction may seem the same, they are not considered equivalent in this model. Figure 2 illustrates a set of relationships between P-E fit and a dependent variable, satisfaction, at this point and indicates that they are not the same construct. Let us consider satisfaction-dissatisfaction as the evaluation of person-environment fit. Curve A represents the case where excess needs of the person (P > E) and excess demands of the environment (P < E) both lead to dissatisfaction (for example, having too much or too little to do on the job may

Figure 2
Three Hypothetical Relationships between Person-Environment Fit and a Response to the Degree of Fit

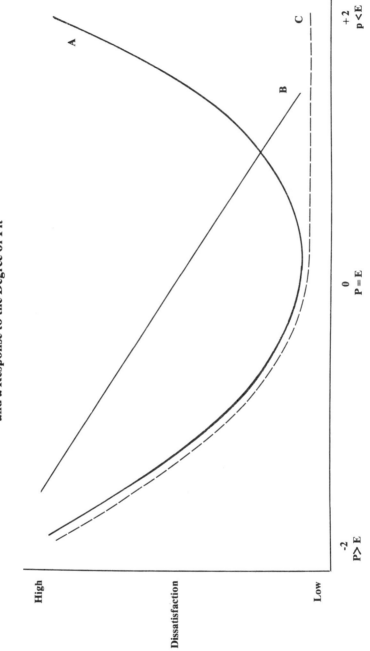

produce dissatisfaction). Curve B represents a linear relationship between the needs of the person and dissatisfaction, regardless of the supplies or demands of the environment (for example, if financial security is extremely important, dissatisfaction lessens as more money comes in, quite apart from the amount needed for minimal security). Curve C represents an asymptotic relationship between misfit and dissatisfaction (for example, some persons need friends for satisfaction, but, once the minimum number of friendships is exceeded, additional friendships may have no further effect on reducing dissatisfaction).

Hypotheses in Figure 1

Arrow 1: Objective fit determines subjective fit. Objective person-environment fit is measured independently of the person's self-report, and ideally, it is free of bias. The perception of objective fit is rarely perfect, and the sources of imperfection are represented by arrows 2 and 3.

Arrow 2: The provision of information increases the accuracy of self-perception and of the environment. French, et al. (1974) refer to these two perceptions as "accessibility of the self" and "contact with reality." Often accuracy may be lost if reliable information sources are inaccessible because the person is unaware of the proper sources or does not know how to gain access to them, or because information is being withheld, sometimes intentionally, to retain control over the person (Crozier, 1964). One intent of counseling is to increase a person's accuracy of perception: "You *do* have enough background for that job as far as math goes. Look how well you scored on the test of mathematical reasoning. However, you should take a course in programming."

Arrow 3: Defensive distortion decreases the accuracy of perception of person-environment fit. A subject may use defenses like denial and projection to avoid confronting certain objective conditions about the environment or about the self. Experimental studies (e.g., Lazarus, Opton, Nomikos, and Rankin, 1965) indicate that these defenses help to reduce the threatening nature of the objective stimuli. As a result, physiological responses typically observed under conditions of threat, such as increased heart rate and galvanic skin response, may be reduced. In the Lazarus et al. study, such defenses were deliberately induced by giving people instructions that led them to use denial or intellectualization in the interpretation of a film showing a shop accident.

Arrows a through e in Figure 1. These dotted arrows provide some of the impetus for the model to be presented in figure 3. The arrows indicate that there have been studies showing associations between either objective or subjective misfit and human responses. A few of those studies are cited for illustration.

Arrow *a* indicates the possible link between objective person-environment fit and outcomes like health and illness. For the most part, available studies deal with objective measures of the environment rather than with objective measures of fit. For example, studies have suggested that occupation (e.g., Guralnick 1963; Cobb and Rose, 1973) and socioeconomic status (e.g., Antonovsky, 1968) are associated with heart disease. Changes in the economy have been linked to mental and physical health (e.g., Brenner, 1973) and to the predisposition of case-finding agencies to identify previously untreated persons (Catalano and Dooley, in a paper presented at this conference). Occupation has also been associated with mental well-being (e.g., Caplan, et al., 1975a; Quinn, Seashore, Kahn, Mangione, Campbell, Staines, Graham, and McCollough, 1971). One study found that the fit between occupational status and the mean status of neighbors was positively associated with low rates of psychiatric illness (Wechsler and Pugh, 1967).

Some of these relationships may be merely associations rather than a means of identifying causal relationships between environment and health. For example, demographic categories such as occupation are probably not stable over time. The blue-collar and white-collar jobs of 30 years ago are different from those of today, different both in terms of the characteristics of the people who are drawn into them and of work settings and job demands. It is therefore preferable to study the effects of person-environment fit, rather than of occupation, on well-being so that this sort of shift in the definition of the predictor variable will be eliminated. Occupational data should be viewed with caution if it uses group-level (occupational category) information to suggest individual level associations. There need not be such a correspondence between group and individual findings (e.g., Caplan, et al., 1975a regarding the ecological fallacy).

As for arrow *b*, there are studies to suggest that perceived misfit or stress is associated with poor mental health (e.g., Kahn, Wolfe, Quinn, Snoek, and Rosenthal, 1964; Gurin, Veroff, and Feld, 1960; Caplan, et al., 1975a; Harrison, 1978) and with physical illness (e.g., Caplan and Jones, 1975; Friedman, Rosenman, and Carroll, 1958). These studies have been conducted at the individual level of analysis, so that their interpretation is not subject to the interpretive problems of group-level data. However, arrow *b*, as well as arrow *a*, does not indicate the *process* by which misfit creates such responses. *Why* is it that misfit (or stress) produces these effects? *What* are the intervening variables? Are there conditions under which people do not show physiological and mental strain even when subjected to it?

Figure 3 will give some hypothesized answers to these questions. For now, consider arrows *a* and *b* open to interpretation. Some of that interpretation may involve causal intervening mechanisms; other interpretations may involve noncausal, coincidental associations.

Arrows *c, d,* and *e,* dealing with social support, a concept that will be defined at length below, also represent associations that have been reported in the literature. Arrow *c* represents the finding that loss of social support can have undesirable effects on well-being. Research has found that loss of a loved one through death, divorce, or separation, can induce depression (Myers, Lindenthal, and Pepper, 1971, for example), increase the incidence of angina pectoris when the work supervisor is nonsupportive (Medalie, Snyder, Groen, Neufeld, Goldbourt, and Riss, 1973), and increase the widower's overall risk of death (Parkes, Benjamin, and Fitzgerald, 1969).

Arrow *d* represents the "buffer hypothesis" of social support. According to that hypothesis, the effects of social stress on well-being are buffered by the presence of social support. In other words, in this hypothesis a person who has social support does not show the expected positive relationship between an increase in stress and an increase in ill health. This hypothesis will be discussed more fully after social support is defined. For now, note that there are a number of studies that appear to support the buffer hypothesis (Cobb and Kasl, 1977; House and Wells, 1977; see the review by Cobb, 1976) and at least one study which fails to support it, (Pinneau, 1975). An elaboration of figure 1, presented later in the paper, will deal with the processes through which social support may effect responses to P-E misfit.

Figure 3: Mediators of Responses to Misfit

On the left side of the figure we again see arrow *1*, indicating the relationship between objective and subjective person-environment fit, and arrows *2* and *3* indicating the roles of information and of defensive perceptions.

Arrows 4 through 6: How the person responds to misfit depends on two response mediators: (a) subjective probability of response, and (b) incentive values for response.

The subjective probability of response depends on the expectation a person has of overcoming the misfit or of reaching a particular level of goal attainment. The value of a response represents its incentive or ability to satisfy certain needs of the person. Norms generate incentives to the extent that the person is not alienated from the norm-producing group and does therefore value the approval of others.

The two elements, expectancy and value, have formed the basis for major theoretical formulations of human motivation (Lewin, Dembo, Festinger, and Sears, 1944; Tolman, 1932; Atkinson and Feather, 1966; Vroom, 1964; Lawler, 1973). These theories state that the motivation to respond in a particular manner is a function of the expectancy that one can respond successfully, multiplied by the value of the outcomes to be derived from such a response.

100

Figure 3
Hypothesized Relationships among Person-Environment Fit, Motivation to Respond to Misfit, and Responses to Misfit

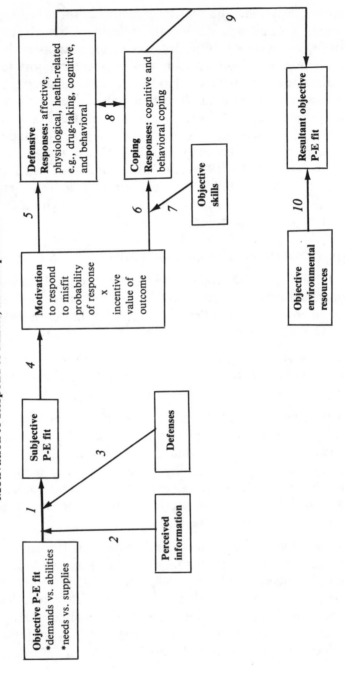

Note: Interactions are represented by the intersection of one arrow upon another.

For readers unfamiliar with expectancy-value models of motivation to respond, here is an illustration. An unemployed person is seeking employment. In this simplified example, the person is mulling over two possible responses to unemployment: applying for a low-paying job which has been listed, or waiting for a better-paying job to be listed.

Let us assume that to take the available job has a subjective probability or expectancy of .8, because the person believes that it will be easy to qualify for the job. Not taking the job will have a subjective probability or expectancy of 1.00, because the person has recently refused similar jobs and knows that it is possible to avoid this job as well.

The person attaches *incentive values* to the outcomes of these responses. On an arbitrary scale ranging from -10 to +10, where +10 equals high positive value and -10 equals high negative value, taking the low paying job will provide some income: value = +6. Taking the job will also be demeaning because the skill level is less than hoped for: value = -5. We will pretend that these are only two considerations, but the procedure could of course be elaborated to include other values. The overall value of taking the low-paying job in this example is (+6) + (-5) = +1.

Not taking the job also has some values associated with it. The further loss of income has a negative value of -3; since the person is still receiving unemployment compensation, the negative value is far from -10. Continued unemployment will be unpopular with spouse and relatives because it will make the person seem to be incompetent as a provider. In this case, a norm, "find a job," is operating in conjunction with personal values about employment. That norm induces a value of only -2 because the largest negative value of failing to secure employment for this reason occurred when the person first was laid off and is independent of the decision to take or not take this particular job. The value of resisting a demeaning job and of preserving one's sense of dignity has a value for this person of +5. So the total value of *not* taking the job is (-3) + (-2) + (+5) = 0. A theory that multiplies the expectancy of being able to perform an act by its value gives the following results in this hypothetical example:

Motivation	Response Alternative	
	Take the job	Don't take the job
Expectancy	.8	1.0
x		
Value	1.0	0.0
= Product (Subjective expected utility)	0.8	0.0

Thus, the act with the strongest product, that is the strongest *positive* motivation or subjective expected utility, is the response of taking the job. The formulations of value x expectancy models can become far more complex, but the illustration serves to point out the key elements that are employed.

The example may conjure up a picture of a calculating, highly rational individual. There are doubtless many behaviors that are governed by such ratiocination, and other behaviors that approach the other extreme and can be called *habit*. Under conditions of habit, the probability of response may be a generalized one relating to a broad range of responses. The incentive value may also be a generalized one relating to a broad range of outcomes.

Motivation and choice. The value-expectancy model may be most useful when a person perceives that there is a choice among alternative modes of response. When there is a lack of perceived choice, additional theoretical formulations become useful predictors of response. Lazarus (1966, Table II) presents a classification of how people respond to what we have called misfit. The classification suggests that when a person perceives no choice to be present because there are no viable responses the person feels competent to make, or when there are strong norms to prevent the making of a choice, then the response will be anger (Maier, 1949) and attack (Smelser, 1963), the classical responses to frustration.

When there is no palatable way to cope with a given situation, depression may be observed as well (Davis, 1952). In some cases defensive distortions may be engaged in, to rationalize away the fact that the demands of the environment are too difficult to surmount or that there is inadequate capability to surmount the misfit (Miller and Swanson, 1960). And in some cases a person may create alternatives by acting in an irrational manner to create the illusion of control (Langer, 1975).

The maintenance of personal control and choice over options has been suggested as a powerful motive, if not the central one, in human behavior (Brehm, 1966). It involves the exercise of choice over the environment, interpretation of events, and decisions in respect to courses of action (Averill, 1973). The concept of "learned helplessness" (Seligman, 1975) has been used to describe the state in which a person, through repeated unsuccessful attempts (such as seeking employment on many occasions without success), has come to accept the belief that choice and control are no longer possible. Reinforcements have become independent of responding (Hiroto and Seligman, 1975). The "helpless" person assumes that any attempt to overcome new problems will probably result in failure; consequently no effort is expended because the person has given up. In such a case, whenever misfit occurs, the generalized belief of helplessness may result in deeper depression (Klein, Fencil-Morse, and Seligman, 1976) rather than in further coping.

Research on the phenomenon of learned helplessness is relatively new, so that little is known about how to intervene and overcome it. Recent work, however, finds that depressives show the learned helplessness response only when they attribute their past failures to their own inability and not to the unreasonable demands of the environment (Klein, et al., 1976; Kuiper, et al., 1978). This suggests that the learned helplessness response might be erased if people could learn to attribute past failures to the nature of the environment and not to their own incapacity to handle them. They would obviously have to be convinced also that the present environment was unlike that of the past.

Although it is reasonable to expect that people will develop attitudes of learned helplessness when faced with certain forms of misfit (one person may expect sure failure if a task requires mechanical aptitude, another if the task involves speaking before an audience), more research on the specificity of helplessness needs to be done. There may be people who approach all life's challenges with a generalized expectancy of helplessness and accordingly cope so ineffectively that they are institutionalized. But for the general population, expectancies are more likely to be limited to specific domains of life.

Intersect of arrows 6 and 7: The quality of the person's coping response is a product of the motivation to respond and of the objective skill of the response. This hypothesis appears widely in the literature on organizational and motivation psychology (for example, Vroom, 1964; Lawler, 1973), where the term "performance" is used for the quality of the response:

$$\text{motivation} \times \text{skill} = \text{performance}$$

Arrow 8: Coping and defensive responses influence each other. It is important to understand the interrelationships among the various responses so that the unique variance of each can be identified and the effects of one response on another studied. For example, the use of drugs may lead to cognitive distortion and reduction of affect, and may, in turn, alter the effectiveness of coping responses. Affective states may lead to the use of drugs; illness and recovery may influence coping and affective states, and so on. A theory of these interrelationships, not formulated here, would be needed if these effects are to be systematically studied.

Arrows 9 and 10: The resultant objective person-environment fit is a function of a person's coping and defensive responses and the objective environmental resources relevant to this fit. The environmental resources refer to physical facilities and the objective demands and resources that bear on a person's objective fit.

The resultant fit can be an important criterion of success for policy-guided interventions. The paths that lead to arrows *9* and *10* may be seen as maps for reaching such a criterion.

This concludes the identification of the immediate determinants of subjective person-environment fit and of responses to person-environment fit. The model has indicated that the responses of the person are a function of the motivation to respond and the skill of response. The motivation has two major components: subjective probability of a successful response and the perceived value of its outcomes. Where the person perceives no responses with acceptable probabilities of success, depression and a sense of helplessness may develop. These resultant states may prevent the person from trying to cope when similar problems appear later. It is most important to discover ways to reduce this feeling of helplessness, so that mastery of and adaptation to a wide variety of environmental challenges may be made possible.

We turn now to the role that other persons play as sources of influences on person-environment fit, motivation to respond to misfit, and the responses themselves. These roles come under the rubric of "social support."

Social Support as a Determinant of Response to Misfit: Definitions

Before considering its effects, the term "social support" must be defined. If one views social support as a mechanism for potential change in certain human conditions, then support takes on the stature of guideline for social interventions. Consequently, a valid definition of social support may need to be more than an exercise in semantics. For this reason, and because there is no widely accepted definition, we shall examine the concept of support in considerable detail.

The term "social support" may be relatively new but the idea has been around for a long time. The concept of love in Biblical texts referred to supportive relations. In the 1940s and 1950s, industrial and organizational psychologists talked of "human relations" (Mayo, 1960), as social mechanisms that could improve well-being and productivity. In the 1960s, "participative management" (Likert, 1961, 1967) and "process-orientation" (Bales, 1950; Blake and Mouton, 1964) were used to refer to ways of relating to people that would make them feel included socially in the systems in which they worked and that would encourage them to contribute to those systems. In the 1970s, "social support" is being used to describe the quality of the social environment in work settings (Caplan, et al., 1975b; Cobb, 1974; Cobb and Kasl, 1977; Pinneau, 1975), and in the community (Caplan, 1974; Caplan and Killilea, 1976; Sarason, 1976). The concept has also been used to examine the effect of the social environment on the behavior of patients in treatment for mental and physical disorders (Baekeland and Lundwall, 1975; Caplan, et al., 1976).

The definitions of social support that appear in the literature show that people tend to have basically the same ideas in mind, but with significant differences—sometimes of degree, but sometimes of the whole frame of reference. This means that there is no unified definition of social support as yet. Here are some of the definitions.

Pinneau (1975) divides social support into three categories: *tangible* support "is assistance through an intervention in the person's objective environment or circumstances . . ." (p. 2). "*Appraisal* or *information* support is a psychological form of help which contributes to the individual's body of knowledge or cognitive system. . . . *Emotional* support is the communication of information which directly meets basic social-emotional needs . . . for example: a statement of esteem . . . a warm embrace." (p. 2)

Cobb (1976, p. 300) excludes tangible support intentionally and defines social support as "information leading the subject to believe that he is cared for and loved, esteemed, and a member of a network of mutual obligations."

Kahn and Quinn (1976) define social support as an *interpersonal transaction* consisting of the *expression* of positive affect including positive evaluation, affirmation or endorsement of the person's perceptions, beliefs, values, attitudes and actions, and the provision of aid including materials, information, time, and entitlements.

G. Caplan (1974, pp. 3 and 4) talks about social support *systems* which reduce "absent or confusing feedback," provide "consistent communications of what is expected of them, supports and assistance with tasks, evaluations of their performance, and appropriate rewards."

Walker, MacBride, and Vachon (1977) define emotional support as "behavior which assures an individual that his personal feelings are understood by others and considered normal in his situation" (p. 36).

Each of these definitions has a slightly different focus: information (Cobb, 1976); interpersonal transactions, expression, and provision (Kahn and Quinn, 1976); assistance, information, and communication (Pinneau, 1975); systems (G. Caplan, 1974); and behavior (Walker, et al., 1977). Many of those who wrote the definitions also talk about linkages of persons that produce social support-networks. Cobb's definition includes information that leads the person to believe that he or she is a member of a network. Cobb, G. Caplan, and Kahn and Quinn suggest that mutuality or reciprocity may be important aspects of support networks. Clearly networks are of interest because they represent two ideas: (1) the person is usually part of a social system larger than a dyad, a system that ought to be studied if we are to understand the effects of social support, and (2) people may have basic needs not only for dyadic relationships but also for a perception of membership in larger clusterings (work organizations, families, and so forth); thus the role of support in providing such inclusion deserves attention.

The topic of networks will not be pursued much further here; Walker, et al. (1977) review some of the literature on social support networks, and Kahn and Quinn provide an extensive set of hypotheses about the effects of the properties of such networks on well-being. The study of networks is one way of trying to answer the question "What creates social support?" That answer will in part depend on how social support is defined.

A discussion of four issues concerning elements of a definition of social support follows. After that, I will suggest a set of definitions for use with the theoretical model of this paper.

(1) *Objective versus subjective social support.* A distinction should be made between social support that is objectively observed and social support perceived by the target of the support. In this way we can distinguish between the pragmatic act of support and its symbolic meaning to the target person (Tannenbaum, 1968).[2]

(2) *Supportive behavior versus relationships.* Concepts such as trust, mutual liking, and inclusion in a social network refer to relationships. Listening to and agreeing with the person's view of self and environment refer to behaviors. Incorporating (1), we can deal with objective versus subjective (i.e., perceived) behaviors and objective versus subjective (i.e., perceived) relationships.

One could operationalize the measurement of objective social support by limiting it to the observation of behaviors such as eye contact, posture, and positive and negative evaluative statements. Attempts to characterize supportive behavior in such terms have been tried. The danger here, however, is that such behaviors may be only an outward expression of a set of caring attitudes held by the giver of social support (for example, Levy, Knight, Padgett, and Wollert, 1977).[3] If people forget this, they may be tempted to believe that they can produce perceived social support in the target person simply by adopting these behaviors or by inducing others to behave in like manner. Accordingly, it is again important to distinguish between the behavior of the support giver and its meaning to the target of support.

Given the choice between using observational data on the behavior of the giver and observational data on the relationship between giver and receiver, the relationship may be a better indicator of the receiver's *felt* social support. But the latter's own

---

2. In some cases the source of subjective social support may be perceived as supernatural (God, a departed relative). If the support is perceivable by the person, even though not objectively measurable, then it should have the same hypothesized impact as any other form of perceived support.

3. If certain attitudes about others, as well as behavioral skills, are required by the giver to produce perceived social support, then programs which attempt to identify only behaviors and to train people in the exhibition of them may not produce so high a quality of perceived social support as is possible. The provider's attitudes and motives toward the target person, if left untouched and if nonsupportive, will probably reduce the skill and sensitivity with which the taught behaviors are exhibited.

reported perceptions, if elicited nondefensively, may be superior to the objective observation of the relationship as an indicator of the receiver's felt social support.

(3) *Unique versus overlapping elements in the definition of support.* It is assumed that social support is multidimensional until shown otherwise. It is also assumed that support's components need not be positively correlated. So far, definitions have not made it clear where they stand on these assumptions and have not stated whether or not all the characteristics of social support need be present or whether any single element is sufficient. For example, must one communicate information about inclusion in a group, esteem, and the fact that one is loved to produce social support, or are these elements interchangeable? Nor is it clear whether or not communication of information about one element of support usually conveys only that fact and no other elements. For example, to give a hitchhiker a ride during a storm probably provides tangible support as well as serving to communicate a helping attitude to the hitchhiker. Is this multiple effect characteristic of social support in general?

At this stage, there is no theory of social support to suggest whether the elements of social support represent factors that are unique or overlapping. The lists of elements of support, therefore, should be regarded as indicators of the width of the domains rather than as indicators of their dimensionality.

(4) *Does "support" embody value judgments?* Let us try a projective test. What is the first word that comes to your mind after you see the words *SOCIAL SUPPORT?* The odds are that you thought of a word that you would evaluate as "good" rather than "bad."

"Support" has a connotation of helpfulness; this is useful in lay language, but it may lead behavioral scientists astray if they tend to define social support in terms of its supposed beneficial effects. Effect-based definitions can present problems. For one thing, they can produce seemingly contradictory deductions. Consider, for example, the following effect-linked definition: support is behavior by the giver that leads the target person to believe that his/her beliefs and perceptions are held by others. Given such a definition, it would be supportive to agree with a suicidal person that life was not worth living, that the basic skills to survive were lacking, and that suicide would be a good response. Second, such definitions make it impossible to test the hypotheses embodied in them. If a certain sort of behavior does not produce the intended effect, one can always say, "Well, that behavior is obviously not social support."

To solve these problems, the effects in effect-based definitions should be recast as *hypothesized* effects of social support rather than as elements of its definition. These effects would then be subject to empirical testing, leaving open the door for the discovery of those effects of social support that were not anticipated on the basis of prior theory or intuition. We would be more likely to study the conditions under which social support did or did not promote human well-being.

Cobb's definition of social support, "information leading the subject to believe that he is cared for and loved, esteemed, and a member of a network of mutual obligations," is an example of an effect-based definition; it can be used to suggest a number of hypotheses that can be tested. Consider the following. Cobb's use of the concept of information suggests that one could study the objective sending of messages with a content of caring, esteem, and inclusion as measures of objective social support. One could also study the perception by the target person that such messages had been sent. Then the following hypothesis could be tested:

Objective behaviors that contain messages about care and love, esteem and value, and acceptance into "a network of communication and mutual obligation" will produce the following respective perceptions in the target person:

(a) "I *am* loved and cared for." This perception differs from the perception, "someone has *told* me that I am cared for."

(b) "I am esteemed." Again we distinguish between another's telling one that one is esteemed and actually perceiving oneself to be so. Self-esteem is positively related to both the objective esteem of others and to the perception that they hold that esteem, but the relationship is *not* perfect (French, Sherwood, and Bradford, 1966).

(c) "I *am* a member of a network of communication and mutual obligation." Again, we would distinguish between perceiving what others have told one and one's perception that "I really *am* a member."

In the long run, social support may come to refer to an area of study dealing with hypothesized effects of behaviors intended to be helpful on the perceptions of such intention, on the feeling of being helped, and on the adaptation, adjustment, and well-being of the target person. By then, we will be less concerned with defining social support and more concerned with predicting those social behaviors that will improve human perceptions of well-being and actual well-being.

A new definition of social support. In one sense the material that follows is not new. From time to time Sidney Cobb, John French, Jr., Robert Kahn, Robert Quinn, and I have exchanged memos and have met to discuss the definition of social support and its hypothesized effects. The following are some working definitions based, in part, on these discussions; I offer them to my colleagues and to the reader as further food for thought, for tinkering and refinement, and with no assumption that they represent the final word.

The concept of "social support" will be altered somewhat here by the addition of two modifiers: "tangible" and "psychological." *Tangible* refers to attributes of the physical environment or, as Cobb (1976) points out, anything that has mass or physical energy (e.g., money, day care, transportation). *Psychological* refers to all those attributes of the person that do not have mass and physical energy, including needs and motives, values, beliefs, perceptions, and emotions.

Objective tangible support will refer to *behavior directed towards providing* the person with tangible resources that *may* (are hypothesized to) benefit the person's mental or physical well-being. Money, shelter, and transportation are examples of such support.

The criteria for mental or physical well-being are *defined by the scientist, policy maker, or practitioner;* one is free to place definitions of well-being here that represent therapeutic goals, although a definition of well-being will not be specified in this paper. Note, however, that some definitions of positive mental health do consider behaviors which may move the person in the direction of person-environment fit—for example, Jahoda's (1958) and Clausen's (1963) concept of environment mastery and Phillips' (1968) concept of adaptation. The target person's criteria of well-being will be considered when subjective social support is defined.

The definition of objective tangible support and the definitions of support that follow, are not effect- or response-based. The behaviors to be watched for should be those which, on the basis of theory and research, appear to promote well-being (Kahn and Quinn, 1976). But, whether or not such goal-directed behavior of the giver does promote well-being in the receiver is a matter for hypothesis testing and not a part of the present definition.

All of the definitions of support proposed here focus on support *behavior* rather than on the concept of supportive relationships. The concept of supportive relationships should, however, be possible to derive from these definitions of behavior. For example, an objective tangible supportive relationship may be defined as the exchange of objective tangible support behavior. Here an observer would look for evidence of reciprocity in the exchange of tangible goods.

Objective psychological support will refer to *behavior* which appears to be directed towards providing the person with *cognitions* (values, attitudes, beliefs, perceptions of the environment) and *affective states* that constitute or are hypothesized to promote well-being. For example, one might provide praise and encouragement as forms of objective psychological support. As with objective tangible support, the social scientist, practitioner, or policy maker retains the responsibility for setting up the criteria for well-being (these criteria might be defined as those set by the target person) and the criteria for judging whether the support provider is directing behavior toward the promotion of the target person's well-being. Whether or not these behaviors that appear to be directed to producing mentally healthy cognitions and affects actually do so is a matter for hypothesis testing, and is not an inherent part of the definition.

It might be of interest to define objective psychological social support as behavior intended to promote the person's well-being or person-environment fit. However, the theory and methodology for inferring intention is not at present well-developed and may not be so for some time to come (e.g., Nisbett and Wilson, 1977). For an observer to judge the goals towards which the provider of social support is striving seems less difficult than for the observer to infer the intentions of the provider. So, to describe the goal-directed behavior rather than the intention of the provider has been suggested as a preferable way to operationalize objective support (J. R. P. French, Jr., personal communication, 1978).

Objective tangible and psychological support can be observed only if one states the specific goals of the support behavior. An observer would code the extent to which such behavior seemed to be directed to these goals. For example, if one wished to help the unemployed to obtain jobs, one might specify that objective tangible support should be directed to putting the person in contact with offices or services that could provide employment information. The dispatch of a mobile office (a van) to a neighborhood hard hit by layoffs might fulfill this objective. One would code the presence or absence of such a unit, the rate at which it could process unemployed people, and other indicators of its tangible support capacity.

The objective psychological support of the van might be judged in terms of whether its personnel were communicating information directed toward:

(a) increasing the unemployed person's perceptions that he or she does have the ability to seek a job or to behave in whatever other way might be stipulated as adjustive and adaptive;

(b) increasing the person's perceptions that jobs are available to match the person's qualifications;

(c) increasing the person's perceptions that others will support job-seeking efforts, creating or enhancing such norms;

(d) increasing the person's perceptions that the person belongs to or has access to a network that will provide needed information and a sense of emotional comfort and acceptance;

(e) increasing the person's perceptions that the pursuit of a job is a worthwhile goal;

(f) increasing the accuracy of the person's perceptions of the correct and incorrect ways to pursue the goal and of the extent to which the person was pursuing the goal correctly; and

(g) decreasing negative affective states.

The observer's ratings of social support behaviors would not be based on success in achieving goals but only on their apparent goal direction. Note that the above list includes many, if not most, of the elements that have been suggested in the definitions of social support by others, reviewed earlier. Research on the patterns of help-giving in self-help groups (Levy, et al., 1977) finds the same elements of goal-directed behavior present, but the emphasis tends to vary with the type of group; for example, behavior control groups tend to use more positive reinforcement than do stress-coping groups.

Subjective tangible support is defined as the *target person's perception* that certain needed physical resources in the environment are being provided by others; the definition is thus based on the target person's point of view. The extent to which the target person's definition of what is needed overlaps with that of the scientist, practitioner, or policy maker may be an important matter for empirical study, but it is of no consequence in defining *subjective* tangible support.

In the further discussion of the theoretical model, following these definitions, the term "perceived information" instead of the concept of subjective tangible support will be used to refer to the perception both of tangible aspects of the environment and of incoming information about the self, including the consequences of particular acts. All these elements are subsumed under perceived information. This simplification will not compromise the major features of the model.

Whereas *objective* psychological support relates to behavior aimed at producing cognitions and affects judged to promote objectively defined well-being, *subjective* psychological support relates to the target person's perception that such behavior on the part of the other person will promote personal well-being. Whether or not the behavior will indeed promote well-being is an empirical question, but it is irrelevant to this definition. The only thing that matters is that the target person believes that the behavior will promote cognitions and affects that will agree with his/her well-being. Subjective psychological support is, in essence, a perception of trust in the other person.

This feeling of trust, or subjective psychological support, is distinguished from any perceptions the target person might have of the messages that the provider of support is sending. For example, the target person may hear the provider saying "You are important," or "Here is a way to gain fame and fortune." These statements may be judged to be objective social support, but only if the target person trusts the sender of such messages; accordingly the perceived content of the messages is not considered subjective psychological support.

Trust may represent an assessment of the motives of the provider for both present and future support. The future perspective is important. Feelings of trust may often be based not so much on what the provider is doing at the moment, but on the belief that if some crisis arose in the future, the provider could be counted on for protection against psychological and physical harm.

This concludes the set of definitions of social support. In the hypotheses to follow, we shall see a framework in which trust serves as an important information gate. It can allow the person access to, or protection from, information from others. Gaining access has a high value because information which gains access influences the person's perceived person-environment fit, motivation to respond to misfit, skill level of responding, and affective states.

Social Support as a Determinant of Response to Misfit: Hypotheses

These hypotheses are shown in figure 4, an elaboration of figure 3.

Arrow 10: Objective tangible support has a positive effect on objective person-environment fit. This hypothesis is repeated here with the substitution of objective tangible support for the objective environmental resources used at the origin of arrow *10* in figure 3. A layoff or job termination would be an example of a loss of objective tangible support which would alter objective fit. The loss of a job may increase misfit in respect to needs for affiliation, recognition, use of one's skills and abilities, and financial security.

Note that the path from objective tangible support to resultant fit does not require that the person perceive support in order to benefit from it. For example, a person whose coping response to unemployment is the filling out of an application form might reduce unemployment misfit by means of both the person's response and external resources. The person may have shown a high degree of competence in completing the form. The employing organization might have facilitated the fit by simplifying the form so that applicants for a job with 10th-grade requirements would not need a college education to fill out the form accurately. Although one might never be aware of such external resources, they could make a significant difference in one's employment chances.

Line 11: Objective tangible support is associated with objective psychological support. This is a noncausal association. It represents the likelihood that the provision of material resources is often a signal to the target person about the attitudes of the giver. The job placement counselor who hands a client a brochure about

Figure 4

**Hypothesized Effects of Social Support on Person-Environment Fit,
Motivation to Respond to Misfit, and Responses to Misfit**

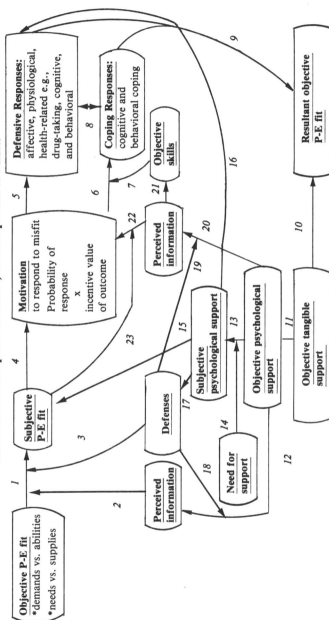

Note: Interactions are indicated by the intersection of one arrow upon another or by the intersection of two arrows with an oval with an x in its center.

the client's occupational interests may be trying to signal to the client, "I want to help you find a job," or alternatively, "I am busy. Read this brochure and you will find out what I don't have time to tell you." Sometimes it may be difficult to tell whether objective tangible support is also objective psychological support or a deliberate *lack* of it.

Arrow 12: Objective psychological support increases the amount of information the person perceives about objective fit. This is a weak hypothesis; a stronger one regarding objective psychological support and perceived information will be presented in the discussion of the intersection of arrows 12 and 18.

Arrow 13: Objective psychological support increases subjective psychological support.

Intersection of arrows 13 and 14: The perceived need of the target person for social support increases the extent to which objective psychological support produces subjective psychological support. The perceived need for social support can be stated in terms of several conceptualizations involving needs for control, reactance, need for independence, and equity, all of which appear to be compatible. These conceptualizations are briefly elaborated below.

The extent to which objective psychological support is perceived as psychologically supportive may depend on whether or not the target person perceives this support as a threat to needs for control or to needs to maintain some decisional choice (Bem, 1972; Nisbett and Valins, 1971; Wickland, 1974; Wortman and Brehm, 1975). Such threats are hypothesized to produce tendencies to reassert one's freedom of choice and control (reactance), even if such a reaction runs counter to one's initial goals. This behavior has been called reactance (Brehm, 1966). For example, Alice brings Tom home to meet her parents. They effusively praise her choice. The next day Alice turns Tom down in favor of Mike. In doing so, she attempts to exert a choice which is not apparently due to the pressure of her parents.

It is likely that persons who have strong needs for independence or autonomy are particularly sensitive to objective psychological support that attempts to control or which may seek to help the target person by providing direct aid rather than enhanced options for choice. On the other hand, if the target person has strong needs for dependence, objective psychological support aimed at *enhancing* freedom of choice may be viewed as psychologically nonsupportive.

The arousal of the need for social support may vary according to the situation, in addition to varying according to the personality disposition of dependence-independence. The target person may believe it legitimate to be given a choice in some situations("I want to be given an array of jobs from which to make my selection") but not in others ("I do not want the surgeon to ask me which scalpel should be used"). To present a person with a choice when you are being counted on to make the decision because of your expertise or legal right may undermine the person's trust in you. These considerations suggest that it is important to define the bases of power (French and Raven, 1968) that are anticipated by the target person in the relationship with the provider of objective psychological support.

Need for social support can also be viewed in terms of *equity* (Adams, 1965). According to an equity theory of social exchange, if the target person perceives objective psychological support in excess of the person's ability to repay it, or in excess of what the person deserves, then psychological tension or discomfort will be aroused. The target person will tend to resist further objective support lest the obligation to repay it be so great as to result in loss of freedom of choice or be excessive. Under such conditions, which may promote reactance behavior, the person's low need for social support will destroy any positive relationship between objective and subjective psychological support.

The proposition that equity is important in determining the acceptance of objective psychological support is congruent with the view of social support relationships as reciprocal (G. Caplan, 1976; Cobb, 1976). Reciprocity allows giver and receiver to maintain an equity of exchange and a sense of freedom from obligation.[4] If obligation exists, then the spontaneity of social psychological support is removed. Spontaneity on the part of the giver may lead the target person to believe that the giver is providing support out of goodness of heart, rather than because "page 32, paragraph 5 of 'Procedures for Dealing with Clients'" says to do so.

Arrow 15: Subjective psychological support increases subjective person-environment fit. The person who feels trust in a relationship may experience increases in person-environment fit on dimensions dealing with social relationships (affiliation, advice, understanding, sharing of responsibilities). The presence of a helpful other will connote that subjective demands will be easier to meet because the other person will provide resources to help meet them. Perceived needs will be seen as better met because of additional supplies provided by the other person.

Arrow 16: Subjective psychological support reduces negative affect. Anxiety and depression should be decreased when subjective psychological support is received. It is possible, however, that this result occurs partly because of the perception that the giver of support is protecting one's choice over options. As was noted earlier, lack of choice may lead to depression.

Arrow 17: Subjective psychological support lowers defensive mechanisms by increasing feelings of security and reducing the need to defend the self from harm. Arrow 17 points to defensive

4. For some persons, the concept of "reciprocity" may mean the exchange of goods or information of like kind ("I hug you, so you hug me") but such a connotation is beyond the meaning of the word. In relationships between professionals and their clients the exchange may involve the trade of goods that are *equivalent only in value* ("You give me advice, and I give you money"). Jackins (1962) has pointed out that in helping relationships that involve self-help networks—like that between acquaintances—the receiver of social support may have equity restored by being able to contribute something useful to the relationship, even if it is housework or helping to repair something which belongs to the giver. Jackins points out that indeed the receiver of social support may need it so badly that it is not psychologically possible for her or him to provide payment in kind, and here bartering arrangements are advisable. In this regard, one might define a supportive host as one who can distinguish between guests who offer to make salads because they feel they are receiving more hospitality than they deserve and wish to restore a sense of equity to the relationship, and guests who make such an offer as a gesture of etiquette fully hoping it will be turned down.

mechanisms, such as filtering, distortion, denial, and projection, that would interfere with a person's ability to accept new information regarding objective person-environment fit. Such defenses might also interfere with accepting information regarding: (a) the person's abilities to cope with misfit; (b) the value or incentives of responding to the misfit in a particular manner; and (c) ways in which response skills can be improved.

Intersection of arrows 12 and 18: Objective psychological support directed to giving information about objective fit will be perceived as valid to the extent that the person's defenses are not aroused by such information.

Intersection of arrows 19 and 20: Objective psychological support directed to providing feedback about abilities to respond to misfit in various ways, the incentive value of each response, and the ways responses can be improved will be perceived as valid to the extent that the person's defenses are not aroused by such information. This hypothesis, like the preceding one, says that if the target person becomes defensive, then information will not be accepted. The defense mechanisms will eliminate the information by methods of selective attention, reinterpretation, and distortion. Such mechanisms will be used to protect the target person from what is seen as information harmful to the self.

When the person trusts the giver of support, defense mechanisms will interfere less with the transmission of information; information will be perceived and viewed as valid even if it does not affirm the target person's perceptions, beliefs, and attitudes. In only one case should affirmation be required: the giver of support must affirm the target person's perception that the giver can be trusted to be a protector from harm.

Arrow 21: To the extent that the person perceives information about how to improve self-performance as valid and as promoting appropriate goals, that information will result in an increase in the person's objective skills in this area. Perhaps this is a reminder to those who are involved in programs designed to increase the skills of certain groups that the mere presentation of didactic information may have no detectable effect on actual skill unless it is accepted as valid and useful. Following arrow *21* back to its antecedents, one sees that the element of trust must be present if instruction is to have the intended effect on actual skill level.

Arrow 22: New information about the probability of successful responses to misfit and about their incentive values will change a person's motivation to respond in certain ways if the information is perceived as valid and as serving felt needs. Following this arrow back, we again see that efforts to increase a person's motivation to respond to a particular person-environment misfit in a particular way (such as a pep talk) may not have their intended effect unless the person trusts the sender of the message and so does not screen out the message by defensive listening.

Intersection of arrows 22 and 23: Information from others perceived as valid and as promoting well-being buffers (conditions) the effects of person-environment fit on responses to misfit by increasing motivation to cope. Cobb (1976) suggests that social support may buffer the effects of stress (misfit) on well-being only when there is a crisis or acute stress, defined as a major and sudden increase in person-environment misfit.

The sharp increase in objective person-environment misfit in the buffer hypothesis is like a trigger. Objective social support should occur only when the increase in misfit exceeds a certain rate over time. No response by the provider of support should be offered until a certain threshold of *change* in misfit is exceeded. Figure 5 shows a hypothetical example.

In figure 5a the nonlinear relationship between rate of increase in misfit and responsiveness of objective social support is shown. In figure 5b the effect of rate of increase in misfit on perceived helplessness is shown to interact with, and to be buffered by, the responsive objective social support. If the social support is nonresponsive, then this hypothesis predicts that no buffering will take place and that the relationship between rate of increase in objective misfit and coping disability, made linear in this example, will remain unchanged.

When buffering does take place, we would expect to find that the perceived increase in misfit will also be great, and that the

123

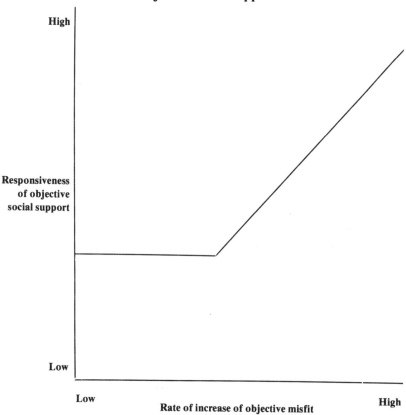

Figure 5a
Hypothetical Relationship between Rate of Increase
in Objective Misfit and the Responsiveness
of Objective Social Support

Figure 5b
Hypothetical Relationship between the Rate of Increase
in Objective Misfit and Coping Disability

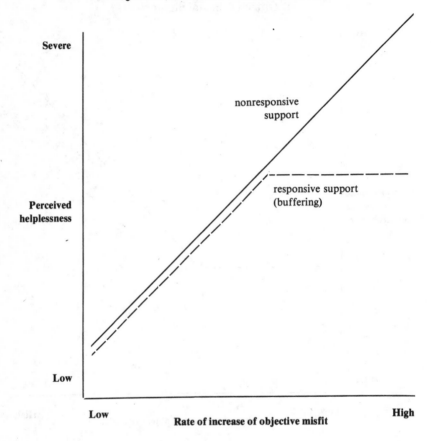

objective psychological support, if responsive, will increase subjective social support. The increase in subjective social support should, in turn, open the person's access to information about resources of psychological security, thus reducing feelings of helplessness and resulting in a perceived ability to cope with the situation.

EVALUATING THE MODEL

In this last section of the paper, three topics are discussed: omissions from the model, the validity of the model, and sources of bias in the model.

What Does the Model Omit?

The following topics are considered briefly: the dimensions of fit and coping to be studied; what other mechanisms of social support buffering may be present; the best sources of objective social support; what it is that supports the support givers; social support networks; and social mechanisms in the improvement of the positive relationship between objective and subjective psychological support.

1. *What dimensions of fit and coping should be studied?* Although there are lists of dimensions, such as Murray's list of needs (1938), the model does not suggest which dimensions are preferable. Other theories, combined with observations of the population to be studied, are required for an informed answer to this question.

2. *Which sources of objective social support are the best?* Should more emphasis be placed on the development of professional services or should we be increasing the skills of the lay network? The model can provide a framework for evaluating this question because the effectiveness of different sources of objective support can be compared. In longitudinal studies the relationship between sources of objective support and perceived support, motivation, responses to misfit, and resultant fit can be examined.

3. *What supports the support givers?* The model in figure *4* is intended to be generically applicable to the explanation of human responses to misfit. Therefore it should be possible to substitute the giver of social support for the target person and to study the conditions that promote and hinder the ability to meet demands of others for social support. In programs of intervention where objective social support resources are to be created, it may be wise to examine the extent to which such programs have social support mechanisms to promote the required role-behavior of support givers (see Caplan, 1979).

4. *What about social support networks?* Kahn and Quinn (1976) have proposed a set of hypotheses about the nature of social networks and social linkages that may allow one to determine those social structures which prevent coping disability. For example, networks of potential providers of objective social support can be described in terms of density (the extent to which the members of the net communicate with one another); size; anchoring (e.g., are they the primary acquaintance of the target person or of the spouse?; are they related as members of some formal organization such as a work setting?; are they related in a professional helping relationship?); stability over time; frequency of contact; and so on.

A recent review of research on the role of networks during the crisis of bereavement (Walker, MacBride, and Vachon, 1977, p. 40) ". . . suggests that there is often a lack of fit between the social and psychological needs of the individual in crisis and the individual's social support network." Studies of the properties of networks could tell us whether or not certain characteristics of these networks are associated with good adaptation. The findings could provide a basis for studies of interventions that sought to change networks or of observed natural changes in network formation. These studies would help to determine whether the networks were a *determinant* of the hypothesized processes that promote adaptive well-being, or were a *symptom* of other influences on adaptive well-being.

If properties of networks are found to vary in their effectiveness according to the type of misfit (for example, Parkes, 1972, suggests that small, dense networks may entrap people during crises of major psychosocial transition by providing limited norms, information, and social contacts), then studies might be justified that describe the distribution of such networks in the population. Such studies could help to identify groups lacking social support resources required for potential management of crises.

5. *Are there social mechanisms that can increase the likelihood that objective psychological support will be perceived as psychologically supportive?* Participation may be an effective social mechanism to produce perceived psychological support. Participation is the amount of a person's influence on decisions and plans that affect the person (after French, Israel, and Aas, 1960). Participation is one way of allowing target persons to indicate the goals on which they want help, and how and when they want to be helped.

Participation as a process allows people to decide how much control they want, and how much control they want others to exert, over a given situation. It avoids the possibility of violating the person's needs for autonomy, or lack of it, by providing an information feedback loop to the givers of objective social support. Participation appears to promote adaptive behavior beneficial both to the target person and to the social system to which the target person belongs (Likert, 1961, 1967; Argyris, 1964; Coch and French, 1948; Morse and Reimer, 1956), providing that such participation is seen as legitimate (French, et al., 1960).

In counseling, participation may consist of permitting the client to exert choice over alternatives. For example, the ultimatum, "You must go to all these job interviews," may be viewed as nonsupportive because it removes choice and may force reactance (dropping out of contact with the job counselor as an act of defiance). By contrast, suppose the counselor were to say, "It may be hard for you to interview for all these jobs. How many would you like to try before coming back to talk with me?" Here the client is being asked to participate in the employment decision and is more likely to view the counselor as someone who can be trusted.

An account of an experiment in which participation was used to improve person-environment fit in social networks is found in the work of Campbell (1973). The procedure was applied to engineers in a federal agency. Participation appeared to work well so long as the dimensions of misfit were not such as to require resources from outside the network. But when adjustments in misfit required a change in demands or resources beyond the network, the process was ineffective. Campbell's study suggests that research on participation, as a mode of building objective and subjective psychological support, should examine the span of control and authority of the social support network, in order to determine the dimensions of misfit that can and cannot be altered by particular networks.[5]

Is the Model Valid?

At the outset it was suggested that a good theory should suggest the targets for an intervention. This model suggests as targets: perceived psychological support; perceptions of abilities and needs and of environmental resources and demands; and perceptions of the incentive values and probabilities of being able to respond to misfit in one manner or another.

To evaluate the effects of any social intervention or policy-guided program, one would need a model that could distinguish between those orders of social support which did and did not lead to desirable levels of objective person-environment fit. One would also want a model that could identify the points in the process between intervention and outcome where less successful interventions failed, so that modifications could be aimed at overcoming these barriers. For example, was an

5. The truly adaptive target person may be one who knows how to link up with those social support networks that are appropriate to the sort of fit needing attention. The truly adaptive organization or society may be one that trains its members how to determine which networks best suit a particular problem; it may also be one that knows how to make these networks available.

unsuccessful outcome due to failure to produce a perception of trust? Did it provide the wrong information about the values of certain types of responses? Did it fail because it did not communicate new information about the norms (for example, did it immerse the person in a peer-support group of those facing the same category of misfit)? Did it fail because, although it produced high motivation and the correct response, it did not deliver the objective environmental resources that were supposed to remove certain barriers to coping?

To answer such questions, a model must have a known or at least reasonably estimated validity. This paper has presented a largely untested model. The following steps would help to determine its validity and therefore its usefulness in answering some of the above questions:

(1) The development of valid measures of objective social support as defined for use in this model and the further development of existing measures of subjective social support.

(2) The development of valid measures of the other elements in the model required for testing its validity: measures of coping, cognitive distortion and defenses, perceived ability, and perceived incentive value of different modes of responding to misfit. The measurement of objective misfit also remains a challenge.

(3) Studies of the effects of social support in samples where some of the respondents will face an acute crisis situation, where other respondents at about the same level of misfit will face a chronic situation, and where still other groups will show normal variation in person-environment fit. Such studies would clarify the role of social support as a buffer of the effects of stress or misfit on responses to misfit (strain, mental and physical illness).

The studies should be longitudinal unless the processes and their effects are considered as occurring simultaneously. For example, Likert (1967) suggests that when participative systems of management are adapted, it may take as long as three years before the benefits are visible. The interval of effect for individuals may vary depending on the coping behavior being studied. In school systems, the shortest time for judging the effects of social support might be a minimum of one semester. In studies of unemployment, estimates of the longitudinal period of study might be based on the current range of time it takes to secure employment or reemployment after a layoff. In studies of child socialization, a research program spanning several years might be desirable.

Is the Model Biased?

This question refers to whether or not the concepts and casting of the model are such that the onus for adaptation and adjustment is placed on the person ("person blame") or on the environment ("system blame"); (Gurin, Gurin, Lao and Beattie, 1969). Do we assume here that the Procrustean bed is in the hands of the environment or in the hands of the person?

The concept of person-environment fit makes no assumptions about who is to do the adjusting. The concept of fit, however, does raise the question about whether fit should be achieved by changing the environment's demands and resources, by changing the person's abilities and goals, or by some combination of the two. The answer to this question is probably dependent upon at least two considerations: the availability and cost of technologies and social mechanisms for improving person-environment fit; and societal values about the use of such technologies and mechanisms. The societal values of interest here are the ones that indicate which aspects of the person should accommodate to society and which should be protected from having to make such an accommodation.

Although the model in figure 4 is not intended to indicate the values we ought to pursue, it (and models like it) may be useful in helping social groups to determine to what extent interventions aimed at increasing person-environment fit do so in socially valued ways. If our models can provide this resource, then we shall have the satisfaction of knowing that we are contributing both to scientific knowledge and to its social utilization.

REFERENCES

Adams, J. S. Inequity in social exchange. In L. Berkowitz (ed.), *Advances in Social Psychology.* New York: Academic Press, 1965.

Antonovsky, A. Social class and the major cardiovascular diseases. *Journal of Chronic Diseases,* 1968, 21, 65-106.

Argyris, C. *Integrating the Individual and the Organization.* New York: Wiley, 1964.

Atkinson, J. W., and Feather, N. T. *A Theory of Achievement Motivation.* New York: Wiley, 1966.

Averill, J. R. Personal control over aversive stimuli and its relationship to stress. *Psychological Bulletin.* 1973, 80, 286-303.

Baekeland, Frederick and Lundwall, Lawrence. Dropping out of treatment: a critical review. *Psychological Bulletin,* 1975, 82, 738-783.

Bales, R. F. *Interaction Process Analysis: A Method for the Study of Small Groups.* Cambridge, MA: Addison-Wesley, 1950.

Bem, D. J. Self-perception theory. In L. Berkowitz (Ed.), *Advances in Experimental Social Psychology.* New York: Academic Press, 1972.

Besant, Walter. *East London.* New York: The Century Company, 1901.

Becker, M. H., Maiman, L. A., Kirscht, J. P., Haefner, D. P., and Drachman, R. H. The Health Belief Model and prediction of dietary compliance: a field experiment. *Journal of Health and Social Behavior,* 1977, 18, 348-366.

Beckman, L. J. Women alcoholics. A review of social and psychological studies. *Journal of Studies on Alcohol,* 1975, 36, 797-824.

Blake, R. R. and Mouton, J. S. *The Managerial Grid: Key Orientations for Achieving Production Through People.* Houston: Gulf Publishing, 1964.

Brehm, J. W. *A Theory of Psychological Reactance.* New York: Academic Press, 1966.

Brenner, M. H. *Mental Illness and the Economy.* Cambridge: Harvard University Press, 1973.

132

Campbell, D. B. A program to reduce coronary heart disease risk factors by altering job stresses. Doctoral dissertation, University of Michigan, 1973. University Microfilms No. 74-15681.

Caplan, Gerald. *Support Systems and Community Mental Health: Lectures on Concept Development.* New York: Behavioral Publications, 1974.

Caplan, Gerald and Killilea, M. *Support Systems and Mutual Help: Multidisciplinary Explorations.* New York: Grune and Stratton, 1974.

Caplan, R. D. Patient, provider, and organization: hypothesized determinants of adherence. In C. M. Clark, Jr. and S. J. Cohen (eds.), *New Directions in Patient Compliance.* Lexington, MA: Lexington Books, 1979, 25-110.

Caplan, R. D., Cobb, Sidney, and French, J. R. P., Jr. Relationships of cessation of smoking with job stress, personality, and social support. *Journal of Applied Psychology,* 1975a, 60, 211-219.

Caplan, R. D., Cobb, Sidney, French, J. R. P., Jr., Harrison, R. V., and Pinneau, S. R. *Job Demands and Worker Health: Main Effects and Occupational Differences.* Cincinnati: National Institute for Occupational Safety and Health, HEW Publication No. (NIOSH) 75-160, April 1975b, 342 pages.

Caplan, R. D. and Jones, K. W. Effects of work load, role ambiguity, and Type A personality on anxiety, depression, and heart rate. *Journal of Applied Psychology,* 1975, 60, 73-719.

Caplan, R. D., Robinson, E. A. R., French, J. R. P., Jr., Caldwell, J. R., and Shinn, Marybeth. *Adhering to Medical Regimens: Pilot Experiments in Patient Education and Social Support.* Ann Arbor: Institute for Social Research, 1976.

Clausen, J. A. Sociology of mental disease. In H. E. Freeman, S. Levine, and L. G. Reeder (eds.), *Handbook of Medical Sociology,* Englewood Cliffs, NJ: Prentice-Hall, 1963.

Cobb, Sidney. Social support as a moderator of life stress. *Psychosomatic Medicine,* 1976, 38, 300-314.

Cobb, Sidney. Physiologic changes in men whose jobs were abolished. *Journal of Psychosomatic Research,* 1974, 18, 245-258.

133

Cobb, Sidney and Kasl, S. V. *Termination: The Consequences of Job Loss.* NIOSH Research Report. U. S. Government Printing Office, DHEW (NIOSH) Publication no. 77-224, 1977.

Cobb, Sidney and Rose, R. M. Hypertension, peptic ulcer, and diabetes in air traffic controllers. *Journal of the American Medical Association,* 1973, 224, 489-492.

Coch, Lester and French, J. R. P., Jr. Overcoming resistance to change. *Human Relations,* 1948, 4, 512-533.

Crozier, Michel. *The Bureaucratic Phenomenon.* Chicago: University of Chicago Press, 1964.

Davis, D. R. Recovery from depression. *British Journal of Medical Psychology,* 1952, 25, 104-113.

Doehrman, S. R. Coping and defense and the impact of the events on mental and physical health. Institute for Social Research, Ann Arbor, MI. Unpublished memo, September 1979.

French, J. R. P., Jr., Israel, J., and Aas, D. An experiment in participation in a Norwegian factory. *Human Relations,* 1960, 13, 3-19.

French, J. R. P., Jr. and Raven, B. H. The bases of social power. In D. Cartwright and A. F. Zander (eds.), *Group Dynamics,* third edition. New York: Harper and Row, 1968.

French, J. R. P., Jr., Rodgers, W. L., and Cobb, Sidney. Adjustment as person-environment fit. In G. V. Coelho, D. A. Hamburg, and H. E. Adams (eds.), *Coping and Adaptation,* New York: Basic Books, 1974, 316-333.

French. J. R. P., Jr., Sherwood, J. J., and Bradford, D. Changes in a management training conference. *Journal of Applied Behavioral Science,* 1966, 2, 210-218.

Friedman, Merton Hirsh, Rosenman, R. H., and Carroll, V. Changes in the serum cholesterol and blood clotting time in men subjected cyclic variation of occupational stress. *Circulation,* 1958, 18, 852-861.

Glass D. C. *Behavior Patterns, Stress, and Coronary Disease.* Hillsdale, NJ: Lawrence Erlbaum Associates, 1977.

Guralnick, Lillian. Mortality by occupation and cause of death among men 20-64 years of age, United States, 1950. *Vital Statistics—Special Reports,* 1963, 53.

Gurin, Gerald, Veroff, Joseph, and Feld, S. C. *Americans View their Mental Health.* New York: Basic Books, 1960.

Gurin, Patricia, Gurin, Gerald, Lao, R. C. and Beattie, Muriel. Internal-external control in the motivational dynamics of negro youth. *Journal of Social Issues,* 1969, 25, 29-53.

Harrison, R. V. Person-environment fit and job stress. In C. L. Cooper and R. E. Payne (eds.), *Stress At Work,* New York: John Wiley, 1978.

Hiroto, D. S. and Seligman, M. E. P. Generality of learned helplessness in man. *Journal of Personality and Social Psychology,* 1975, 31, 311-327.

House, J. S. and Wells, J. A. Occupational stress, social support and health. Paper presented at the conference "Reducing Occupational Stress." White Plains, NY, May 10-12, 1977.

Jahoda, Marie. *Current Concepts of Positive Mental Health.* New York: Basic Books, 1958.

Kahn, R. L. and Quinn, R. P. Mental health, social support, and metropolitan problems. Ann Arbor, MI: Institute for Social Research, 1976, unpublished multilith, 79 pages.

Kahn, R. L., Wolfe, D. M., Quinn, R. P., Snoek, J. D., and Rosenthal, R. A. *Organizational Stress: Studies in Role Conflict and Ambiguity.* New York: Wiley, 1964.

Klein, D. C., Fencil-Morse, E., and Seligman, M. E. P. Learned helplessness, depression, and the attribution of failure. *Journal of Personality and Social Psychology,* 1976, 33, 508-516.

Kuiper, N. A. Depression and causal attributions for success and failure. *Journal of Personality and Social Psychology,* 1978, 36, 236-246.

Kulka, R. A., Mann, D. W., and Klingle, D. M. School crime as a function of person-environment fit. Chapter prepared for forthcoming volume on school crime. National Council on Crime and Delinquency. Davis, CA, 1977.

Langer, E. J. The illusion of control. *Journal of Personality and Social Psychology.* 1975, 32, 311-328.

135

Lawler, E. E. *Motivation and Work Organizations.* Monterey, CA: Brooks-Cole, 1973.

Lazarus, R. S. *Psychological Stress and the Coping Process.* New York: McGraw-Hill, 1966.

Lazarus, R. S., Opton, E. M., Nomikos, M. S., and Rankin, N. O. The principle of short-circuiting of threat: further evidence. *Journal of Personality,* 1965, 33, 622-635.

Levy, L. H., Knight, B. G., Padgett, V. P., and Wollert, R. W. Patterns of help-giving in self-help groups. Paper presented at the American Psychological Convention, San Francisco, September, 1977.

Lewin, K. *Field Theory in Social Science.* In D. Cartwright (ed.), New York: Harper, 1951.

Lewin, K., Dembo, Tamara, Festinger, Leon, and Sears, P. S. Level of aspiration.In J. McV. Hunt (ed.), *Personality and the Behavior Disorders.* New York: Ronald, 1944, 333-378.

Likert. R. *New Patterns of Management.* New York: McGraw-Hill, 1961.

Likert, R. *The Human Organization: Its Management and Value.* New York: McGraw-Hill, 1967.

Maier, N. R. F. *Frustration.* New York: McGraw-Hill, 1949.

Mayo, E. *The Human Problems of an Industrial Civilization.* New York: Viking Press, 1960.

Medalie, J. H., Snyder, M., Groen, J. J., Neufeld, H. N., Goldbourt, U., and Riss, E. Angina pectoris among 10,000 men: 5-year incidence and unvariate analysis. *American Journal of Medicine.* 1973, 55, 583-594.

Miller, D. R. and Swanson, G. E. *Inner Conflict and Defense,* New York: Holt, Rinehart, and Winston, 1960.

Morse, Nancy C. and Reimer, Everett. The experimental change of a major organizational variable. *Journal of Abnormal and Social Psychology.* 1956, 52, 120-129.

Murray, H. A. *Explorations in Personality,* New York: Oxford University Press, 1938.

Myers, J. K., Lindenthal, J. J., and Pepper, M. P. Life events and psychiatric impairment. *Journal of Nervous and Mental Disorders.* 1971, 152, 149-157.

Nisbett, R. W. and Valins, S. Perceiving the causes of one's own behavior. In E. E. Jones, et al. *Attribution: Perceiving the Causes of Behavior.* Morristown, NJ: General Learning Press, 1971.

Nisbett, R. E. and Wilson, T. D. Telling more than we can know: verbal reports on mental processes, *Psychological Review,* 1977, 84, 231-259.

Palmblad, J., Cantell, K., Strander, H., Froberg, J., Karlsson, C. G., and Levi, L. Stressor exposure and human interferon production. *Reports from the Laboratory for Clinical Stress Research,* Karolinska sjukhuset, 1974, 35.

Parkes, C. M. *Bereavement: Studies of Grief in Adult Life.* New York: International Universities Press, 1972.

Parkes, C. M., Benjamin, R., and Fitzgerald, R. G. Broken heart: a statistical study of increased mortality among widowers. *British Medical Journal,* 1969, 1, 740-743.

Pervin, L. A. Performance and satisfaction as a function of individual-environment fit. *Psychological Bulletin.* 1968, 69, 56-68.

Phillips, Leslie. *Human Adaptation and its Failures.* New York: Academic Press, 1968, Chapter 1.

Pinneau, S. R. Effects of social support on psychological and physiological strain. Doctoral dissertation, University of Michigan, 1975. University Microfilms No. 76-9491.

Quinn, Robert, Seashore, Stanley, Kahn, Robert, Mangione, T., Campbell, D., Staines, Graham, and McCollough, M. *Survey of Working Conditions: Final Report on Univariate and Bivariate Tables* (Document No. 2916-0001). Washington, DC: U.S. Government Printing Office, 1971.

Rosenman, R. H. and Friedman, M. Behavior pattern, blood lipids, and coronary heart disease. *Journal of the American Medical Association,* 1963, 184, 934-948.

Sarason, S. B. Community psychology, networks and Mr. Everyman. *American Psychologist,* 1976, 31, 317-328.

Seligman, M. E. P. *Helplessness.* San Francisco: Freeman, 1975.

Selye, Hans. *The Stress of Life.* New York: McGraw-Hill, 1956.

Smelser, N. J. *Theory of Collective Behavior.* New York: The Free Press of Glencoe, 1963.

Tannenbaum, A. S. Control in organizations: individual adjustment and organizational performance. In A. S. Tannenbaum (ed.), *Control in Organizations.* New York: McGraw-Hill, 1968. Pp. 307-314.

Tolman, E. D. Principles of performance. *Psychological Review,* 1932, 62, 315-326.

Vroom, V. H. *Work and Motivation.* New York: Wiley, 1964.

Walker, K. N., MacBride, A., and Vachon, M. L. S. Social support networks and the crisis of bereavement. *Social Science and Medicine,* 1977, 11, 35-41.

Wechsler, H. and Pugh, T. F. Fit of individual and community characteristics and rates of psychiatric hospitalization. *American Journal of Sociology,* 1967, 73, 331-338.

Wicklund, R. A. *Freedom and Reactance.* New York: Wiley, 1974.

Wortman, C. B. and Brehm, J. W. Responses to uncontrollable outcomes: An integration of reactance theory and the learned helplessness model. In L. Berkowitz (ed.), *Advances in Experimental Social Psychology.* Vol. 8, New York: Academic Press, 1975.

5
ROLE ADAPTATION AND THE APPRAISAL OF WORK-RELATED STRESS

MARC FRIED

Introduction

The importance of work for economic life is self-evident. Whether viewed in the aggregate as the basis for sustaining the physical existence of a society or more humanly as the necessary condition for meeting the subsistence requirements of a population or for enhancing standards of living, work activities are the foundation of a social order. By the same token, the loss of productivity due to unemployment and its consequences for the availability of goods and services in a population would also appear to be self-evident. Nonetheless, one can only view those economic and business analyses of unemployment that see advantages in moderate levels of unemployment, if only periodically, as a reflection of the distortions of a rational, economic order.

That the activities, relationships, and accomplishments associated with work are also critical components of social experience and personal development is less widely recognized. While the importance of the non-economic functions of work is a fundamental tenet of contemporary social science, neither the basic human significance of work nor, correspondingly, the deleterious consequences of unemployment, is universally accepted. Charles Booth, almost a century ago, was startled to learn that many of London's lower class population were poor because they earned so little money or were unable to find jobs and were not merely avoiding work. His observations did not

139

140

entirely convince that cynical socialist, George Bernard Shaw, for whom "the undeserving poor" were at least a segment of the lower classes. It is more disturbing to realize that despite many studies of work and the job, despite the evidence that most people want to work and would be willing to work except under the most disadvantageous conditions, there is a persistent disbelief in any widespread motivation for employment. In parallel fashion, there is extensive ignorance concerning the damaging consequences of job loss for individuals and families, except for the more obvious features of economic deprivation.

Social science investigation has, unfortunately, failed to contribute its due to a clarification of these issues. Apart from studies of unemployment during the great depression, only during the last few years have several close empirical analyses of the impact of job loss been unveiled. There are, of course, many subtle and complex issues involved which complicate the study of these problems and the interpretation of findings. Moreover, the basic conceptual and theoretical apparatus for guiding the analysis of these issues is quite rudimentary. It is primarily this inadequacy of concepts, models, and theories essential for understanding psychosocial phenomena like work and unemployment that is the major impetus to the present effort.

The general significance and specific forms of work and unemployment in modern societies derive from the larger social structure and the social system values, and are embedded within the entire array of roles and experiences of people within the small social systems of daily life. As a consequence, the development of micro-level concepts and models for understanding the processes and experiences of work must take account of the diverse spheres of daily behavior and of their interrelationships with one another. In turn, this implies that the very effort to understand work and unemployment must be initiated at a more abstract level, far removed from the concrete phenomena of the world of work. With this in mind, I shall give little attention to jobs, work experiences, and job loss at the outset and will only return to these concrete foci in order to exemplify and develop further some of the abstract formulations.

I start with the view indicated above: the nature of work itself and of attitudes toward work are largely a function, ultimately, of macro-level politicoeconomic and sociocultural forces. While they may be sustained and even modified by specific experiences within different types of organizations, these represent mainly variations on a larger societal theme. Marcuse (1964, 1966), following several lines of thought developed by Freud (1961a, 1961b), has vividly characterized the ways in which these macro-level forces dominate and direct our psychic apparatus. The broad brush strokes of Marcuse's formulation are not sufficient, however, for close empirical analysis, but they provide a meaningful vantage point and important suggestions about dimensions to be considered. Despite the need for further theoretical clarification of the mechanisms by which macro-level forces impinge on individuals, I shall give only scant attention to this problem. I shall attempt, rather, to develop and specify the parameters of micro-level psychosocial analysis. Since it is primarily for individuals as role participants in small social systems and collectivities that the impact of macro-level forces is most potent, I shall devote much of my attention to the development of role analysis.

To the extent that the role concept can be formulated so that it has facets, dimensions, and dynamics, it may well serve as a critical link between the operation of social system forces and the commonalities or idiosyncracies of psychological process in explaining behavior. Indeed, since internal and external structural and dynamic forces interact and impinge on individuals, a specification of role concepts can, in principle, provide the most stable basis for explaining aggregate behavioral patterns or individual variability. To accomplish this conceptual objective, it is essential to formulate the parameters of roles and to generate theoretical propositions about the dynamics of role systems and about the determinants and consequences of these dynamics. Ultimately, it is necessary to demonstrate that the regularities or irregularities of role behavior explain and predict the continuities and discontinuities in human functioning better than do the social and psychological processes from which role behaviors derive.

To initiate such an inquiry, I will focus attention on the concept of *role adaptation* as the conceptual expression of changes in role behavior in response to internal or external forces. In order to clarify the concept of role adaptation, however, it is necessary to develop the language of role behavior and to specify the ways in which roles are interrelated in forming the small social systems of daily functioning. Given these definitional and conceptual formulations, I will extend the conceptual apparatus to propositions concerning the impact of external forces on role behavior and the process of role adaptation. Particular emphasis will be given to those external forces that can be conceived as stress. Greater attention is given to external events than to variability in psychological reactions, partly as a function of the available literature, and partly because of philosophical predisposition. Both sets of forces, however, must be invoked in developing the concepts of stress and strain before applying these formulations to the phenomena of work and unemployment and to the role adaptations generated by stress in these spheres of experience.

Since a great part of the discussion is necessarily conceptual, a brief synopsis of the substantive argument is desirable. Borrowing the concept of a stress-strain ratio from applied physics, I shall argue that the impact of stress influences the role behavior of individuals through the strain developed in role functioning. These individual experiences of strain, however, have repercussions far beyond the individual as they affect other individuals whose roles are intertwined in the small social systems of daily life. Moreover, not only do external social, economic, and political forces initiate most of the stresses that are subjectively transformed into strains of different degrees of severity, but these same forces constrain the options available for role adaptation. Thus, while the range of adaptational responses for coping with stress are, in principle, almost infinite, the conditions of life substantially narrow the possibilities and produce residual or even additional stresses, conflicts, and strains in the very process of adapting to the initial stress. Many of these secondary stresses, conflicts, and strains are often submerged beneath apparent adaptational achievements in response to the initial stress. But this should not obscure either the existence of these stressful residues or their evaluation in a meaningful human cost-benefit analysis. The stresses associated with work in our society and, even more strikingly, those entailed by unemployment, reveal most sharply the interrelationships among role adaptations in different spheres of functioning and the consequences of stress and adaptation to stress for small social systems.

Role Conceptualization: Alternative Approaches

A recent news dispatch reported that Johnny Weismuller, the erstwhile Tarzan of many films, had been hospitalized because he had taken to shouting that he was Tarzan, expressing himself in the savage gutterals of that jungle denizen, trying to swing from hanging reminders of jungle vines, and reliving in many ways his famous movie role.

Occasionally, with the depersonalization that sometimes characterizes sociological analysis, the concept of role is formulated by analogy with drama. Such terms as role-taking and role-playing imply such artifice and, to this degree, mock the objective conformity and subjective investment associated with role behavior. What is lost in the dramaturgical conception is that the drama and the art of acting evoke the reality within the role for a brief moment in time and only in a specific context. Moreover, it is the reality *within* a role and not the reality *of* a role. Only with the repetition of the same dramatic role, evoking the same reality with regularity, and only for those individuals who can fulfill themselves through the reality within dramatic roles, can the play become an encompassing experience. Sean Connery, I understand, refused to be 007 in the James Bond movies any longer for fear of becoming 007 both in subjective reality and in the eyes of his audiences. He may, thus, have averted Johnny Weismuller's fate, a retrogressive debasement of a secret identification that went beyond dramatic necessity.

But while this exaggeration of a familiar phenomenon reveals the tenuousness of a dramaturgical conception of roles in daily life, it also reminds us that similar forms of secret identification which exceed social necessity arise occasionally in other conditions. Merton (1957) presents a telling form of such identification and its overload of commitment to rules in his analysis of bureaucratic structure and personality. Goffman's social analyses (1959, 1971), while often verging on Daumier-like caricature, also capture the essence of distorted identifications with the formal definition of roles, sometimes reduced to their ultimate absurdities. A psychodynamic analysis is essential for clarifying the processes by which such over-commitment takes place and for analyzing the individuals who find fulfillment or, at least, security in such role investment. However, there is also a more evident social condition common to these situations.

Such identifications appear mainly to occur when the role represents an organizational position endowed with substantially more power than the incumbent can ever hope to achieve in his or her own right. By pursuing all of the formal rigidities of rule-defined role behaviors, individuals can indulge themselves in reflected glory and, at the same time, believe themselves to be expressing the unexpressed will of those with true authority. The price they frequently pay is that, having borrowed their strength without proper license, they must then go on feigning the power they do not possess. The excessive identification with the roles of bureaucrat, professor, executive, public official, or doctor cannot bear confrontation with the reality of diminished power in other roles and relationships. A process that may have started innocently as dedication to a work role, supplemented by exaggerated esteem for and rigidification of establishment standards, results in a total persona modeled on the role. The person within the persona readily vanishes.

Fortunately, most people do not become so intensly identified with single roles, nor do most role situations encourage such excessive commitment to single roles. While such over-identification with roles is frequent enough to warrant some attention in dealing with the pathologies of role behavior, a general conceptualization of role functioning must be based on principles that characterize role behavior more regularly in daily life. Apart from the dramaturgical model, several different conceptions of role are widely used.

The role concept has been defined, categorized, and deployed in many diverse ways. Common to all of them is the view that role represents the intersect between social and psychological processes and vantage points. However, relatively little conceptualization, theoretical formulation, or empirical analysis explicitly develops this potential. Numerous critics have, in fact, rejected the role concept on the grounds that it has proved of little theoretical or empirical value (Coulson, 1972; Preiss and Ehrlich, 1966; Sarbin, 1954). But a concept can have little theoretical or empirical merit in its own right. Concepts like intelligence, electromagnetic force, or social networks have significance primarily because they have dimension and are incorporated within propositions that can be used for theoretical development or empirical evaluation. While there are several examples of efforts to engage the concept of role beyond initial definitions (e.g., Bates, 1956; Gross et al., 1958; Nye et al., 1976; Parsons and Shils, 1952; Popitz, 1972; Turner, 1970), there has been a paucity of such effort, with few attempts to generate the dimensions and framework for role analyses. Nonetheless, a brief consideration of several of the dominant approaches to role conceptualization helps to place the present formulation in context.

Three different conceptual styles and corresponding differences in the conceptualization of roles are evident. The most familiar of these stems from structural-functional theory in sociology (Goode, 1960; Merton, 1957; Parsons, 1951). This approach conceives of roles as the primary units of social organization defined in functional terms. Each role is the functional correlate of a structural unit conceptualized as a status. This structural unit itself is based on norms regarding the rights and obligations associated with specific, designated positions in the social system. In this conception, the structural features of statuses define many of the regularities of the function of such roles as parent, friend, colleague, teacher; and, in this respect, the structural-functional approach gives priority to structural determinants of role behavior. Since the relationship between structure and function is reciprocal, functional features are, by no means, neglected.

Nonetheless, this approach tends to rigidify conceptions of roles and role behavior unrealistically.

The various forms of interactional analysis adopt a very different view of role in which the classification and analysis of role behavior is oriented to the psychosocial function of roles within a given setting (Goffman, 1961; Turner, 1962). Since roles are viewed as emergent phenomena within specific interactional conditions, their interpersonal functions are given priority. This is reflected in interactionist role terminology which characterizes roles by such features as facilitator, antagonist, provocateur, or conciliator. In effect, it is the function of the role in developing the emergent processes of action and interaction that is its defining characteristic. Regularities of role, therefore, stem from similarities in the conditions of action and from general principles of social participation.

The social psychological tradition of role conceptualization is more diverse and does not lend itself so neatly to a summary statement. Two main strands of theoretical role formulations appear in the work of Sarbin (1965, 1968) and in the work of Kahn and a series of collaborators (Katz and Kahn, 1966; Kahn et al., 1964; Kahn and Quinn, 1970). In both instances, the approach to role theory tends to emphasize the normative features of role functioning and of the stressful or conflicted components of role patterning. The social psychological conceptualization and the corresponding terminology is more formal than that of the interactionist role formulations in dealing with characteristic situational forces that condition role behavior. At the same time, this approach gives greater attention to the dynamics of role behavior than appears in structural-functional analysis by virtue of its emphasis on specific organizational or contextual factors that influence roles.

In the present view of role concepts and theory, each of these approaches provides a distinctive contribution to role analysis. In its treatment of rights and obligations, normatively defined, as central features of roles, the present formulation is closest to the structural-functional conceptualization. However, it differs from the structural-functional conception in several respects. Since roles are conceived, in the present approach, as themselves structural-functional entities, there is no particular need for a distinction between statuses and roles.[1] Moreover, while a role is defined on the basis of its most critical social functions, there is considerable variability and, indeed, flexibility in the supplementary functions served by given roles. In this respect, this conceptualization leans toward the interactionist formulation and gives particular priority to the role relationship in defining supplementary role functions and in determining many of the properties of the role. On the other hand, the more specific interpersonal or group functions of roles often addressed by interactionist analysis are not considered in the present formulation. These attributes of role behavior represent a different dimension of analysis, an aspect of group process only incidentally linked to role functioning. The present formulation is similar to that of the social psychological approach in its simultaneous concern with social and individual functions of roles. However, to the extent that social psychological role analysis has focused on role dynamics internal to the role system, it reflects only one of the several sources of influence on role functioning. The present approach is as much concerned with macro-level external forces and with internal micro-level forces as with those inherent in the system of roles as determinants of role behavior.

Several issues arise in role conceptualization apart from the different general theoretical frameworks within which role concepts are embedded. One fundamental problem concerns the contrast between normative and behavioral definitions of roles. The normative conception defines roles primarily in terms of rights and obligations. The behavioral conception defines roles primarily in terms of regularities of functioning in roles. Given a normative definition, there remains the question of whose norms are involved or, more generally, as Gross et al. (1958) point out, the degree and form of consensus regarding role norms. Moreover, two other issues remain problematic within the normative conception: (1) are the different rights and obligations associated with a role equally potent or do they represent different degrees of

---

1. For a view expressing similar doubts about the value of maintaining the distinction between status and role, see: Jackson, 1972.

requiredness? and (2) are there not other features of role behavior that may reflect social expectations but are not quite obligations or rights? A behavioral definition avoids the problem of variability and flexibility in role conceptions, but it does not confront the issue of normative requiredness, of consensus associated with common features of role functioning. Thus, we are led to the view that a normative definition of roles involves a necessary but insufficient basis for distinguishing and delineating roles. In addition to an (unknown) level of normative consensus concerning major role obligations and rights, definitions also involve: (a) variations in the behavioral translation of obligations and rights; (b) differences in the potency of different obligations and rights associated with a role; and (c) supplementary role behaviors that may be widespread or highly variable but are sustained by structural or dynamic forces other than norms.

Another issue that occasionally arises and has important if subtle implications for the style and scope of role analysis concerns the extent to which the different roles in which individuals participate encompass all of individuality (Jackson, 1972; Popitz, 1972). The present formulation conceptualizes roles to include all spheres of behavior. This implies, in turn, that all behavior is role-related. However, individual differences and, in its most essential sense, individuality, may be expressed in several different aspects of role functioning: in developing an individual variant of normative conceptions of role functions; in the specific behavioral expression of those functions; in the manner of linking those functions to the functions of role partners; and in the total patterning of different roles. But the problem of individuality in the midst of omnipresent roles must itself be understood as a function of the orientation of role concepts and role analysis.

Role is universally conceived as an interface concept, one that lies between and is directed toward social and psychological analysis. However, the types of role concepts employed, the role terminology used, and the types of role behavior subjected to analysis may reflect a primary emphasis on the societal function of roles or on the individual function of roles, or may be explicitly directed toward the dual, psychosocial aspect of roles. In societal analysis, the role is the unit of aggregation, and the individual necessarily becomes irrelevant as we move to higher levels of social organization. In individual analysis, the social function of roles becomes incidental, and individuals experiencing and responding to role expectations are primary considerations. Psychosocial analysis, which conceives the dual reference of roles as the core problem of analysis, must invoke several dimensions of role functioning to deal with this complexity. The formulation of a model of integrative levels of role functioning is designed to link up with the different system units involved. At the same time it is clear that individuals, of unique physiological and psychological composition, coordinate the different integrative levels of role functioning.

Although I shall argue that most physiological and psychological attributes are incorporated within roles and are significant socially only to the extent that they affect role behavior, I believe there is a realm of private experience that can only be viewed properly in individual terms. Even though these private experiences may stem from behavior in roles, and even though such subjective states may eventually influence role functioning, they are reflected in the fact that they cut across roles and are common to the diverse behaviors of an individual rather than to the common or diverse features of a given role. Moreover, they are represented as the subjective experiences which are residues of daily role behavior, if only in dreams, play, and fantasy. But the frequency with which such individuality is manifest *within* the very process of role functioning is itself a reflection of the social order. The extent to which human behavior is encompassed by roles, or represents the expression of individuality in the pursuit of role commitments, is an important aspect of the fundamental freedom or constraint within a society or within classes in society.

Role Analysis: Structure and Dynamics

Role will be defined as the set of normatively-motivated behaviors that subserve specific institutional or social system functions and through which individuals fulfill physiological, psychological, and social needs and desires. Roles are socially defined through the behavioral expectations of society, and their associated sanctions concerning the functions individuals must and can fulfill within the small social systems of daily life. To the extent that these behavioral expectations are conceived as essential features of the role, they comprise the responsibilities and prerogatives of the role. However, the degree of requiredness of different role functions and the range of functions that a given role may serve or fail to fulfill can vary considerably.

The norms and expectations about role behavior provide some guarantee that socially necessary or desirable functions will be accomplished and will be coordinated with the roles and functional activities of role partners and other members of small social systems. To a considerable extent, higher levels of the social system influence human functioning and control role conceptions through influencing normative expectations, through confining choices and options, and, in the extreme, through providing sanctions to encourage conformity. Contemporary structural forces supplement socialization processes during childhood and adulthood to lend impetus to role conformity. Nonetheless, there are many variations in the clarity, consensus, and rigidity of normative expectations and structural constraints regarding role fulfillment. Moreover, larger social system forces may be viewed as setting the boundary conditions for role behavior since numerous other influences serve to specify expectations and structural options and constraints.

Since normative expectations regarding role functions and behavior are reflections of cultural orientations, sub-cultural differences among social classes, ethnic groups, age groups, and even regions of the country are likely to result in variations in role norms. Of even greater importance, however, albeit partly as an aspect of subcultural differences, the role system in which roles are embedded can markedly influence role conceptions and role behaviors. In particular, role partners and the entire role set ordinarily have powerful effects in offering support for or modifications of role expectations.

Apart from the various social forces impelling at least a modest degree of role conformity, a major (and often neglected) determinant of role fulfillment stems from the fact that most of the socially necessary or desirable functions designated by role definitions also serve to meet individual human needs and desires. I have already indicated that an inevitable consequence of social organization is that the accomplishment of more personal physiological, psychological, or social objectives must largely be contained within the opportunities and constraints of socially-defined roles. Thus, the meshing of individual motives to fulfill personal needs, whether for food, sex, or sociability, and the social organization of functions within roles, is fundamental for social conformity.

There are conditions, however, in which there is a marked gap between social demands and individual needs, in which individual needs may be minimally fulfilled through social role behavior or the role requirements may even be antithetical to human desires. It is evident, for example, that blue-collar jobs generally fail to meet the desires of workers for intrinsic productive satisfaction but, nonetheless, labor force participation is sustained by the necessity of earning a living. When role conditions do not provide such internal pressures and are not merely transitory, severely restrictive sanctions are necessary to insure role performance. Such discordances between role demands and personal needs can be major sources of strain in a society although, as in the case of many class-related role variations, these may be obscured by social mechanisms that control potential conflict. At the other extreme, the degree of flexibility in role definitions allows individuals to utilize these roles even for idiosyncratic personal fulfillments. But the possibility of such individuality in role behavior is a function of the options and constraints in normative definitions, on the one hand, and of individual motivation and adaptational skills, on the other.

While roles may be the elementary units of the larger institutional structure and dynamics of a society, they are concretely carried out within the small social systems, collectivities, and environments of daily experience. These small social systems, collectivities, and daily environments can be classified as distinctive clusters of role systems: work/occupation, family/

household, extra-nuclear interpersonal relations, cultural/recrea-
tional participation, and social/personal maintenance. Since these
clusters include a complex of component roles, they can be viewed
as role complexes. It is within these role complexes that roles and
role behavior can be conceptualized in functional terms.

Although the organization and coordination of roles entails a
number of social processes, the component roles in role complexes
can be visualized and named on the basis of several criteria. Such
distinctions among roles are reasonable only if several conditions
are met: (a) different instrumental or core role functions are
involved (e.g., household maintenance in contrast with companionship); (b) the different functions can vary independently of one
another along several dimensions of performance (e.g., effective
and cooperative household maintenance along with minimal
intra-household companionship); and (c) any one of the core
(instrumental) role functions may be carried out, at least in
principle, in different role complexes (e.g., companionship in the
family, at work, or in the neighborhood).

Roles within the family or household can be categorized
functionally as: household maintenance, sexuality, sociability,
childrearing, and companionship. These roles within the
household or family are generally carried out by the same
individuals with the same role partners and are most evident in a
single role complex in our society. Nonetheless, in this and in other
instances, it is essential to maintain the distinctiveness of different
roles since, as Bates (1956) has pointed out, the same role may be
carried out in different positions or role complexes. Indeed, the
interrelationships among the different roles within a role complex,
and the degree to which specific roles are rigidly bound within or
excluded from specific complexes, are important features of
empirical social analysis.

Few role complexes regularly include so diverse a set of
(potential) roles as occur within the family/household complex.
Work/occupation roles are clearly less numerous and can be
divided into productivity roles (serving social/organizational and
individual needs for accomplishment of production goals) and

income-gaining roles (serving individual and/or household support functions). However, sociability and companionship roles frequently occur within the work/occupation complex. Roles within other role complexes are generally less clearly named, can be less clearly disguised, and are less sharply defined by normative expectations or structural conditions. This variation has frequently been conceptualized as a difference in the levels of role crystallization (Jackson, 1966).

One of the central features of this model of role functioning involves the hierarchical organization of different components of role behavior. I shall refer to this hierarchical organization as the different *levels of integration* of role behavior. Each successively higher level involves increasing ties to other individuals, networks, groups, and organizations. Since higher levels of role integration entail greater social coordination, the constraints on individual variability in role behavior are greater than at lower levels. By the same token, reactions to stress that are similar to homeostatic adjustments ordinarily are initiated at the lower levels of role integration. But when they are ineffective, either because they fail to fulfill role functions adequately or generate internal or interpersonal conflict, the stress may invade higher levels of role integration. Under these conditions, individual or social problems of a more serious nature may result. For present purposes, I will restrict the levels of role integration to five major forms of coordination. While there are levels of role integration beyond these, other forms of role integration are relevant mainly for macrosocial analysis and carry the analysis beyond the small social system.

(1) *Role Activities* are the elementary, concrete units of role behavior and, thus, of role analysis. They consist of the discrete decisions and tasks in which people engage whether these be regular, occasional, or rare behaviors. Individual activities may, of course, be pleasurable or onerous in varying degrees and the desirability of the behavior is bound to influence the frequency with which it is carried out. However, much of the individual and social meaning of the activity derives not so much from the nature of the activity itself as from the role functions these activities

subserve. Thus, even when an activity is intrinsically pleasurable it can suffer interference if the role function is a source of conflict. Conversely, onerous activities are regularly pursued if they are in the service of accepted, important role functions.

Most activities are guided by a primary role purpose or function. However, any activity may serve several different role functions and some activities may simultaneously meet the prerequisites of different roles. Thus, friendliness among co-workers may facilitate the task performance of an individual and, at the same time, help to coordinate the work of a team. Or collaborative household chores carried out by husband and wife can get the work done more efficiently and, at the same time, implement the companionship role relationship between spouses. It is reasonable to assimilate all behaviors to roles because no matter how private or personal, all behaviors are influenced by structural conditions, role expectations, and role commitments. Only in viewing them as role-related behaviors is it possible to appreciate the sociocultural or politicoeconomic influences that determine why a given behavior is carried out in a particular way at a particular time or in a particular place. Moreover, while this may not account for some of the specific, individualized choices of activity or forms of behavior that differentiate people, conceptualizing the behavior in role terms provides a context for understanding the extent and type of individual contribution. Even highly individualistic behaviors, including efforts to escape from norm-dominated patterns, are most informative when understood as variant patterns of role functioning. Some activities, however, retain a considerable degree of autonomy from incorporation within roles, like autoerotic behavior, private hobbies, or day-dreaming. A role framework may not be sufficient, but it is essential for a full appreciation of the frustrations and aspirations, the conflicts and gratifications that have sociocultural as well as individual meaning even for such autonomous behaviors.

(2) *Role Functions* represent the next higher level of role integration. Of particular importance are the core, instrumental role functions which form the main basis for classifying or naming

roles. The core instrumental role function serves several simultaneous objectives: (1) it insures the fulfillment of basic societal activities through the distribution of various role functions within the small social systems which, in the aggregate, comprise the social organization of a society; (2) it provides for the fulfillment of basic physiological, psychological, and social needs in a normatively acceptable form despite the flux of motivation; (3) the incorporation of role functions within small social systems involves the individual in at least minimal forms of interaction with others in the role system, and, thus, facilitates social participation; and (4) in allowing some flexibility in the role activities through which role functions are performed and in permitting personal variations in the manner of defining the role function, there is the possibility of achieving more personal, individualized objectives.

Although roles are defined by their core, instrumental functions, many supplementary role functions may be fulfilled within the same role. Some of the attributes of role behavior that are occasionally distinguished as separate roles are more appropriately conceived as peripheral or supplementary role functions. Such functions as expressiveness, communication, nurturance, or control are always accomplished in the process of carrying out core role functions or as adjuncts to activities that subserve core role functions. While secondary to the main normative societal objectives of the role, they may be critical for individual objectives, for the relationship between role partners, or for the interactions among members of the role set.

Role activities may be the elementary, concrete units of role behavior and of role analysis, but role functions are focal points of societal and individual maintenance. In this respect, role functions form the base for all role behaviors and, consequently, for role analysis. To the extent that role functions are intertwined within role systems, higher levels of role integration have particularly potent influences on role behavior. But even within such role systems and despite some interchangeability of role functions among the members of role relationships, the link between roles and role functions is generally quite distinguishable.

Moreover, some roles and role functions are less thoroughly integrated into higher levels of role organization than are others. Thus, while consumer roles are coordinated with salesperson roles in role relationships, these are not ordinarily as closely contingent on one another as are the various roles within the family. Seen in a different light, when the impact of stress results in the direct loss of a role function (e.g., due to unemployment) or in secondary incursions on role functions (e.g., a decline in sexual activity as a result of unemployment), there are likely to be repercussions throughout the entire role system as well as consequences (physiological, psychological, and social) for the total person. In this sense, despite the importance of higher levels of role integration, role functions are particularly critical points of investigation in role analysis.

(3) *Role Relationships* represent a higher level of role integration involving the interactions, associated affects, and supplementary reciprocal role functions between role partners. Since the same individuals may be role partners in different roles serving different instrumental role functions (e.g., household maintenance, sexuality, and companionship between husband and wife), it is best to reserve the concept of a role relationship for partnerships associated with specific roles or instrumental role functions. While the significance of the role relationship varies with the degree of binding between roles, those role relationships which are highly contingent upon one another are major determinants of role behavior and essential aspects for role analysis. Indeed, including both closely contingent and loosely coordinated forms of interaction within roles, the role relationship is, in a fundamental sense, the societal microcosm. The social norms that influence role behavior are concretely conveyed and enforced or modified through role relationships and the structural constraints on role behavior are largely reflected in the role relationship.

Like the role function itself, the patterns of role relationships are largely determined by social structural forces and widespread norms. However, concrete role relationships involve transactions, negotiations, alliances, and reciprocal adjustments between role partners. On the one hand, therefore, they define the specific ways in which role functions are actually allocated and performed within the small social system to fill the social objectives of the role. On the other hand, they establish the likelihood of fulfillment or failure of fulfillment of psychological needs and desires for all role partners. In these respects, the interactionist approach has been more sensitive to the emergent nature of role behavior than the structural-functional approach. Not only is the role relationship itself an emergent phenomenon, bounded but not truly determined by structural and normative considerations, but the influence of the role relationship on role functions and role activities is a primary aspect of social variability.

Although role concepts tend to present an image of greater stability and homogeneity than is represented in actual functioning, it is particularly within the role relationship as it develops and changes over time that the processes producing change and heterogeneity are most evident. Role relationships are themselves, for most people, primary sources of gratification or conflict. Indeed, in many situations, it is the role relationship that helps to sustain the performance of role functions. Its significance, however, becomes most strikingly apparent in conditions of stress or deficit. When these stresses arise from sources internal to the individual (physiological, psychological) or from sources external to the small social system, role partners can be major sources of social support or of concurrent stress. This may extend to helping or hindering individuals in performing their role activities and may involve fairly extensive alterations in the allocation of role functions within the role system. At the same time, when stress begins to go beyond interference with role activities and role functions and invades the role relationship, the dangers of disruption of role behavior become most potent.

Sets of role relationships comprise the small social systems within which people function in daily life. Beyond these, however, there are several further levels of integration which link the small social system more clearly and concretely to other social units. Two of these, in particular, are so closely intertwined with the small social system that they deserve consideration in micro-level role analysis: the role array and role set interactions.

(4) The *Role Array* is the total set of different roles in which a person engages and the degree of investment in each of these roles. On the continuum of levels of role integration, the role array represents a step beyond the role relationship in two respects: (a) each role in the array has a bearing on all other roles and on the role activities, role functions, and role relationships of the total set, and (b) the role array forms one type of transition between small social systems and the wider society since it is a link between different small social systems in which people engage. However, it is the individual who is the coordinating unit between different roles in different small social systems. While there may be characteristic role array patterns in a society or in a class or ethnic group, there is generally some variability in role choice, in role investment, and in the influence of one role upon another among different individuals.

The role array involves individuals in a variety of role functions in a diversity of social units. Thus, it is a reflection of the extent and type of social participation. However, even when the roles are structurally independent of one another, the fact that a single individual engages in the different roles creates interdependence among them. This may take many different forms. On the one hand, one role may place structural constraints on the nature of role behavior in other roles. One of the more striking examples of this set of interrelationships which is currently undergoing society-wide change concerns relationships between work roles and parental roles for both men and women. On the other hand, the different roles may reinforce one another; joint sociable activities between husbands and wives can supplement their sexual and companionship role relationships even in the midst of a very busy schedule. From an individual viewpoint, the array of different roles provides an expanded opportunity for achieving satisfaction in diverse situations. Indeed, given the many constraints on role functioning in several different spheres, the different roles provide an opportunity for compensatory gratification in one role which is unattainable in other roles (e.g., close intimacy with neighbors and friends as an alternative to marital intimacy). More generally, a critical dimension of role analysis and, specifically, of the strains generated in role functioning, involves the congruence or discrepancy between the demands of different roles and the subjective importance of these roles.

(5) *Role Set Interactions* represent another dimension of the extension of the small social system of regularized behaviors into a wider network of roles and relationships. In introducing the concept of the role set, Merton (1957) pointed to the varied roles that may be either central or peripheral to the small role system but which influence both the normative conceptions and actual behaviors of role system members. The role set involves structurally-determined inter-systemic linkages. Role set interactions attain their significance by virtue of the fact that the roles that are outside of, but interconnected with, the small social system are generally "representative" roles. That is, the roles represent a wider or more powerful system and, as a consequence, carry some degree of actual or potential authority. In the case of the school superintendents studied by Gross et al. (1958), the role set may include school board members, citizen constituencies, representatives of the teachers, other school board members, other representatives of the teachers, other school superintendents, or officials from higher administrative levels within the educational hierarchy. On the job, loosely- or tightly-organized teams of co-workers form the small role system but can be markedly affected by foremen, inspectors, or representatives of the higher authority system of a factory or of the union. Even within so private a role system as the family, family members are involved in external affairs that affect family functioning: with kinspeople, with neighbors, and with school teachers.

Role Analysis: Measurement Issues

This effort to define a set of role concepts and to relate them to one another through a model of integrative levels of role functioning must, ultimately, be supplemented by more precise operational formulations and measurement procedures. While it would carry the discussion far afield to engage in a detailed consideration of these issues, it is useful to present some directions for measurement. Two main aspects of measurement are essential for the quantitative analysis of the different integrative levels of role functioning: (a) the dimensions along which each concept can be measured, and (b) a theoretical framework for incorporating the dimensional analysis into a larger analytic scheme. I will touch briefly on both of these although further theoretical and empirical work is evidently essential for clarifying these issues.

While each of the five levels of role functioning involves a number of different dimensions, in each case one particular aspect of role functioning appears most critical for the influence of one level upon another.

(1) Role Activities can be measured as *pleasurable vs. onerous.* While onerous activities may have to be carried out, they are likely to occur regularly only if the role function involved is of major importance. Moreover, the flexibility inherent in many decisions about most role activities, the alternative means of fulfilling a given role function, allows for choices based on the pleasure experienced or anticipated in the activity in its own right.

(2) Role Functions represent the major social meaning of the role. But a number of different role functions can be associated with any role, some of which are more integral to the social definition of the role than are others. Thus, role functions (or more concretely the associated role activities) can be measured on a *central-peripheral* scale with respect to the core instrumental role function(s) that define the role.

(3) Role Relationships are implicitly investigated in almost every study of social interaction and social behavior. Yet, in view of the paucity of formal analyses of role relationships, one can only conjecture about the most important dimensions for analysis. However, a dimension of great generality (which may, nonetheless, have different meaning in different sociocultural conditions) is the relative weight of *sharing vs. separation* between role partners in carrying out role activities that fulfill the role functions of the partners.

(4) The Role Array depends on the hierarchy of investment in different roles. Thus, retaining our focus on the role activity as the primary unit to be measured, the different role activities and the amount of time devoted to each (as a proxy for personal investment) can be allocated to the different roles involved. Alternatively, one can assess the degree of investment in different roles (or, perhaps more precisely in different role activities) on the basis of their subjective importance.

(5) Role Set Interactions must be measured along different dimensions depending on the purpose of the analysis. To the extent that our primary interest lies in the analysis of the effectiveness of adaptation within roles and the overt or covert cost-benefit ratio entailed by such adaptations, a major analytical dimension is the *conflict vs. consensus* revealed by the interactions between a role incumbent and members of the role set. It seems likely, however, that some consideration must be given to the power of different members of the role set, since conflicted interactions with one role set member may be trivial but may be a source of major stress with other role set members.

While supplementary information is occasionally necessary or, at least, desirable, most of the measurement is oriented toward gauging attributes of the role activities, the most concrete aspect of role behavior. At each level of role integration, we are concerned with measuring the relative weight of each dimension along an implied continuum. Thus, the basis for the analysis of role behavior lies in the relative weight of:

(a) pleasurable vs. onerous role activities (intrinsically pleasurable/onerous),
(b) central or peripheral to core instrumental role functions, indicating
(c) shared vs. separate role relationships between role partners, bearing on
(d) high or low priority roles, involving
(e) conflict or consensus in interactions with role set members.

Several alternative methods of aggregating the data are possible as a basis for assessing role behavior. Fundamentally, however, as we shall see in the discussion of role adaptation, the adult developmental process can be seen in light of an expansion or contraction of those features or role activities that hypothetically produce more highly coordinated and satisfying forms of social participation through role functioning. Three hypotheses are involved:

(1) pleasurable role activities that are central to core instrumental role functions, that entail shared role relationships, that focus on high priority roles, and that achieve consensus among role set members are most effective for adaptation since they optimize social participation and individual fulfillment,

(2) in view of the possibility that these desirable forms of role behavior may themselves be in conflict with one another and require either compromises within a given dimension or opting for less preferable choices along one dimension in order to achieve more desirable role activities along another dimension, the measure has to be based on the net result of role activities in the entire role array, and

(3) since role adaptation is a process, it is primarily the *expansion* or *contraction* of pleasurable, central, shared, high priority, consensual role activities that is the major criterion of adaptation.

From a general theoretical point of view, it is evident that (a) the range of choices of role activities is limited; (b) that various forces within the role system as well as forces outside the role system and internal to individuals create pressures for a narrow range of role decisions; and (c) that there is great variability along all the parameters of social inequality (class, sex, ethnicity, age, etc.) in the options available. In this light, it must be assumed that any assessment of role adaptation along these dimensions can only be meaningfully achieved relative to specified sociodemographic or sub-cultural groups. Indeed, for purposes of cross-sectional analysis, it is possible to compare the scores of individuals along all these dimensions relative to a similarly defined sub-population. It is also possible to compare sub-populations on the basis of their aggregate scores, a method that permits one to estimate inequalities in the range of role options and constraints. However, as previously indicated, a more dynamic analysis requires the comparison of scores of individuals (or aggregates) at different points in time. Only in this way is it possible to evaluate the degree and type of expansion or contraction of desirable forms of role behavior over time or under different conditions.

Stress, Strain, and Role Adaptation

In developing several concepts and a model of role functioning, I have occasionally used the terms stress, strain, and role adaptation. Subsequently, this paper will provide more formal definitions of these concepts and relate them to one another in a provisional model. However, since the discussion of these concepts and of the model becomes quite intricate, some preliminary comments may serve as a useful guide. The model is quite similar to other models involving stress; it is mainly distinguished from them by its decomposition of a complex process into a number of components and the formulation of propositions concerning the relationships of components to one another.[2] In this way, I hope to reduce a problem that has proved virtually intractable to a set of difficult, but by no means intractable, theoretical and empirical issues.

The main proposition of the model, stated broadly and in oversimplified overview form, proceeds from one component of the process to the next. (See figure 1 for a graphic view of the model.)

(1) Stress is initiated by a number of systems that impinge on individuals.

(2) Stress is defined by its ultimate effects on *changes in role behavior at* any level of role integration or, more mediately, by its effects on subjective experiences of *strain.*

---

2. Needless to say, there is always a danger that one may take the decomposition too literally and view the components as real or the relationships among them as fixed and linear. The physical as well as the social sciences have often fallen into this trap. The decomposition of continuous processes solves one set of problems but introduces other, hopefully less difficult, ones.

164

Figure 1
Provisional Model of Relationships between Stress, Strain

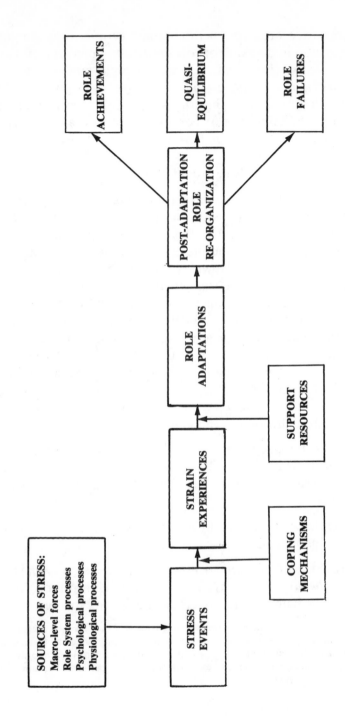

(3) A major intervening process, operating through automatic but individually-variable *coping mechanisms,* tends to reduce (and, thus, to obscure) the effects of stress.

(4) The residual stress effects experienced by the individual in various forms can be abstractly conceptualized as *strain.*

(5) Thus, strain is the most *direct and immediate determinant* of changes in functioning.

(6) The effect of strain on changes in role functioning can be modified by supplementary *stresses* that tend to exacerbate the strain or by *support resources* that tend to reduce strain.

(7) The consequent changes in role functioning can be conceived as role adaptations which can involve any level of role integration.

(8) The internal analysis of role adaptation, involving the different levels of role integration that may be affected, provides a major *terminal point* in studying the effects of stress and of the various intervening processes.

(9) Role adaptations frequently lead to further role re-organization by the individual or by the role system members.

(10) Role adaptations and/or subsequent role re-organization can result in new levels of *role achievement,* a temporary *quasi-equilibrium,* or *deficits* in *role behavior* and further stress.

Stress can arise from many sources: from the body itself, from psychological processes, from conditions within the role system, or from the external environment. All of these sources of stress have been studied and all have been implicated in pathological sequelae. Indeed, during recent years research on stress has proliferated.[3] Despite several points of disagreement, much of the

3. Discussions of stress have been visible during the last few years even in the popular media. The most extensive research has been done on life event stress and its effects on physical and mental illness. Two extensive recent volumes present some of the major issues and the research of major investigators: Dohrenwend and Dohrenwend, 1974; and Gunderson and Rahe, 1973. Several more recent articles update this perspective: Barbara Dohrenwend et al., in press; Dohrenwend and Dohrenwend, 1978; Gersten et al., 1977; Hurst et al., 1978; and Myers et al., 1975. For an alternative approach, see: Coelho et al., 1974.

current work reflects considerable convergence in conceptualization and analysis. While I will draw a number of analogies from applied physical mechanics in formulating conceptions of stress and strain, the approach is essentially congruent with the main body of recent analyses.

In applied physics, the concept of stress derives from the concept of force: stress is the force per unit area. The concept of force, basic to modern physics, had a long metaphysical history and gave both Galileo and Newton much difficulty (Burtt, 1932). Newton found an operational solution in defining force on the basis of its *effects:* The "something" which causes the motion of a body to change in any way, either in direction or in speed and overcomes the resistance (mass) of that body. To carry the discussion of force much further would lead us astray.[4] Nonetheless, a crudely equivalent definition of psychosocial force is a useful starting point: a psychosocial force is any event that causes the activity of an organism to change in any way—in direction, in frequency, or in speed. But it may be best to reserve the term force for its main current use in social science: as a generic term for structural or dynamic sources of change acting directly *or* indirectly on organisms. From this vantage point, the concept of stress can be limited to those immediate events that eventually cause changes in role functioning. Thus, a given generic force, e.g., unemployment rates, may result in stress, e.g., job loss or threat of job loss, but would not itself be called a stress (or stressor); the job loss or threat of job loss is the stress.

Generic social forces and more discrete stresses are omnipresent. To the extent that their effects are not detectable, however, we must neglect them or seek methods for magnifying their presumed

---

4. At a more basic, theoretical level, further consideration of the concept of force might well prove useful. It is, after all, a concept we use loosely in all the social sciences. But the fundamental failure of Kurt Lewin's brilliant effort to accomplish such a conceptualization may be instructive (see: Lewin, 1926, 1936, 1938). In physical science, the formulations were developed over centuries in an effort to conceptualize concrete observations and experiments. Lewin's attempt, and other similar efforts to develop broad and encompassing conceptual and theoretical systems in the social sciences, divorced from such constant and step-wise interaction with diverse empirical problems and phenomena, remains too abstract for translation into the realities of organismic or social life.

effects. This can pose a problem which, for the time being, we can recognize without resolving. If stresses cumulate in some linear or non-linear fashion, a stress that may be trivial under most circumstances could prove critical in precipitating major sequelae. This is a special and more difficult case of a more general observation: uniform stresses do not necessarily evoke uniform effects. A major source of such variability seems to stem from differences in the operation of systemic, "homeostatic" mechanisms that reestablish organismic equilibrium and keep changes within pre-defined bounds. In physiology, these have been described by Cannon (1932) who called the process homeostasis. The existence of similar equilibrating mechanisms in psychological and social functioning are sufficiently clear to allow the concept to be generalized.[5] To link the concept to more familiar psychosocial terminology, I will refer to these immediate equilibrating responses which counteract, compensate, or other-wise diminish the impact of stress as coping mechanisms. Since coping mechanisms reduce the impact of stress, they diminish the possibility of measuring subtle or covert reactions to stress. For the time being, we can only accept this fact if we are to proceed with the analytic process. However, it is important to recognize the possibility that substantial, hidden costs may be entailed by the rapid and automatic nature of such adjustment processes. Among these costs is the negation of the positive, "motivating" potential of stress due to rapid, equilibrating adjustments.

Cannon concentrated on the general process of homeostasis and its mechanisms, but there is considerable evidence for individual *differences* in coping behavior (Coelho, Hamburg, and Adams, 1974). Thus, despite the general effectiveness of coping mechanisms in reducing the visible effects of many daily stresses, residual consequences may persist for some people. Moreover, many events do not allow for such rapid, short term homeostatic coping mechanisms and leave marked residues more widely for

---

5. In a fascinating epilogue to his well-known summary volume, Cannon (1932) attempts to translate physiological homeostatis into social processes. His effort, however, is devoted to macro-level parallels. Moreover, it assumes an equilibrium model for long periods of time, a dubious assumption if extended beyond the rapid and immediate mechanisms he actually studied.

many people. Stress events may vary along many dimensions: severity, persistence, cumulative potential, and system-wide repercussions. The extent to which each of these dimensions is implicated in longer term residual consequences of stress is, of course, an empirical question. Such residues of stress that are not eliminated by coping adjustments lead to a continued state of imbalance.

Stress, as I have defined it, must be conceived as *uniform* for any given event. Thus, on the basis of measurements of widespread effects, or by alternative rating procedures, a stress value can be assigned to any event.[6] This stress value refers to the average change potential or probability of continued imbalance due to specific stress events. But it is evident that while a specific stress event may be assigned a probable effect, there will be many actual deviations from this value. This variability in the effect of specific stresses derives from differences in coping which, in turn, result in differences in the residual effects. It is these residual effects that I will refer to as *strain*.

In applied physics, engineering, and metallurgy, strain is defined as the deformation of a material as a consequence of stress. The deformation may be temporary, in which case the material returns to a prior state when the stress is removed, or it may be permanent in varying degrees. The utility of the concept is most clearly manifest in generating empirical stress: strain ratios. These permit one to estimate the degree of stress a category of materials or an individual object can tolerate without excessive or permanent deformation. An analogous formulation in psycho-social terms also provides a basis for empirical work. Stress:strain ratios can be estimated for average levels of strain in response to different types of stress and for individual variability in strain after a common stress.

---

6. Holmes and Rahe (1967) initiated a procedure for assigning such "population" stress values to different events on the basis of ratings by expert judges. More recently, Barbara Dohrenwend et al. (in press) have pursued this form of assignment with a modified approach. An alternative method involves similar assignments on the basis of direct or indirect measurements of stress effects with large samples.

Psychosocial strain can be defined as stress-induced disruptions of regularized, anticipated, or motivated behavior. Subjectively these are experienced as anxiety, tension, dissatisfaction, or uncertainty. Strains appear to represent several different types of discordance: between desires and opportunities, between needs and resources, or between functional requirements and functional capacities. These strains or disruptions of actual or anticipated continuity are the most immediate determinants of changes in role functioning or of role adaptations. While the measurement of stress has been widely discussed in the literature, the concept of strain has received little methodological attention.[7] In practice, however, a great deal of effort has been devoted, both in clinical and in field research, to estimating those subjective states included here in the descriptive definition of strain. More often than not, however, these states of discordance are viewed as pathological or as evidences of emotional disturbance. I see these, rather, as quite frequent reactions to daily life events, individually variable in severity and persistence, but basic components of the processes leading to social action. Thus, the potential for pathology lies not in strain itself but in the degree and kind of effect of strain on role behavior.

Nonetheless, it is almost certainly the case that as the level of strain increases, the likelihood of effective adaptational responses is diminished. Indeed, it it possible to chart a hypothetical stress:strain curve to characterize the probable relationships between increasing increments of stress and increasing levels of strain (figure 2). I suggest that the curve is exponential in form for several reasons. The significance of the exponential curve for the impact of stress on strain is that (a) over the course of increasing increments of stress there is a gradual but slowly accelerating increase in strain; (b) at a certain (unknown) point, the point colloquially referred to as the straw that broke the camel's back,

---

7. There is potential confusion in the fact that some authors (Selye, 1956; Pearlin and Schooler, 1978) have used the concept of stress to refer to the subjective or internal responses to noxious stimuli. Indeed, Pearlin and Schooler use the term strain for the objective events or stimuli that produce internal changes. Apart from the emphasis on roles in this presentation, I have preferred to retain the language used by most authors in conceptualizing stress as an objective event and strain as an internal (residual) experience.

there is a sharp upward turn of strain in response to increments of stress; (c) this point we shall refer to, as in physics, as the *elastic limit* of the organism, defined by the fact that the effects of stress beyond this point are irreversible, that the organism (or metal) can no longer entirely recover its former elastic or flexible properties; and (d) from this point on, the curve goes rapidly to infinity, which is to say that the relationship between increasing units of stress and strain responses becomes indeterminate.

Figure 2
Hypothetical Stress: Strain Ratios

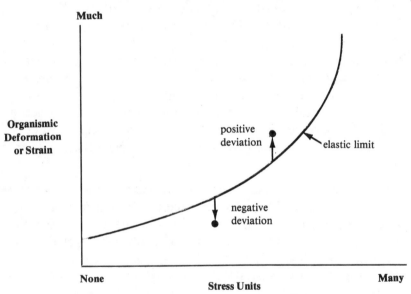

Stress:strain curves, I have suggested, allow us to calculate the average level of strain induced by a discrete stress in a population, to determine the average curve of increments of strain produced by adding stresses in a population, or to estimate the variability in strain among individuals in response to one or more stresses. We assume that the discrete scores of individuals will be dispersed around these means. For any individual it is, thus, possible to determine the negative or positive deviation from the mean at any given level of stress. In an experimental situation, we might actually chart the discrete level of strain in response to unit increments of stress. In clinical medicine, as in applied physics, such a procedure is used to evaluate levels of physical tolerance for different levels of physical stress. If this model of role adaptation is appropriate in this respect, the measurement of stress:strain ratios provides a basis for population predictions. However, it can readily prove grossly inaccurate for individuals since it does not take account of subsequent phases of responses to stress-induced strain. To consider this issue further, it is necessary to turn to the processes of role adaptation.

RESPONSES TO STRAIN: ROLE ADAPTATION

Role adaptation is here defined as the modification of role behavior in response to changes in psychological or physiological processes or to changes in sociocultural, politicoeconomic, or environmental conditions. The definition includes the motivational impetus of changes within the role system itself, which may result from the impact of events outside the role system on any role partner.

Several assumptions lie behind this definition. (1) All behavior can be relegated to different social roles whether they are central or peripheral to these roles. (2) Discrete, short term changes may occur in psychological, physiological, or social processes without requiring role adaptation, or automatic, coping responses to minor changes may eliminate the need for role adaptation. (3) Through prior role adaptations and role system constraints, individuals develop relatively stable patterns of role functioning which tend to resist adaptational change and can result in new or additional sources of stress. (4) Stable role behavior represents the establishment of concordance between individual and environment; only those internal or external changes that produce discordance beyond an individually-variable tolerance threshold and/or beyond the immediate coping capacities of the individual entail further adaptational effort.

For evaluative purposes, it is necessary to designate the success or failure of adaptational efforts in achieving concordance. While the term adaptation is often used to indicate successful change, such usage confounds the process and its consequences. In retaining the neutrality of the concept of psychosocial adaptation, we can avail ourselves of the term *maladaptation* to indicate adaptational failure. The obverse term, *bonadaptation* can signify effective adaptational efforts. Bonadaptation and maladaptation, I suggest, can be measured as the degree of *role satisfaction or dissatisfaction weighted by the subjective importance of that role.*[8] This can be extended to include situational satisfactions that affect role behavior (e.g., housing, community) or generic satisfactions (e.g., satisfaction with political process, life satisfactions).

Adaptation itself is conceived as a "satisficing" rather than an "optimizing" process. When the individually-variable minimal threshold of concordance is reached, most people are willing to accept sub-optimal conditions. Most people develop a sense of satisfaction in achieving a quasi-equilibrium, even if it is far from initial expectations or ideals. Difficulties in effecting inner or outer change, normative pressures toward conformity, and the attention demanded by the many stresses of daily life all require economizing of role effort and limit the attainment of optimal role adaptations. Moreover, numerous conditions limit the likelihood of achieving optimal adaptations. Many role behavior changes involve unanticipated consequences. And if the change in role behavior is of any import, it is likely to involve supplementary changes in role functioning to subserve the major change, or it

---

8. Although I do not want to pass lightly over this issue, a detailed justification would require extensive discussion. Yet merely to assert that this is the operational definition I am employing for adaptation would not do justice to it. Briefly, if we view discordance between individual and environment (whether expressed directly or as an internal conflict) as the critical issue in bonadaptation, it implies the absence or negation of strain. Such discordances or concordances pose insuperable problems of measurement. But it is reasonable to view satisfaction as an expression of the absence of strain with respect to discrete issues or spheres of role functioning. On the other hand, I would reject the view that such satisfaction can be designated "well-being" as Campbell, Converse, and Rodgers (1976) have done. The expression of satisfaction may reflect an assessment of the lack of potential for change but may still be a far cry from providing a sense of personal fulfillment.

may have consequences and reciprocal effects on the partners in the role relationship.

In describing adaptation as a process of "satisficing" rather than "optimizing," I have extended the idea that there are costs as well as benefits entailed by adaptation processes. Bonadaptation signifies that, given the available external options and constraints, as well as the internal resources and expectations that guide decision, the net benefit:cost ratio has proved favorable. Total satisfaction with an outcome of choice behavior is infrequent under the best of conditions. As Freud noted, for social beings, conflict and the necessity for reciprocity in interpersonal relationships involve the surrender of some desires or aspirations in pursuit of other, presumably prepotent, objectives.

Previously I said that the expansion or contraction of pleasurable, central, shared, high priority, and consensually validated role activities is a primary measure of the process of role adaptation. From an evaluative viewpoint, the expansion of these role attributes is the benefit side of adaptation while the cost is represented by the contraction of these role attributes. Naturally, both may occur simultaneously so that the contractions or the costs must be weighed against the expansions to produce an individual cost:benefit ratio.

It is evident from these observations that the costs and benefits of adaptation must be estimated for the entire array of roles. While a given stress is likely to affect one role initially and directly, its repercussions may lead to role alterations of diverse types. This is due both to the relationships among roles (e.g., income-gaining at work subserves household maintenance) and to the fact that a single individual is the link between different concrete roles in the role array. Adaptational failure in one role may be simultaneous with success in another role, and the two must be weighed in a full analysis. Similarly, a process of invasion in response to stress may affect only one role or may result in deterioration of role functioning across the entire array of roles. The evaluation of role adaptation must, therefore, be made on the basis of the benefits and costs entailed by role changes (including foregone opportunities) and the residual stresses after role alteration has occurred.

It is possible to develop another theoretical fragment concerning the process by which stress impinges on an organismic system and produces differing degrees of bonadaptation or maladaptation. For the sake of simplicity, I will limit myself to the case of maladaptation. If the formulation of the different levels of role integration is a reasonable reflection of human and social processes and structures, then we can say that the different role integration levels represent a progressive series of opportunities for personal and social fulfillment. Whether from the point of view of the individual or from the vantage point of the small social systems in which role functioning occurs, each successively higher level is increasingly important for objective stability or subjective satisfaction.[9]

Since each successively higher level of role integration is more closely coordinated as an endogenous system and bolstered by constraints and supports within the system, higher levels of role integration are less responsive to the immediate impact of stresses that might affect the individual.[10] In this sense, a stress such as unemployment would first affect the level of role activities and, only as it became more severe a situation or experience, might it begin to modify role functions, role relationships, the role array, and the role set. Clearly, the higher the level of role integration involved, the wider the ramifications for additional role functions, additional role relationships, and additional role systems.

I have already referred to this process as *invasion*. It implies that there are successive incursions of stress-induced strain on different levels of role integration. As a stress event persists or increases in severity or as several stresses supplement one another, the level of strain increases. This increases the likelihood of a gradual modification of higher levels of role functioning. This spread from lower levels to higher levels of integration is the invasion process

9. I should note, at least in passing, that while a principle of inertia may operate for human beings as it does for physical objects in Newton's first law, the idea of a body as rest is foreign to organismic functioning. A meaningful principle of constancy can only be conceived as *continuity* rather than a static form of stability.

10. This model of the integrative levels of role functioning is similar, in many respects, to Sherrington's (1920) formulation of integrative levels in the nervous system.

itself. At each successive level, the problems of maladaptation become more serious because a wider set of activities, more central functions, and a larger number of people and systems become involved. However, at any point in the sequence, other factors may enter to modify the invasion process and to impede or accelerate its progress.

A discrete role activity may be impaired (that is, carried out without the requisite or expectable regularity, efficiency, or supplementary functions) without being a major impediment to the social functioning of the individual or the social unit. Of course, the more central the role activity is to the core role function, the more ramified its effects. More generally, however, a worker may perform one particular task badly without generating sanctions either by co-workers or by the foreman. A wife does not ordinarily evoke marital conflict if she performs some of her marital role activities inadequately but only as these begin to proliferate and move toward more central or core role functions. The process of invasion first spreads to a wider array of role activities or behaviors which are of greater importance to the role function. As the role function begins to undergo attrition, it places an increasing burden on the role relationships. There are compensatory mechanisms available. Other people may supplement the halting performance of a role function. A wife may go to work when her husband becomes unemployed, or she can otherwise diminish the significance of the impact on herself or on the family. Friends and neighbors may draw closer to a person who has lost a job in the hope of counteracting the strains due to overt loss or to the lack of opportunity. But to the extent that the role relationship represents an integral component of a structured social unit, such measures are mainly transitory. Unless there is a re-organization, such as might occur with a better job, most social units in our society do not have the flexibility or resources to sustain a member who fails to fulfill central role functions or is manifestly seeking new roles or role relationships. Under the impact of continued role failure, role relationships themselves are likely to become disrupted.

176

There is yet another dimension to the process of invasion of role impairments or achievements. In addition to moving through the hierarchy of integrative levels of role behavior, the invasion process may move through diverse role spheres. For our purposes, we can limit these role spheres to the major broad social activities in daily life. There is no evident hierarchy among these since different people, in different life situations, and in different sociocultural contexts, may give quite different priorities to these role spheres. Thus, it is the number of spheres that are invaded, along with the hierarchical level of invasion, that is an indicator of the degree of impairment or achievement in social behavior.

These concepts and propositions need further development. The measurement procedures need to be further concretized. The concepts can be defined more precisely. And the propositions (if not the assumptions) need to be expanded, formalized, and validated. Nonetheless, even in their current form, they offer some promise of allowing more accurate and richer formulations and measurements of the impact of stress and of adaptational responses to strain.

Macro-Level Influences on Work and Unemployment

In presenting an analytic framework for studying the effects of stress on adaptation, I have traced a major sequence of determinants of role functioning. I have also suggested that macro-level sociocultural and politicoeconomic forces are primary determinants of stress, albeit less visible than the immediate events that engage us and demand a response. But I have said little about the reasons for their special importance or about their significance for narrowing the range of options available to people in their efforts to cope with and adapt to stress. Despite the great influence of these processes on human adaptation, I can only make a few suggestions about directions for further work, supplemented by examples from the phenomena of work and unemployment.

A major problem emerges in trying to apply macro-level social theory to the processes of adaptation. This stems from the failure to make explicit a distinction widely recognized in other systems between structural, dynamic, and developmental models. As in the relationship between anatomy, physiology, and embryology, or between psychic structure, psychodynamics, and psychological development, they can be treated separately even though each formulation assumes critical features of the other mode of explanation. A structural social model accounts for the relatively stable, established, and regularized patterns of role functioning which can readily be formulated as aggregate patterns with variations. A dynamic model deals with situational, fluid, or transitional forces affecting individual role functioning although large-scale movements or trends may arise if the forces are sufficiently widespread in their impact. A developmental model concerns itself with the process of child and adult socialization, the "internalization" of values, rules, and role expectations, the organization of alternative relations between individual and society, and the generation of conformist, variant, or deviant trends in populations.

The power of macro-level forces results, in part, from the diverse routes through which they influence behavior. Throughout childhood there are direct and indirect preparations for work roles at home, at school, and even among peers. During late adolescence and early adulthood, some of the realities produced by economic needs begin to impose themselves. Participation in the labor force introduces additional influences at the organizational level and within the work role system among co-workers which also bear the marks of macro-level forces. Since the work role is only one among a number of roles in the role array, other societal forces that bear on work role functioning are transmitted through diverse forms of social participation. Conventional role conceptions and the likelihood of specific forms of coping and adaptation might well be described as "overdetermined" by social mechanisms that insure a high degree of conformity. But some role conceptions and orientations have greater societal primacy than others, and those that influence work roles are among the most critical.

The most striking feature of macro-level structural forces affecting work is encapsulated in the view that *the production of*

178

goods and services is the primary function of a society. All other
objectives must be subordinated and, if possible, geared to this
goal. This value is so embedded in our society that it is difficult to
recognize it as debatable, even in a technologically-advanced
society that can produce material abundance with a fraction of the
population engaged in work. At the micro-level, the primacy of
the value of production is reflected in the central significance of
work roles in daily life. Since many of the requirements of work in
our society are often antithetical to other human dispositions and
other role demands, the sanctions for non-performance are severe.
While starvation is no longer explicitly sanctioned in our society,
and the poor-house and the work-house have fallen out of
fashion, there are powerful pressures linking the instrumental role
functions of *productivity* and *income-gaining.* That there are
frequently contradictions between productivity and income-gaining is evident and in these cases the criteria for productivity or for
income-gaining must be lowered. Thus, artists frequently feel they
cannot both earn a decent living and be optimally productive and
must often choose between them. Many blue-collar workers also
see an intrinsic conflict between these component roles but have
few opportunities to select a preferred mix.[11] While the lives of
most people are encompassed by income-gaining activities, a
corresponding sense of productivity is a ready dividend for only a
small proportion of the population.

Clearly, production is necessary for an economic system. But
the overall conception of production values and the relationship
between values of production and other social values is
enormously variable among different types of societies.[12] Since
productivity itself is motivationally supported, there would be no
conflict if opportunities for fulfillment were widely available. It is

11. Since productivity roles are also encouraged by motivational, if not external sources,
many workers go to extraordinary lengths to envision or strive for some intrinsic meaning
in work (Fried, 1966, 1973).

12. Polanyi's (1944) discussion of different orientations to the value of economic
production has, unfortunately, been neglected in recent years. Another fascinating
formulation of relationships between economic and non-economic activities is presented in
Wolf's (1966) effort to develop a conceptual basis for understanding present economic
systems.

the meager availability of work conditions encouraging productivity which, in a fundamental sense, necessitates the use of
income as a reward for work. Even at a concrete level, it is
apparent that some jobs or forms of job organization provide such
minimal elements of productivity roles that income rewards must
be increased to retain a work force (e.g., the automobile assembly
line). That the union movement in the United States has persisted
in its concern with extrinsic work conditions to the virtual
exclusion of attention to productivity roles has been a source of
major frustration to many workers and to ''job expansion''
theorists.

Role functions in all roles depend upon fulfilling human
physiological and psychological needs in the course of subserving
social objectives. Macro-level forces, however, define the norms
and the actual conditions that govern role decisions and choices.
Thus, until recently the organization of jobs and the conditions of
child-rearing in our society necessitated a choice for most women
between working and having children, a situation of potential
conflict that has been modified but not resolved. Similarly, the
low levels of participation in family life among men are
encouraged by fixed-schedule, eight hour days, as the flexible
work schedule advocates have pointed out. Nonetheless, as stable
patterns embedded within the entire fabric of society, these
structural macro-level principles and policies are taken for
granted, and the ensuing contradictions, conflicts, stresses, and
more distant repercussions are lost to view. Only in the case of the
convergence of several dynamic changes that supplement one
another, as in the case of the growing engagement of women in
labor force activities, do these dynamic forces produce a mass
social movement that engenders system-wide changes. Indeed,
until the last few years, women who wanted both to work and to
bear and rear children suffered many of the stresses of responding
to dynamic forces without systematic mechanisms of social
support.

When we pursue several problems posed by the link between
productivity and income-gaining further, we note some of the

deleterious consequences of maintaining its priority status despite the many contradictions involved.

(1) Capitalist societies retain some of the legal prerogatives of aristocratic societies in allowing wealth or property to substitute for productivity as a source of income. There persists a class for whom the relationship between productivity and income is, at best, tenuous. When members of this class do income-gaining work, their incomes can only be assigned on the basis of an arbitrary conception of the contribution of their jobs to the value added in the process of production. Executive salaries provide one example of the arbitrary determination of value. However, with the prerogatives of wealth, this privileged class also has unique power opportunities. One of the most serious sociopolitical consequences is that the members of this class are free to undertake and often have access to central economic, political, and sociocultural positions with relatively modest income but great power. As a consequence, in the United States we have developed two houses of lords to legislate some of the forces that govern our daily lives.

(2) Housekeeping wives (or husbands) are considered "dependents" whose productive activities are assumed to guarantee the income-gaining functions of the other spouse. There is minimal relationship between the value added by their activities and their incomes (via the earnings of their spouses). The attractions of income-gaining work, encouraged by life-style aspirations, the economic reality of continued inflation, and the movement(s) for women's liberation have had to struggle against sociocultural and politicoeconomic forces designed to supplement traditional patterns of economic organization and family roles. Prior to industrialization, the interplay of productivity and income-gaining roles was more flexible for a larger proportion of working class men and women. Industrial organization and technology led to an increased division of labor and, along with it, increased segregation of male and female work roles. Labor legislation, directed toward relieving conditions of work for women and

children, also served to decrease the employability of women.[13] Such temporal shifts in social process and population patterns invoke the dynamic model of explanation. While the process may be engendered by structural changes that create complexities and contradictions in the system, there is generally a long time lag before the changes initiated are re-integrated within stable values, institutional patterns, and roles.

(3) Developmental models are necessary, if not sufficient, to account for the structural stability of many incongruous phenomena in the sphere of work. In technologically advanced societies, children are largely free of the necessity of gaining income. Child-rearing is a social investment that insures a future labor force for production. The sense of fulfillment provided by children to their parents ordinarily is sufficient to guarantee that the needs of the economy will be met. The socialization process inducts young people into the social system by encouraging them to *want* (or at least to *expect*) what they will *have* to do. They will have to work in order to live; and they will have to conform in order to work. But encouraging children and adolescents to want to work, in spite of low levels of opportunities for productivity, is fraught with difficulty and strain. Observation of and identification with close adults in role behavior is a major source of learning to cope with balancing inner needs and outer demands. Punitive actions are also available for those who have not observed or cannot identify with the role situations of the adults they know best. The schooling process prepares the way more overtly by linking productivity in school with income-like rewards in the form of grades and prerogatives (as well as punishment for nonconformity). The ostensible orientation of formal education is one of reward for productivity. In practice, however, with an unconscious recognition of the true situation, the causal sequence is generally reversed. Thus, for most young people the goals are

13. The increased demand for marriage as a precondition for sexual intercourse also appears to have developed at the same time. Divorce and separation may well have become more difficult during the mid-nineteenth century. The cultural significance of maintaining non-working wives, hitherto a phenomenon of upper and latter, of middle class life, gradually became a symbol of masculine pride among working-class people as well.

oriented toward reward (which requires production) rather than productivity (which incidentally entails reward).

(4) Frequently, dynamic forces serve to "adjust" or "compensate for" imbalances resulting from structural rigidities without altering those structural rigidities themselves. These generally involve numerous individual-level stresses. That the inequalities in income in our society are structured with excessive rigidity is evident to many observers of the social class system. The income inequalities (not to mention inequalities of wealth) are vast; there is a strong propensity to the inheritance of class positions; and economic position is a powerful determinant of social and political position and a host of supplementary rewards or deprivations. Moreover, despite enormous changes in technology, in educational levels, in the status of occupational titles, and in the development of a graduated federal income tax, the relative distribution of incomes in the United States has remained virtually unchanged since at least the early 1930s. There is even some evidence of an increase in inequality in recent years. Yet until the past five years, most people felt that they had already achieved an improvement in social class position and anticipated further gains. Two dynamic forces appear to be primary in encouraging these views and, in the process, diminishing the conflict between aspirations and achievements. The rising standard of living, on the tide of post-World War II technological advances along with an increase in secondary workers in the household led to improvements in the life styles of most people. That increases in the national income were as inequitable or more inequitably distributed than the prior structure of inequality is a fact that only social scientists concerned with these matters observed. Subjectively, this appears to have been experienced as "upward mobility." But in a more literal sense, opportunities for upward social mobility through education and occupation, restricted though they may be, also serve as encouragement to aspirations and negate some of the sense of anger. Self-blame and a sense of inadequacy are more likely responses to failure to achieve mobility than hostility toward the system of structured inequality. But even for those who are, in fact, upwardly mobile, the ostensible

adaptational achievement is attended by many stresses and by a long term process of role change at all levels of role integration.

While all of these considerations touch on the ways in which both structural and dynamic forces generate stresses and define the narrow range of options for coping and adaptation, these macro-level forces also assert an influence on the most concrete features of work experiences. Adaptation to some of the less gratifying features of blue-collar jobs reflects the end-product of major structural forces in the organization of work in our society. The most typical adaptational problems of blue-collar work involve adapting to constraint. The prototype is the assembly line, although this mode of production has influenced conceptions of blue-collar work roles far beyond the actual assembly line. Not only is the definition of core instrumental work role functions extremely narrow and confining but this is bolstered by restrictions on associated role activities on the job: hours of work, coffee breaks, supervisor-worker contacts, peer relationships. Inevitably these conditions reduce the potential for a sense of productivity or pleasure in work. And since the options for coping with on-the-job stresses are so limited, there are many residual strains that are carried into non-work roles. Moreover, to exacerbate the problem, there are generally few intrinsic rewards to encourage a sense of productivity which might compensate for other stresses and their residual strains.

I have already mentioned the influence of work role definitions on child-rearing participation. Similarly, there is a marked confinement of leisure, recreation, and cultural activities, a split between on-the-job social interaction and after-work social relationships, and a fundamental conflict between subsistence needs and personally gratifying activities. Moreover, subjective experiences on the job influence the quality of participation in other roles. Extremely hard physical labor or the performance of tasks that are psychologically demanding with little sense of productivity, readily diminish involvement in other roles and role relationships. The patterns can vary considerably. The carryover may involve role behavior in the household that compensates for neglected needs or imposed constraints at work. Enforced compliance and a sense of powerlessness on the job readily lead to exaggerated aggression and power manipulations at home. Or, as an earlier example indicated, the power "borrowed" from a work role may be precariously extended into an exaggerated bid for authority in other roles. Conversely, the frustrations and stresses at work frequently evoke a depressive orientation that is contained by a few beers or passive television viewing. These are all costs, often submerged, that must be weighed against the benefits in evaluating alternative organizational principles that might affect blue-collar work roles. But since they are highly structured and bolstered throughout the system, they tend to be impervious either to the influence of dynamic forces or to any form or rational plea for more productive or more humane work conditions.

The stresses associated with unemployment provide a very different example of processes that derive from dynamic forces that are almost as stable as structural forces, but are bolstered only by ad hoc solutions. The result is that, even though it is no longer a "rare event," coping and adaptation are individual-level processes with little systematic economic or social support provisions. While the deleterious consequences that have been attributed to unemployment are still matters of debate, on theoretical grounds they appear entirely reasonable and may even underestimate the seriousness of the problem.[14]

Stresses from structural forces differ from those stemming from dynamic forces in a number of respects, with corresponding differences in consequences. Structural stresses tend to be more widespread and to affect a larger proportion of the population. Indeed, when stresses from dynamic sources become very widespread, they begin to take on many of the characteristics of structural stresses as is the case with inflation and energy problems. And the very few structural resources for dealing with dynamic forces that produce stresses like unemployment originated during the 1930s with massive unemployment. Thus, another distinction lies in the societal mechanisms designed to

---

14. See Brenner, 1973, 1976; Catalano and Dooley, 1977; Cobb and Kasl, 1977; Fried, 1969.

mitigate the overt stresses and to facilitate rapid coping processes when the stresses stem from structural forces. These are less readily available for stresses from dynamic sources. Seen from another vantage point, structurally-derived stresses are often experienced in common with many other people and there is a sense of shared strain. Dynamically-derived stresses, on the other hand, even when relatively widespread, tend to be conceived and to function for individuals and role systems in isolation. The repercussions develop subtly, through the ramifications of role change at micro-level as these proliferate through the role system and beyond. Finally, stresses of structural origin are more likely to be anticipated than those from dynamic origins, providing increased opportunities for effective coping behavior.[15]

Except for relatively recent and highly suggestive, but not entirely conclusive, studies of job loss and the large literature from the great depression, the extent and details of the effects of unemployment are not well understood. In describing the consequences of unemployment in terms of stress and role adaptation, therefore, there is necessarily a large admixture of conjecture with evidence.

As with many stresses, and especially those from dynamic sources, the initial impact of job loss occurs at the level of role activities. Despite the fact of a loss of role functions, perhaps even of a role, the work role is subjectively retained as an integral feature of the role array. The income-gaining role is partly compensated through unemployment insurance coverage. The meager productivity roles experienced by many people in work are displaced onto the job search. For many people, until the ramifications of unemployment are confronted more fully, there may even be a sense of relief from the oppressive features of work. Thus, the phenomena of stress, coping, and residual experiences of strain are initially reduced but subtly and individually variable. The real confrontation begins to arise when other jobs are not readily available and when the realities of trying to maintain a prior standard of living on drastically reduced income become

---

15. See Janis (1958) for the significance of anticipation in coping with stress.

evident. Additional stresses may occur to exacerbate the problem, either independent of the job loss or indirectly linked to it. One would suspect that, for many people, a mechanism of denial operates to diminish the strain until the impact of job loss on individual roles and the role system becomes unavoidably clear. At higher status levels, in fact, there is evidence that the denial can persist for long periods of time, bolstered by the adoption of pseudo-work roles with little if any current job income (Buono, 1976). On the other hand, in rare instances, the loss of an undesirable job can lead to efforts at career change or even to intensified upward mobility strivings.

Although there is much variation in duration as well as rates of unemployment among different sociodemographic groups, these coping mechanisms may suffice until a new job is found. Whether there are longer term effects of short term unemployment is likely to be a function of the ease of locating a new job and the differences between the two jobs. To the extent that even short term unemployment precipitates or exacerbates individual strain in the role system, of course, a relatively small loss may result in magnified consequences. But the tolerance for periods of unemployment is likely to vary with many individual and role system differences linked to economic, social, and personality attributes. From a more theoretical viewpoint, the problem becomes potentially serious when the lack of a job begins to operate both subjectively and objectively as the loss of the work role. At that point, the management of the stress through a variety of coping devices including job seeking is diverted to other psychic, physiological, or role system issues. Or the causal sequence may work in the opposite direction: the prominence of psychic, physiological, or role system stresses may result in the deterioration of the work role. The phenomena of discouraged workers and underemployment may well result from such a history.

Regardless of the precise conditions that operate, it is not so much the loss of work role activities per se, but rather the development of an equilibrium position around the loss of the instrumental role functions of work, productivity and income-gaining, that portends further role changes. And these further role changes, from all of the evidence that is available concerning unemployment, begin to manifest the forms of role adaptation that I have referred to as the invasion process. Certainly, a quasi-equilibrium can be established at any one of the different levels of role integration. But, once the major instrumental role functions associated with work are lost, the extent to which and the form in which further invasion or stability is attained is a function of the small role system. Any major change of this nature is bound to induce stresses within the family and may well engender stresses in other role systems as well. Thus, as the stresses invade diverse role relationships, the opportunities both for compensatory support and for exacerbating stress expand.

Characteristically, however, the options available for individual and role system adaptations to continued unemployment appear extremely limited. These can include a gradual contraction of life style characteristics, a shift in family roles associated with new income-gaining roles by spouse or children, continued efforts at productivity without commensurate income-gaining roles, or the disruption of the role system(s) like the conjugal family that rests on the income-gaining role of a single member. Whichever route is taken, however, a major set of role adaptations is most often involved. The problem rests, not merely on the stress of unemployment nor even on the loss of a role which is critical for subsistence and essential for a sense of productive social participation, but on the narrow range of options available for role adaptations to either of these losses. Therefore, despite occasional exceptions, the predominant result is in the form of a contraction of all the meaningful dimensions of role functioning, a process of maladaptation. It becomes a function of the isolated individual or of the separate role systems to stem the processes of role invasion or to allow them to continue to the point of disruption of other roles and role systems. And it is these considerations, as much as any discrete consequence of continued (and perhaps even short term) unemployment that lends theoretical credence to the evidence accumulated by Brenner (1973, 1976) on aggregate data, of the deleterious effects of unemployment on physical and mental illness.

That unemployment is viewed and continues to be seen as a dynamic feature of socioeconomic processes rather than as an endemic and, thus, a structural aspect of our system which requires structural solutions poses serious difficulties for the effective functioning of many individuals and role systems in our society.

REFERENCES

Bates, Frederick, Position, Role and Status: A Reformulation of Concepts. *Social Forces,* 1956, 34: 313-321.

Brenner, M. Harvey, *Estimating the Social Costs of National Economic Policy: Implications for Mental and Physical Health, and Criminal Aggression.* A Study Prepared for the Use of the Joint Economic Committee of Congress, Washington, DC: U.S. Government Printing Office, 1976.

Brenner, M. Harvey, *Mental Illness and the Economy.* Cambridge, MA: Harvard University Press, 1973.

Buono, Anthony F., *The Impact of Joblessness on the Psycho-social Functioning of Middle-Aged Business Executives.* M.A. Thesis. Chestnut Hill, MA: Boston College, 1976.

Burtt, Edwin Arthur, *The Metaphysical Foundations of Modern Science.* Garden City, NY: Doubleday, 1954.

Campbell, Angus, Converse, Philip E., and Rodgers, Willard L., *The Quality of American Life: Perceptions, Evaluations, and Satisfactions.* New York: Russell Sage, 1976.

Cannon, Walter B., *The Wisdom of the Body.* New York: W. W. Norton, 1932.

Catalano, Ralph and Dooley, David, Economic Predictors of Depressed Mood and Stressful Life Events in a Metropolitan Community. *Journal of Health and Social Behavior,* 1977, 18, 292-307.

Cobb, Sidney and Kasl, Stanislav V., *Termination: The Consequences of Job Loss.* DHEW (NIOSH) Publication No. 77-224. Cincinnati, OH: U.S. DHEW, Division of Biomedical and Behavioral Science, 1977.

Coelho, George V., Hamburg, David A., and Adams, John E., eds., *Coping and Adaptation.* New York: Basic Books, 1974.

Coulson, M., Role: A Redundant Concept in Sociology?: Some Educational Considerations, in J. A. Jackson, ed., *Role.* Cambridge, England: Cambridge University Press, 1972.

Dohrenwend, Barbara S. and Dohrenwend, Bruce P., eds., *Stressful Life Events: Their Nature and Effects.* New York: Wiley, 1974.

Dohrenwend, Barbara S., Krasnoff, Larry, Askenasy, Alexander R., and Dohrenwend, Bruce P., Exemplification of a Method for Scaling Life Events: The PERI Life Events Scale. In press, *Journal of Health and Social Behavior.*

Freud, Sigmund, *Civilization and Its Discontents.* London: Hogarth Press, 1961. (Standard Edition, Vol. XXI, First Published 1930.)

Freud, Sigmund, *The Future of an Illusion.* London: Hogarth Press, 1961. (Standard Edition, Vol. XXI. First Published 1927.)

Fried, Marc, The Role of Work in a Mobile Society, in Sam Bass Warner, Jr., ed., *Planning for a Nation of Cities.* Cambridge, MA: MIT Press, 1966.

Fried, Marc, Social Differences in Mental Health, in John Kosa, Aaron Antonovsky and Irving Kenneth Zola, eds., *Poverty and Health: A Sociological Analysis.* Cambridge, MA: Harvard University Press, 1969.

Fried, Marc, et al., *The World of the Urban Working Class,* Cambridge, MA: Harvard University Press, 1973.

Gersten, Joanne, Langner, Thomas C., Eisenberg, G., and Simcha-Fagan, Ora, An Evaluation of the Etiological Role of Stressful Life-Change Events in Psychological Disorders, *Journal of Health and Social Behavior,* 1977, 18, 228-243.

Goffman, Erving, *Encounters: Two Studies in the Sociology of Interaction.* Indianapolis, IN: Bobbs-Merrill, 1961.

Goffman, Erving, *The Presentation of Self in Everyday Life.* Garden City, NY: Doubleday, 1959.

Goffman, Erving, *Relations in Public: Microstudies of the Social Order.* New York: Basic Books, 1971.

Goode, William J., A Theory of Role Strain, *American Sociological Review,* 1960, 25, 483-496.

Gross, Neal A., Mason, Ward S., and McEachern, Alexander W., *Explorations in Role Analysis.* New York: Wiley, 1958.

Gunderson, Ellsworth K. and Rahe, Richard H., eds., *Life Stress and Illness.* Springfield, IL: C. C. Thomas, 1974.

Holmes, T. H. and Rahe, R. H., The Social Readjustment Rating Scale, *Journal of Psychosomatic Medicine,* 1967, 11, 213-218.

Hurst, Michael W., Jenkins, C. David, and Rose, Robert M., The Assessment of Life Change Stress: A Comparative and Methodological Inquiry, *Psychosomatic Medicine,* 1978, 40, 126-141.

Jackson, Jay A., Conceptual and Measurement Model for Norms and Roles, *Pacific Sociological Review,* 1966, 9, 35-47.

Jackson, Jay A., Role—Editorial Introduction, in J. A. Jackson, ed., *Role.* Cambridge, England: Cambridge University Press, 1972.

Janis, Irving L., *Psychological Stress: Psychoanalytic and Behavioral Studies of Surgical Patients.* New York: Wiley, 1958.

Kahn, Robert L. and Quinn, Robert P., *Mental Health, Social Support, and Metropolitan Problems.* (Unpublished) Ann Arbor, MI: Institute of Social Research, 1976.

Kahn, Robert L. et al., *Organizational Stress: Studies in Role Conflict and Ambiguity.* New York: Wiley, 1964.

Katz, Daniel and Kahn, Robert L., *The Social Psychology of Organizations.* New York: Wiley, 1966.

Lewin, Kurt, Comments Concerning Psychological Forces and Energies, and the Structure of the Psyche, in David Rapaport, ed., *Organization and Pathology of Thought.* New York: Columbia, 1951.

Lewin, Kurt, *The Conceptual Representation and the Measurement of Psychological Forces.* Durham, NC: Duke, 1938.

Lewin, Kurt, *A Dynamic Theory of Personality.* New York: McGraw-Hill, 1936.

Marcuse, Herbert, *Eros and Civilization.* Boston: Beacon Press, 1966.

Marcuse, Herbert, *One-Dimensional Man.* Boston: Beacon Press, 1964.

Merton, Robert, The Role Set: Problems in Sociological Theory, *British Journal of Sociology,* 1957, 8, 108.

Myers, Jerome K., Lindenthal, Jacob J. and Pepper, Max P., Life Events, Social Integration and Psychiatric Symptomatology, *Journal of Health and Social Behavior,* 1975, 16, 421-427.

Nye, F. Ivan, Bahr, Howard M. et al., *Role Structure and the Analysis of the Family.* Beverly Hills, CA: Sage Publications, 1976.

Parsons, Talcott, *The Social System.* Glencoe, IL: Free Press, 1951.

192

Parsons, Talcott and Shils, Edward A., eds., *Toward A General Theory of Action*. Cambridge, MA: Harvard University Press, 1952.

Pearlin, Leonard I. and Schooler, Carmi, The Structure of Coping, *Journal of Health and Social Behavior*, 1978, 19, 2-21.

Polanyi, Karl, *The Great Transformation*. New York: Farrar and Rinehart, 1944.

Popitz, Heinrich, The Concept of Social Role as an Element of Sociological Theory, in J. A. Jackson, ed., *Role*. Cambridge: Cambridge University Press, 1972.

Preiss, J. and Ehrlich, H., *An Examination of Role Theory: The Case of the State Police*. Omaha: University of Nebraska Press, 1966.

Sarbin, Theodore R., Role Theory, in Gardner Lindzey, ed., *Handbook of Social Psychology*. Cambridge, MA: Addison-Wesley Press, 1954.

Sarbin, Theodore R. and Allen, Vernon L., Role Theory, in Gardner Lindzey and Elliot Aronson, eds., *The Handbook of Social Psychology*. Reading, MA: Addison-Wesley Press, 1968.

Selye, Hans, *The Stress of Life*. New York: McGraw-Hill, 1956.

Sherrington, Charles S., *The Intergrative Action of the Nervous System*. New Haven: Yale University Press, 1920.

Turner, Ralph H., *Family Interaction*. New York: Wiley, 1970.

Turner, Ralph H., Role-Taking: Process versus Conformity, in Arnold M. Rose, ed., *Human Behavior and Social Processes: An Interactionist Approach*. Boston: Houghton-Mifflin, 1962.

Wolf, Eric R., *Peasants*. Englewood Cliffs, NJ: Prentice-Hall, 1966.

6
ECONOMIC DEPRIVATION, SOCIAL MOBILITY, AND MENTAL HEALTH

LOUIS A. FERMAN
JOHN GARDNER

The work of M. Harvey Brenner and A. Pierce has recently provided the impetus for a variety of studies exploring the psychological and social effects of aggregate economic changes (e.g., unemployment rates). While the findings are important in themselves—the inverse correlation between suicide and the composite stock index, and even more significant, the inverse correlation between the manufacturing employment index and the incidence of admissions to mental hospitals over a fifty-year span—these studies have erected a framework for further work. Figure 1 is a simple diagram which proposes a set of hypothesized relationships and indicates which connections have been examined.

What is striking here is the lack of information about how large-scale economic change translated into loss of work moves toward non-economic life stress, on to adverse psychological change, and then to large-scale psychological and social disorder. What is in the "black box" that intervenes between aggregate measures of economic change and aggregate measures of psychological and social disorder? Specifically, what economic, social, and psychological processes link economic change to subsequent social and psychological functioning? There may be more than one answer to these questions; and one can imagine a number of competing (and even overlapping) perspectives on what is in the "black box." What is crucial, however, is to gather, analyze, and eventually augment those pieces of research that can

193

194

Figure 1
Hypothesized Relationships Between Economic Change and Indicators of Psychological Change

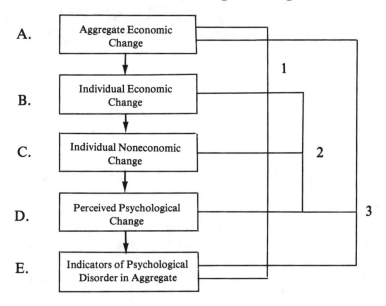

1. Relationships between A and E measured by Pierce[1] and Brenner.[2]

2. Relationships between B and C, C and D, and B, C, and D measured by others in Dohrenwend and Dohrenwend.[3]

3. Relationships between A, B, C, D, and E either assumed or described nonquantitatively by Bakke,[4] Angell,[5] Komarovsky,[6] and others.

1. A. Pierce, The Economic Cycle and the Social Suicide Rate. *American Sociological Review*. 1967, 32, 475-482.

2. M. H. Brenner, *Mental Illness and the Economy*. Cambridge: Harvard University Press, 1973.

3. B. S. Dohrenwend and B. P. Dohrenwend, eds., *Stressful Life Events: Their Nature and Effects*. New York: John Wiley and Sons, 1974.

4. E. W. Bakke, *The Unemployed Man*. New York: E. P. Dutton and Company, 1934.

5. R. C. Angell, *The Family Encounters the Depression*. New York: Charles Scribner and Sons, 1936.

6. Mirra Komarovsky, *The Unemployed Man and His Family*. New York: The Dryden Press, 1940.

provide an understanding of the individual and social dynamics involved in personal, family, and community responses to economic change, so that policies designed to intervene in this succession can be based on an understanding of the total life situation and problems of the worker who experiences some form of economic change.

Focus of the Paper

In an effort to develop an explanatory scheme for aggregate economic change and its physical and mental health outcomes, we have started with a number of assumptions. The first is that economic change—whether contraction of the economy, plant shutdowns, increased rationalization and automation of work, plant mergers, or productivity gains—results either immediately or eventually in the loss of work for certain groups of people. Thus, an explanatory scheme must deal with the fact that numbers of people will change jobs (some voluntarily, others involuntarily) and will be without work for varying periods of time. An explanatory scheme, then, may begin by postulating that economic changes initiate patterns of "bumping" and "skidding" in the labor market. This process involves the displacement and replacement of some workers by others (bumping) and the taking on of jobs that provide less status, offer less income or fewer fringe benefits, or less protection from arbitrary work practices (skidding). There is already some evidence that bumping and skidding trigger psychological reactions that may be related to mental health. What is needed is a new view or model of the labor market that focuses primarily on bumping and skidding. More traditional models of the labor market, which have not been concerned with relating aggregate economic changes to aggregate psychological changes, have failed to consider this behavior.

A second assumption is that some of these workers will find themselves, to varying degrees, in financial trouble, as savings are depleted and debts mount. They may find it necessary to curtail expenditures, find new sources of income, or to rely on other members of the family in producing income. All these options can impose strains on the worker and his family. Therefore, a

196

significant situational stress for some of these displaced workers will be resource insufficiency and economic deprivation.

Third, workers who lose jobs will subsequently show different career patterns. Some will find immediate reemployment; others will remain unemployed; and still others will move from job to job. The work career patterns following economic change may be highly indicative of the stresses and instabilities that arise when changes in work status are involved. The work career pattern is a *summation* of labor market experiences rather than a picture of a status level at any one time; thus it may be a somewhat more sensitive measure of individual adjustment to economic change.

The fourth assumption is that economic deprivation and work career patterns will be *predictors* of physical and mental health outcomes. We would argue that these changes would create considerable disruption in the lives of affected workers and that their consequences would be apparent in the functioning of the individual. We would also argue that these changes affect not only the individual directly involved but also the members of his family indirectly. These changes can alter role sets and reciprocal role behavior, passing changes in the affected worker on to other family members, as well, by a "ripple effect." This point will not be dealt with in this paper but is germane to the comments by Marc Fried on role behavior.

The focus in this paper, then, is on the roles played by economic deprivation and job mobility in the life organization of the individual. Basic to this discussion is the belief that aggregate economic change will result, for large numbers of individuals, in skidding and bumping and that in turn would influence both social and psychological functioning.

In specific terms, a plant shutdown may cause considerable bumping and skidding in the local labor market as the displaced workers seek new jobs. The patterns of labor force participation for these workers will vary so that a number of worker mobility patterns will be experienced. These will be directly linked to the degree of economic deprivation suffered by the worker and in turn to the worker's psychological states and social adjustments.

We can plot, then, the following sequence of events and the linkages between them:

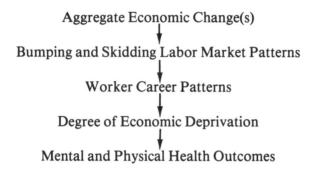

Aggregate Economic Change(s)

↓

Bumping and Skidding Labor Market Patterns

↓

Worker Career Patterns

↓

Degree of Economic Deprivation

↓

Mental and Physical Health Outcomes

Skidding and Bumping

Since we have postulated that mobility patterns and their consequences are essential determinants of the physical and mental health of workers, our initial point of reference will focus on a new perspective and model of the labor market based on bumping and skidding.

An individual who loses his job as the result of an aggregate economic change may: remain unemployed while searching for a new job; leave the labor force altogether; or may find another job quickly. The new job may be comparable to, or even in some respects better than, his previous one, but he may find that it could be performed by a worker with less skill, intelligence, experience, or training than were needed on his previous job. The new job may also pay less or be less prestigious than the old one. This less than desirable outcome of a change of jobs would seem to be most likely to occur during recessions, when reemployment opportunities are limited. If such "skidding" by one worker either causes employed workers of less skill or education to be laid off or prevents the hiring of unemployed workers, those people who become or remain unemployed are said to have been "bumped."

The hypothesis offered here is that this pattern of reaction, if not predominant during recessions, is nevertheless sufficiently important that its recognition and study will lead to improved understanding of the dynamics of aggregate employment and unemployment and their relationship to aggregate patterns of mental health.

The process can be illustrated as follows. In figure 2, jobs are ranked according to the ability required to perform them, and individual laborers are ranked according to whatever ability they possess, lower numbers indicating higher levels of ability in both cases. A comparison of the rankings of jobs and of laborers shows that in periods of high employment, enough jobs are available to employ workers with ability gradations 1-20. Of these, 1 and 2 are employed in top-level (I) jobs, 3-5 in second-level (II) jobs, and so forth.

If we assume that skidding characterizes all employment adjustment, the job ranking for low employment levels would show the differential between recession and prosperity. At each job level, fewer people are employed; people with the lowest qualifications at each level lose their jobs and skid to the next lower level of employment. Thus, grade 2 workers lose their level I jobs and skid to level II. Similarly, grade 4 and 5 workers, who had been employed at level II, have now skidded to level III.

If no skidding occurred at all, the situation would be as shown in figure 3. The number of level I jobs has been reduced, so that grade 2 workers are unemployed. Similarly, grade 5 workers become unemployed because level II jobs have been reduced. The total increase in unemployment is the same in either case; the distribution of job reductions among job types is the same. But the incidence of unemployment is different.

A comparison of the two diagrams also illustrates the part played by bumping in the adjustment process when skidding is involved. As figure 3 shows, grade 5 employees would have lost their level II jobs even if skidding had not occurred. But grade 4 workers would have remained at their level II jobs if grade 2 workers had not skidded but instead had become unemployed. Thus, the skidding by grade 2 workers has bumped grade 4 workers into level III jobs. Similarly, employees of grades 7 and 8 have been bumped into level IV, and those of grades 16-19 have been bumped into unemployment.

Figure 2
Employment Adjustment - Complete Skidding

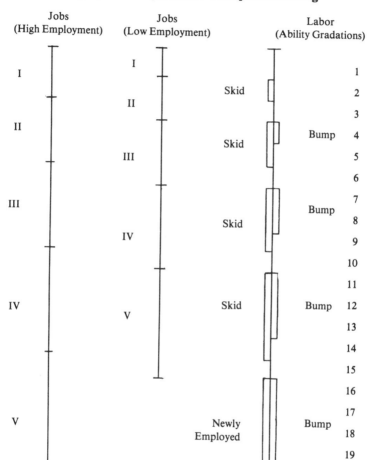

Jobs (High Employment)	Jobs (Low Employment)		Labor (Ability Gradations)
I	I		1
		Skid	2
	II		3
II		Bump	4
		Skid	5
	III		6
III			7
		Bump	
		Skid	8
	IV		9
			10
			11
IV		Skid Bump	12
	V		13
			14
			15
			16
			17
V		Newly Employed Bump	18
			19
			20
			21
			22
	Previously Unemployed (or out of the labor force)		23
			24
			25

200

Figure 3
Employment Adjustment (Without Skidding)

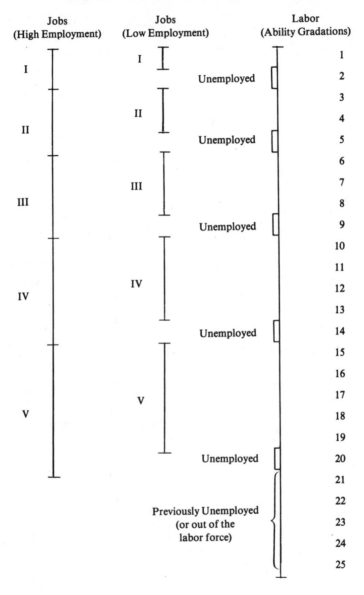

The explanation of labor market adjustment to recession that is presented in figure 2 is similar to the queue theory of labor markets developed by Thurow[7] to explain the incidence of poverty and by Mangum[8] to explain the differences in employment experiences of various demographic groups. Melvin Reder offered a similar model to explain cyclical changes in occupational wage differentials.[9] Figure 3 represents workers' behavior that seems to be implicit in most discussions of unemployment in recession and recovery, but they are too vague for this point of view to be attributed to specific economists or economic observers.

These two views can be contrasted with still another framework: the dual labor market approach.[10] In that case the process described in either figure 2 or 3 characterizes primary employment. The lowest level of jobs, however, is more appropriately represented by a reservoir of undesirable, low-paying jobs that require little or no education, skills, or experience. These jobs are in fact so ephemeral that it is difficult even to count them. The low-grade laborers who hold them constantly bounce between employment, unemployment, and nonparticipation. In recession, even the lowest grades of workers who normally belong to the primary sector may find themselves in secondary jobs. In most discussions, it is not clear whether the adjustment process that the authors have in mind for the primary sectors follows the skidding model or its alternative. Figure 4 shows the dual market view if skidding occurs. Most adherents of the dual labor market approach will believe that some skidding may occur, but that in most cases it would be from primary job levels to secondary ones. That is, they would see the process in the primary sector as more nearly like figure 3, but with "unemployment" replaced by "unemployment or (temporary) secondary employment."

7. L. C. Thurow, *Poverty and Discrimination.* Washington, DC: Brookings, 1969.
8. G. L. Mangum, Economic Growth and Unemployment. In J. Kreps, ed., *Technology, Manpower, and Retirement Policy.* Cleveland: World Publishing Co., 1966.
9. M. W. Reder, The Theory of Occupational Wage Differentials. *American Economic Review.* 1955, 64, 833-852.
10. See G. C. Cain, The Challenge of Segmented Labor Market Theories to Orthodox Theory: A Survey. *JEL,* 1976, 14, 1215-1217; P. B. Doeringer and M. J. Piore, *Internal Labor Markets and Manpower Analysis.* Boston: Heath, 1971; and M. L. Wachter, Primary and Secondary Labor Markets: A Critique of the Dual Approach. *Brookings Papers on Economic Activity,* 1974, 3, 637-680.

202

Figure 4
Employment Adjustment - Dual Labor Market (With Skidding)

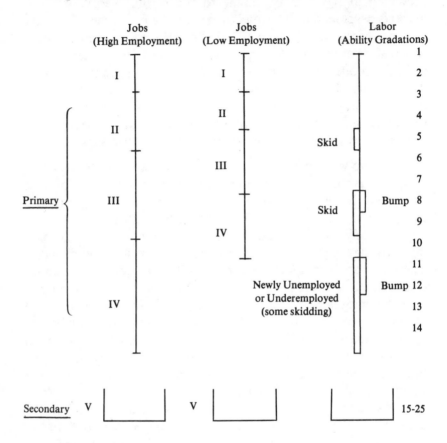

Of course, these views are ideal ones, and no one view describes the workers during all employment transitions. The point is the relative usefulness of these different approaches and the emphasis that should be placed on each analysis in each case. The appropriate emphasis can be determined only by going further, beyond the skeletal descriptions of labor market adjustment that are presented in the diagrams above.

A schematic diagram describing the employment adjustment process may help to identify the outstanding issues. The diagram in figure 5 indicates the three states in which a person may find himself with respect to the labor market and the broadly defined ways in which this status may change. In this framework, people are employed, unemployed, or nonparticipants. Employed people may change their status by retiring, quitting, being laid off, or separating from work for other reasons. People who quit or are laid off are usually unemployed, at least for a short time, and those who retire or otherwise separate usually become nonpartici-pants. Entrance to employment takes place as people are newly hired or rehired; thus, some of them are new entrants or re-entrants to the labor force. The labeled arrows in figure 5 indicate these flows, but they are not meant to imply that other patterns (such as movement from employment to nonparticipation *via* layoff) will not take their place. Accessions and separations continuously take place at all levels of this pyramid, and one can think of steady-state rates of these flows that maintain both the size and the structure of this stock of jobs.

In a steady state, although the number and structure of jobs do not change, any particular worker's position in the hierarchy is unlikely to remain the same. This change of position will probably follow a certain pattern. Most people enter employment nearer to the bottom on the pyramid than to the top. Vroman finds, for instance, that about 80 percent of working teenagers obtain their early experience in retail trade and services, where they fill low-paying jobs for the most part—those requiring little skill or previous experience.[11] As they acquire experience, they tend to

11. Wayne Vroman, Worker Upgrading and the Business Cycle. *Brookings Papers on Economic Activity,* 1977, 1, 236.

Figure 5
Labor Force Participation Patterns

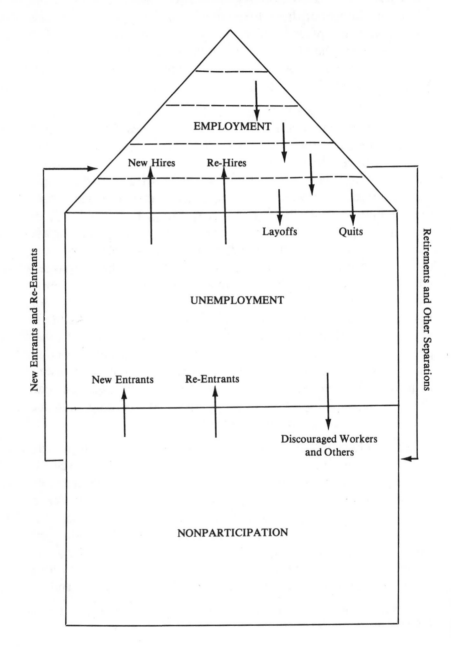

move to higher strata in the pyramid as vacancies occur. Also, while advancement is the movement usually desired, some people will move laterally or downward in this process of change within the steady state. For those who advance, upward movement occurs on well-defined job ladders. Others improve their position by changing firms or even by changing occupations. Sommers and Eck found, for example, that between 1965 and 1970, 32 percent of those employed changed their occupations,[12] presumably reflecting improvements in their situations. It is typical for some industries, like retail trade, to serve as "feeder" industries for others, like durable mnufacturing.[13]

For some individuals, however, employment consists of frequent accession and separation, with little opportunity for advancement. This pattern may obtain because the individual has only a transient attachment to the labor market (e.g., teenagers in school) or because he lacks the skill or education requisite for advancement. Periods of expansion or recession add another dimension to this continual flow of people into, out of, or within the employment state. In expansion or recession, the stock of jobs will change. That such changes have different effects on different strata of employment has been well documented. It has been observed that unemployment rates for blue-collar workers, operatives, non-farm laborers, and craft workers are more cyclically sensitive than those for white-collar workers, professional and technical workers, and managers.[14] Additional direct evidence appears in the finding that the employment of production workers in manufacturing fluctuates proportionately more over the cycle than does the employment of managerial or supervisory employees.[15] Within particular industries, the employment of lower-wage workers is found to be more cyclically sensitive.[16]

12. Dixie Sommers and Alan Eck, Occupational Mobility in the American Labor Force. *Monthly Labor Review,* 1977, 100, 3-19.

13. Wayne Vroman, *op. cit.,* p. 237.

14. P. M. Ryscavage, Impact of Higher Unemployment on Major Labor Force Groups. *Monthly Labor Review,* 1970, 93, 21-25.

15. W. U. Oi, Labor As a Quasi-fixed Factor. *Journal of Political Economy,* 1962, December, 550.

16. Oi, pp. 547-549 and Vroman, Table 1, p. 235.

Across industries, Okun has found that high-wage manufacturing industries eliminate or increase jobs at a higher rate than total manufacturing industries do.[17] Thus, the lower strata of the pyramid expand or contract more than proportionately with the higher strata.

Taken by themselves, these different patterns of cyclical response across strata imply that the people who hold low-level jobs will have more frequent periods of unemployment, with their accompanying economic deprivation, than will occupants of high-level jobs. More frequent unemployment helps to explain the generally higher levels of unemployment rates in these groups, but this need not be strictly a cyclical phenomenon. In the steady state, unemployment would occur more often if the low-level jobs were so undesirable that people left them more often. This is the explanation given by dual labor market theorists. However, if the cyclical aspects are important in themselves, then one would expect to observe that low-level workers have larger absolute (but not necessarily larger proportionate) increases in periods of unemployment in the downturn of the cycle.

There is evidence for both the steady state and for the cyclical patterns described above. Higher-level jobs tend to be dominated by prime-age white males and low-level jobs by disproportionate numbers of women, teenagers, and prime-age black males. Thus, demographic groups can serve as rough proxies for groups of occupants of particular job strata. Hall finds that blacks have more frequent spells of unemployment at a given level of aggregate unemployment than do whites. Blacks and low-skilled workers are more likely at any time to become unemployed than are whites or more highly skilled workers.[18] At any given aggregate unemployment rate, periods of unemployment decline with age for all race and sex groups; within each age group, white males

---

17. A. M. Okun, Upward Mobility in a High Pressure Economy. *Brookings Papers on Economic Activity*, 1973, 1, Table 2, 220-221.

18. R. E. Hall, Turnover in the Labor Force. *Brookings Papers on Economic Activity*, 1972, 3, 717-718.

have the lowest number of such periods.[19] To the extent that broad age classifications (16-19, 20-24, 25-44, 45-59) reflect differences in experience, these results too are consistent with the predictions above.

Evidence with respect to the additional implications of the cyclical pattern is not conclusive. It is consistent with the preceding predictions that Perry finds that women and teenagers generally show larger absolute (but smaller proportionate) increases in average periods of unemployment as the aggregate unemployment rate rises.[20] But if one looks instead at the cyclical sensitivity of the probability of an employed person becoming unemployed, that probability changes more (both absolutely and relatively) for prime-age white males than for some other demographic groups and is the principal reason why the unemployment rates of primary labor force groups increase.[21]

This ambiguity may be resolved in part by considering the cyclical adjustment process in more detail. A reduction in the number of low-level jobs will cause some people to lose their jobs outright. But an even larger impact is likely to be felt by those who seek employment at job levels where contractions are greatest. That is, the flow of new hires and rehires will be perhaps more affected by the employment reduction than the flow of layoffs will be.

The empirical evidence on this point seems to support the cyclical pattern. For instance, Perry finds that the probability of leaving unemployment is more responsive to changes in the aggregate unemployment rate for teenagers and women than for prime-age males.[22] Perry's figures do not differentiate between a

19. S. T. Marston, Employment Instability and High Unemployment Rates. *Brookings Papers on Economic Activity*, 1976, 1, Table 2, p. 176, and calculations by the authors from Table 5, p. 186.

20. G. L. Perry, Unemployment Flows in the U.S. Labor Market. *Brookings Papers on Economic Activity*, 1972, 2, 259.

21. Marston, *op. cit.*, p. 186 and R. E. Smith, A Simulation Model of the Demographic Composition of Employment. In R. G. Ehrenberg, ed., *Research in Labor Economics*, Volume 1, 1977, p. 273.

22. Perry, *op. cit.*, Table 2, p. 250.

person who leaves unemployment because he finds a job and one who leaves the labor force.But when Marston does take this difference into account, he finds that the most important reason for increased unemployment for women, teenagers (except black males), and black prime-age males is the reduced probability of finding a job. Both the likelihood of successful labor force entry and the likelihood of finding a job after unemployment are reduced less for prime-age white males than for almost any other group.[23] Smith's estimates of these same probabilities do not agree so consistently with the above implications. His estimates show that the elasticity of successful entry for prime-age white males with respect to changes in the ratio of aggregate vacancies to aggregate unemployment is as great as for other groups. But the likelihood that an unemployed person will obtain a job is affected less in the case of white prime-age males than in that of any other group.[24]

Employment changes across occupational groups in the 1974-75 recession provide additional insight into a predictable pattern. Between January 1974 and January 1975, while total employment fell by over one million, employment of professional and technical workers, clerks, and other service workers increased. At the same time, nearly a half-million jobs were lost both for craftsmen and for non-transport operatives, over 300,000 for non-farm laborers, almost 100,000 for transport operatives, and nearly 200,000 for managers and administrators. The pattern for clerks, other service workers, and managers appears inconsistent with the hypothesized tendency for lower strata to be more cyclically sensitive. But the other categories do conform to the expected pattern. And a large portion of the apparent inconsistencies can be explained. Nearly half the employment loss for managers occurred among self-employed people outside the retail trade. Such positions may well be nearer the bottom of the employment pyramid than the top. And the employment of clerical and service workers would seem to reflect strong underlying secular trends rather than to

---

23. Marston, *op. cit.,* Table 6, p. 187.

24. Smith, *op. cit.,* p. 279. The sole exception is a rather strange estimate for the coefficient for white female teenagers.

contradict the main thrust of the hypothesized pattern of adjustment.

Finally, when one combines the changes in probabilities of losing current jobs and of finding new ones, the impact is greater for secondary labor-force groups than for prime-age white males.

From this evidence one could suggest two reasons for the higher unemployment rates suffered by secondary labor-force groups:

1) The poor quality of low-level jobs and the looser labor-market attachment of secondary workers result in more frequent periods of unemployment for those groups.[25]

2) The greater cyclical sensitivity in the stock of those jobs in which secondary groups are concentrated leads to greater sensitivity of the unemployment rates of those groups to change in aggregate labor-market conditions. The first reason is a static one that explains only differences in levels of unemployment rates. The second explains differences in cyclical sensitivities as well.

This greater sensitivity in the stock of lower-level jobs is usually attributed to the investment a firm makes in high-level employees. The higher the level of the job, the more likely it will be that the worker will develop form-specific knowledge and experience that will permit the firm to pay wages higher than the worker's opportunity wage but lower than the value of his marginal product to the firm. This excess of marginal product over wage allows the firm to continue to employ specifically trained workers even during periodic reductions in product demand when less highly trained workers may be laid off.[26]

The skidding and bumping process suggests, however, that there may be an additional (as distinct from an alternative) reason both for the higher level of unemployment rates and for the greater cyclical sensitivity of certain rates. If a recession is severe enough

---

25. Whether worker quality or job quality is responsible for this looser labor market attachment or whether all three factors are mutually reinforcing is not at issue here. See D.M. Gordon, *Theories of Poverty and Underemployment: Orthodox, Radical, and Dual Labor Market Perspectives.* Lexington: Heath, 1972.

26. Oi, *op. cit.,* J. H. Pencavel, Wages, Specific Training, and Labor Turnover in U.S. Manufacturing Industries. *Indian Economic Review,* 1972, 13, 53-64.

to affect the stocks of high-level jobs, and if some of the people who lose those jobs (usually primary workers) skid into low-level positions, not only are there fewer low-level jobs overall, but the influx of skidders reduces even further the number of such jobs available to secondary workers.

Thus, aggregate economic conditions influence the frequency and severity of exposure to economic deprivation for all labor force groups. They affect the lowest strata of the labor force primarily through the frequency and duration of spells of unemployment, since the low quality of the jobs open to them will not greatly change. Economic conditions affect the higher strata in a similar way, but they have a less pronounced impact. To the extent that skidding takes place among those holding jobs of the higher strata, however, another dimension of influence will be added, which will be reflected in downward job mobility as well as in higher unemployment rates. To focus on unemployment rates alone may be to understate the impact.

Economic deprivation and job mobility are not independent. In any individual case they may occur separately or together. This section has emphasized that the likelihood of deprivation and/or mobility will be affected by aggregate economic conditions and may be affected in different ways for different groups in the labor force. The relation between individual deprivation or mobility and individual non-economic change is the subject of the following sections.

Economic Deprivation

The use of situational and mobility factors as determinants of social behavior reflects two distinct traditions in sociological research.[27] Mobility variables refer to the movement of individuals from one stratum to another or shifts in the relative size or position of whole strata in social groups. Following the direction of Durkheim's research on suicide, students have attempted to

27. M. Janowitz, Some Consequences of Social Mobility in the United States. *Transactions of the Third World Congress of Sociology.* Vol. 3. London: International Sociological Association, 1956, p. 194.

trace the specific psychological and social outcomes of such changes.[28] The crucial assumption in this schema is that social mobility requires the individual to rationalize his status change both psychologically (by the use of coping mechanisms) and socially (by the adoption of new ideologies and styles of life). In contrast, the situational approach places little emphasis on the individual's developmental or social history and emphasizes instead the adjustment to the strains and stresses inherent in the immediate social situation. These two traditions are not operationally discrete; in any specific research some attention is paid to both sets of variables, and an attempt is usually made to clarify their interaction effects.

There is an old Jewish adage that says "whether you are rich or poor, it is good to have money." Translated into the concerns of this conference, we can speculate that resource *sufficiency or insufficiency* for any unemployed worker—professional or blue collar, skilled or unskilled, white or black, male or female—can have a strong influence on mental health. Resource availability in a period of unemployment performs three important functions: (1) it stabilizes and maintains an existing style of life; (2) it permits continued contact with primary and secondary groupings where adequate finances may be a condition for participation; and (3) it imparts a feeling of control over the environment.

The concept of economic deprivation has been measured in various ways. Pope, for example, concerned with a working profile of economic loss, indexed economic deprivation by the number of months of unemployment in the worker's career.[29] Street and Leggett, emphasizing the situational dimension, used the employment status of the respondent—working or not working—as a measure of economic stress.[30] It is apparent, however, that situational economic stress most closely reflects the

28. E. Durkheim, *Suicide: A Study in Sociology.* J. A. Spalding and G. Simpson, trans. Glencoe, IL: The Free Press, 1951.

29. Hallowell Pope, Economic Deprivation and Social Participation in a Group of Middle Class Factory Workers. *Social Problems,* 1964, 11, 290-300.

30. David Street and J. C. Leggett, Economic Deprivation and Extremism: A Study of Unemployed Negroes. *American Journal of Sociology,* 1961, 67, 53-57.

worker's access to economic resources. The availability or lack of such resources is a function not only of employment status but of other factors as well, such as the earnings of other family members, eligibility for pension or transfer payments, and income from property. To obtain approximations of the situational strains and stresses felt by the worker after the loss of a job, Aiken, Ferman, and Sheppard constructed a three-item index of economic deprivation for use in the study of unemployed workers. The index summarized the responses to three questions:

Are you better off or worse off than a year ago in respect to savings;

Are you better off or worse off than a year ago in respect to debts;

Have you had to cut back on important expenditures (e.g., food or clothing).

The Index of Economic Deprivation has now been widely used. Aiken, Ferman, and Sheppard, in their study of displaced auto workers, found that the index correlated with a broad variety of attitudinal and interactional measures.[31] The index was more powerful than any other study variable in explaining the variance of three mental health measures: Srole's Scale of Anomia; Index of Satisfaction with Life; and Social Participation with Friends or Relatives. High scores on the index (meaning a high degree of economic deprivation) were related to a high degree of anomia, low satisfaction with life, and a lowered degree of participation with friends and relatives. Respondents with high scores on the index were most likely to report changes for the worse in the preceding three years, while respondents with low scores were more likely to report changes for the better. Furthermore, high-score respondents were more likely to report deterioration in jobs and income and to worry more about money matters.

In 1962, Harold Sheppard used this index in a study of displaced auto workers after the shutdown of the Studebaker Plant in South

---

31. M. Aiken, L. A. Ferman, and H. L. Sheppard, *Economic Failure, Alienation and Extremism*. Ann Arbor: University of Michigan Press, 1968.

Bend.[32] Again, the measure of economic deprivation proved to be the strongest predictor of variance in variables associated with mental health (satisfaction with life, anomia, and social participation with friends and relatives). In our current research on unemployed workers in Detroit, we have used this economic deprivation measure once more.[33] Respondents with high scores on the index tended to report more physical symptoms than others and to have low morale scores. Furthermore, high scores of deprivation were associated with reports of sickness or malaise in the preceding two weeks as well as with reports of anxiety over financial problems and of increased smoking. Anxiety over financial obligations, strongly associated with economic deprivation and undoubtedly a derivative of it, was strongly linked to physical and emotional problems. The correlations are not strong but they consistently move in the same direction. High anxiety as to an ability to maintain obligations manifests itself in reports of poor general health and of more days of feeling ill; in reports of more specific physical and somatic symptoms; in reports of more feelings of dissatisfaction and negative moods. This group has had a higher tendency to high blood pressure and increased smoking since unemployment. The index is associated with short-term physical and mental health problems but not with chronic illnesses or long-standing health problems.

The importance of resource sufficiency in maintaining well-being in the face of economic adversity has been suggested by other researchers. Little, in his study of unemployed professionals in 1976, noted that individuals with financial reserves evidence less emotional stress than the financially strapped.[34] According to Little, the financial cushion, supplemented by an education edge, may allow unemployed professionals to see unemployment as a rather welcome career change and an opportunity for advancement.

32. H. L. Sheppard, *The Studebaker Plant Shutdown.* Unpublished manuscript, 1965, pp. 10-11.
33. "Family Adjustment to Unemployment in an Urban Setting (The Detroit Unemployment Study)." Department of Health, Education and Welfare, PHS-G-5R011MH26546.
34. C. B. Little, Technical-Professional Unemployment: Middle Class Adaptability to Personal Crises. *Sociological Quarterly,* 1976, 17, (Spring), 262-274.

Economic deprivation is not spread equally among labor force participants. What are the antecedents of economic deprivation? Among ex-Packard workers in 1958, length of unemployment and the employment status at the time of the interview were the best predictors of economic deprivation. The findings in the study of ex-Studebaker workers in 1962 corroborated these findings. In our current research on unemployment in Detroit, we again found that the number of months of unemployment together with the employment status were the best predictors of economic deprivation. Cobb and Kasl, using a five-item expanded measure of the Index of Economic Deprivation, found that economic deprivation was best predicted by the number of months unemployed and the employment status at the time of the interview.[35] They felt that this relationship was strong in the early stages of unemployment but grew weaker as the number of months of unemployment increased; possibly because some long term adjustment had been made in expenditures, savings, and debts to reduce the degree of economic deprivation.

In summary, then, the situational stresses generated by resource insufficiency can have profound effects on the physical and mental health of the unemployed worker. The available evidence indicates that the impact is immediate and short term. We have no indication, as yet, of long term "scarring effects" of resource insufficiency. What is being suggested is that the length of unemployment and reemployment experiences do not by themselves have a direct negative effect on mental health, but rather that such effects are heavily linked to resource insufficiency.

Social Mobility

Durkheim postulated a direct relationship between the sudden and frequent status changes inherent in mobility experiences and a consequent social malaise and disorientation of the individual.

---

35. S. Cobb and S. V. Kasl, Termination: The Consequences of Job Loss. NIOSH Research Report. Washington, DC: U.S. Government Printing Office. DHEW (NIOSH) Publication #77-224, 1977.

Surprisingly, few researchers have tried to test this hypothesis in regard to changes in jobs and income that are associated with economic changes (e.g., contraction of the economy or plant shutdowns). Wilensky and Edwards studied "skidders," using a sample of non-supervisory factory workers.[36] Two broad patterns of skidding were identified: intergenerational skidders and work-life skidders. The former group were now blue-collar workers although their fathers had been white-collar workers. The latter group had entered the factory as blue-collar workers although their previous jobs had been white-collar. The researchers found significant changes in political and personal orientations as compared to non-skidders. The skidders became more politically conservative and more pessimistic about work opportunities. Bettelheim and Janowitz studied veterans of World War II who had expected to return to their old jobs but had been bumped.[37] They found that this group as a whole had become more hostile toward minority group members and had more interpersonal difficulties in everyday social relationships. Aiken, Ferman, and Sheppard undertook a test of the Durkheimian hypothesis in their study of displaced automobile workers in 1957.[38] Two measures of job mobility were used: (1) shifts between levels of skilled, semi-skilled, and unskilled jobs and (2) shifts in wages. Starting with the long term stable job at the Packard Motor Company, the researchers charted every job change made in the 27-month period under study. At the 27th month, a considerable amount of information was elicited from the respondents on social, psychological, and economic adjustments. The job career data yielded three types of mobility categories: never reemployed—remained without a job during the 27-month period; reemployed, not working now—obtained a job but subsequently lost it (in a sense a "two-time loser"); and reemployed, still working—obtained a job and still on it at the time of the interview.

36. H. L. Wilensky and Hugh Edwards, The Skidder: Ideological Adjustment of Downward Mobile Workers. *American Sociological Review*, 1959, 24, 216-231.

37. Bruno Bettelheim and M. Janowitz, *Dynamic of Prejudice*. New York: Harper, 1950.

38. Aiken, Ferman, and Sheppard, *op. cit.*

Using three measures associated with the mental health concept (satisfaction with life, anomia, and participation with friends and relatives) the researchers found significant influences from the mobility measures. The workers who had become reemployed and remained so had the most positive mental health scores. The workers who had remained unemployed had intermediate scores, while the two-time losers had the lowest scores of all. Four respondents had been "three-time losers" (i.e., lost three jobs in the 27-month period) and each one had scores indicative of extremely poor mental health.

The findings of the Packard Motor Car study indicate that reemployed displaced workers who experience job mobility in terms of wages are less well integrated socially than are those reemployed workers who do not experience changes in wages or than those who remain unemployed. Job mobility had its most deleterious effects on the upwardly mobile two-time losers. These findings are consistent with Emile Durkheim's theories as to the social consequences of changes and fluctuations in the economic order. Job fluctuation and change, as well as labor market failure, are found to result not only in strong feelings of anomia and political alienation but also in a circumscribed social life, as measured by the frequency of social interaction with relatives, friends, and co-workers.

Among the ex-Packard workers, it was the individual who had to adjust to status changes more than once who had the highest anomia scores, the greatest alienation from political institutions, and the lowest social participation. Since all the workers had undergone at least one status change—the shutdown experience itself—it would seem that it is repeated status change, inherent in reemployment (coupled with the demand for consecutive dramatic adjustments) that is more likely to weaken individual ties to the social order. It is ironic that the workers who were not reemployed in any job were better integrated than the workers who had experienced successive changes in reemployment. Prolonged unemployment was undoubtedly unpleasant, but it was marked by a relative stability of expectations that was clearly not present in the case of workers called on to make adaptations to successive changes. Although a single status change, such as job displacement, may place strains on the individual's attachment to accepted groups and values, it is the successive changes inherent in reemployment that pose the greatest threat because they generate a milieu of uncertainty about the worth of existing group ties and values.

Interaction Between Economic Deprivation and Social Mobility

Both economic deprivation and mobility patterns are predictors of mental health responses. The data set in the Packard study showed that the situational factor (the degree of economic deprivation) was more important than the mobility factor (post displacement job pattern) in shaping the attitudes and behavior of the displaced workers. Economic deprivation produced greater alienation in attitudes and behavior (anomia, dissatisfaction with life, and withdrawal from contact with kin and friends) than job mobility. It is the absence or presence of financial strains that shapes the displaced worker's outlook on life and social participation, not the tragedies of his past work history.

It is interesting to examine these findings in the light of Durkheim's hypothesis about the relationship between social mobility and the social posture of the individual. Durkheim postulated a direct relationship between the sudden and frequent status changes inherent in mobility experiences and the consequent social malaise and disorientation of the individual. His followers have largely accepted this hypothesis and have given little thought to the role of situational variables in inhibiting the consequences of sudden status changes. Janowitz has raised a question about the role of primary and secondary group structures in modifying the consequences of social mobility, and Kornhauser has analyzed the importance of these group variables in social mobility and status change.

Our findings suggest that another dimension of the worker's situation is important in the modification of the consequences of mobility; namely, the degree of economic deprivation. It is likely that the number and intensity of group memberships and social contacts are directly related to the worker's financial resources. Many primary group activities with kin and friends demand material or social reciprocity, which is dependent on the availability of financial resources. Lack of resources may also lead to exclusion from secondary groups (e.g., the lodge, church membership, the neighborhood clubhouse). The exact nature of the interaction is not clear without further study, but our data suggest that a lack of financial resources may produce reactions of anomia (or alienation), psychic states that place severe limitations on social interaction. Reduced interactions may well produce more intense anomia and further weaken the individual's social ties. Second, the lack of financial resources may severely restrict access to various forms of group life, which may lead to further economic as well as social isolation.

It is not change in itself that triggers attitudinal and behavioral reactions but rather the significance given to these changes by the dimensions of the worker's immediate situation (e.g., economic deprivation). Changes in jobs, positive or negative, may be a minor influence on the worker's life if he continues to exercise some control over his social environment. This control is maintained partly through the availability of economic resources. It may well be that it is necessary to reexamine the Durkheim hypothesis and to specify further the conditions under which the effects of mobility may be modified.

Unemployment Careers and Mental Health

The worker's adaptation to economic change must be viewed not in terms of a single event or labor market experience but rather as a series of events that begin with job loss and continue through a series of labor market experiences until a new adjustment is made to the world of work. Adaptation in this sense is a process than can be illustrated by examining the aftermath of job layoff for a group of workers.

"Unemployment careers" differ according to the patterns of employment, unemployment, and underemployment. These career patterns serve as measures of experiences in the labor market and in the aftermath of job loss. Unemployment careers may be investigated over a period of weeks, months, or years, and they gain their importance from the fact that career stability or instability may be strongly associated with mental health. Causation may run in either direction: poor mental health may generate unstable careers, or unstable careers may be a precursor of poor mental health. The important consideration is that unstable careers can be an important link between aggregate economic change and subsequent personal functioning.

The pattern of labor market experience after job loss may influence the mental health of workers. Some workers may experience continuous unemployment; others may return to work immediately; still others may alternate among episodes of employment, unemployment, and underemployment. There may be shifts in job type, in industry affiliation, or in place of employment. These patterns all come under the heading of "unemployment careers," and they have a three-fold importance for mental health. First, career instability (successive and sudden job changes) can jeopardize predictable day-to-day living by creating constant anxiety about job tenure, income, and the meeting of essential demands. Second, unstable careers can make for unstable relationships with family and friends. The worker's influence in the family can decline if family members are faced with constant shifts in expectations about the worker's ability to provide for daily needs. Finally, disruptive and frequent shifts in employment status can have a marked effect on the worker's self-esteem and self-image, since he questions more and more his capacity to control future events and his own sense of worth.

In our current University of Michigan study of unemployment, a preliminary look at the survey data indicated that the married men in the sample could be placed in groups according to their career patterns after an initial episode of job loss. It was decided to select three respondents from each group and to interview them again and again in an effort to identify personal and circumstantial correlates of such patterns. The respondents were chosen in such a way as to provide a diversity of types for each category. Repeated detailed interviews in the home were conducted by Leslie Dow of the University's Anthropology

Department. The following observations are based on three interviews and are highly tentative and preliminary.

Six unemployment career patterns were suggested by the data from the initial field surveys and were studied by Dow as they pertained to mental health.

1. *Those who had remained unemployed since losing their last job.*

The life situations of the men in this group were remarkably similar. The three respondents were all older workers (in their sixties), skilled, and in poor health. They had sought work repeatedly but were rebuffed because of age and poor health. The pattern indicates that a worker's health record, once questionable, thereafter becomes a significant barrier to reemployment. The men felt that poor health was robbing them of their last years of productive life. They felt keenly the frustration of having to lose years of income, and most or all of their pensions, because of events beyond their control. Each felt that his current work situation had contributed to his health problems. They were bitter toward their former employers and the "system"—a bitterness continually fueled by shrinking incomes in the face of inflation. Even though these men had suffered serious illnesses, they felt that loss of employment was a more severe crisis. The men expressed resignation to their plight but were resentful about the blind unfairness of life.

2. *Those who had returned to their former jobs.*

These three men were periodically unemployed but within the year following the loss of work they returned to their former jobs. At the time of Dow's interviews they reported that their current situation was improving but that during the year they had been beset by a wide range of personal problems attributable to joblessness: marital strife, drinking, deterioration of personal relationships within the family. Two of the men had significant money problems before their reemployment, while the third was able to manage by a combination of unemployment insurance and Supplemental Unemployment Benefits. Even though they had financial resources, personal strain was evident. The men were wary of the future but hopeful. It was obvious that sudden unemployment and the uncertainty that followed it had had a "scarring effect."

3. *Those who found a new job and remained in it.*

Of all the career patterns observed by Dow, this one seemed to be the one most fraught with peril. Without exception, these workers believe that the layoff period has been the most difficult challenge of their lives. Also, without exception, each one had adjusted to new employment with a determination never again to suffer the humiliation and defeat of losing both job and income. These men had never hoped to be reemployed at their former jobs. Their firms or businesses had gone bankrupt, or automation had made their skills obsolete. Accustomed as they were to steady employment, they found job loss devastating to themselves and to their families.

All the men had had periods of doubting that they would ever work again and of facing the nagging realization that financial security might permanently elude them; they had been pessimistic about ever being hired again. The sense of hopelessness and a common sense of depression and anxiety distinguished these workers from those in type 2 above. Indeed, their uncertainty about the future took perhaps as heavy a toll in human misery as did reduced income. The men now report that they have recovered markedly from their symptoms, agree that they remain less optimistic and more cynical, but are more thankful than ever before to be working.

4. *Those periodically in and out of work with the same employers.*

For each one of the workers in this group, periods of work and of joblessness were clearly predictable. Unemployment was accompanied by Supplemental Unemployment Benefit payments and rarely last for more than a few months, so that financial problems were minimal. Under such conditions, unemployment resembled something closer to a vacation than a crisis. They did not all express pleasure at these periods of unemployment, but their reactions were so mild as to present an important alternative view to a usually dark picture. The experiences of these men were different from those of the other groups. Unemployment could be a pleasant interlude, a planned-for respite from the drudgery of nine-to-five work, if a man were sure that he could work again at will.

5. *Those periodically in and out of work with one new employer.*

The career pattern of these workers is superficially similar to those in the fourth category in the sense that they established patterns of employment, unemployment, and reemployment. In the case of this fifth group, the pattern was established only after losing a job with a first employer and being employed by a new one. Workers in this group seldom received Supplemental Unemployment Benefit payments to tide them over. Hence it was unlikely that they had enough financial flexibility to pick and choose their next jobs.

The basic difference between workers in groups 4 and 5 is seen in their contrasting reactions to unemployment. Type 4 workers tended to view it as a slight bother at worst, and a welcome vacation at best. Type 5 workers shared little of this attitude, since they had to struggle to supplement their unemployment insurance with some form of income. While it is true that periods of unemployment for the type 5 worker might have been just as temporary and just as short as those experienced by type 4, the former's lack of Supplemental Unemployment Benefit payments created an economic crisis that the latter did not have to endure; accordingly unemployment was not a welcome respite. But neither did it bring about the agony of uncertainty faced by workers in the first three career patterns. The men in this group made more use than others of the irregular economy ("off-the-books employment") to supplement their incomes while unemployed.

6. *Those periodically out of work with more than one employer.*

Workers in this group had the most chaotic career patterns. They not only experienced repeated layoffs but each layoff followed a job with a different employer. It is difficult to generalize about their attitudes and behavior. Each person had his own reaction to the pattern. One viewed it as a way of life; to be expected. Another felt these changes were consistent with his attempt to find the right job or "strike it rich." However, all three workers were in less desirable jobs than before, and financial deprivation had become a part of life.

Other scattered career patterns are evidenced but they are idiosyncratic and defy classification. The classification is admittedly crude, but it offers a starting point for in-depth investigation of the adjustments made by workers who have undergone economic change.

Implications

It is obvious from our discussion that we consider economic deprivation a central concept in explaining and understanding the relationships between economic change and mental health. The territorial unit of analysis must be the local labor market, conceptualized in terms of manpower flows between levels with the specific objective of identifying patterns and rates of skidding and bumping. We are not seeking to identify the causes of all mental health problems in this way, but we believe that a significant number of them—whether short or long term we can only guess—can be approached in this way.

An analysis of economic change and mental health would first require that affected workers be identified (or sorted) in terms of risk characteristics for reemployment (e.g., age, education, skill level). The second step would be the determination of labor market outcomes for these workers in terms of number of months of unemployment, or mobility patterns. A third consideration would be the use of these latter variables as predictors of the magnitude of economic deprivation. Finally, there is the use of economic deprivation measures to predict specific physical and mental health outcomes. This logic suggests that we can build up predictive tables on the magnitude of economic deprivation as well as on the prevalence of mental health problems.

Our intervention goal would be to reduce the magnitude of economic deprivation; the development of alternative jobs with adequate income is one obvious method. Intervention with social supports of various kinds draws us into uncharted waters. Cobb and Kasl did not find that social support reduced economic deprivation to any significant extent,[39] but the support measure they used was limited to psychological support from the spouse. It seems more likely that economic deprivation would be reduced through functional resource supports (money, services, and goods). In this sense, economic deprivation might be significantly reduced through access to various kinship or neighborhood-based resource networks, or forms of "off-the-books" employment. At this stage, this is speculation; we probably should conclude that, as of now, we know little about the actual impact of social support.

---

39. Cobb and Kasl, *op. cit.*

7
ECONOMIC CHANGES AND
MENTAL ILLNESS: A COMMENTARY

ROBERT L. KAHN

The discovery of large empirical regularities is almost always exciting. Finding out that certain things "go together" can flood with light an assortment of previously murky details. More often, locating a couple of seemingly related bright spots makes the intervening darkness more localized, more conspicuous, and more tempting for exploration. Some explorations have been highly successful. Generations of economics students learned about the corn-hog ratio and the research and theorizing stimulated by its discovery. (A similar regularity between the world price of wheat and oil used to be alleged, but has not been mentioned recently.)

Harvey Brenner's 1973 book, *Mental Illness and the Economy,* asserts one of those large co-variations in human events, gives considerable evidence for it, and proposes that the relationship is essentially causal: economic "bad times" are somehow responsible for increases in mental illness. Elsewhere in this volume Berg and Hughes refer to Brenner's work as admirable, pathbreaking, and underspecified. All three adjectives are well-chosen, and the papers by Ferman and Gardner, Fried, and Caplan reflect all three. Their authors accept Brenner's work, concur in its importance, and address in rather different ways the problem of underspecification.

Brenner's work does not merely reaffirm the correlation between low socio-economic status and vulnerability to mental illness. It is dynamic and demonstrates that, with appropriate time lags, fluctuations in various macroeconomic measures are followed by similar fluctuations in aggregative measures of mental illness. His interpretation, modified with various contingent clauses, is that economic decrements cause increases in mental illness.

There are, as the methodological saying goes, plausible alternative hypotheses. Moreover, there are formidable problems even if one accepts Brenner's interpretation in the main. For one thing, mental illness is not the modal response to poverty, sudden or prolonged. Most people do not become mentally ill when the economy dips. Economic downturns may be considered causal, but they cannot be considered sufficient causes.

For another thing, cross-national economic differences do not fit the naive interpretation of Brenner's data; no one would claim that by ordering the nations of the world in terms of material prosperity we would also be ranking them in terms of mental health. Finally, the long term trend data in the United States require different, or at least additional, explanations to that of Brenner's central proposition. From the end of World War II to the 1970s, economic gains in the United States were large, widely experienced, and only occasionally interrupted in serious degree. The incidence of mental illness may have been responsive to the fluctuations in the economy, as Brenner proposes, but the same relationship does not hold for the long term trend. If it did, other things being equal, we should have had an ascent in mental health two generations long.

Brenner is aware of such issues, and so are the authors of the three papers now before us. They accept Brenner's proposition that economic downturns evoke mental illness—accept it not naively or uncritically, but as worthy of investigation and elaboration. All three papers can be regarded as independent efforts at elaborating and explicating the Brenner hypothesis. That hypothesis is at the societal level: the incidence of mental illness follows variations in the economy. The economic concepts that Brenner uses are macro-level variables; his measures of mental illness are also at that level, although they are mostly aggregates of individual events (admissions to mental hospitals, for example).

The explication of this relationship between two distant sets of macro-data is a double task. The first is to provide the intervening links in the presumed causal chain. We require a set of hypotheses between proximate pairs of variables that will lead us from economics to mental illness. The second part of the explicative task is to link the macro- and micro-levels, to bring together societal and individual events. To advocate this is not merely to betray a taste for reductionism. Brenner's data suggest that adverse economic events cause some people to "change" (or to be reclassified) from mentally competent to mentally ill. Since most people are not so affected, questions immediately arise that can be answered only at the individual level. Which people are most affected by economic downturns? How much of their response depends upon their vulnerability to such changes—to their past experience, their resources, their personality? How much depends on their particular location in the economic structure: is vulnerability to economic change a property of the situation rather than the person?

Ferman, Gardner, Fried, and Caplan all deal with these explicative questions, but in somewhat different ways. Ferman and Gardner are nearest to Brenner in two respects: they are concerned with the immediate effects of economic downturns on labor market dynamics and they are working very largely at the societal level. Their model of labor market dynamics is an attempt to show the far larger gross movements that are indicated in part by net changes in unemployment rates or GNP. Fried's paper is less concerned with labor force dynamics or other events at the societal level. Fried takes the loss of the work role as the immediate consequence of economic recession for many and uses the language of role theory to link economic causes at the societal level to social-psychological outcomes at the individual level. His main effort is to describe the processes of role adaptation and integration that are initiated after economic adversity strikes. Caplan's paper is more individualistic than the others. The environment and the changes in it are not neglected, but the emphasis is on the ways in which different individuals cope with environmental stresses, whether those stresses are economic in origin or originate in other ways. The concern is with psychodynamics rather than labor market dynamics.

A schematic representation of these three papers in relation to Brenner's work is presented below. The vertical dimension represents the level of conceptual emphasis, from individual to society. The horizontal dimension, from left to right, represents the causal sequence that Brenner asserts, from changes in the economy to changes in the rate of diagnosed mental illness.

This schema is, of course, an oversimplification. The papers are not so neatly compartmentalized nor so limited in their level of discourse. Ferman and Gardner, for example, not only propose a model of labor force dynamics, they are also concerned with career patterns. The diagram, however, serves to locate the center of gravity of each paper and to suggest what seems to me to be the main relevance of each to Brenner's work.

Levels:

Societal	Ferman and Gardner		
Role		Fried	
Individual			Caplan

Properties of the Economy ⎯⎯⎯⎯⎯⎯⎯⎯➤ Mental Illness

With that schema before us, let us turn to a closer consideration of the three papers, keeping in mind a set of questions that apply to all three: Are the authors talking about the same things and dealing with the same underlying problems? If so, are they offering different ideas and information about those problems or merely using different vocabularies? To the extent that they are indeed telling us different things about the connection of economics to mental illness, are their contributions additive; can they be integrated? Finally, what do these papers imply for the

Brenner hypothesis, for our research priorities, and for our advocacy in the realm of policy?

Ferman and Gardner

The main contribution of this paper is to propose a model of the labor market that shows the ramifications of adverse economic change. The key concept that links these labor market dynamics to mental illness is economic deprivation—reduction in the quantity and steadiness of one's income. Unemployment is the most obvious example of economic deprivation resulting from fluctuations in the economy as a whole, but counting the unemployed understates the impact of those fluctuations. Ferman and Gardner argue that an economic downturn kicks off a complex set of events in the labor market, and that the experience of economic deprivation is more widespread than appears in the unemployment count. The mechanisms of this spread of deprivation they call bumping and skidding, processes by which some men and women who lose jobs at one level of skill or status find jobs that are less attractive and well-paid, and in doing so displace workers of lesser ability or seniority.

Aggregate economic change of a negative kind thus involves economic deprivation of some people at virtually all levels in the employed sector, although the duration and frequency of unemployment is greatest in the groups of lowest status. Moreover, the experience of downward mobility—skidding—adds to the strain of economic loss itself. How often such experiences occur in the course of a worker's life or in the working life of a given age cohort is not known, nor do we know to what extent repeated cycles of such deprivation leave a residual psychological scarring. Ferman and Gardner have some case-study evidence, however, that suggests the cumulative damage of such cycles at the individual level. The two- and three-time "losers" in plant closings seemed most affected by the process. For those at the end of the bumping and skidding chain, such alternation between employment and unemployment is the predicted consequence of economic downturns. Ferman and Gardner's model would identify them as the population at greatest risk of mental illness.

The relationship between aggregate economic change and aggregate indicators of psychological disorder is thus seen as involving four main hypothetical links—from aggregate economic change (downturn) to altered labor market patterns (bumping and skidding), from those to individual experiences of downward mobility, from those mobility patterns to economic deprivation, and from the degree of economic deprivation to negative effects on physical and mental health.

Fried

Fried gives least emphasis to the things that Ferman and Gardner emphasize most—the phenomena of the labor market and the ways in which aggregate economic changes are encountered as events in the work life of individuals. He takes the importance of work for economic life as self-evident, and its importance for social expression and personal development as no less in degree but less recognized and less understood. Where Ferman and Gardner make *economic* deprivation the key concept in their discussion of job loss and its psychological impact, Fried wants a framework that accommodates *non-economic* deprivations as well. In developing such a framework, he is at once more abstract and yet more individualistic than Ferman and Gardner. Fried's central concept, role adaptation, applies to individuals but it is, as he says, "far removed from the concrete phenomena of the world of work."

In a sense Fried takes up where Ferman and Gardner leave off. He accepts it as given that negative changes in the economy are manifested as "stress events" in the lives of individuals and are experienced as strain. Strain, however, does not in itself constitute pathology in Fried's model; pathology is the effect of strain on role behavior.

Let us recapitulate the main elements in the model. Roles consist of normatively motivated behaviors that serve system functions and fulfill individual needs. For each role that an individual holds, the work role, for example, we can distinguish the required behaviors themselves, the functions that their performance serves for the individual and the society, and the relationships with others that the performance of the role entails. Moreover, the life of each individual consists of an array of such roles. The individual strives for concordance, which is a kind of optimization of need-satisfaction across the whole array of his or her roles. That striving toward concordance is behavioral; it is observable as role behavior. It may be successful or unsuccessful and the modes of behavior it entails may be acceptable or unacceptable to others and to the larger society. Fried proposes maladaptation and bonadaptation as terms to indicate the failure or success of such role behaviors.

The impact of economic downturn enters this model at the point of job loss. Unemployment hits certain role activities immediately and is then hypothesized to "invade" other roles and relationships. The invasive process is partly economic and partly social-psychological. The longer it persists, the more likely it is to involve the entire hierarchy of role integration. The individual's efforts to adapt to such role disruption may or may not be pathological, depending on the duration and severity of the invasion, the coping mechanism of the person, and the supportive resources that are made available.

Caplan

This paper is the most "psychological" of the three, although it has a good deal in common with Fried's. Like Fried, Caplan begins with the point at which some aggregative economic movement enters the life of the individual. Like Fried, he assumes that individuals seek to optimize the satisfaction of their needs; Fried's concordance is Caplan's P-E (person-environment) fit. And like Fried, Caplan attempts to develop a general model of stress and behavior at the individual level, rather than a model specific to economic changes and work disruption. There is in Caplan's model less emphasis on role and the array of roles that constitute individual life, although that view is perhaps implicit. There is more emphasis on the distinction between objective events and their perception by the individual, and much more emphasis on social support as a buffer against the effects of stress.

Caplan incorporates a good deal of criticism and evaluation in his paper. He notes that social support can have negative effects (learned helplessness) as well as positive outcomes. He reminds us that empirical work on social support does not always confirm its buffering against stress. He raises the question of whether the model itself is biased, in the sense of reducing economic events at the societal level to problems of individual coping and competence. He emphasizes the need for valid measures of social support (tangible and psychological), for the study of other intervening elements in coping with external stress, and for the study of both chronic and acute stresses.

Implications and Recommendations

Let us conclude by risking a few statements that seem consistent with all three papers. Work is neither a sovereign remedy for mental illness nor a general preventive against it. Work is often stressful and sometimes pathology-inducing. Nevertheless, for many men and women work has many positive aspects, and nonwork—the lack of paid employment—is far worse. Economic fluctuations that create unemployment are stressful both because unemployment typically implies economic deprivation and also because it implies loss of relationships and opportunity for meaningful activity.

The pathogenic effects of economic changes are characteristically underestimated, for a number of reasons. More people are affected (by bumping and skidding) than are revealed by counts of unemployment. Repeated cycles of job-getting and job-loss are likely to be cumulatively damaging. People differ in their vulnerability to such experiences, in their ways of coping with them, and in the support that is available to them from other sources. As a result, conspicuous pathological behavior is not the modal response to the stresses of job loss. Moreover, our social accounting tends to be compartmentalized, in ways that make it difficult to add up the total costs of economic downturns. The corporate "bottom-line" does not take account of changes in the city's welfare rolls nor the state's expenditures for mental illness, and neither the private nor the public accounts take notice of family and intergenerational effects of job loss.

Finally, as research workers we cannot pretend that such costs are known to us in full or that certain remedies are at hand. We particularly need longitudinal analyses that incorporate both economic and social-psychological data. Some such data are available and can, with ingenuity, be pieced together; more remain to be developed. The strength of the Brenner research is its demand for explanation. Each of these papers is a partial response to that demand.

8
PSYCHOPHYSIOLOGY
OF STRESS

GEORGE C. CURTIS

This chapter will examine the usefulness of physiological "stress" as an intervening variable linking econometric measures to illness statistics. It has been reported that downturns in the economy forecast increases in illness-related statistics (1,2). Some evidence suggests that upturns may do the same (1,3,4,5). These findings raise the question of whether the link is economic deprivation or something less obvious. There are similar questions at the clinical and physiological levels. Distressing situations may provoke physiological discharges, but so also may simple change, novelty, or uncertainty (6). Psychological distress has long been thought to play a role in illness; recent evidence suggests that change per se may be equally important (7).

There is no generally accepted definition of stress, but most definitions have several elements in common. Among these are: (a) that it is a psychophysiological response of the organism, not a provoking situation; (b) that the provoking situation entails harm or threat; and (c) that the response is the same, regardless of what provokes it; i.e., that it is non-specific.

It turns out that many so called "stress" responses are in some way involved with accelerating catabolism; i.e., the breakdown of tissue, the combustion of stored fuel, and the expenditure of energy. This concept has an immediate intuitive appeal as a solution to the problem at hand. Economic downturns cause "stress"; "stress" causes tissue breakdown and depletion of energy stores. These in turn make organisms more vulnerable to disease. Although things are not really that simple, the catabolic theory of stress has shown a remarkable capacity to survive in the face of difficulties. Its successes and failures make up the dominant theme of stress research.

"STRESS" AS A CATABOLIC REFLEX

Cannon's Fight-Flight Reaction

Although Cannon rarely used the word "stress," his work with the autonomic nervous system laid the foundations for the catabolic theory of "stress" (8). The sympathetic and parasympathetic divisions of the autonomic nervous systems send nerve fibers to most of the same structure: to exocrine glands that produce digestive juices, sweat, and sexual secretion; and to smooth muscle in the digestive tract, heart, blood vessels, bronchi, and pupils. The sympathetic system also sends fibers to the adrenal medulla, stimulating it to secrete adrenaline into the bloodstream. After Cannon's time it was discovered that both the adrenal medulla and the sympathetic fibers themselves also secrete noradrenaline into the bloodstream. Parasympathetic nerves stimulate the pancreas to secrete insulin into the bloodstream. Where sympathetic and parasympathetic fibers supply the same organ, their effects are usually opposite. Sympathetic stimulation speeds the heartbeat and elevates blood pressure; parasympathetic stimulation slows the heartbeat and lowers blood pressure. Sympathetic stimulation slows secretion of digestive juices and motility of stomach and bowel; parasympathetic stimulation speeds them. Sympathetic stimulation relaxes bronchial constrictor muscles thus increasing the diameter of the airways. Parasympathetic stimulation does the opposite. The effects on blood vessels are complex but the usual overall effects are that sympathetic stimulation diverts blood from the abdominal organs into skeletal muscles and parasympathetic stimulation does the reverse. Sympathetic stimulation transfers fuel from tissue stores to bloodstream. Parasympathetic stimulation does the opposite.

Although the evidence was and remains rather scant, Cannon suggested that the central controlling mechanisms are organized for reciprocal inhibition of the sympathetic and parasympathetic systems. This means that each input to the central controller has a double effect. Inputs which increase sympathetic activity simultaneously decrease parasympathetic activity, and vice versa.

Another key element of Cannon's theory was that all branches of the sympathetic system respond in unison, exerting their effects more or less simultaneously on all organs which they supply. The parasympathetic system was seen as responding in discrete units, affecting various organs more or less independently of each other.

Cannon found evidence of sympathetic discharge in response to muscular exertion, cold, asphyxia, hemorrhage, pain, and "great emotion," such as "fear and rage," as shown by dogs and cats when they confront each other. He described the total package of responses—emotional behavior, sympathetic stimulation, and presumably parasympathetic inhibition—as a reflex, and suggested that it can be conditioned to many different stimuli by Pavlovian procedures. By implication, the subjective experience of emotional arousal also could be taken as part of the reflex. The reflex itself has most of the features we currently ascribe to "stress." It is a response of the organism, provoked by harm or threat, and its physiology is the same across a range of provoking agents.

Cannon noted further that the net effects of sympathetic stimulation are to withdraw fuel from tissue stores and to speed the transport of fuel and oxygen to muscles. The net effects of parasympathetic stimulation are to facilitate digestion, deposition of fuel stores, reproductive function, and excretion of wastes. More generally, the net effect of sympathetic stimulation is catabolic and the net effect of parasympathetic stimulation is anabolic. Hence, the catabolic physiological response during "great emotion" appears to have adaptive utility by preparing for muscular exertion, which is often required for survival at times of great emotion.

238

Selye's "Stress"

Selye (9) found evidence of increased adrenocorticotrophic hormone (ACTH) secretion* from the anterior pituitary gland into the bloodstream in response to bone fractures, thermal burns, x-radiation, cold, other noxious situations, and also emotional excitement. ACTH stimulates the adrenal cortex to secrete several hormones into the bloodstream. A group of these, including cortisol and cortisone, are known as glucocorticoids. They cooperate with adrenaline and sympathetic stimulation in promoting catabolic processes. Selye formally introduced the word "stress" into physiology. He distinguished between local stress and general stress, using the former to refer to local changes in injured tissues and the latter to refer to changes in the organism as a whole. Although details of the systemic changes varied with the provoking stimulus, Selye found ACTH secretion to be a feature common to all. Therefore, he limited his definition of general stress to the secretion of ACTH and the extensive biologic changes which occur as a consequence of ACTH secretion. In addition to the catabolic effects caused by glucocorticoids, these changes include effects on wound healing, water and electrolyte balance, inflammatory responses, and resistance to infection. Selye referred to inciting stimuli as "stressors" to distinguish them from responses of the organisms.

Selye's concept of "stress" is distinct from Cannon's "fight-flight" concept. Nevertheless, they share several common features: diversity of stimuli, constancy of response, catabolic consequences, harm or threat, and an emotional component which by itself seems capable of provoking the physiological changes.

Subsequently it emerged that the pituitary, long recognized as the master endocrine gland, is under direct control of the brain.

---

*ACTH stimulates the adrenal cortex to secrete several hormones, the most important of which is hydrocortisone (cortisol) in man and corticosterone in the rat. There are many methods of estimating ACTH and adrenal cortical secretion. To be biochemically precise about these would be unduly confusing for nonspecialists. For the remainder of this article the cover term "ACTH secretion" will be used to refer to what all are attempting to estimate. Estimates of ACTH secretion and of adrenal hormone secretion do not parallel each other perfectly, but for present purposes the differences can be ignored.

This means that not only the autonomic nervous system and the adrenal medulla, but the entire endocrine system is under neural control and potentially subject to psychological influences. Because of technical ease of measurement, the largest volume of psychoendocrine work focused on the pituitary-adrenalcortical (ACTH and cortisol secretion) system, while autonomic studies focused mainly on easily measured organ changes such as heart rate, galvanic skin response (GSR), and indicators of blood vessel dilation and constriction such as skin temperature or finger volume. Perhaps the single experiment which best epitomizes, summarizes, synthesizes, and offers an interpretation of this large volume of research is one by Mason and his co-workers (6).

Mason's Catabolic-Anabolic Sequence

These investigators observed a coordinated, multi-hormonal response in rhesus monkeys facing a variety of challenges, including muscular exercise, adaptation to restraining chairs, or performing an operant avoidance task (6). The response included increased secretion of noradrenaline, adrenaline, ACTH, growth hormone, and thyroid hormone, and suppressed secretion of insulin, male sex hormones (androgens), and female sex hormones (estrogens). All the hormones that were increased in these situations have the catabolic effect of mobilizing short-chain fatty acids from tissues stores, and some also mobilize glucose. Fatty acids are the main muscle fuel burned during exertion, and glucose in the principal brain fuel. Insulin, which was suppressed, has powerful anabolic effects, antagonizing the glucose and fatty acid mobilizing actions of the hormones with "catabolic" actions. Androgens and estrogens, which were also suppressed, also have some anabolic actions. The simultaneous stimulation of the "catabolic" group of hormones and suppression of the "anabolic" group suggested the possibility of reciprocal innervation of catabolic and anabolic systems. This idea extended Cannon's suggestion of reciprocal innervation of the sympathetic and parasympathetic nervous systems. After termination of the avoidance task the "catabolic" hormones returned to baseline values. The "anabolic" group rebounded above baseline before returning to pre-experimental levels. This suggested a biochemical preparation for fuel consumption during the stress procedure and replenishment of fuel stores afterward. Mason called the total response pattern the "catabolic-anabolic sequence." The findings shared with those of Cannon and Selye some degree of nonspecificity, provocation by psychological as well as physical events, and the apparent shift of the body economy toward catabolism with the capacity for serving as preparation or support for muscular exertion.

Taken together, Cannon's, Selye's, and Mason's proposals amount to a theory of stress as a catabolic reflex, consisting of a fixed package of component responses. Emotional arousal in the psychological sense, or some component of it, is seen as either a component of the total reflex or as a stimulus releasing the package of physiological responses. This theory accounts for at least the predominant effect of most stressors on most physiological variables. There are, however, findings which it has difficulty in handling. We turn now to a consideration of these.

DIFFICULTIES FOR THE CATABOLIC REFLEX THEORY

Low Correlations Among "Catabolic" Response Measures

The hypotheses that (a) all branches of the sympathetic nervous system and all the "catabolic" hormones discharge as a unit and that (b) the "catabolic" and "anabolic" systems are reciprocally innervated, predict high and consistent correlations among variables such as heart rate, blood pressure, adrenaline, ACTH, and blood glucose, assuming a reasonable degree of control over interfering variables. Simultaneous measurements of groups of these variables frequently show trends, sometimes significant, in the expected direction, but the correlations tend to be low and variable (10,11).

Effects of Mild Stimuli

Mild, seemingly trivial situations that are novel, ambiguous, and convey uncertainty or perhaps vague threat, are particularly potent as stimuli for stress-related physiological variables. Their effects may rival or even exceed those seen in situations that would seem more appropriate for "great emotion." In the autonomic field these responses are studied as the "orienting reflex" (12). In the psychoendocrine field they are often called "novelty," "anticipation," or "first time" effects (6). The fact that they may coincide with slight increases in psychological measures of emotion provides some justification for regarding them merely as mild versions of "great emotion" effects. However, their disproportionate effectiveness becomes increasingly difficult to ignore.

Small Effects of Great Emotion

Cannon and most subsequent investigators have felt that "great emotion" such as "pain, fear, and rage" is a sufficient stimulus to provoke a catabolic reflex. A minimum requirement for testing this hypothesis is an independent means of determining whether and to what extent emotion is present. Cannon used the combination of situational criteria (cats were exposed to dogs) and his own judgment of the emotional state of the animal, based on its observed general behavior. If only the situational criteria had been used, the conclusions would have been different. Some cats did not appear to be upset by the dogs, and they did not show physiological signs of fight-flight reactions. This finding suggests that situational criteria are incidental and that emotional behavior is what matters.

Subsequently, the matter of independent criteria for emotion became problematic. In animals, emotion can be inferred from situational criteria, from general behavior, or from specific conditioned behaviors. In human subjects all of these can be used, plus the person's description of his subjective state. This in turn can be used either as a criterion in itself or as a basis for judgment by another person. No great difficulties are presented when all the criteria converge toward one conclusion. However, different criteria can and often do diverge toward different conclusions. For example, in Mason's studies the conditioned avoidance situation appeared to be a more effective stimulus to ACTH secretion than

242

some other situations which produced more clearcut gross behavioral arousal (13,14). Natelson et al., found plasma ACTH and growth hormone levels to be poor correlates of gross behavioral arousal, whether produced by electrical brain stimulation (15) or by conditioned avoidance (16).

Human studies have also been somewhat supportive of the "great emotion" hypothesis, but the results with human subjects have been especially weak, disappointing, and subject to great individual variability (6). Some of these disappointing results could be due to the necessarily weak stimulus situations often used in human research, to the failure of some subjects to become upset in apparently upsetting situations (like some of Cannon's cats), or to a protective effect of psychological defenses in preventing emotional arousal (6). If this were the case, strong and consistent stimulation of "catabolic" responses should occur in situations where all independent criteria converge toward the conclusion that a strong emotional response has occurred. As Mason (6) insisted, this hypothesis cannot be tested by the use of situational criteria alone. The psychological response must be independently assessed by psychological methods.

Among the more heroic efforts to study strong emotional stimuli in human subjects were two studies of combat situations during the Viet Nam war. One concerned a small special forces combat team encamped in enemy controlled territory near the Ho Chi Minh Trail and receiving intelligence reports indicating that the group was soon to be attacked and overrun by a superior force (17). The other (18) concerned helicopter ambulance medics who flew under fire into combat areas to evacuate wounded. All of the subjects had chronic ACTH indices below the mean of established norms. During the times of maximum danger only two subjects showed any ACTH increase, and several showed further suppression. Although emotion and defenses were not formally assessed, informal observations suggested to the authors that defenses may have played a role in blocking emotional responses.

The development by Marks et al. (19) of "flooding in vivo" as a method for treating phobias appeared to provide a situation where several independent criteria converge toward the conclusion that "great emotion" exists. Persons with phobias have an irrational morbid fear of some object, situation, or activity. They avoid the phobic stimulus, often at the expense of great constriction of their lives, and they experience anxiety or panic when unable to avoid it. The treatment consists of persuading them to approach the phobic situation, together with the therapist, and to endure the anxiety or panic until the phobic situation is no longer frightening. A total of several hours of exposure is often necessary before fear and the urge to avoid are extinguished. By selecting patients with phobias for small objects such as snakes, dogs, or insects, it is possible to insert treatment sessions into the design of a controlled experiment and to raise or lower the anxiety level at will by introducing the phobic object into the laboratory with the subject or by removing it.

Using this approach Curtis et al. (20,21) found that during flooding in vivo, estimates of ACTH secretion were sometimes elevated, but more often not, even when independent criteria indicated that anxiety was strong. Adaptation to the laboratory and anticipation of the treatment were more reliable stimuli for ACTH secretion than was the treatment itself, even though anxiety by independent criteria was much higher during actual treatment. Plasma growth hormone was never elevated during adaptation to the laboratory but was elevated during treatment in about two-thirds of the subjects (22). However, plasma levels remained near zero in some subjects even when subjective and behavioral criteria suggested very intense anxiety.

The accumulated evidence is difficult to reconcile with three hypotheses derived from the catabolic reflex theory: (a) that the component physiological responses of the catabolic reflex occur as an unvarying package; (b) that novelty and anticipation responses are mild versions of the "great emotion" response; and (c) that "great emotion" constitutes a sufficient condition for secretion of either ACTH or growth hormone.

Damping

Cannon did not do systematic studies on the effect of repeating painful or arousing stimuli in the same animals. Sutherland and

Zbrozyna (23) carried out such a study on one component of the fight-flight reaction (i.e., skeletal muscle vasodilation). They found that when cats were repeatedly exposed to dogs, the vasodilation response extinguished after a few trials, although the cats' behavior continued to suggest emotional arousal. Sidman et al. (14) found that painful electric shocks stimulated ACTH secretion in monkeys only on the first few trials and that subsequently the same stimulus produced no effect. Mason et al. (6) also found that the ACTH response to Sidman avoidance diminished and disappeared after several repetitions. Natelson et al. (16) found ACTH responses to be poorly correlated with emotional behavior during Sidman avoidance and that emotional behavior persisted after ACTH responses disappeared. Curtis et al. made a similar observation in phobic patients treated by flooding (20,21).

These results suggest not only that novel stimuli are especially effective in provoking "catabolic" responses, but also that pain and great emotion are more effective when they themselves are novel.

Paradoxical Effects

Cannon (8) noted that bowel hypermotility, defecation, or diarrhea during emotional excitement suggest parasympathetic rather than sympathetic effects, and he could not reconcile this finding with his theory. Fainting during fear or anxiety is another paradoxical reaction in which there is a sudden fall in blood pressure and slowing of the heart rate (24). These changes are opposite to those predicted by the catabolic reflex theory. Examples of suppressed ACTH secretion during apparently stressful states have been reported by Bourne et al. (17,18), Mason et al. (25), Curtis et al. (21, 26), and by Caplan, Cobb, and French (27). When Mason et al. (6) repeated the Sidman avoidance procedure at weekly intervals, the ACTH response diminished progressively, disappeared, and then reversed. This is an especially striking finding, since the investigators went to great length to assure very low pre-avoidance levels which they defined as "basal." Nevertheless, the repeated avoidance procedure resulted in further suppression below this carefully obtained low baseline level.

Negative Feedback

Negative feedback probably accounts for some masking or blurring of expected catabolic reflex effects (28). If heart rate, blood pressure, or blood sugar, to name only a few, should increase, reflex mechanisms are activated to bring them back up. Under stress the actual level of a variable which is subject to negative feedback control probably reflects the balance between stimuli displacing it from its setpoint and stimuli tending to restore it to its setpoint. Blood levels of cortisol, thyroid hormones, estrogens, and androgens are also subject to negative feedback control as are body temperature, blood acidity, blood osmotic pressure, and many others. Other variables, such as secretion of saliva or gastric juice, are not subject to negative feedback control. Some research designs have managed to unmask responses by means of statistical corrections for negative feedback (10).

Another type of negative feedback effect is the rebound overshoot: an initial response in one direction is followed by an overshoot in the opposite direction before the variable returns to baseline. This could be a mechanism in fainting: elevated blood pressure and rapid heart beat followed by overcorrection in the opposite direction, resulting in a temporary drop in blood supply to the brain (24). Some of the paradoxical effects on ACTH secretion mentioned above could result from measurements timed to coincide with a corrective overshoot of the system controlling plasma cortisol levels.

Whereas negative feedback would tend to cancel out, or even reverse, the effect of a catabolic stimulus input, reciprocal innervation, as postulated by Cannon and by Mason, would tend to enhance it. This is because reciprocal innervation would inhibit, rather than activate, responses antagonistic to the stimulus input.

Although it is not clear whether there really is a reciprocally innervated catabolic reflex, the proven existence of numerous negative feedback loops does not rule it out. One and the same system could have both features. In that case the net behavior of the system would reflect the balance between the two mechanisms.

Specificity

Specificity hypotheses are modifications of the theory of the stereotyped catabolic reflex, attempting to reconcile it with the fact that stress responses are not all alike. Individual-Response (I-R) specificity is a proposal that each individual has his own response profile which is consistent for him across time and across situations. For example, one person might be predominantly a heart rate responder, another might be predominantly a blood pressure responder, another a thyroid responder, and yet another a large intestine responder. Stimulus-Response (S-R) specificity is a proposal that each stimulus produces a characteristic response profile which is consistent across individuals and on repetition within individuals. There have also been proposals that different emotions (anger and fear, for example) produce characteristic physiologic profiles. If one sees emotions as stimuli and physiological profiles as responses, then these proposals might also be classified as S-R specificity hypotheses. If one sees both emotions and physiological profiles as responses (the view advocated here) then these proposals might be classified as Response-Response (R-R) specificity hypotheses.

Evidence supporting all of the above mentioned types of specificity has been reported (29,30,31). Probably the type most frequently and consistently observed has been I-R specificity. The types of specificity are not mutually exclusive; one study actually showed both I-R and S-R specificity in a single group of subjects (30).

Learning of Discrete Responses

Another alternative to the theory of the invariant catabolic reflex is to view each of its many components as separate responses, each capable of being elicited, conditioned, and extinguished separately from the others. No component response (whether subjective, behavioral, or physiological) need be an unconditioned stimulus for any other, but any component might become a conditioned stimulus for any other. The only difference between this concept and the classical catabolic reflex theory is the composition of the response which is conditioned. According to the classical theory, a total integrated package is conditioned. According to this proposal, it is not the total package but its separate components which are conditioned.

There is now strong evidence that increases or decreases in blood sugar can be conditioned by classical Pavlovian methods (32), using sugar administration or insulin administration as unconditioned stimuli. Depending upon experimental details, the conditioned response may be either similar or opposite to the unconditioned one, apparently through conditioning either of primary response or its compensatory reflex. Conditioned suppression of ACTH secretion has been reported in rats, using water administration to thirsty animals as the unconditioned stimulus and the sight of an empty water bottle as the conditioned stimulus (33). Even conditioned suppression of an antigen-antibody response has been reported (34) and partially confirmed (35).

Discrete conditioning and extinction would provide a mechanism for assembling and dismantling "stress" responses with specific profiles, having anticipatory and adaptive functions as Cannon and Mason suggested, but tailor-made to the psychological and metabolic experience of the individual. Such responses might or might not include subjective and behavioral components, and they might be either similar or opposite in direction to those predicted by the theory of the catabolic reflex.

Beyond Catabolism

Psychophysiological stress responses involve far more than catabolism. This topic is sufficiently complex that only a few illustrative points can be made. The discussion is based on a more detailed, yet still fragmentary analysis of the subject by Mason (6).

248

First, each hormone has many different effects on many different biochemical processes. Cortisol, for example, affects the metabolism of carbohydrates, fats, proteins, sodium, potassium, phosphate, chloride, calcium, magnesium, and water. It also affects acid-base balance, and it inhibits growth, wound healing, inflammation, immunological response, and resistance to infection. Secondly, any one biochemical process is affected not by one hormone, but by many. For example, blood levels of glucose and fatty acids are affected at least by cortisol, adrenaline, noradrenaline, growth hormones, thyroxine, and insulin. Therefore, the rate of a hormonally regulated process is not determined by the level of a single hormone, but by the overall hormone balance. Thirdly, the effects of different hormones on a given process are sometimes synergistic, sometimes antagonistic, and sometimes permissive. (Permissive effects mean that one hormone must be present in at least some minimum quantity in order for another to exert one of its effects.) Fourth and finally, hormones which are synergistic in their effect on one biochemical process may be antagonistic in their effect on another.

There is no cell, tissue, or process anywhere in the organism beyond the reach of the autonomic nervous system and the overall hormone balance. By activating components of the "catabolic reflex" in flexible combinations, an almost infinite range of adaptive and maladaptive biochemical effects could be produced.

PSYCHOSOCIAL FACTORS AND DISEASE

The material reviewed above indicates that machinery exists whereby disease, either physical or mental, could be significantly affected by sociophysiological pathways. It is easy to see, and possible to demonstrate, how activation of all or part of a catabolic reflex might affect some diseases. In diabetes mellitus, for example, there is a deficiency of insulin production. Activation of a complete catabolic reflex would inhibit any remaining insulin secretion and stimulate secretion of most of the known insulin antagonists. Clinically significant effects of emotional stress on the insulin requirement of diabetic patients and on occurrence of the dangerous complication known as diabetic ketoacidosis have been demonstrated both in the laboratory and in the clinic (36,37). Paradoxical effects have also been observed in which emotional stress appears to reduce blood sugar or the insulin requirement (36). It is easy to imagine, though not yet demonstrated, how chronic activity of a catabolic reflex might convert a person only predisposed to diabetes into one with the fullblown disease. It is also easy to understand and possible to demonstrate clinically significant effects of emotional stress on the course of illness in persons with heart disease (38) and hypertension (39). There is good evidence for psychological predisposition to arteriosclerosis leading to myocardial infarction (40). The relation to the catabolic reflex is less clear, but a link through reflex effects on fat metabolism is possible. The list of potentially affected diseases does not end here, but the possible physiological mechanisms become increasingly unclear. There is even evidence to suggest that psychological stress may affect resistance to experimental infections (41). Depending on the strain of infectious organism and on details of the experimental procedure, the effect may be either to increase or decrease host resistance. Once again this is reminiscent of physiological effects of stress which may go in either direction.

Moving a step closer to economic indicators, there is now substantial evidence that several psychosocial events significantly affect the risk of physical and mental illness. Risk is increased by separation from significant others, grief (42), and life change of any sort (7). The accumulation of life change events tends to accelerate in the months preceding illness onset. Social support appears to buffer against these risk factors (43). It is conceivable that major economic events might affect the health of individuals by affecting their life change events, their social support networks, and their psychophysiological responses.

SUGGESTIONS FOR RESEARCH

Change, both "good" and "bad," emerges as a major variable of interest, being one of the more reliable stimuli for physiological events, and one of the better predictors of illness onset.

Concepts of "stress" as a fixed package of component responses, invariant across a wide range of stimuli, and whose effects on health are all detrimental, require critical reevaluation. There are many documented examples in which the same variable can change in either direction, or perhaps first in one direction and then the other, in states of "stress." This alone might suggest the possibility of either detrimental or beneficial effects on health, but clinical observations to the same effect are available. Rather than defining "stress" as a response in any one direction, perhaps it would be better to regard stress as referring to a state of a system driven to function in opposition to its negative feedback loops. This would allow for bi-directional effects on many variables, and suggests that it might be as meaningful to look for changes in range and variance in the data of "stressed" populations as to look for mean differences.

Concerning biological variables, few if any are beyond the reach of "stress."

REFERENCES

1. Brenner, M. H. *Mental Illness and the Economy.* Cambridge: Harvard University Press, 1973.

2. Brenner, M. H. Economic changes and heart disease mortality. *Am J Public Health* 61:606-611, 1971.

3. Eyer, J. Prosperity as a cause of death. *Int J Health Serv* 7:125-150, 1977.

4. Catalano, R. and Dooley, D. Does economic change provoke or uncover behavioral disorder? A preliminary test. NIMH Conference on Mental Health and Economic Change. Hunt Valley, MD, June, 1978.

5. Pierce, A. The economic cycle and the social suicide rate. *Am Sociol Rev* 32:457-462, 1967.

6. Mason, J. W. Organization of Psychoendocrine Mechanisms: A Review and Consideration of Research. In *Handbook of Psychophysiology.* Greenfield, N. S. and Steinbach, R. A. (eds). New York: Holt, Rinehart, and Winston, Inc., 1972. pp. 3-91.

7. Rahe, R. H. Life Crisis and Health Change. In *Psychotropic Drug Response; Advances in Prediction.* May, P. R. A., Wittenborn, J. R. (eds). Charles Thomas, 1969. pp. 92-125.

8. Cannon, W. B. *Bodily Changes in Pain, Hunger, Fear and Rage.* Boston: Charles T. Branford Company, 1953.

9. Selye, H. *The Stress of Life.* New York: McGraw-Hill, 1956.

10. Lacey, J. I. The evaluation of autonomic responses: Toward a general solution. *Ann NY Acad Sci* 67:123-164, 1956.

11. Hofer, M. A. The Principles of Autonomic Function in the Life of Man and Animals. In *American Handbook of Psychiatry, Vol 4.* M. F. Reiser (ed). New York: Basic Books, 1975. pp. 528-552.

12. Sokolov, E. N. Higher nervous functions: The orienting reflex. *Ann Rev Physiol* 25:545-580, 1963.

13. Mason, J. W., Brady, J. V., and Sidman, M. Plasma 17-hydroxycorticosteroid levels and conditioned behavior in the Rhesus monkey. *Endocrinology* 60:741-752, 1957.

14. Sidman, M., Mason, J. W., Brady, J. V., and Thach, J. Quantitative relations between avoidance behavior and pituitary-adrenal cortical activity. *J Exp Anal Behav* 5:353-362, 1962.

15. Natelson, B. H., Smith, G., Stokes, P. E., and Root, A. W. Plasma 17-hydroxycorticosteroids and growth hormone during defense reactions. *Am J Physiol* 226:560-568, 1974.

16. Natelson, B. H., Krasnegor, N., and Holaday, J. W. Relations between behavioral arousal and plasma cortisol levels in monkeys performing repeated free-operant avoidance sessions. *J Comp Physiol Psychol* 90:958-969, 1976.

17. Bourne, P. G., Rose, R. M., and Mason, J. W. 17-OHCS levels in combat. Special forces "A" team under threat of attack. *Arch Gen Psychiat* 19:135-140, 1968.

18. Bourne, P. G., Rose, R. M., and Mason, J. W. Urinary 17-OHCS levels. Data on seven helicopter ambulance medics in combat. *Arch Gen Psychiat* 17:104-110, 1967.

19. Marks, I. Perspective on flooding. *Seminars in Psychiatry* 4:129-138, 1972.

20. Curtis, G. C., Buxton, M., Lippman, D., Nesse, R., and Wright, J. "Flooding in vivo" during the circadian phase of minimal cortisol secretion: Anxiety and therapeutic success without adrenal corticol activation. *Biol Psychiatry* 11:101-107, 1976.

21. Curtis, G. C., Nesse, R., Buxton, M., and Lippman, D. Anxiety and plasma cortisol at the crest of the circadian cycle: Reappraisal of a classical hypothesis. *Psychosom Med.* In press.

22. Curtis, G. C., Nesse, R. Buxton, M., and Lippman, D. Plasma growth hormone: Effect of anxiety during flooding in vivo. *Am J Psychiat.* In press.

23. Sutherland, C. J. and Zbrozyna, A. W. Extinction of the vasodilator component of the defense reaction in the cat. *Experientia* 30:49-59, 1974.

24. Graham, D. T., Kabler, J. D., and Lunsford, L. Vasovagal fainting: A diphasic response. *Psychosom Med* 24:493-507, 1961.

25. Mason, J. W. A review of psychoendocrine research on the pituitary-adrenal cortical system. *Psychosom Med* 39:576-607, 1968.

26. Curtis, G. C., Fogel, M. L., McEvoy, D., and Zarate, C. The effect of sustained affect on the diurnal rhythm of adrenal cortical activity. *Psychosom Med* 28:696-713, 1966.

27. Caplan, R. D., Cobb, S., and French, J. R. P. White collar work load and cortisol: Disruption of a circadian rhythm by jobb stress? Unpublished manuscript. Institute of Social Research, University of Michigan, Ann Arbor, Michigan.

28. Cannon, W. B. *The Wisdom of the Body.* New York: W. W. Norton and Company, Inc., 1932.

29. Lacey, J. I., Bateman, D. E., and Van Lehn, R. Autonomic response specificity: An experimental study. *Psychosom Med* 15:8-21, 1953.

30. Engel, B. T. Stimulus-response and individual-response specificity. *Arch Gen Psychiat* 2:305-313, 1960.

31. Silverman, A. J., Cohen, S. I., Shmavonian, B. M., and Kirshner, N. Catecholamines in psychophysiologic studies. *Recent Adv Biol Psychiat* 3:104-117, 1961.

32. Woods, S. C. and Kulkosky, P. J. Classically conditioned changes of blood glucose level. *Psychosom Med* 38:201-219, 1976.

33. Levine, S. and Coover, G. D. Environmental control of suppression of the pituitary-adrenal system. *Physiol Behav* 17:35-37, 1976.

34. Ader, R. and Cohen, N. Behaviorally conditioned immunosuppression. *Psychosom Med* 37:333-340, 1975.

35. Rogers, M. P., Reich, P., Strom, T. B., and Carpenter, C. B. Behaviorally conditioned immunosuppression: Replication of a recent study. *Psychosom Med* 38:447-451, 1976.

36. Hinkle, L. E. A summary of experimental evidence relating life stress to diabetes mellitus. *J Mount Sinai Hosp* 19:538-570, 1952.

37. Baker, L. and Barcai, A. Psychosomatic aspects of diabetes mellitus. In *Modern Trends in Psychosomatic Medicine, II.* Hill, O. W. (ed), New York: Appleton Century Craft, 1970. pp. 105-123.

38. Chambers, W. N. and Reiser, M. F. Emotional stress in the precipitation of congestive heart failure. *Psychosom Med* 25:38-60, 1953.

39. Reiser, M. F., Rosenbaum, M., and Ferris, E. B. Psychologic mechanisms in malignant hypertension. *Psychosom Med* 13:147-159, 1951.

40. Rosenman, R. H., Brand, R. J., Sholtz, R. I., and Friedman, M. Multivariate prediction of coronary heart disease during 8.5 year follow-up in the western collaborative group study. *Am J Cardiol* 37:903-910, 1976.

41. Friedman, S. B., Glasgow, L. A., and Ader, R. Psychosocial factors modifying host resistance to experimental infections. *Ann NY Acad Sci* 164:381-461, 1969.

42. Jacobs, S. and Ostfeld, A Epidemiological review of the mortality of bereavement. *Psychosom Med* 39:344-357, 1977.

43. Cobb, S. Social support as a moderator of life stress. *Psychosom Med* 38:300-314, 1976.

9
SOME MENTAL HEALTH CONSEQUENCES OF PLANT CLOSING AND JOB LOSS

STANISLAV V. KASL
SIDNEY COBB

This report is based on the findings of a completed study, the results of which have been presented in some detail in a National Institute for Occupational Safety and Health Research Report (Cobb and Kasl, 1977). Additional analyses, not described in the NIOSH publication, were carried out for this report and/or for subsequent scientific meetings (e.g., Kasl et al., 1977).* The results of this study of job loss are exceedingly complex and defy easy summary; for example, the outcomes were influenced by the urban setting of the one and the rural setting of the other of the two plants that closed down, and also by the varying degrees of social support experienced by the men who lost their jobs. Moreover, many anticipation effects were evident; that is, there were elevations in physiological indicators or on measures of psychological distress at a time when the men were aware of the impending shutdown although the work loss had not yet taken place.

What follows, then, is a selective presentation of findings that document the mental health impact of the loss of job. Because of the current high visibility of research on unemployment and because the results of such research have a high potential for

*This research was supported, in part, by the following grants:

Nos. K3-MH-16709 and K5-MH-16709 from the National Institute of Mental Health;
Nos. 5-R01-CD00102 and 5-R01-HS-00010 from the U.S. Public Health Service;
No. 91-26-72-23 from the U.S. Department of Labor
NIOSH Purchase Order 76-1261.

affecting governmental planning and policy, we are acutely aware of the need to avoid either exaggeration or minimization of evidence for adverse mental health influences. The findings discussed below reflect our best judgment as to how to describe this impact most clearly. Nevertheless, the reader is urged to consult the original NIOSH Report and to arrive at his/her own assessment of the extent of the evidence.

METHODS

The study is a longitudinal investigation of the health and behavioral effects of job loss and ensuing unemployment and/or job change experience. It reflects a research strategy in which significant social events of a stressful nature, which are predictable and thus open to study in their natural setting, can be identified with sufficient scientific rigor. The design may also be seen as a way to study life events which is complementary to the more usual approach of adding up life events into one global score without examining any one event in depth (e.g., Dohrenwend and Dohrenwend, 1974).

We were able to identify two plants that were about to shut down permanently and dismiss all their employees. In this way, we were able to establish a cohort of men whom we could then follow at regular intervals for up to two years as they went through the successive stages of anticipation of job loss, plant closing and employment termination, unemployment (for most), probationary reemployment, and stable reemployment. Our target population was composed exclusively of male blue-collar workers who were married, in the age range of 35-60, and who had worked at one of these two plants for at least three years. Of the men eligible for study, 79 percent agreed to participate.

The men were visited in their homes by public health nurses, on the following schedule:

Phase 1: The first visit took place some four to seven weeks before scheduled plant closing; the men were still on their old jobs, but they were already well aware of the impending shutdown. We have called this the Anticipation Stage.

Phase 2: The second visit took place some five to seven weeks after plant closing. At this point the men were either unemployed or else had found new employment where they were still in the probationary period.

Phase 3: Here the visits took place some four to eight months after plant closing. Some men were seen only once; but for some 60 percent of the men there were actually two nurse visits during the period. For these men, the average of the two values for each study variable is used in data analysis. During Phase 3, more and more men found new jobs; some were still unemployed, and a few had already made another job change.

Phase 4: Here the visits took place one year after plant closing. Most men had achieved a stable re-employment situation, but some were experiencing further job changes and a few remained unemployed.

Phase 5: The last nurse visit took place some two years after the original plant closing. By then, a sizable minority had experienced additional job changes and unemployment during the preceding year.

In our presentation of results, we refer to these five phases as: Anticipation, Termination, 6 Months, 12 Months, and 24 Months, respectively.

During the course of each visit to the man's home, the nurse collected blood and urine specimens, took blood pressure, pulse rate, height and weight, and used a structured interview schedule to collect diverse social-psychological and health data. These included: his current employment situation, his economic circumstances, his subjective evaluation of his job and financial situation, questionnaire measures of mental health and affective reactions, and physical health data. Because there was a great deal of data collected at each phase, two nurse visits were necessary; these visits came two weeks apart and during this period the men kept a diary with a daily record of the state of their health.

Most of the data that we collected are based on standardized, explicit (pre-coded) interview schedules and questionnaire measures, developed over a period of some four months of pretesting. The public health nurses, all of whom were experienced interviewers, received some additional two to three weeks of training in the use of the study's interview schedule and questionnaires. This training was directed primarily to ensuring uniform interview behavior and strict adherence to the interview schedule, its questions, and its built-in probes.

The design of the study also called for the use of *controls*, men who were continuously employed in comparable jobs. They were followed for almost the same length of time under exactly the same assessment procedures.

The men who lost their jobs came from two companies. One was a paint manufacturing plant located in a large metropolitan area. The men were largely machine operators, laboratory assistants, and clerks in shipping departments; the work was relatively light for most of them. The other plant was located in a rural community of some 3,000 people. It manufactured display fixtures used by wholesale and retail concerns, and the men were machine operators, assembly line workers, and in a few cases, tool and die workers.

The controls came from four companies and were quite comparable to the actual cases in respect to major demographic characteristics, type of work, and the rural or urban location. One setting was the maintenance department in a large university, and the men were largely machinists and carpenters. The second company manufactured parts for heavy trucks; it was located in a large metropolitan area, and the men were machine operators and assembly line workers. The other two companies were both rural manufacturing concerns where the men again were primarily machine operators and assembly line workers.

Table 1 presents the major socio-demographic characteristics of the terminees—the men who lost their jobs—and the controls. The two groups are quite comparable, and none of the differences in table 1 is significant. It is worth noting that the terminees had worked for the company almost twenty years, on the average. Given their age, this would suggest that the plant closing meant for

Table 1
A Comparison of Terminees and Controls

	Terminees	Controls
Companies involved	1 urban 1 rural	2 urban 2 rural
Number of men in study	100	74
Initial participation rate (% of target population)	82%	75%
Mean age	48.1	50.1
Mean years of schooling	9.5	10.0
Mean number of children	2.9	3.3
Percent non-white	8%	11%
Mean years at (original) company	19.4	21.1
Mean hourly wage (initial)	$2.96	$3.58
Mean Duncan code of occupational status	28.2	32.2
Mean employability (combines age, education, nurse's rating of health, and Duncan code of highest previous job held)	2.5 ($\pm$0.5)	2.6 ($\pm$0.5)

Terminees and Controls also comparable on:

    a) Need for social approval (Crowne-Marlowe scale)
    b) Ego resilience (Block)
    c) Flexibility-rigidity (California Psychological Inventory)
    d) Self-rated health (on initial visit)

most of them a separation from their primary place of employment during their adult working careers.

The bottom of table 1 shows that terminees and controls were also comparable on diverse additional variables, such as: a) The Crowne-Marlowe measure of the Need for Social Approval (Crowne and Marlowe, 1964), useful as a measure of defensiveness in self-report; b) Block's Ego Resilience Scale, a measure of general adjustment (Block, 1965); c) The CPI Flexibility-Rigidity Scale (Gough, 1957); d) Readiness for Illness Behavior, an index based on Mechanic's brief scale (Mechanic and Volkart, 1961); e) global self-rating of health on the initial visit. There was only one measure on which the cases and controls were found to be significantly different: on a health history of 15 chronic illness/symptoms, the controls acknowledged slightly more of them (mean of 2.1 vs. 1.6 for terminees). We tentatively attributed this difference to recruitment of subjects: terminees were asked to join the study because we were studying job loss, whereas controls were told only that we were studying blue-collar workers, their work and their health.

In this report we shall present results with two indices of the person's economic state, both of which are adopted from a previous study of plant closings and unemployment (Aiken et al., 1968).

Relative Economic Deprivation: a 2-item index based on pre-coded, scaled answers to two questions (1) How difficult is it for you and your family to live on your present total family income? and (2) How does your present family income compare with that of most of your friends and neighbors? High score = high sense of deprivation.

Relative Economic Change: a 5-item index based on questions dealing with changes in total family income, in family debts, and in family savings, and the experience of having to cut expenses and obtaining loans from friends and relatives. For each question, the time referent is "last 3 months." High score = high change.

Another group of variables for which we shall present some findings are what we have come to call *Work Role "Deprivation" Scales,* in which the respondent rates his current life situation: "How things look to you now," as well as "How you would like things to be." For each of the twelve dimensions, the score reflects the difference between the actual and the desired situation. The dimensions deal with: physical activity, keeping busy, doing interesting things, use of valued skills, security about future, perceived respect from others, socializing with others, being able to talk over problems with friends, and so on. These dimensions are called "work role deprivation scales" since they reflect the various possible dimensions of satisfaction that the job and the work setting may provide.

Finally this report presents the results for several indicators of *mental health*. The nine scales here are based on a factor analysis of a large pool of items, with some five or six items defining each scale. Because items have been heavily borrowed from existing measures, these scales may be viewed as highly typical of what is available in the research literature. The nine scales, with illustrative items in parentheses, are as follows: 1) Depression ("Things seem hopeless"); 2) Low Self-Esteem ("I am inclined to feel I am a failure"); 3) Anomie ("These days a person doesn't really know whom he can depend on"); 4) Anxiety-Tension ("I often feel tense"); 5) Psychophysiological Symptoms ("I am bothered by my heart beating hard"); 6) Insomnia ("I have trouble falling asleep"); 7) Anger-Irritation ("I lose my temper easily"); 8) Resentment ("I feel I get a raw deal out of life"); and 9) Suspicion ("I used to think most people told the truth but now I know otherwise").

All the measures are scored in such a way that a high score indicates poor economic circumstances, high deprivation, high distress, poor mental health, or low sense of well-being. Moreover, all scales have been converted into standard scores (mean = 0, S. D. = 1.0), with the data on consistently employed controls (men in comparable blue-collar jobs who faced neither the threat nor the actuality of plant closing) used as a basis for standardization.

In some of the analyses, we utilize a control variable that we call *Perceived Social Support*. This is a 13-item index, consisting of: six items on perceived social support from wife, two items on perceived social support from friends and relatives, three items on frequency of social interaction with friends and relatives, and two items dealing with the perceptions of the social environment as one in which sociability can be expressed and problems can be discussed. Information about additional brief measures introduced in this report will be given at appropriate places in the results section.

Let us briefly characterize the unemployment experience of the men during the two-year follow-up period. Overall, the men experienced an average of about fifteen weeks of unemployment during the 24 months; for most of them, this was the period between plant closing and the time they started on a new full-time job. However, 20 percent of the men were unemployed twice or oftener. In the urban setting, the experience during the first year was less severe: 25 percent experienced no unemployment (i.e., they found a new job at once), and another 50 percent had less than two months of unemployment. In the rural setting, the men had more difficulty in finding a job; even some three to four months after plant closing, one-third of the men were without a job. By the end of the first year, the men in the rural setting had experienced an average of twelve weeks of unemployment, in contrast to seven weeks for their urban counterparts. During the second year, the situation was reversed, and more men in the urban than in the rural setting had additional periods of unemployment. Thus by the end of the two-year period, the cumulative experience of the men in the two companies was about the same.

A separate analysis of the social context of the two companies (Gore, 1973) has revealed that in the urban setting, where the men's homes were scattered throughout the city, the plant itself was an important focus for a sense of community and social support. When the plant closed down, this "community" died (see also Slote, 1969). But in the rural setting, the small town itself and the people in it were the major source of a sense of community and social support for the men, while the plant had never become fully integrated into the community life. When the plant closed, the community and its social organization remained largely intact, and social interaction with former co-workers who had been friends was not so severely disrupted. These differences in the severity of the unemployment experience and in the social setting of the urban and rural companies have to be kept in mind as the results are presented and discussed.

RESULTS

We shall begin by presenting some descriptive data that deal with the men's perceptions and evaluations of the job loss experience. The intent here is to treat such data not as indicators of impact, but simply as providers of additional information about the plant closing and job loss experience. In table 2, some results with three measures are presented. The first two are based on the questions: "First, could you tell me how you would rate this job loss?" and "Now, could you tell me how long you think it took you before things got pretty much back to normal?" The third measure derives from a procedure in which the respondent was presented with a "ladder" from 0 to 100 in which certain events and corresponding values, obtained from the Holmes and Rahe (1967) Social Readjustment Rating Scale, were listed in order to provide anchors.

Table 2 presents the results separately for the urban and rural settings and gives the men's perceptions at one year and at two years after plant closing. In general, the men rate the experience between "somewhat disturbing" and "very disturbing," and indicate that it took them, on the average, somewhere between "a few months" and "around half a year" before their lives normalized. As a "life event," the job loss experience was rated comparable to "getting married;" 27 percent of the ratings placed it as high as "divorce," or higher. The intercompany differences and changes over time are not reliable.

Table 3 explores some of the correlates of perceptions and evaluations of the job experience in relation to three indicators: a) the amount of unemployment experienced during the first year; b) the number of job changes (including transitions from part-time to full-time status) during that year; and c) a comparison of the old and new job on seven job dimensions (those seen in table 5). The ratings at one-year follow-up include: a) the three dimensions seen in table 2; b) a total job loss "stress index" which combines the three dimensions, plus one additional item based on a graphic chart of "ups and downs;" and c) the scores on the brief index of Relative Economic Deprivation.

Table 2
Some Perceptions and Evaluations of the
Job Loss Experience at 12 Months and 24 Months

Evaluation		12 Months		24 Months	
		Urban	Rural	Urban	Rural
Rate job loss					
1 = hardly bothered me at all					
2 = upsetting a little bit	Mean	3.4	3.2	2.9	3.0
3 = somewhat disturbing					
4 = very disturbing	S.D.	1.4	1.3	1.4	1.4
5 = changed my whole life					
How long before normal					
1 = about a week or so					
2 = about a month	Mean	3.4	3.9	3.1	3.6
3 = a few months					
4 = around half a year	S.D.	1.4	1.1	1.5	1.3
5 = not yet back to normal					
Plant closing and job loss as "Life Event"					
10 = traffic ticket					
30 = trouble with in-laws	Mean	49.6	55.3	43.7	51.8
50 = getting married					
80 = divorce	S.D.	25.7	36.0	30.2	29.5
100 = death of wife					

The results in table 3 reveal that the most pertinent objective index of severity in the job loss experience—number of weeks unemployed—shows moderate correlations with the subjective ratings, but this is true only for the urban setting. In the rural setting, the correlations are small and not significant; in fact, several are in the opposite direction and are significantly different from the correlations based on the urban men. The second variable, number of job changes, does not have much influence on the perceptions and evaluations of the job loss experience in either setting. The third variable, comparison of the old and new jobs, reveals some tendency for the men to rate the job loss experience in both companies as less stressful to the extent that they prefer the

Table 3
Correlates of Perceptions and Evaluations of the
Job Loss Experience by Urban vs. Rural Setting

Ratings at 12 months	Number of weeks unemployed during first year		Number of job changes during first year		Comparing old and new job, average on seven job dimensions*	
	Urban	Rural	Urban	Rural	Urban	Rural
Rate job loss	.21	.01	-.01	-.06	.14	.03
How long before normal	.39	.03	.16	-.06	.35	.32
Plant closing and job loss as "Life Event"	.43	-.17	.05	.07	.06	.28
Total job loss "stress" index	.45	-.12	.13	-.03	.43	.32
Relative economic deprivation	.38	-.06	-.03	.08	.25	.27

*Based on a five point rating scale, where 1 = new job is much better than old one, and 5 = new job is much worse than old one.

new job to the old one. Both correlations with the total job loss "stress" index are significant.

Some limited information was collected on the men's perceptions of where blame for being unemployed should be assigned: "Who do you think is to be blamed for the fact that you are not working right now? We would like to know how much you think each of the following is responsible for your unemployment." The relevant results are presented in table 4. Since this question was asked only of men not working at the time of a particular visit, numerically meaningful data are available for Termination and for six months only. At Termination, when over half of the men were not working, the men attributed most of the blame to the management of the company, some blame to the business situation and the government, and decreasing amounts of blame to the union, automation, and themselves. This pattern of attributed blame is about as realistic as one could find. The company management's decision, indeed, closed the plant down; automation was not the reason and they themselves were not responsible. The business situation made it more difficult to find prompt re-employment. By six months, there is a tendency to blame self somewhat more and all the other possible sources somewhat less. This again seems "realistic" in that continuing to be unemployed can be attributed more to personal characteristics (higher age, poorer health, lower skills) and less to the original cause for the plants' closing.

Overall, we were impressed by the fact that the men who were not working had a realistic appraisal of the reasons for their unemployment and were able to avoid blaming themselves. (For example, at Termination, 85 percent of the men chose "not at all" as the degree of own responsibility for not working.) This has implications for the analysis and interpretation of psychological effects presented below. It may also be in contrast to the observations made in unemployment studies of the 1930s (e.g., Bakke, 1940a and 1940b; Cavan and Ranck, 1938; Ginzberg, 1943; Komarovsky, 1940), where many men who became unemployed blamed themselves for the loss of their jobs.

Table 4
Perception of Blame for Being Unemployed
at Termination and at 6 Months

Focus of Blame*	Termination		6 Months	
	Mean	S.D.	Mean	S.D.
The business situation	2.5	1.6	2.4	1.1
The company management	4.1	1.4	3.5	1.7
You yourself	1.4	1.0	2.1	1.5
The union	1.9	1.2	1.4	0.9
The government	2.3	1.2	1.7	1.1
Automation	1.6	1.1	1.1	0.2

*Asked only of men who were unemployed at time of visit. The five degrees of perceived responsibility were: 1 = not at all, 2 = slightly, 3 = somewhat, 4 = quite a bit, and 5 = completely.

The next table presents subjective data relevant to the comparison between the original job and the job held at 12 and 24 months. The seven dimensions are the traditional basic job satisfaction dimensions. The overall trends in table 5 suggest that the men viewed the new job more favorably than the old one; this is particularly true at 24 months. The smallest differences in perceptions involve pay, which was "realistic" since their reported hourly wage on the new job was, on the average, about the same as on the old job. The largest differences involve co-workers and supervision. Testing for statistical significance may be done by assuming that responses which are not "ties" (new job same as old one) should be equally distributed into "better than" and "worse than" categories. The following distributions are significantly different from this chance expectation: a) job as a whole, 24 months; b) co-workers, both occasions; c) supervision, both occasions; d) content of job, 24 months; e) opportunities for promotion, 24 months; and f) opportunities for skill utilization, 24 months.

These results can be taken as a very general indication that the men are *not* looking back on their old jobs with a nostalgia and

Table 5
Respondents' Views of Original Jobs in Relation
to Current Jobs at 12 Months and 24 Months

Job satisfaction dimensions and phases	Better than old one (%)	Same as old one (%)	Worse than old one (%)
Job as a whole			
12 months	37	30	33
24 months*	60	27	13
Pay			
12 months	38	19	43
24 months	48	21	31
Co-workers			
12 months*	32	60	8
24 months*	31	64	5
Supervision			
12 months*	37	57	6
24 months*	47	45	8
Content of job			
12 months	34	37	29
24 months*	47	41	12
Promotion opportunities			
12 months	36	44	20
24 months*	37	50	13
Opportunities for skill utilization			
12 months	34	43	23
24 months*	43	45	12

*Significantly different from an equal distribution of "better" and "worse."

fondness that might lead to dissatisfaction with their new jobs. Yet, the extent to which these ratings may have been anchored in reality cannot be determined. Objective data on pay do support the lack of significant differences on subjective ratings of pay. However, the data on co-workers and supervision are curious: after some 19 years (on the average) in the old jobs, one might expect that these two social aspects of the work environment would have been rated more unfavorably on their current jobs. The results are opposed to this intuitive expectation and would argue against any strong assertion that the men particularly missed their former co-workers when they looked back to their old jobs.

We are now ready to present data on the psychological impact of the experience. In the next six figures, the results are expressed in the following format. One hundred terminees are split into two groups, below and above median on the number of weeks (approximately five) unemployed during the first year. Each group is further divided according to a median split on Perceived Social Support. Since these two control variables are essentially uncorrelated, the resulting four groups are of about equal size. The means on six selected dependent variables are then given for each of the four groups by the five phases of the study. The means are presented in standard scores (mean = 0, S. D. = 1.0), with the data on controls as the basis for standardizing the raw-scale scores. The purpose of this analysis is to define the influence of the severity of unemployment and of the level of social support on the impact of the job loss experience over time. Of particular interest is the notion that the adverse impact may be concentrated in the Low Social Support-High Unemployment Group of men.

Figure 1 presents the data on Relative Economic Change. The results suggest the following: 1) There is no anticipation effect, with all four groups starting out at a point near that of the controls. 2) The effects of job loss are seen only in those two groups who had more unemployment; moreover, the effect is most striking at Phase 2, Termination. 3) The level of social support does not seem to have influenced the effects over time of the severity of unemployment; however, there is some evidence of interaction at Phase 5 (24 Months) with the two low social support groups showing a relatively wide separation in means due to the effect of unemployment.

There is a serious limitation to the index of Relative Economic Change when used in longitudinal studies such as this one. It measures *change* rather than the state of affairs at one point in time. This means that the measure is most sensitive in describing change but is relatively insensitive in describing stabilization at a new, altered level of behavioral adaptation. In figure 1, the men who have undergone more unemployment, irrespective of the level of social support, report adverse changes in financial circumstances and economic behavior between Anticipation and

270

Figure 1

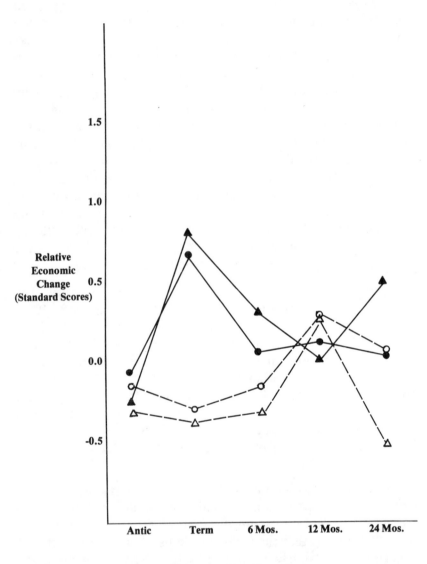

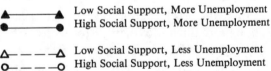

Low Social Support, More Unemployment
High Social Support, More Unemployment

Low Social Support, Less Unemployment
High Social Support, Less Unemployment

Termination. If these men stabilize at this new level of more precarious financial circumstances, then at six months they will report few changes in the "last three months" and will receive low scores, comparable to those of the controls. But their financial situation may be no better than at Termination. For this reason we feel that figure 1 should be examined only for the means at Anticipation and Termination, where the interpretation is unambiguous.

Figure 2 presents the data for Relative Economic Deprivation. This is a less "objective" measure of economic well-being than the previous one, but it is fully suitable for repeated administrations in a longitudinal follow-up. The results suggest that: 1) At Anticipation, the four groups start out rather close together and, on the average, somewhat below the level for controls. It is possible that they felt at that moment relatively well off, compared to what they knew was soon coming (plant closing), even though their objective financial circumstances were comparable to those of the controls. 2) Men with more unemployment clearly experienced more deprivation; the effect is greatest at Termination, but even at 24 months the men with more unemployment are about one-third of a standard deviation above controls. 3) Social support interacts rather clearly with levels of unemployment; in low levels of unemployment it has no effect, whereas at higher levels low social support contributes significantly to a sense of relative economic deprivation.

The next two figures present the results for two scales from the group of measures called *Work Role "Deprivation" Scales.* The wording is as follows: "Do you have a feeling of *security* when you think about the future; and how much *security* do you feel about the future now?" "How much do you feel you are doing important things, so others notice you and *respect* you for what you do?" A high score on these two scales indicates a high discrepancy between a man's rating of his actual life situation and the desired situation.

The results in figure 3 reveal a rather striking separation of one group of men—Low Social Support and More Unemployment—

Figure 2

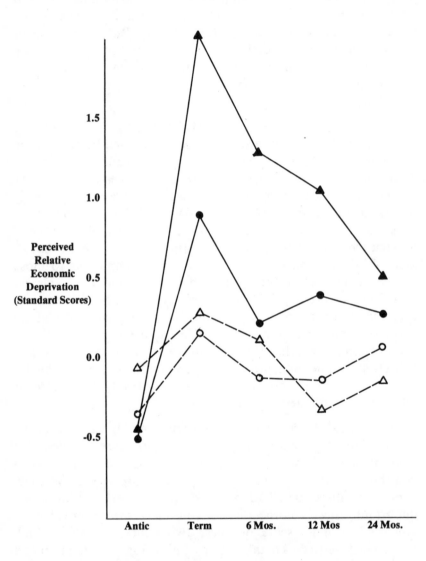

Perceived
Relative
Economic
Deprivation
(Standard Scores)

1.5

1.0

0.5

0.0

-0.5

Antic   Term   6 Mos.   12 Mos   24 Mos.

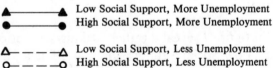

▲━━━━▲ Low Social Support, More Unemployment
●━━━━● High Social Support, More Unemployment

△-----△ Low Social Support, Less Unemployment
○-----○ High Social Support, Less Unemployment

Figure 3

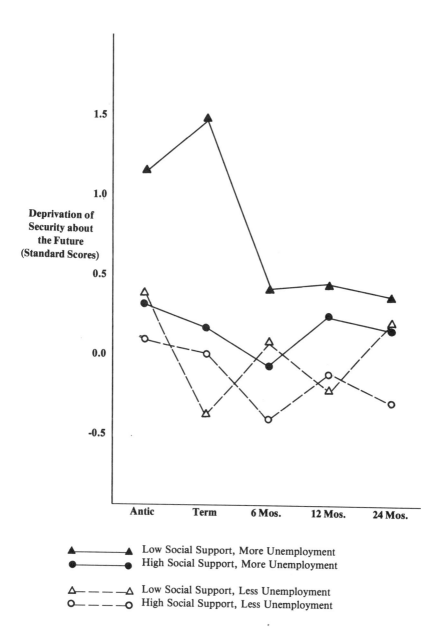

Deprivation of Security about the Future (Standard Scores)

1.5

1.0

0.5

0.0

-0.5

Antic   Term   6 Mos.   12 Mos.   24 Mos.

▲————▲ Low Social Support, More Unemployment
●————● High Social Support, More Unemployment

△ — — —△ Low Social Support, Less Unemployment
○ — — —○ High Social Support, Less Unemployment

from the other three. The latter show a modest anticipation effect, with prompt leveling off at slightly below the mean for controls (0.0) and some chance fluctuations. But the first group shows a large anticipation effect, additional rise at Termination, a sharp decline, and a leveling off at a point not significantly higher than that of the control mean. The results in figure 4 are suggestively similar in that the same group of men, Low Social Support and More Unemployment, again stands out. The results are somewhat different in that: a) the other three groups do not show any anticipation effect; b) the High Social Support and More Unemployment Group shows a good deal of fluctuation from phase to phase without any overall trends (this may be genuine instability in the men's sense of respect in that high social support and more unemployment may exert opposite pressures on their sense of respect, thus preventing a stable equilibrium); c) the elevation in the Low Social Support and More Unemployment Group is more enduring, persisting through the one-year follow-up; d) at 24 months, the four groups show a good convergence, stabilizing somewhat below the control mean.

The data in figures 3 and 4 are superficially consistent with the expectation that one group of men, low on social support and with more severe unemployment, will show the greatest impact of the job loss experience. However, because this group of men is already distinct at Anticipation, before the actual start of the unemployment experience, the simple interpretation of an impact is imperiled. Let us for the moment concentrate on the Anticipation phase in figure 4. The highly significant interaction can be described as follows: a) among men low on social support, having higher levels of a sense of loss of respect from others is *predictive* of subsequent longer unemployment; b) among men high on social support, lower levels of the deprivation of respect from others are slightly predictive of longer unemployment. The results in figure 3 at Anticipation show a similar interaction, but no reversal of the predictive association in the high support group.

We believe that the most plausible interpretation of the data in figures 3 and 4 is: among men with low social support, anticipating the plant closing with a high sense of deprivation

Figure 4

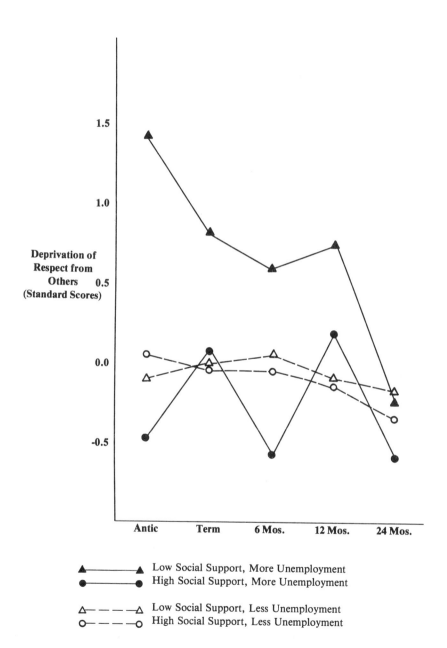

Deprivation of
Respect from
Others
(Standard Scores)

increases the likelihood of longer subsequent unemployment. It is possible, then, that in the context of low social support, initially high levels of a sense of deprivation constitute an obstacle to prompt reemployment.

At least two other interpretations of these data are possible. One is that the men with *characteristically* high levels of a sense of deprivation, and with low social support, are the ones who take longer to find a job following plant closing. However, this interpretation is contradicted by the eventual decline, from the initially high levels, seen at 24 months. Thus, the self-selection into longer unemployment among men low on social support appears to be due to the acute response to the anticipation period rather than to characteristically or consistently high levels of those men. The second possible interpretation is that at Anticipation, the men were able to predict reasonably well the difficulty they might have in finding a new job and, the more difficult they thought it would be, the more they felt a sense of "deprivation" even before plant closing. However, the index of employability (see bottom of table 1), which was a reasonably good overall predictor of amount of unemployment ($r = -.39$, p $.001$), was not found to be correlated with levels of a sense of deprivation at Anticipation; thus we are inclined to discount this interpretation as well.

The data on the next two figures (5 and 6) deal with two mental health indicators, depression and anomie. They were selected because the general unemployment literature seems to suggest that these would be the most sensitive indicators. The results once again reveal the sharp separation of the one group of men, Low Social Support and More Unemployment, from the other three. However, in contrast to figures 3 and 4, the levels of depression and anomie in this group never show a decline, even at 24 months. This pattern of results, therefore, may suitably be interpreted as a self-selection phenomenon among those with *stable* or characteristically high levels of depression or anomie. In other words, among men low on social support, those who have characteristically high levels of depression or anomie are the ones who will have the more difficult time in finding a job; among men high on social support, levels of depression or anomie are not particularly predictive of the subsequent amount of unemployment. This, then, is tantamount to saying that unemployment did not have a detectable impact on depression or anomie in this analysis, but that depression and anomie did have an impact on unemployment among the subset of men with low social support. It must be acknowledged that we cannot reject an alternate hypothesis: among men low on social support, those who respond to the anticipation period with a sharp increase in depression and anomie (from hypothesized average levels at some prior "baseline" period) have greater difficulty in finding a job, which then prolongs their psychological reactions so that they do not return to normal levels within the two-year period of follow-up. This is the same interpretation that was applied to figures 3 and 4, except that the anticipation-based reaction is presumed to persist beyond 24 months. We do not feel that this second interpretation is as compelling as the first, but in the absence of true baseline data prior to any anticipation of a plant's closing (an ideal design foolishly written into the original proposal but impossible to implement), we cannot reject it with confidence.

It is instructive to contrast the pattern of results in figures 2 vs. 3 and 4 vs. 5 and 6. All of them show an interaction with the levels of social support, but the inferences about the impact of plant closing and job loss are different. In figure 2, the four groups start out at a comparable level and show near convergence at 24 months; here the inference that job loss had an impact is rather compelling. In figures 3 and 4, because of the group differences at Anticipation but with convergence at 24 months, the inference is that, among men low on social support, the degree of the anticipatory reaction is predictive of severity of unemployment. In figures 5 and 6, because of the group differences at Anticipation and the failure to converge at 24 months, the inference is that among men low on social support, stable or characteristically high levels of depression and anomie are predictive of longer unemployment.

At this point we felt that the analyses carried out so far, although they revealed the interactive effect of the level of social support satisfactorily, might not have been the optimal ones for detecting the impact of job loss. Accordingly, additional analyses

278

Figure 5

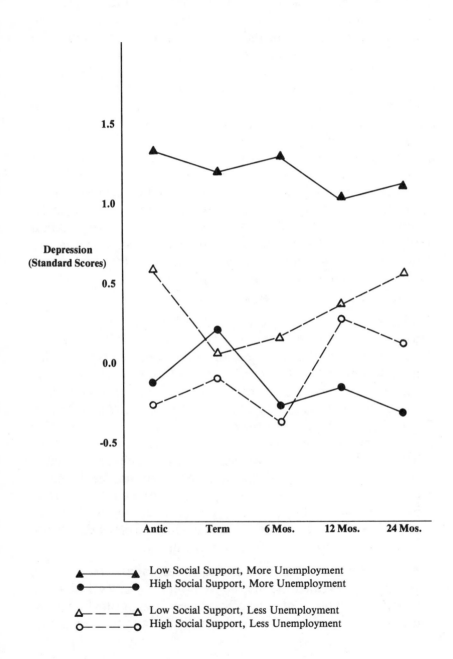

Low Social Support, More Unemployment
High Social Support, More Unemployment

Low Social Support, Less Unemployment
High Social Support, Less Unemployment

Figure 6

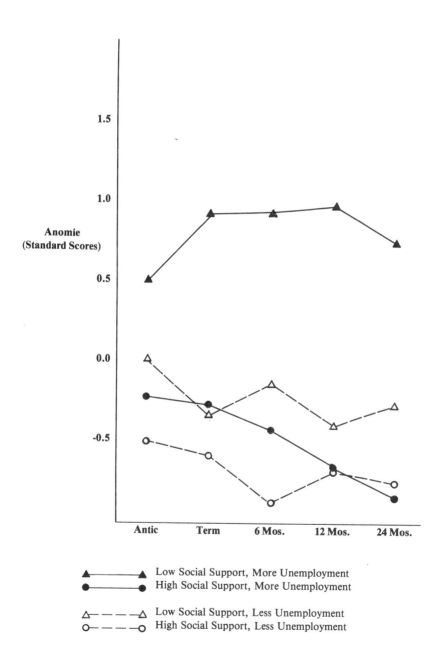

were made in order to pinpoint more effectively the role of anticipation and the effect of working vs. not working on the various indicators of deprivation and mental health. The basic findings are given in table 6. The first column presents the mean values (in standardized scores) for the various measures collected at Phase 1, Anticipation. The data in the second column are based on later home visits (Termination, six months, 12 months, 24 months) whenever the respondent was unemployed.For 51 of the men, one or more of the scheduled home visits took place when the man was unemployed; for the other 49 men, either none of the visits coincided with the time they were unemployed or they might not have been unemployed at all (12 percent of the sample). The data in the third column are based on all visits when the man was reemployed; there were five men who remained unemployed during all the subsequent follow-up visits. The values in columns two and three are means of 51 and 95 scores, respectively, where each score itself is an ipsative (intra-person) mean whenever two or more scores were available for one individual for periods of unemployment and re-employment. The last column is based on the computation of an intra-person difference between the ipsative mean for all occasions of unemployment and the ipsative mean for all occasions of employment; there were 46 individuals for whom these intra-person differences could be computed.

An examination of anticipation effects can be made either by studying the means in the first column and noting which are significantly different from the control mean of zero, or by comparing the first column with the third column, which gives the means for the occasions of re-employment. By the first criterion, the anticipation effects could be described as higher insecurity and depression, and lower suspicion; but only the first variable—insecurity—satisfies also the second criterion, significantly higher levels in comparison to the means for occasions of re-employment.

The impact of unemployment (i.e., of not working) on these indicators of mental health and well-being can be examined in several ways: a) compare means in column 2 with controls (i.e., a mean of 0); b) compare columns 2 and 3; c) examine means in column 4, which may be viewed as the most sensitive approach

Table 6
Changes in Mental Health and Well-Being Associated with Anticipation of Plant Closing, Being Unemployed, and Being Re-employed

	Mean values for anticipation	Mean values for all occasions when unemployed	Mean values for all occasions when employed	Amount of intra-person difference between all occasions when unemployed and when employed
Relative Economic Deprivation	-.23	1.23	.17	.96
Work Role "Deprivation" Scales				
Security about the future	.44	.58	-.02	.54
Getting ahead in the world	-.20	.66	-.25	.96
Respect from others	.10	.46	-.10	.52
Use of one's best skills	.18	1.56	.31	1.26
Things are interesting	.16	.53	.03	.61
Summary scale of 12 dimensions	.25	.94	-.03	.94
Mental Health Indicators				
Depression	.35	.55	.23	.18
Low self-esteem	.15	.34	.03	.14
Anomie	-.04	.05	-.19	.01
Anxiety-tension	.12	.17	-.16	.28
Psychophysiological symptoms	.03	-.09	-.06	-.30
Insomnia	-.07	-.08	-.08	-.14
Anger-irritation	.03	-.11	-.15	.02
Resentment	.15	.25	.03	.05
Suspicion	-.31	-.35	-.38	-.28
N	100	51	95	46

*See text for description of measures and explanation of computation of mean scores.

since it compares unemployment and re-employment values intra-individually. However, all comparisons roughly tell the same story: on indices of deprivation (economic, in the work role), the impact is clearcut and highly significant (all differences in column 4 at $p < .005$ or lower). Thus, for example, on "use of one's best skills," the discrepancy between "actual" and "desired" when the men are unemployed is one and one-quarter of a standard deviation above the discrepancy values for occasions when the men are later reemployed. However, the mental health indicators show little impact. In column 2, only three means are suggestively different from those of the controls: high on depression and low self-esteem, and below expected on suspicion. But the last column (intra-person differences) does not yield statistically reliable differences for these 3 scales. In fact, in column 4 there are only two significant intra-person differences: anxiety-tension and psychophysiological symptoms. Moreover, the latter scale reveals an opposite effect: fewer symptoms were reported during periods of unemployment. Overall, then, the impact of unemployment on these mental health indicators seems rather weak.

The data in table 7 explore the notion that the impact of not working may be different in the urban vs. the rural setting. Essentially, the means seen in the last column of table 6 are recomputed separately for the urban and the rural men. The results in table 7 suggest the following: 1) The impact on the two economic indicators is roughly the same in both settings; 2) The impact on the work role "deprivation" scales is suggestively stronger in the rural setting; 3) The impact on the indicators of mental health appears stronger in the urban setting; 4) The physiological data suggest a setting difference only for serum uric acid. The other indices of work role "deprivation" and mental health showed urban-rural differences similar to those shown in table 7 but somewhat smaller in magnitude. Consequently, the overall separation of the two settings in terms of differential impact is not as sharp as suggested by the psychological scales selected for table 7.

Any interpretation of these urban-rural differences is hampered by the ambiguity and multidimensionality of that contrast. We have already noted two aspects reflected in that contrast: a) In the rural setting, the job market was quite limited, and thus, the unemployment experience of the rural men was more severe. b) In the urban setting, the friendship network of co-workers was plant-based and when the plant closed down, this network was severely disrupted because of the scattered residential locations of the former co-workers in the metropolitan area. (Geographical distance is a more powerful obstacle to social interaction among blue-collar workers (Kasl, 1977).) On the other hand, the friendship networks of co-workers in the rural setting were community-based and were thus less severely disrupted by the plant closing; consequently, there was a greater potential for sharing of the job loss experience among those going through it. In addition to these two aspects of the contrast, there is also some evidence that small town workers are less alienated from middle-class work norms than are urban workers (Hulin and Blood, 1968; Turner and Lawrence, 1968); this greater attachment to the work role among the rural workers would thus suggest the potential for a greater impact due to the loss of the work role among them. Overall, the results in table 7 are consistent with the following interpretation: the greater attachment to the work role among the rural workers may explain the greater impact on the work role "deprivation" scales, while the lesser disruption of the social and friendship networks—and the consequent greater potential for sharing and emotional support—may explain the lesser impact on mental health among them.

The data presented in table 6 appear to lead to the general observation that the impact of not working is seen primarily on the work role "deprivation" scales, and that the impact on mental health appears attenuated at best. This is quite congruent with the results of many studies showing that the impact of the work environment on blue-collar workers is seen much better on indices of job satisfaction than on indicators of mental health status (Kasl, 1974, 1979). Nevertheless, we still felt uneasy about the conclusion of only a limited mental health impact, and consequently pursued the issue of impact one step further. We settled on an additional data analysis procedure which we feel is

Table 7
Some Effects of Unemployment by Urban vs. Rural Setting

	Intra-person differences between occasions when subject was unemployed vs. when re-employed in standard scores*						
	Mean Change		Significance of Change				Interaction (difference between settings)
Selected Outcomes	Urban	Rural	For urban	For rural	For both		
Economic Indicators							
Relative Economic Deprivation	1.09	0.91	—	—	<.001		n.s.
Relative Economic Change	0.74	0.92	—	—	<.001		n.s.
Work Role "Deprivation" (discrepancy between actual and desired)							
"Using one's best skills"	0.40	1.59	n.s.	<.001	—		<.01
"Things one does are interesting"	0.11	0.82	n.s.	<.005	—		<.10
"Getting ahead in the world"	0.18	1.28	n.s.	<.001	—		<.005
Indices of Well-Being							
Anger-Irritation	0.41	-0.13	<.10	n.s.	—		<.05
Resentment	0.83	-0.26	<.025	n.s.	—		<.001
Anomie	0.55	-0.12	<.05	n.s.	—		<.05

Physiological Indicators

Serum Cholesterol	0.64	0.96	—	—	<.001	n.s.
Serum Uric Acid	0.57	0.09	<.001	n.s.	—	<.025
Pulse Rate	0.53	0.21	—	—	<.005	n.s.

*Values for occasions when subject is re-employed are subtracted from values when subject in unemployed. Positive change indicates values for episodes of unemployment are higher. Values are standardized, using data on controls as the basis (mean = 0, S.D. = 1.0). Mean change of 0.50 indicates 1/2 of a standard deviation separates unemployment and re-employment values.

most sensitive to the actual temporal process of adaptation to job loss, unemployment, and re-employment (Kasl et al., 1977). Essentially, the procedure is as follows. Between Phases 1 and 2, Anticipation and Termination, the men either experience a transition from anticipation to unemployment (N = 53) or from anticipation to fairly prompt re-employment (N = 46). Any differential changes in the dependent variables may be viewed as reflecting the impact of an acute or brief "stress." For example, men experiencing the transition to unemployment may show a rise in a particular variable reflecting deprivation or distress if there was no anticipation effect, or they may stay high if there was an anticipation effect. But men experiencing the transition to prompt re-employment may be expected to stay low (or average) if there was no anticipation effect, or show a drop if there was an anticipation effect. In any case, the two groups should show differential trends.

Now let's follow these men to their next visit at Phase 3, some 4 to 6 months after plant closing. The men unemployed at Phase 2 may still be unemployed (N = 15) or they may have found a job, a delayed re-employment group (N = 37). The men who were employed at Phase 2 are continuing to stabilize their re-employment situation (N = 34). (There were also 11 men who were employed at Phase 2, but by Phase 3 they had experienced additional job changes and/or episodes of unemployment; they do not fit the notion of stabilized re-employment and are omitted from this particular analysis.) Now any differential changes in the dependent variables across these 3 groups would suggest the impact of more prolonged stress. In particular, the group continuing to be unemployed should continue being elevated or might even show some additional increases. The delayed re-employment group should show a drop in indices of deprivation and distress, while the stabilized re-employment group should continue being low or perhaps show some additional decreases. The data relevant to these expectations are presented in the next two tables.

In table 8 we see that one scale, Relative Economic Deprivation, shows results fully consistent with the hypothesized impact of both

Table 8
Changes in "Deprivations" by Duration of Unemployment

| | | Amount of Change From | | | | |
| | | 1-Anticipation to | | 2-Unemployed to | | 2-Reemployed to |
		2-Unemployed	2-Reemployed	3-Still Unemployed	3-Delayed Reemployment	3-Stabilized Reemployment
Relative Economic Deprivation	Mean change*	1.74	0.11	0.33	-1.02	-0.23
	Significance of change	<.001	n.s.	n.s.	<.001	n.s.
	Significance of group differences		<.001		<.025	
"Deprivation" Scales						
Chance to Use One's Best *Skills*	Mean change*	1.89	0.27	-0.88	-1.84	-0.25
	Significance of change	<.001	n.s.	<.07	<.001	n.s.
	Significance of group differences		<.001		<.005	
How Much Time Filled with Things to Do: How *Busy*	Mean change*	1.24	-0.15	-1.07	-1.28	-0.60
	Significance of change	<.001	n.s.	<.01	<.001	<.025
	Significance of group differences		<.001		n.s.	
Chance to Talk with People Around You and *Enjoy* Yourself	Mean change*	-0.14	0.08	-1.13	0.64	-0.53
	Significance of change	n.s.	n.s.	<.01	<.05	n.s.
	Significance of group differences		n.s.		<.025	
Feelings of *Getting Ahead* in the World	Mean change*	0.98	0.02	-0.47	-1.30	0.14
	Significance of change	<.001	n.s.	n.s.	<.001	n.s.
	Significance of group differences		<.001		<.005	
Feelings of *Respect* from Others	Mean change*	0.33	-0.09	0.43	-0.97	0.31
	Significance of change	n.s.	n.s.	n.s.	<.005	n.s.
	Significance of group differences		n.s.		<.01	

Note: n.s. = not significant.

*Positive score indicates an increase in deprivation over time; negative score indicates a decrease. Values are in Z-scores ($M = 0$, $S.D. = 1$) based on normative data from controls.

brief and prolonged stress. Between first and second rounds, the men who go on to unemployment go up almost two standard deviations in Relative Economic Deprivation, while those who become promptly re-employed show essentially no change. Between round 2 and 3, men continuing in unemployment status show an additional slight rise, while those continuing to stabilize on their job show a slight decline; and the delayed re-employment group shows, as expected, a significant decline in economic deprivation, since for them this represents a transition from unemployment to re-employment. Interestingly, this decline isn't as large as the earlier increase between Phases 1 and 2.

In striking contrast to these results are the findings for the work role "deprivation" scale labelled "How Much Time Filled with Things to Do; How Busy." Here, there is a clearcut effect of brief stress only: men who go on to unemployment at Phase 2, increase their sense of idleness, of not having enough things to do to keep busy and to fill the time. But this feeling of deprivation does not last with continued unemployment, for between Phase 2 and 3, the "still unemployed" group comes down almost as much as the group experiencing delayed re-employment. Two other scales ("Chance to Use One's Best Skills," and "Feelings of Getting Ahead in the World") show the same patterns, but it is somewhat less striking.

Another variable, "Chance to Talk with People Around You and Enjoy Yourself," shows still another pattern, one which is also very interesting. Essentially, there is no impact of the briefer stress and the prolonged stress actually *benefits* those continuing to be unemployed and adversely affects those in the delayed re-employment group. This would suggest that at the minimum, lengthier unemployment does not reduce enjoyable social interactions and may provide an opportunity for increasing them.

Only one of the work role "deprivation" scales, "Feelings of Respect from Others," suggests an impact of the more prolonged stress: with continued unemployment, there is an increase in the sense of not being respected by others, in contrast to the perceived gain in respect among the delayed re-employment group.

Table 9 presents the relevant results for four physiological variables and four selected mental health indicators. As can be seen, all four physiological variables show a sensitivity to the briefer stress, but none show reliably different trends associated with the longer lasting stress; only diastolic blood pressure reveals a pattern of trends consistent with sensitivity to prolonged stress, but the differences are not significant. Of the four mental health indicators, three show the predicted sensitivity to the impact of briefer stress; interestingly, this is more due to a decline from an anticipation effect among the promptly re-employed than due to a rise among those going on to unemployment at Phase 2. In any case, all four indicators reveal a decline in the group which continues being unemployed (between round 2 and 3) and, therefore, none show the predicted sensitivity to more enduring stress. Of particular interest is the Psychophysiological Symptoms Scale, which comes closest to measuring the same content as the Langner scale (Langner, 1962), which up to now has been the most frequently used index of "psychiatric impairment" in mental health epidemiology studies. We can see that the only significant result with this scale is, unexpectedly, the decline in reported symptoms among the men who continue being unemployed between Phases 2 and 3.

Overall, the results in tables 8 and 9 suggest that these blue-collar workers did not maintain a state of arousal, distress, and sense of work role deprivation as long as the unemployment experience lasted; instead, they showed evidence of adaptation so that following an initial period of unemployment those continuing to remain unemployed could not be distinguished—in terms of changes on the many indicators—from those finding a new job. It appears that adaptation to the loss of work role among most middle-aged blue-collar workers does not take a long time, except for the economic aspects. Elsewhere (Kasl, 1979), we have noted the similarity of these results to the data on another loss of the work role, retirement, and suggested that perhaps the significant adaptations among many low skill blue-collar workers are those which take place earlier in their work career: coming to terms with the dull and monotonous job which they have and giving up any expectations that work per se will be a meaningful human activity.

Table 9
Changes in Physiological and Mental Health Indicators by Duration of Unemployment

| | | Amount of Change From | | | | |
| | | 1-Anticipation to | | 2-Unemployed to | | 2-Reemployed to |
Indicator	Measure	2-Unemployed	2-Reemployed	3-Still Unemployed	3-Delayed Reemployment	3-Stabilized Reemployment
Pulse Rate (beats/min.)	Mean change*	2.43	-2.22	-3.36	-0.97	-1.65
	Significance of change	<.05	<.05	<.05	n.s.	n.s.
	Significance of group differences		<.005		n.s.	
Diastolic Blood Pressure (mm Hg)	Mean change*	1.36	-3.07	1.36	-1.65	-0.22
	Significance of change	n.s.	<.005	n.s.	n.s.	n.s.
	Significance of group differences		<.01			
Serum Uric Acid (mg/100 ml)	Mean change*	0.09	-0.55	-0.37	-0.23	-0.01
	Significance of change	n.s.	<.001	n.s.	n.s.	n.s.
	Significance of group differences		<.001			
Serum Cholesterol (mg/100 ml)	Mean change*	9.24	-2.40	-6.21	-18.97	-2.63
	Significance of change	<.025	n.s.	n.s.	<.001	n.s.
	Significance of group differences		<.05			
Psycho-Physiological Symptoms (Z-scores)	Mean change*	-0.18	-0.30	-0.71	0.38	0.10
	Significance of change	n.s.	n.s.	<.05	n.s.	n.s.
	Significance of group differences		n.s.		<.05	
Depression (Z-scores)	Mean change*	0.30	-0.43	-0.39	-0.09	0.07
	Significance of change	<.10	<.05	n.s.	n.s.	n.s.
	Significance of group differences		<.01			

Anxiety-Tension (Z-scores)					
Mean change*	0.19	-0.45	-0.51	-0.05	-0.14
Significance of change	n.s.	<.025	<.10	n.s.	n.s.
Significance of group differences		<.01		n.s.	
Suspicion (Z-scores)					
Mean change*	0.17	-0.55	-0.56	0.12	-0.04
Significance of change	n.s.	<.01	<.05	n.s.	n.s.
Significance of group differences		<.05		n.s.	

Note: n.s. = not significant.

*Positive score indicates an increase over time; negative score a decrease.

The final set of analyses, undertaken to further increase our confidence in the general conclusion of only a limited mental health impact of job loss, were those involving various correlates of Relative Economic Deprivation. The reasoning here is that this is the one scale which is consistently showing an impact of unemployment and that, therefore, it is the best candidate for exploring its role as a possible intervening variable, mediating between the objective experience of job loss and unemployment and the impact criteria of mental health and work role deprivation. The results of these additional analyses are summarized in the following four major points. As will be apparent, the general conclusion of a limited impact remains unchallenged by these additional results.

(1) Cross-sectional correlations (i.e., within a particular phase) between Relative Economic Deprivation and the various impact criteria revealed many significant correlations (mostly in the high .20's to mid .30's) among the terminees. However, since controls showed many correlations of similar magnitude, it is difficult to implicate specifically the job loss experience in such associations. For example, the correlation between Depression and the economic index is .27 for controls; for terminees, the highest intra-phase correlation is .34. This suggests no more than that the two measures share an underlying construct or a common response tendency.

(2) When the terminees did show some cross-sectional associations which were suggestively higher than the baseline correlations for the controls, this was almost never true for the occasions at which Relative Economic Deprivation showed elevated levels, i.e., Termination and 6 months. For example, Deprivation on Feelings of Respect from Others did not correlate with the economic index among controls (r = .02); the highest correlation for terminees was .37. However, this was obtained at 24 months when both variables have essentially returned to normal levels. Thus, it is again difficult to implicate the job loss experience per se.

(3) Analyses over time using the notions of lagged correlations in longitudinal data (e.g., Cook and Campbell, 1976) led just as

often to the inference that prior mental health causally influenced Relative Economic Deprivation as they did to a conclusion that the economic index causally influenced later mental health status. In short, the causal picture was completely indeterminate.

(4) Analysis of change scores between adjacent phases did not reveal a single significant correlation between change in Relative Economic Deprivation and change in any of the physiological, mental health, or work-role "deprivation" indices.

CONCLUDING COMMENTS

The findings which have been presented are based on complementary and overlapping analyses which yielded an internally consistent set of results: the mental health impact of job loss and unemployment appears to be a limited one, both in terms of its magnitude as well as in terms of its duration.

The primary purpose of this section is to discuss the likely limitations of these findings. One set of limitations inhere in the circumscribed nature of the phenomenon studied. For example, there is no question in our mind that the results obtained could have been different had we studied some group of men other than low skilled blue-collar workers. Stated differently, it is likely that our results are generalizable only to other groups who have a weak attachment to the work role and whose work is not a particularly meaningful activity. Secondly, we studied the closing of an entire plant where everybody (outside of a few in higher levels of management) lost their jobs. This may have created a situation in which self-blame was at a minimum. Moreover, since the entire cohort of the workers was going through the experience together, the potential for sharing of the experience among those affected and for the building of community support structures could have been greatly enhanced. All of these aspects of the phenomenon could have attenuated the mental health impact. Thirdly, the length of unemployment for most of the workers was relatively brief. It is possible that the unemployment experience has to exceed some threshold duration before an impact is manifest. Similarly, the financial impact of the job loss experience was

294

reduced by the existence of a severance payment, which the men received if they worked through the last day of the plant's existence. However, the men lost their seniority and their retirement benefits, which they would have then to build up on their new jobs. Thus, it is quite possible that there will be a delayed impact of the experience, beyond the two years of observation. Specifically, the men may have a more unstable work career in their late 50s and 60s, and a lower post-retirement income.

There were certain selection criteria which were applied to the employees of the closing plants which defined the eligibility for participation in the study: male, age 35-60, married in blue-collar jobs, three or more years of seniority. The rationale behind these criteria was to define a homogeneous subgroup, of a sufficiently large number, in which the impact of job loss might be particularly strong. For example, men are still presumed to be, in the dominant U. S. culture, the primary breadwinners in the family; hence, job loss in men should have more of an impact than in women. Similarly, being married implies the presence of financial responsibility for one or more other members of the family, which again may be presumed to increase the impact. Middle-aged status and many years of seniority imply a longer attachment to the work role and to a particular work-place, as well as a certain stabilization of a work career; here again, the plant closing may be thought of as being more disruptive. However, since the criteria were chosen mostly on an intuitive basis, the prudent viewpoint is to see them as defining the limits of generalizability of the findings, rather than as convincingly defining a particularly vulnerable subgroup. It could be, for example, that the increased responsibility due to being married is more than compensated for by the increased potential for social support. Similarly, an average of twenty years of seniority at a plant might just as well reflect boredom and readiness to move on, as a great attachment to the particular place of work.

Additional limitations to the generalizability or interpretability of the findings may inhere in the study design. As noted already, the study began at the point of anticipation of plant closing and ended two years after plant closing. A longer observation period prior to the event and following the event might have established better baseline data and better evidence regarding long term effects. The impact on other members of the family and other members of the community in which the plant closed down was not examined. The role of the general economic climate in the geographical areas of the plants could not be assessed. Some of these limitations, of course, simply reflect the limits of what can be reasonably accomplished within one study and the limits imposed on the investigator's access to the phenomenon (e.g., true baseline data prior to any anticipation). These limitations are not overcome as much by trying to design a better and larger study, but by carrying out a variety of studies in a variety of settings. It should also be noted that study designs usually represent implicit or explicit trade-offs. For example, studying a total plant closing enables the investigator to have a good hold on various possible self-selection biases, but prevents him from studying job loss in the context of strong self-blame.

We are quite aware that our results, indicating a limited mental health impact of job loss, do not particularly agree with the ecological analyses which have related cyclical fluctuations in the economy to some aggregated indicator of mental health status of a population, such as rate of psychiatric hospitalizations. This approach, made visible most recently by Brenner (1973, 1976), has itself had its ups and downs in popularity (e.g., Dayton, 1940; Henry and Short, 1954; Hovland and Sears, 1940; Hurlburt, 1932), ever since the pioneering analyses carried out by Durkheim. However, it would be unfortunate if this approach were to sink once more into disuse and obscurity (among non-economists) without it being first subjected to a thorough-going evaluation of its rationale, its methodology, and its complex data manipulations. Ideally, such an explication of the strengths and weaknesses of this approach should come from its most devoted practitioners. In the meantime, we shall have to be satisfied with the progress of other investigators who have subjected the approach to partial criticism and evaluation, and who have introduced useful innovations and variations on the basic approach (e.g., Catalano and Dooley, 1977; Dooley and Catalano, 1978a, and 1978b; Liem and Liem, 1978; Marshall and Funch, in press).

Discrepant, or partially discrepant, results are not a rare phenomenon in the social sciences. In such circumstances, progress, rather than stalemate and confusion, is still possible if the different methodologies are examined for their strengths and weaknesses. When discrepancies due to methodological short-comings are discarded, what may remain are genuine leads pointing toward new areas of inquiry and toward as yet ignored processes or risk factors. However, it is difficult to see how results from methodologically sound studies of individuals could be discarded because of discrepant results from ecological analyses. Rather, it would appear that results of methodologically sound ecological analyses could point toward as yet unexamined variables and processes in the studies of individuals.

REFERENCES

Aiken, M., Ferman, L.A., and Sheppard, H. L. *Economic Failure, Alienation, and Extremism.* Ann Arbor: University of Michigan Press, 1968.

Bakke, E. W. *The Unemployed Worker.* New Haven: Yale University Press, 1940(a).

Bakke, E. W. *The Unemployed Workers.* New Haven: Yale University Press, 1940(b).

Block, J. *The Challenge of Response Sets.* New York: Appleton, 1965.

Brenner, M. H. *Mental Illness and the Economy.* Cambridge: Harvard University Press, 1973.

Brenner, M. H. *Estimating the Social Costs of National Economic Policy: Implications for Mental and Physical Health, and Criminal Aggression.* Report to the Congressional Research Service of the Library of Congress and the Joint Economic Committee of Congress. Washington, DC: U.S. Government Printing Office, 1976.

Catalano, R. and Dooley, D. Economic predictors of depressed mood and stressful life events in a metropolitan community. *J. Health & Soc. Behavior,* 1977, 18, 292-307.

Cavan, R. S. and Ranck, K. H. *The Family and the Depression.* Chicago: University of Chicago Press, 1938.

Cobb, S. and Kasl, S. V. *Termination: The Consequences of Job Loss.* Cincinnati: DHEW (NIOSH) Publication No. 77-224, 1977.

Cook, T. D. and Campbell. D. T. The design and conduct of quasi-experiments and true experiments in field settings. In Dunnette, M.D. (ed.) *Handbook of Industrial and Organizational Psychology.* Chicago: Rand McNally, 1976, 223-326.

Crowne, D. P. and Marlowe, D. *The Approval Motive.* New York: Wiley, 1964.

Dayton, N. A. *New Facts on Mental Disorder.* Springfield, IL: C. C. Thomas, 1940.

Dohrenwend, B. S. and Dohrenwend, B. P. (eds.) *Stressful Life Events: Their Nature and Effects.* New York: Wiley, 1974.

Dooley, D. and Catalano, R. Economic change as a cause of behavioral disorder. Unpublished manuscript. Irvine, CA: Public Policy Research Organization, University of California, 1978(a).

Dooley, D. and Catalano, R. Economic, life, and disorder changes: Time series analyses. Unpublished manuscript. Irvine, CA: Public Policy Research Organization, University of California, 1978(b).

Ginzberg, E. *The Unemployed.* New York: Harper, 1943.

Gore, S. *The Influence of Social Support in Ameliorating the Consequences of Job Loss.* Philadelphia: University of Pennsylvania, unpublished doctoral dissertation, 1973.

Gough, H. *The California Psychological Inventory Manual.* Palo Alto: Consulting Psychologists Press, 1957.

Henry, A. F. and Short, J. F., Jr. *Suicide and Homicide: Some Economic, Sociological, and Psychological Aspects of Aggression.* Glencoe, IL: The Free Press, 1954.

Holmes, T. H. and Rahe, R. H. The social readjustment rating scale. *J. Psychosom. Res.,* 1967, 11, 213-218.

Hovland, C. I. and Sears, R. R. Minor studies of aggression: VI. Correlations of lynchings with economic indices. *J. Psychol.,* 1940, 9, 301-310.

Hulin, C. L. and Blood, M. R. Job enlargement, individual differences, and worker responses. *Psychol. Bulletin,* 1968, 69, 41-55.

Hurlburt, W. C. Prosperity, depression, and the suicide rate. *Amer. J. Sociol.,* 1932, 37, 714-719.

Kasl, S. V. Work and mental health. In O'Toole, J. (ed.) *Work and the Quality of Life.* Cambridge: The MIT Press, 1974, 171-196.

Kasl, S. V. The effects of the residential environment on health and behavior: A review. In Hinkle, L. E., Jr. and Loring, W. C. (eds.) *The Effect of the Man-Made Environment on Health and Behavior.* Atlanta: DHEW Publication No. (CDC) 77-8318, 1977, 65-127.

Kasl, S. V. Epidemiological contributions to the study of work stress. In Cooper, C. L. and Payne, R. (eds.) *Stress at Work.* Chichester: J. Wiley and Sons, 1978, 3-48.

Kasl, S. V. Changes in mental health status associated with job loss and retirement. In Barrett, J. E. (ed.) *Stress and Mental Disorders.* New York: Raven Press, 1979, 179-200.

Kasl, S. V., Cobb, S. and Thompson, W. D. Duration of stressful life situation and reactivity of psychological and physiological variables: can one extrapolate chronic changes from reactivity to acute stress? Paper presented at the annual meeting of the American Psychosomatic Society, Atlanta, March 1977.

Komarovsky, N. *The Unemployed Man and His Family—The Effect of Unemployment Upon the Status of the Man in Fifty-nine Families.* New York: Dryden Press, 1940.

Liem, R. and Liem, J. Social class and mental illness reconsidered: The role of economic stress and social support. *J. Health & Soc. Behav.,* 1978, 19, 139-156.

Marshall, J. R. and Funch, D. P. Mental illness and the economy: A critique. *J. Hlth. & Soc. Behavior,* in press.

Mechanic, D. and Volkart, E. H. Stress, illness behavior and the sick role, *Amer. Sociol. Rev.,* 1961, 26, 51-58.

Langner, T. S. A twenty-two item screening score of psychiatric symptoms indicating impairment. *J. Hlth. & Hum. Behavior,* 1962, 3, 269-276.

Slote, A. *Termination: The Closing at Baker Plant.* Indianapolis: Bobbs-Merrill, 1969.

Turner, A. N. and Lawrence, P. R. *Industrial Jobs and the Worker.* Cambridge: Harvard University Graduate School of Business Administration, 1968.

10
THE SOCIAL IMPACT
OF STRESS

PETER MARRIS

All civilizations have been founded upon deeply stressful relationships, where people have simultaneously feared and depended upon each other; where men have intimidated women and parents have put the fear of God into their children; where the weak have feared the strong and the strong have feared their rivals; where beyond the sea, the mountains, or the river the enemy is always forming. Human labor is so valuable that the temptation to commandeer it has always overwhelmed that other ideal of a golden age where people live together in harmony and affection. By force of arms, indebtedness, slavery or serfdom, by the capture of resources or the assertion of sexual or parental rights, people have been driven to work for others, to defend themselves by their own petty tyrannies, to mingle their mutual dependence and love with mutual fear. Societies unlike this are the curiosities of anthropologists: remote shy glimpses of human possibilities caught only in legends and utopian fantasies.

Nor has this fearful organization ever overcome the abiding natural dangers of famine and disease. Only in the last hundred years have doctors learned how to cure; only in the last two hundred have farmers discovered how to multiply their yield; and these achievements have been matched with new and even more terrifying fears of global devastation—fears so monstrous that we can still scarcely grasp their evident possibility.

The ways we deal with these fears profoundly influence the nature of a society, and this is what I mean here by the social impact of stress. Stress, as the outcome of experiences we share through the relationships we create, generates ideological and institutional reactions that, in their turn, change those relationships. I want to suggest that these reactions are not characteristically concerned with the causes of stress, but that they justify them, compensate for them, and ritually allay them; and so they not only inhibit those actions which might reduce the stresses of life, but glorify and entrench them instead. I believe this to be as true, here and now, as it has ever been.

In the first place, stress seems to be more bearable when we can accept its inevitability. Once suffering is given purpose, we can find reasons to live in spite of it. When people are severely bereaved, for instance, the meaninglessness of life without the dead at first plunges them into the despair of grief. Only as they can gradually reconstruct a sense of meaning in their lives does the psychic energy to go on living return, and that meaning has to incorporate loss, to enfold suffering in an unbreakable strand of purpose. It is, I think, this urgent need to find and hold to a reason for living that makes people so often accomplices in sustaining the ideology of their own exploitation. To wear oneself out in labor for others, to be rejected, is the will of God, service for the greatest good of all, the justice of democracy, the biological destiny of women or of inferior races; whatever the reasons, they invite resignation to hardships that have taken on meaning in some larger scheme. If you deny those reasons, you deny the fundamental need to suffer what you cannot change. It takes the courage of uncommon conviction to affirm a purpose for which the institutions, the texts and symbols, and the everyday expectations have not yet been created. Because it is an interpretation so unrealistic, so foolish and self-destructive, in the end it is destructive of others and therefore wicked. Hence, one aspect of stress is that it becomes incorporated into the social ideology as a necessary virtue: we believe it hardens, purifies, enobles us. Then, the culture begins to generate stressful situations, even where they are not necessary—as in education or play—to inculcate these virtues. A traditional English public school education, with its beatings, fagging, loneliness and emotional repression once represented, it seems to me, an endurance test for the creation of men who would bear, honorably, the "white man's burden," and so could claim the moral right to demand suffering of others.

But stress also generates psychological withdrawal. We imagine ourselves, once we have passed through this life, reborn into immortal happiness; or we dismiss misery as mere appearance, irrelevant to the inner core of being. In his essay on contemporary India, *A Wounded Civilization,* V. S. Naipaul suggests the influence of both these defenses on the impoverishment of Indian social thought.

Men had retreated to their last impregnable defenses: their knowledge of who they were, their caste, their *karma,* their unshakable place in the scheme of things; and this knowledge was like their knowledge of the seasons. Rituals marked the passage of each day; rituals marked every stage of a man's life. Life itself had been turned to ritual; and everything beyond this complete and sanctified world—where fulfillment came so easily to a man or to a woman—was vain and phantasmal.

Kingdoms, empires, projects . . . they had come and gone. The monuments of ambition and restlessness littered the land, so many of them abandoned or destroyed, so many unfinished, the work of dynasties suddenly supplanted. India taught the vanity of all action, . . .

Only India, with its great past, its civilization, its philosophy, and its almost holy poverty, offered this truth; India *was* the truth. So to Indians, India could detach itself from the rest of the world. The world could be divided into India and non-India. And India, for all its surface terrors, could be proclaimed, without disingenuousness or cruelty, as perfect.[1]

The American derivatives of this quietism declare: it's all right, anything can be beautiful, no one need feel guilt because there is

1. V. S. Naipaul, *India: A Wounded Civilization* (New York: Vintage, 1978), p. 26.

nothing to be guilty of. Reality is not an independent creation but uncovers its many faces to the attuned. Without the responsibility for its relief, stress itself belongs with the illusion of mere appearance.

Thirdly, we exorcise stress with rituals: offering sacrifices, concocting magic, acting for the sake of action, even when we no longer believe in the logic that once, perhaps, gave these rituals a sufficient purpose. If one reaction to stress is passive acceptance, its complement is a compulsion to be doing something to combat it: to propitiate danger with burnt offerings, prayers, scapegoats, research, or conferences. And then, to challenge the usefulness of all this activity becomes subversive.

Each of these reactions represents, I believe, a deeply embedded human response to stress. Apathy, restlessness, the search for an escape into consoling states of being, and the need for ritual are all apparent in the behavior of the bereaved; they seem to be, indeed, necessary to the working out of grief. I suspect we will always look for such defenses to palliate anxiety. But the inevitability of suffering is a personal experience. When these defenses are projected into the ideology, institutions, and culture of society their effect is to justify, make sense of, or absolve suffering in a context where it becomes no longer inevitable but contrived by the collective outcome of human actions. And so these impulses inhibit the will, the conceptions, and the actions which might attack the causes of suffering.

Many aspects of modern American society offer characteristic responses to stress: the glorification of competitiveness, as the necessary and therefore admirable requisite of prosperity; of masculine aggression and feminine self-sacrifice, as the natural and therefore mature expressions of sexuality; the relentless exploitation of anxiety by advertisers who offer patently irrelevant goods to palliate our fears of being unloved, dishonored, unsuccessful; the new doctrines of narcissistic nonattachment, variously blended of quietism, meditation, psychotherapy and hype; and perhaps above all, the ideal of the American home—haven, as Christopher Lasch puts it, in a heartless world.

It was Catherine Beecher who, with the publication of *The American Woman's Home,* in 1869, most explicitly defined the home as at once the engine of capitalist society and a retreat from its harshness.[2] As Dolores Hayden writes, Catherine Beecher saw the home as "a Christian 'commonwealth,' where the woman is the 'minister of the home.' As head of the 'home church of Jesus Christ,' she can inculcate 10 to 12 offspring with the idea of 'work and self-sacrifice for the public good' and 'living for others more than for self.' Exaggerated gender differences reinforce the notion of a worldly, competent male needing the spiritual presence of an other worldly, domestic female. The woman establishing herself as minister of Salvation in the home finds her parish, her office, and her life identically bounded."[3] Catherine Beecher described this ambience as "the true Protestant system . . . the Heaven-devised plan of the family state." Within the shell of a Gothic cottage, neat, unpretentious and functionally efficient, she conceived a way of life that at once inculcates a rationalization of and submission to all the stresses of industrial society, provides endless busy work to allay its anxieties, and insulates the home as a spiritual retreat against the inevitably aggressive, cruel world of men. She even recommended, with a frankness few advertisers would dare to copy, insatiable consumption: "The use of superfluities, therefore, to a certain extent, is as indispensable to promote industry, virtue and religion as any direct giving of money or time."

This is the home, stripped of its overtly Christian symbolism, we still know so well: with its mortgage we cannot really afford; its quiet neighborhood no longer altogether safe; its endless gadgets and playthings we do not need; its harassed, rarely present father, frustrated, isolated mother, and bored, spiritually undernourished children, who wonder what it is all for. Yet though a teenage daughter may be pregnant, a son taking drugs, though there's a gun in the desk and another in the glove box of the car, and the

2. Dolores Hayden, "Catherine Beecher and the Politics of Housework" in Susana Torre, ed. *Women in American Architecture* (New York: Watson-Guptil, 1977).

3. Catherine Beecher, *The American Woman's Home* (1869) and *A Treatise on Domestic Economy* (1841), quoted in Dolores Hayden above.

parents may be heading towards their second divorces, the myth that somehow home could be a tranquil, loving reward, a final affirmation after all the struggles and humiliations, remains very powerful. And so, of course, sometimes it is—often enough to make the hope seem possible to realize. But home remains at best a relief from a compensation for, and a justification of, a profoundly stressful structure of relationships it makes no attempt to change. The inequalities of race and class and sex are compounded by the residential patterns it imposes, harnessing people to the competitive grind by its relentless costs and so itself becoming infected and corrupted by the societal strains it seeks to escape.

But there is another aspect to American ideology, and that is a secular, pragmatic refusal to accept the necessity of suffering. No other people seem so unreconciled to ill health, unhappiness, even mortality itself. Only an American president would, I think, have announced that a modest appropriation designed to help some poor communities would constitute a war to eradicate poverty in the United States, as if to admit that no prompt, wholesale solution was at hand would be an unacceptable confession of failure. The very idea of discussing stress—not this stress or that, but stress as any and every manifestation of the pain and anxiety of life—seems to me to represent a readiness to challenge the need for suffering that is peculiarly American. Most societies have in the past turned to religion to justify and compensate for the hardships of living; out of American Protestantism evolved a worldly individualism uniquely dedicated to the ideal that happiness was a realizable pursuit for all. In this sense, the arrival of a seriously and traditionally religious president reintroduces into American politics a reactionary spirit of resignation.

Yet this positivism is still largely modern magic: a methodical, solemn ritual for curing evils which it cannot, from the nature of its assumptions, effectively change. Its structure of thought prevents positivism from acknowledging the nature of stress. Because it denies the need for suffering, it is impatient with grief, scarcely understanding it or assigning a place to it, and so does not reach its underlying cause. Let me try to explain, very briefly, what I think that cause is.

We experience stress, I suggest, when we lose confidence in our ability to handle relationships, either with the physical world or with each other. This loss of confidence arises from an inability to control, a breakdown of expectations, a sense of being at the mercy of unpredictable and indomitable forces, from complexities and contradictions we cannot master. Hence we continually try to secure, as best we can, predictable and controllable relationships; and those who have more power will tend, characteristically, to secure the predictability of the relationships that benefit them at the expense of those who have less power.

Yet to secure the predictability of relationships involves much more than a simple prediction of events; it involves an ability to classify events, each of which is in some sense unique, into regularly related sets, so that we can react to them and manipulate them purposfully. It requires a structure designed to represent and reproduce a conception of reality. In part, this structure may be highly generalizable, as common language, a shared religion and science, custom and convention. But, in part too it is unique to each individual, because it has been organized around the specific purposes and relationships that each man and woman has grown into. That is, many of our most crucial purposes are not generalizable but are attached to unique, irreplaceable circumstances. We become bonded to each other as parent and child, as lovers; we come to love a place, become (as we say) wedded to a particular ambition. And the specific meaning of our lives is embedded in these crucial relationships. Whenever we cannot create or sustain this meaning, either because the relationships lose their reliability or because the purposes that have organized its structure disintegrate, we undergo stress. So, for instance, an unfamiliar society becomes stressful because we do not understand how it works; disappointment is stressful because it robs us of an expectation around which we had organized our world; the loss of someone to whom we are intimately attached is deeply stressful because it disrupts both relationship and purpose, so that life seems at once unintelligible and aimless.

Correspondingly, we cannot change or venture without stress. Only when we experience incompetence, embarrassment and anxiety are we learning; but these situations can be tolerable when we choose them on our own terms and can contain them. As we grow up, we try to consolidate a meaning to our lives in thought and feeling and the relationships that embody them, secure against fundamental disruption. But the search for inviolable meaning leads in partly contradictory directions. We are impelled to protect the bonds of affection through which our capacity to love and care becomes realized, since without them nothing would matter anymore. Yet we also seek to abstract and generalize our principles of understanding so that they can encompass whatever may happen, since then we would never be at a loss. What we call wisdom is, I think, essentially an awareness of this interplay of thought and feeling in the structure of our lives, a sense of how general principles become realized in emotional attachments, and how these attachments in turn inform the purposes of generalization; of how each life is at once unique and organized by universal truths.

I am suggesting, then, that stress arises from loss of confidence in our ability to handle our circumstances—whether out of the fear that crucial resources are failing, that we are at the mercy of capricious or malign forces, that those we love may be taken from us, or that we cannot master what we need to learn. Our confidence rests on an organization of reality into manageable relationships, which is as much a synthesis of our purposes and attachments as a representation of the principles on which we operate. So to avoid stress we must reach an understanding at once universal enough to make sense of any event we are likely to encounter, and yet rooted in those specific relationships from which meaningful purposes arise. And those needs conflict. Once we commit ourselves we are vulnerable; the circumstances in which life will have a vital and confident meaning become particularized. But systematic thought that hopes to embrace all understanding cannot do more than make sense of abstractions; we cannot live by it. So we try, with more or less success, to balance the rational, instrumental, and emotionally committed aspects of meaning. We try to love, but not blindly.

The dominant structure of thought, and therefore of organization, represented by American positivism seems to frustrate that interplay. Its science manipulates generalizable orders of relationship, abstracting form from content in more and more inclusive systems, in search of an ultimately indomitable, universal competence. It operates by reducing content to undifferentiated elements which can then be recombined to stand for any complex actual events whatever, according to the formal properties of the relationships abstracted from it. Physical science is only the most sophisticated achievement in our pursuit of an invulnerable ordering of reality. In every aspect of experience—in economic and political relationships, the psychology of human behavior, in social organization—we look for the elements of a system that in the end will merge with every other in a completed cosmology. Accordingly, unique experiences, like learning something, loving someone, making something, are reduced to the universal elements from which they can be compounded.

The power of this mode of understanding stems from the most basic principles of human learning. But it does not by itself create meaning, unless it is informed by that other bonding of purpose to specific attachments. Whenever this method of understanding is applied in social action, it requires that any event be treated as equivalent to any other event in its class. The more scientific social intervention seeks to be, the more it treats behavior and satisfactions as interchangeable. So, for instance, scientific management tries to break work down into discrete processes that can be accomplished indifferently by any one of a class of workers; rational administration conceptualizes relationships as a formal interaction of roles, where people are substitutable; comprehensive policy analysis reduces actual choice to a calculation of costs and benefits. Even when this science recognizes that people will not willingly be regimented as undifferentiated units, its response is simply to incorporate another generalizable satisfaction and to mass produce personalized products, management techniques, and sympathetic environments. A science fiction story by Frederick Pohl recounts the frustrations of a patient locked in contest with his computer

310

therapist, whose agreeable, adaptable appearance of humanity only makes the layers of scientific impersonality more impenetrable.[4]

This positivism leads toward a society dominated by an operating logic where to make use of its theoretical grasp, people must be interchangeable. If it makes sense to close a factory here, open another there, to shift resources from region to region or nation to nation, human labor must be substitutable from one place to another: workers must either move or be replaced. If inflation or recession is to be regulated in accordance with monetary theory, people must be reduced to units of consumption whose aggregate behavior can be forecast. If someone has suffered a loss, the solution is to find a replacement. Any generalizable system that operates so as to maximize benefits presupposes that outcomes can be expressed in the sum of equivalent units, whether of profit or economic growth or welfare.

This preoccupation with aggregate results discounts the significance of personal attachments. Our distress at change is blamed on our inability to adapt, not on the changes themselves. We ought to accept whatever is more profitable, efficient or productive, however it upsets our lives. Grief is sickness; love of the familiar, ignorance. We should retrain, relocate, remain flexible. Such an ideology of responsiveness to change is persuasive, because it advocates qualities valuable in individual learning. But as a societal attitude, it implies that people should continually adapt to the logic of management, that large-scale, aggregate problem-solving must always set the conditions of any response. Such an ideology clearly benefits the greatest concentrations of economic and political power, since to realize that power, to manage huge and complex enterprises successfully, a systematic reduction of reality to relatively simple, aggregable elements is crucial. Correspondingly, the more sophisticated the techniques and theories of management, the wider becomes the possible scope of concentrated control.

4. Frederik Pohl, *Gateway* (New York: Ballantine, 1977).

The more exclusively this whole conceptual structure of operation comes to predominate, the more it creates stress. It uproots people from the context in which their lives have meaning by its indifference to the specific nature of attachment. Personal relationships become literally unintelligible. They can only be understood systematically as relationships of exchange, in which the need for sex, companionship, nurturing, or support becomes an object of psychic barter: and as such, its fulfillment would still leave us deeply lonely. The true nature of our needs remains unprotected in the scheme of adaptation. At the same time, the concentrations of power that derive from and exploit the possibilities of science create enormous inequalities of control: and, as I suggested earlier, these inequalities will be reflected in vulnerability to uncertainty. The powerful, in managing relationships so as to secure for themselves the most highly predictable environment they can, inevitably make that environment less predictable for the weaker. Power is, above all, the ability to transfer the burden of risk to others.

Thus positivism, seemingly so intolerant of suffering, becomes distorted into a system of control that imposes, very unequally, a highly stressful ideology of adaptation. Since it cannot take into account those conditions that would create and sustain personal goals, it constantly undermines them. As the concentrations of economic power grow, so does the scale of social maladjustment—devasted city neighborhoods, new cities and regions overwhelmed by ephemeral booms as their resources are exploited, rising unemployment, inflation, and taxes. The responses to that lack of adaptation become increasingly ruthless, as policy analysts begin to talk not only of how to help, but whom: which of the wounded shall be left to die?

In reaction, people are seeking to reassert control over their circumstances by grabbing defensively at whatever seems to protect them against these remote, uncontrollable forces. Cities enact moratoria on growth, refusing to release sewer hookups or building permits; human barricades gather to guard familiar landmarks from the bulldozers; highways stop before stiffening neighborhood resistance. And they are in revolt against taxes.

Proposition 13 went before the voters in California—a simple-minded measure to roll back property taxes and hold them, by law, to a fixed and modest level. I can understand why it won: that last sanctuary of security, owning one's own home, carried a constantly doubling burden of taxation that threatened to price it beyond reach. And the symbolic appeal of this revolt against government seemed to draw even renters into support, though they had nothing to gain and something to lose by it.[5]

Such reactions are the counterpart of impersonal rationalism—simplistic, emotional, and no more capable of affecting the underlying causes of stress. I doubt very much whether homeowners will, as a whole, benefit from Proposition 13: they will pay the same taxes somehow, or if they do not, they will confront other stresses such as impoverished schools and services. The gesture is, too, just as arbitrary in the hardships it imposes. Suddenly, unpredictably, the careers of teachers and social workers, as well as the services on which many depend, are threatened. Similarly, the moratorium on sewer hookups in Bolinas did not prevent growth or preserve the quality of a way of life; it created new patterns of illegal building, a beleagered psychology, and a fantasy of village life borrowed from the very people it had expropriated. These defenses are characteristically selfish, crude, and intemperate. They resemble the obstinate negations of people who feel at bottom helpless, and can only cling desperately to the defensive strategies within their grasp. So an overweaning positivism provokes a correspondingly distorted, popular conservatism.

I have argued that societies characteristically deal with stress by justifying its necessity, as America glorifies the competitive struggle; by psychological withdrawal and compensatory fantasies, as America idealizes the suburban family home; and by creating a cosmology capable, in principle, of grasping reality as a whole—a universal religion to provide both explanation and

---

5. The information about Proposition 13 comes from *The Los Angeles Times,* May 27th, and about Bolinas from David Dubbinch (research in progress). I discuss the relationships between grief and loss of meaning much more fully in my *Loss and Change* (New York: Anchor Books, 1975).

response. Ours, I suggest, is a religion of scientific adaptation. The social impact of stress, in its largest sense, is the consequence of these ideological strategies. Though they make stress more manageable, they also compound it, because they inform, justify, and promote the ways of thinking, the institutions, and regulative operations of a structure of social relationships that is inherently stressful.

Yet there are traditions of thought, from the myth of a lost Eden to communism, which constantly return, in faith or nostalgia, to the roots of stress in human organization. Raymond Williams, in *The Country and the City* traces pastoral lament for a once whole and happy way of life from contemporary writing to the poetry of ancient Greece.[6] I think that as idealists we are attracted to these traditions, and as intellectuals, suspicious of their naivete—confused by a social science that tries to incorporate both radicalism and social engineering.

Of all the contemporary American endeavors to tackle the roots of stress, I think the women's movement comes closest to a practical radicalism, as much because of, as in spite of the ambiguities it contains. It recognizes that the fundamental causes of stress lie in uncertainty of meaning—the contradictions which beset a woman's search for identity and purpose and the deeply embedded structure of relationships that imposes, exploits, rationalizes, and yet undermines them. But it also recognizes that the restructuring of these relationships has to come about in the context of intimate personal relationships, in the everyday language of exchanges between men and women; without that affirmative action, or promotion of women executives merely draws a few women into complicity with the masculine pattern of competitive dominance and exploitation. Hence the movement has to struggle to change the distribution of opportunities between the sexes, while remaining profoundly critical of what those opportunities stand for. To sustain this ambivalence, it has created a network of support, of sympathy, and learning, that tries to interrelate many different levels of action and awareness. In this

---

6. Raymond Williams, *The Country and the City* (New York: Oxford University Press, 1975).

sense, it understands the interplay between the need for conceptual organization and the need to interpret the meaning of those conceptions in the everyday circumstances of individual lives with a greater sensitivity and a fuller understanding of the ambiguities inherent in all change than other social movements.

It seems to me that the women's movement is creative, where so many other reactions are merely defensive, theoretical, or withdrawn, and we can learn from it what questions to ask. What are the roots of stress in human relationships? How are they rationalized and perpetuated? How can people use a radical ideal in circumstances where it can be realized only through a long process of understanding and change? How can they live with the practicable actions that fall short of their ideal, without becoming either co-opted or isolated? How do they find the courage and support to exchange resignation to stress for the stress of rejecting a structure they cannot at once change? I hesitate to call these questions for research; that sounds too uninvolved, too detached from the feelings and attachments which alone give intellectual endeavors themselves any meaning. But they are, I think, the crucial questions, and they need to be understood through the evidence of empirical enquiry.

11
DISCUSSION

JAMES S. HOUSE

Ivar Berg has told us that he advises students to avoid problems in which neither the independent nor dependent variables are clearly defined. A certain lack of clarity in either the independent or the dependent variables can be tolerated, but not in both. This is good advice; yet if we had all been students of Ivar's we would not be here today, because the problem of the economy and mental health plainly involves loosely conceived independent and dependent variables. And unfortunately, to bring in the concept of stress does little to alleviate that problem and perhaps only makes it worse. The papers of Dr. Curtis, Stan Kasl, and Peter Marris illustrate both the promise and the problems that characterize the issues with which we are dealing, and help to explain why we continue to work on these issues despite their often difficult and even frustrating nature. I hope to show that these three very different papers have three common concerns or themes. My comments will not so much seek to present new points as to emphasize concerns already discussed here.

First, as a set, the papers exemplify, perhaps as strongly as one could wish, the multidisciplinary and multilevel nature of the problem at hand. Dr. Curtis, a psychophysiologically oriented physician, directs our attention to the ways in which an individual responds to stimuli behaviorally, psychologically, and physiologically, the specificity versus the generality of the effects of such responses across stimuli, across individuals, and across different types of responses. Stan Kasl takes the sociopsychological perspective that has been most familiar to us in this conference and presents an excellent and innovative longitudinal study of how the immediate social environments of individuals—their work situation, family and community setting—affect their physical and mental health. Finally, Peter Marris presents an important sociological and anthropological perspective on how social institutions develop in response to the ubiquitous stresses of human life and in turn influence the ways that people experience and deal with these stresses.

Thus, these papers cover a wide range from the societal down to the hormonal and so illuminate, if not the range of each of our individual concerns, at least the range of our collective preoccupations. This multidisciplinary, multilevel nature of the field is an element that attracts researchers to this area, although it also contributes to its difficulty as an area of concentration.

Bob Kahn attempts to develop linkages between the various levels, particularly between macro-economic phenomena and individual well-being. In his words, the crucial issue is "what's in the [black] box" that converts events at the macro-economic level into effects on individual well-being. His comments, and the accompanying papers and discussion in general, deal with the immediate social situation of individuals, e.g., role relations, social supports, or personal economic deprivations. As a social psychologist myself, I believe we are much in need of such formulations.

It is well to recognize, however, that there are really multiple black boxes here. There is at least a partial black box in our conceptions of how social and psychological stimuli are translated into physiological reactions. Dr. Curtis ably reviews the limits of our knowledge in this area. And, as a number of comments indicated, we need to elaborate the phenomena and linkages at the macro end of the scale, an endeavor of value both scientifically and as a means to develop a knowledge base that will be useful in planning policy interventions at the various levels of social organizations.

This will entail further elaboration of the nature of the "economy," as Eliot Sclar has suggested. This can best be done by economists and macro-sociologists, but clearly the economy encompasses a great deal more than unemployment rates, which indeed (as Sally Bould has suggested) may not be the most significant aspect of the economy. The economy involves levels of personal income and characteristics of the occupational structure, of particular jobs, and of the labor market, as well as other phenomena. I am concerned that there may be other variables closely related to unemployment rates (e.g., levels of personal income) that may correlate just as strongly—or more strongly—with the health consequences that Harvey Brenner has so dramatically linked with unemployment. The seeming contradiction between Brenner's aggregate analysis of the effects of unemployment and those of Stan Kasl and Sidney Cobb at the individual level clearly indicate a need to consider a wide range of the various aspects of the economy. We need to consider, and not just as control variables, other social institutions such as union formation and activity, community integration, or government labor or health policies, which may play roles in the effect of the economy on health and/or on how individuals react to the economy. Elaborating our conception of the economy will also involve making a greater differentiation between levels of the economy, such as national versus state versus local. The nature of the labor market at any given time may be very different at different levels or across different units (e.g., states) at the same level.

The second common theme of these papers is their focus on stress, clearly one of the most plausible mechanisms for the understanding of the impact of macro-economic forces on individual mental health. A variety of stress hypotheses has been implicit in most of our discussions. But we must recognize that "stress" is not a unitary explanatory concept and is only one of several possible factors that link the economy to health. Consider the effects of an increase in the unemployment rate in a metropolitan area, resulting in job loss for a number of individuals; certainly the loss of a job will have a variety of consequences. Some of them involve what we define as stress—e.g., the loss of meaningful work, or of self-esteem, or of social ties. However, job loss may have other consequences, such as the loss of income and of those fringe benefits that had previously sustained good nutrition and ensured good medical care, considerations that can be deleterious to health regardless of the level of stress experienced. Further, as Catalano and Dooley suggest, economic change can alter or modify the social processes by which persons become identified as mental health cases, thus yielding apparent changes in mental health that may have nothing to do with the effects of unemployment on individuals or households.

In sum, we need careful evaluation of a wide range of alternative explanations of exactly how the macro-economy does affect health. Understanding what is "in the box," that is, which explanation is correct, is a critical factor in policy interventions (other than those affecting the macro-economy itself) that seek to alleviate the harmful impacts of economic changes on mental health. If loss of meaningful work or self-esteem is the major consequence of unemployment, the policy implications are quite different from those that emerge if the problem is, say, loss of income and medical benefits. Various "stress" hypotheses are among those, although they are not the only ones, that could be considered and evaluated. Furthermore, we must specify the type of stress that becomes problematic for particular workers.

Finally, let me note that these three papers all underline, though in different ways, the validity of looking at the health effect of stress—and probably of the economy more generally—as a process occurring *over time.* Only in this way can we clearly document the causal impact of the economy on health, whether through stress or other mechanisms, and gain some comprehension of how individuals adapt to stress. Curtis has approached these issues experimentally, Kasl has utilized a longitudinal field study, and Marris has taken an historical and observational approach. But all three of them study stress as a process occurring over time.

The three themes common to the three papers point to a number of directions that should broaden our research in terms of social time and space. First, we need more research that will examine multiple levels and aspects of the phenomena of economy and health. For example, we must bridge the gap between studies of individual-level versus aggregate data and bring together in the *same* studies data on individuals and on different levels and aspects of the social environments to which they are exposed. We need to look at how individual health varies as a function both of employment status and of the unemployment rates in the localities, states, and regions in which the workers live. We should measure the availability of social support as it is perceived by individuals and as it is manifested in their objective social networks and in the integration of their neighborhoods and communities. Such efforts require social psychologists to develop a more macro-orientation, while requiring of economists and macro-sociologists a more micro-orientation.

Second, we need more examination of data over time at the individual as well as at the aggregate level. If we are to firmly establish the impact of the economy on health, we must achieve *at the level of individuals* the time ordering of variables that is characteristic of aggregate time series data. A major deficiency in our knowledge of the economy and health, and more generally of stress and health, is the lack of solid longitudinal data. Such data are challenging and expensive to collect and to analyze. But without them, we are condemned to the indeterminacy that presently prevails, for example, in our understanding of the relationship between socioeconomic status and mental health.

One useful way to obtain such longitudinal data would be to assess more fully the health consequences of naturally occurring social change. Social experiments have been carried out in respect to the negative income tax, social and technological redesign of jobs and organizations, and employment training and placement. Why not assess the health consequences of such experiments along with their other economic and social consequences? Finally, as Peter Marris suggests, we should experiment with reducing social and economic stress in order to improve health, and carefully evaluate the results.

Third, as Bob Kahn points out, and as I have already indicated, a central goal of both interdisciplinary or multilevel research and longitudinal research should be to specify those linkages or mechanisms "in the box" that link the economy and other aspects of the social environment to health.

In conclusion, we need not only more research of the sort we have been doing, but also research of the kind we have largely not been doing. This will not be an easy task. We are all more comfortable dealing with concepts and data at the level typically employed in our disciplines, but the question we wish to answer cuts across these levels and disciplines. We do not have wide experience or great expertise in analyzing data on the same individuals at several points in time, though we are learning. Nevertheless we must begin to move in these unfamiliar directions, with due regard for our limited competence, if we are to achieve the advances in socially useful knowledge that may accrue from them.

12
DOES ECONOMIC CHANGE PROVOKE OR UNCOVER BEHAVIORAL DISORDER? A PRELIMINARY TEST

RALPH CATALANO
DAVID DOOLEY

ABSTRACT

Recent analyses (Brenner, 1969, 1969a, 1976; Marshall and Funch, 1979; Sclar and Hoffman, 1978) of annual archival data suggest that admission to mental hospitals is significantly associated with prior macroeconomic changes. These findings have been criticized (Dooley and Catalano, 1977) on several grounds, the most important of which is failure to identify intervening variables. Subsequent research (Catalano and Dooley, 1977; Dooley and Catalano, 1978a) has suggested that two intervening variables, stress in day-to-day life and mental depression, vary with economic change. The research has not, however, been designed to discriminate between two competing hypotheses: i.e., whether economic change serves to uncover existing untreated cases or to provoke symptoms in persons previously normal. This paper, based on data collected in one metropolitan community during the early 1970s, describes a method that seeks to determine which hypothesis will better explain the relationship between economic change and mental hospitalization. Limitations inherent in the available data emphasize the need for further replication, but the implications of the preliminary findings, for mental health service delivery and for primary prevention, are examined here.*

*The order of authorship was determined by coin flip. The research was supported by National Institute of Mental Health Grant MH-28934-10A1.

The authors wish to thank Mary Keebler of the Department of Mental Health of the State of Missouri, Lois Tetrick of the Western Missouri Mental Health Center of Kansas City, Deidre Klassen of the Greater Kansas City Mental Health Foundation, and Lori Radloff and Don Rae of the National Institute of Mental Health for their patience and assistance in helping us obtain the case opening data employed in this analysis. We also thank the Center for Epidemiologic Studies, Division of Biometry and Epidemiology of the National Institute of Mental Health for earlier assistance in providing the survey time series used in this secondary analysis. Appreciation is also expressed to Sig Fidkye and Norm Jacobson for their computational work.

321

Scientific notice of the impact of economic change on human well-being dates back at least to the late 19th Century (Durkheim, 1897). Empirical analyses of relationships between macroeconomic variables and health and behavioral problems appear regularly, although not frequently, in the literature (see Dooley and Catalano, in press, for a comprehensive overview of research in this area). By far the most exhaustive study has been made by M. H. Brenner (1969, 1973), who measured the influence of economic conditions on mental hospital admissions in New York State from 1913 to 1967.

Brenner's data and methods have been described in detail elsewhere (Dooley and Catalano, 1977; Catalano and Dooley, 1977; Eyer, 1977). He found that, controlling for long term and cyclic trends, first admissions to mental hospitals rose as New York State's economic well-being declined, and vice versa. The relationship was strongest when the dependent variable "lagged" one or two years behind the economic variable. This relationship was found to be reversed for persons of less than grammar school education, as well as for women with high school educations, and for the elderly. Brenner's explanation here was that economic downturns provoke a behavioral pathology that leads to increased confinement in institutions. The minority who do not react in this way experience, according to him, relative deprivation when the economy expands and relative improvement when it shrinks.

Catalano and Dooley (1977) have noted that while Brenner adopts a "provocation" explanation, his findings do not exclude a rival "uncovering" hypothesis, which assumes that the incidence of behavioral disorder is random or is constant over time, and that economic change can influence institutionalization through such factors as reduced tolerance in the home or a lessened ability to care for the behaviorally disordered there.

Catalano and Dooley (1977) then tested the hypothesis that monthly economic changes in a metropolitan area would prove to be significantly related to variations in the amount of stress and depression reported by representative samples of the population. Using data collected in an earlier longitudinal survey of the municipal population in Kansas City, Missouri (Roth and Locke,

1973), they found that life events were positively related to measures of previous absolute (as opposed to algebraic or directional) change in the size and structure of the metropolitan economy. Mood was significantly related to previous change in directional (e.g., unemployment) measures of economic conditions. Catalano and Dooley described their findings as consistent with Brenner's provocation hypothesis, but noted that this did not rule out uncovering.

Provocation vs. Uncovering

The social-psychological mechanisms implicit in the concepts of provocation and uncovering are not fully understood. Emerging scholarship on such topics as the sick role (e.g., Mechanic, 1977; Segall, 1976), social support (e.g., Cobb, 1976; Kaplan, Cassel, and Gore, 1977), and life change and stress (e.g., Dohrenwend and Dohrenwend, 1974; Rabkin and Streuning, 1976) suggests a tentative differentiation of the two models. The most elaborate portrayal of provocation can be found in the literature dealing with life events and stress. Despite methodological difficulties, the life-event literature implies that major or frequent life changes, particularly undesirable ones, can lead to psychological disequilibrium. While some individuals adapt to or cope with their life changes, others report feelings of distress which may take the form of maladaptation to reality, health problems, or psychological difficulties. Individuals who have little in the way of social support, psychological stability, or other coping resources are of course most vulnerable to heightened life change (e.g., Cobb and Kasl, 1977; de Araujo, Van Arsdel, Holmes and Dudley, 1973; Myers, Lindenthal and Pepper, 1975; Nuckolls, Cassel, and Kaplan, 1972). Turbulence in the community owing, for example, to economic change, tends to produce changes in the lives of the population (Catalano, 1979). Highly vulnerable individuals whose life changes are most extreme are the most apt to suffer adverse psychological symptoms, which in turn makes it more probable that they will appear as cases in the mental health system.

Unlike provocation, the uncovering explanation rests on the sociological notion of role (Sarbin, 1969; Scheff, 1966).

Epidemiological surveys (e.g., Srole, Langner, Michael, Opler, and Rennie, 1962) repeatedly reveal numbers of untreated individuals who have psychological symptom levels high enough to warrant psychotherapy. Presumably these persons fill niches or roles for which their diminished level of functioning is adequate, even if only marginally so. Turbulence in the socioeconomic system presumably jars not only individuals, but also the interpersonal relations that define social roles. As a consequence, borderline individuals may find that changes in the niches they occupy will bring them to the attention of the mental health system. Indeed, they may seek care because of perceptions altered by environmental changes. That is, existing symptoms are relabeled "abnormal." Family, friends, or neighbors may no longer be able to meet the social or material needs of the individual because of heightened costs of adaptation imposed on them by socioeconomic changes. Possibly because of a reduction in the insulation of the borderline individual, his usual coping efforts may, for the first time, catch the attention of public service gatekeepers such as the police, mental health outreach workers, or social welfare agents.

Since uncovering and provocation are both plausible explanations for Brenner's findings and are not mutually exclusive, why is it important to choose between them? The practical answer is that the two call for quite different economic policies and mental health strategies. If either one is the dominant link between economic change and treated disorder, it is crucial that it be identified before scarce intervention resources are committed.

The provocation explanation suggests that to moderate economic change, perhaps particularly undesirable change, would serve as a primary prevention of mental disorder; but such a policy would, by definition, have no impact on total disorder (treated plus untreated) in the case of uncovering. Indeed, economic change may be desirable to the extent that it locates mental cases among the symptomatic. An appropriate policy for the uncovering case might be the study and improvement of secondary preventions (e.g., crisis intervention and early identification of and care for those individuals who are in the early stages of disorder).

HYPOTHESES

A test of the relative validity of the provocation and uncovering hypotheses is available if the Catalano and Dooley analyses, alluded to above, are extended to include an inpatient facility utilization variable that is similar to Brenner's. If monthly variations in the number of new inpatient cases in the Kansas City mental health system are compared with variations in the economic environment and surveyed symptoms, this should provide a stronger support for either the uncovering or the provocation hypothesis. The Kansas City survey data, coupled with case opening counts and archival economic data, provide the following variables appropriate to a discriminating test: monthly change in 1) the metropolitan economy; 2) the frequency of self-reporting of symptoms; and 3) use of inpatient mental health facilities.

The pattern of longitudinal relationships among these variables should indicate which hypothesis is the more accurate. Figure 1 shows the several patterns of relationships that can be expected if either hypothesis is accurate, or if both are at work. Since the relations between economic change and service utilization would be similar across all three possible causal paths, column 1 is not discriminating. That relation, which has not been widely tested at other than the statewide level (Sclar and Hoffman, 1978) is central to the underlying assumption that Brenner's findings may be generalized in a metropolitan community over monthly periods and is therefore measured.

If the uncovering hypothesis is viable, there should be no longitudinally significant relationship between symptoms and inpatient case openings since the latter is assumed, according to Brenner, to be associated with economic change, and the former is assumed to be constant or stochastic. The relationship between economic change and service utilization, controlling for symptoms, should be similar in magnitude to their simple correlation. This is true because symptoms are assumed, by the uncovering hypothesis, to be unrelated to service utilization.

326

Figure 1
The Pattern of Correlational Relationships to be Expected
Among Test Variables for Each of the Contending Hypotheses

Hypothesis	Economic Change X Inpatient case openings	Symptoms X Inpatient case openings	Economic Change X Inpatient case openings controllings for symptoms
Uncovering	significant	none	significant
Provocation	significant	significant	none
Both	significant	significant	significant

If the provocation hypothesis alone were accurate, the pattern would be those shown in row 2 of figure 1. Symptoms would be positively related to service utilization. There should not, however, be a significant relationship between economic change and service utilization controlling for symptoms since economically provoked symptoms are assumed to be the intervening link.

If both uncovering and provocation contribute to the relationship between economic change and the use of mental health services, a third pattern should emerge. Symptoms and service utilization should, again reflecting the provocation hypothesis, be related. Economic change and service utilization, controlling for symptoms, should also be related due to the uncovering processes.

Brenner's (1973) findings as well as those of Dooley and Catalano (1977) indicate that age, sex, and income groups are differently affected by varying dimensions of economic change. While total first admissions were negatively related to his directional measure of economic change, Brenner found, as noted earlier, that the relationship of several subgroups was positive. The fact that some subgroups appear to be counter intuitively affected by an expanding economy can be explained by either hypothesis, and does not axiomatically support one at the expense of the other. The finding does suggest the possibility that economic changes provoke disorder in some groups while uncovering it in others. The case opening data, described below, allow figure 1 to be constructed for the total population: male, female, old, middle-aged, and young. Unfortunately, an income breakdown was not possible.

Based on Brenner's (1973) interpretation of his inpatient findings and Catalano and Dooley's (1977) findings that adaptation demands and measures of depressed mood were positively related to economic change, the working assumption is that provocation is correct. It is therefore hypothesized that the pattern of relationships exhibited by the total population and by each of the analyzed demographic subgroups will be consistent with row 2 of figure 1.

METHOD

The Psychological Symptoms Variable

As described by Markush and Favero (1974), fresh weekly probability samples of adult residents (18 years or over) of Kansas City, Missouri were interviewed between October, 1971 and January, 1973. The approximately hour-long personal interviews covered a variety of health, mental health, life event, and demographic variables. Of the 1,140 respondents who completed the life event and symptom sections of the interview, 449 were male and 691 were female. With respect to age, 345 were between 18 and 30; 392 were between 31 and 50; 398 were 51 or over; ten declined to give their ages. In terms of ethnicity, 848 were white; 279 were black; 13 fell into all other ethnic groups combined. Socioeconomic status was estimated from self-reported annual income: 466 reported less than $8,000 to $15,999; 159 reported $16,000 or more, with 77 declining to state their incomes.

The Midtown Scale of psychophysiological symptoms (Langner, 1962) was administered in the Kansas City survey. While the Midtown Scale has been severely criticized as a measure of untreated mental disorder (Dohrenwend and Crandell, 1970; Seiler, 1973), it has proved useful as a measure of psychological distress and as a predictor of formal help-seeking (Mechanic and

328

Greenley, 1976). Since the Midtown Manhattan study (Srole, et al., 1962), the scale and its variants have in fact been the most widely used survey measures of untreated psychopathology.

If the Midtown Scale were to serve as a test of the present hypotheses, it had to be sensitive to short-term changes in community symptomatology. It was of concern, therefore, that the Midtown Scale asked whether any of 22 symptoms had been experienced during the *past year*. Nevertheless, the scale does appear to be sensitive to current emotional status. For example, in the Kansas City survey, the Center for Epidemiologic Studies Depression measure (CESD), which taps mood over the preceding week, was positively correlated with the Midtown Scale. The association of these two symptom measures held both within individuals ($r = .56$, $p<.001$, n = 1,140) and over consecutive monthly sample means ($r = .77$, $p<.001$, n = 16), controlling for linear trends and seasonal variability.

The Case Openings Data

For information on Kansas City mental health case openings over the period corresponding to the epidemiological survey, the authors turned to the National Institute of Mental Health, which had provided the survey data. The NIMH files led back to the Greater Kansas City Mental Health Foundation which had conducted the survey and in turn to the Western Missouri Mental Health Center (WMMHC), the dominant public provider of mental health services in Kansas City, Missouri. With the permission of WMMHC, the statistical section of the Missouri State Department of Mental Health in St. Louis recreated the monthly case opening counts of WMMHC for the period of time that bracketed the survey period by one month, i.e., September 1971 through February 1973. Inter- and intra-institutional transfers or patient status transactions were excluded to avoid counting patients twice. Inpatient admissions were disaggregated by age (young = 18 to 30, middle-aged = 31 to 51 +) and by sex.

Despite the considerable effort invested in their discovery and reconstruction, the resulting case opening variables are incomplete in several respects. First, they represent only the public mental health sector. A cross-sectional inventory of private care in the test community was conducted in the late 1960s (Udell and Hornstra, 1975). Results indicated that 40 percent of the requests for services were made in the private sector. Second, the data reflect only that part of the public sector belonging to WMMHC. The extent to which other public institutions engaged in mental health treatment (e.g., public hospital emergency ward care or essentially psychiatric care) was not measured. Third, WMMHC is located in the central part of the Missouri section of Kansas City. Neither the survey nor the case openings data represents Kansas City, Kansas. Because of the incomplete nature of the data, attention should be focused on the variability of patient admissions over time rather than on their absolute level. The interpretation of the resulting analyses hinges on the assumption that variability in WMMHC case openings is proportional to the variability in total mental health case openings for the period in question.

Several possible weaknesses in the variability of the admissions data were corrected. To correct for the varying lengths of the months, the admission counts were broken down into daily figures. To control for possible linear trends and seasonal variations, the per diemized admissions were, as discussed below, residualized using temporal order (for linear trend) and average monthly temperature (as a surrogate for the seasons) in multiple regression analysis.

The Economic Variables

Three dimensions of change in the metropolitan economy were measured for this analysis. The first was monthly metropolitan unemployment, which is a measure of the economy's ability to provide employment acceptable to those who consider themselves to be in the labor market. While the unemployment rate is a widely reported index of economic well-being, its nature is frequently misunderstood. Because it measures the portion of the *potential* work force that is not employed, a rise in the unemployment rate does not necessarily mean that fewer people are working nor does a drop mean that more are working (Ginzberg, 1977). These fluctuations could reflect an increase or decrease in the number of persons who are actively seeking work. It should also be noted that the unemployment rate is not necessarily sensitive to the amount of job change in a given economy. Two consecutive months of five percent unemployment could mean that the same people were unemployed in both months or that all those unemployed in the first month were employed in the second but were "replaced" in the unemployment rolls by newcomers to the labor force combined with those who had lost their jobs.

A second measure of economic change was devised to compensate for the fact that unemployment rates do not capture the extent of job loss or gain in a discrete time period. The measure is a variant of Catalano and Dooley's (1977) absolute change in the size and structure of the economy. The latter variable is the sum of the absolute monthly differences in the number of employees engaged in each exclusive category of the Standard Industrial Classification System (U.S. Office of Management and Budget, 1972). For the purposes of this analysis, the deseasonalized and detrended Catalano and Dooley absolute change measure was weighted by multiplying it by the deseasonalized and detrended signed first difference of the total work force for the appropriate months. This weighting produces a measure that taps not only total job change but also the degree to which the change left the economy with fewer or more jobs. Unlike the unemployment rate, which is confounded by the expansion and contraction of the potential labor force, weighted absolute change of the work force measures the expansion or contraction of the work force itself.

The difference between the unemployment rate and weighted absolute change is best shown by the fact that it is possible for both to increase in value for the same time period. This apparent contradiction is solved by realizing that while the number of jobs in the economy increased, the increase in the number of persons seeking jobs but not finding them was greater. The two variables are inversely but not strongly related over time (r-.40, $p<.05$, n = 18).

The third economic measure used was Catalano and Dooley's (1977) absolute change in the size and structure of the Metropolitan work force. The measure, described above, was added to the analysis to determine if change per se was predictive of outcome measures for any of the subgroups.

Analyses

Because various investigations of the effect of economic change on behavior (Brenner, 1973; Catalano and Dooley, 1977) have found that relationship to be "lagged" (i.e., economic change occurring in time period 1 shows its effect in period 1 + n), correlation and partial correlations needed to complete figure 1 had to be computed in more than just the synchronous configuration. While both the Brenner and the Catalano and Dooley analyses used only lag procedures, recent work (Mark, 1979) has suggested a cross-correlational technique. This technique, which goes at least as far back as 1901 (Hooker), involves the computation of as many lead (dependent variable preceding the independent variable) as lagged correlations. The temporal pattern of the resulting coefficients should fit the hypothesized causal path. In the case of the hypotheses listed above, the lead coefficients should be insignificant and random, while the lagged coefficients should climb to significance at some point and then decline to insignificance. The cross-correlation technique leads to more conservative, but more compelling, causal inferences (Lee, 1977).

Each of the dependent and independent measures is a time series and therefore likely to exhibit cycles and linear trends. Any association found between two such series could be due to their common trend rather than to any causal relationship. To reduce this confusion, each measure was regressed on a linear trend variable and on monthly mean temperatures. The residuals of the regression were used as the test variables.

The reader may be curious as to why multiple regression techniques were not used to remove trend and seasonal cycles from both the dependent and independent variables, and thus simplify the findings. The method described above is more appropriate because the dependent and independent variables are times series of various lengths, and it is therefore illogical to use one weather variable for deseasonalizing. Generating the leads and lags of the economic variables, for example, required 32 months of data (18 months synchronous with the case opening data, 7 leads and 7 lags). The weather values for the lead and lag months were not the same as those for the 18 months of case opening, or for the 16 months of survey data, making it inappropriate to control for season by using a single weather variable in multiple regression format. The simplest alternative would be to regress each variable on the appropriate weather values and trend for the full extent of the time series and then to separate the residuals into appropriate leads and lags.

To reduce further the chances of inferring a true relationship from a spurious trend-related correlation, each of the significant coefficients was subjected to the Durbin-Watson test for serial autocorrelation (Durbin and Watson, 1950, 1951). Since the null hypothesis is no-autocorrelation, the .05 level of significance is more stringent than .01 (Koutsoyionis, 1973). The note of no-autocorrelation in tables 1 through 3 indicates that the coefficient passed the Durbin-Watson test at the .05 level.

RESULTS

Detrending and deseasonalizing removed considerable proportions of the variance in the case opening data. Table 1 shows the change in R^2 attributable to trend and season for total inpatient case openings and for each of the subgroups.

The reader, when considering the correlation coefficients in tables 2 through 4, should note that squaring the coefficients will yield variance that is explained after detrending and deseasonalizing. The product of the squared correlation coefficient and variance remaining after deseasonalizing and detrending will yield the proportion of the original variance in case openings accounted for by a particular economic or symptom variable. For example, table 2 shows a simple r of .67 for female case openings lagged six months after weighted absolute change. This means that the economic variable accounts for 16.2 percent of the original variance of case openings for women [$(.67^2)$ $(1-.63) = 16.2\%$].

Table 1
Proportion of Variance (R^2) Removed from the Inpatient Case Openings Data by Detrending and Deseasonalizing

	Total	Male	Female	Young	Middle aged	Old
Trend	40%[a]	29%[a]	49%[a]	63%[a]	24%[a]	8%
Season	11%	13%	14%[a]	0	30%[a]	8%
Total	51%[a]	42%[a]	63%[a]	63%[a]	54%[a]	16%

a = $p<.05$ (n = 18 months)

All three explanations (provocation, uncovering, or both) of Brenner's findings assume that economic change is associated with subsequent recourse to inpatient services. As shown in table 2, the expected relationship is found for each of the considered subgroups. The relationship is not, however, uniformly strong across economic predictors. The best of the economic predictors was weighted absolute change, which was significantly related to lagged service utilization for each group. Each correlation passed the Durbin-Watson test and, since no confounding lead relationships appeared, an ideal cross-correlational pattern emerged. The relationships varied in direction across groups. The total population was related at both a one-month (-.47, $p<.05$) and six-month lag (.49, $p < .05$). The paradox of the opposite signs may be due to differences in the subgroup findings. Males reacted inversely at a one-month lag (-.51, $p < .05$) while females reacted, as Brenner found, positively at six months (.65, $p < .05$). The old and middle-aged showed significant correlations (-.47, $p < .05$, and -.53, $p < .05$ respectively) at one-month lag, while the young showed a positive relationship (.67, $p < .05$) at the six-month lag.

Table 2
Cross-Correlations Between Two Measures of Economic Change and Inpatient Case Openings

	Dependent Variable														
	Preceding (Months)							Synchronous	Following						
	7	6	5	4	3	2	1		1	2	3	4	5	6	7
All Case Openings															
1 = Unemployment	-.11	.12	-.20	-.06	-.69ac	-.49ab	-.19	.04	.12	.01	.00	.01	-.01	.56ab	.30
2 = Weighted Change	.20	.03	-.29	.06	.09	.21	-.21	.25	-.47ab	-.22	.14	.00	-.05	.49ac	-.28
Males															
1...............	.00	.16	-.21	-.16	-.73ab	-.54ab	-.19	.15	.09	-.08	.16	.05	.13	.56ab	.23
2...............	.24	.03	-.34	.10	.16	.22	-.22	.08	-.51ab	.14	.01	.01	-.23	.32	-.17
Females															
1...............	-.25	-.05	-.14	.13	-.28	-.19	-.06	-.21	.04	.21	.02	.02	-.29	.26	.20
2...............	.10	.07	-.15	.14	-.04	-.13	-.02	.43	-.24	-.14	-.13	-.29	.28	.65ab	-.38
Young															
1...............	-.26	.08	-.01	.23	-.12	-.12	-.00	-.16	.11	.16	-.05	-.05	-.45	.05	-.04
2...............	.31	.15	-.19	.08	-.16	-.12	-.02	.40	.00	-.18	-.03	-.03	.00	.67ab	-.26
Middle-Aged															
1...............	.04	-.04	-.42	-.11	-.56ab	-.41	-.29	-.01	.06	.00	.13	.13	.17	.49ab	.22
2...............	.03	.06	-.17	.02	.14	.09	-.21	.29	-.53ab	.22	-.11	-.11	-.09	.42	-.16
Old															
1...............	-.06	.26	.03	-.25	-.86ab	-.59ab	-.02	.27	.03	-.10	.00	.00	.15	.65ac	.38
2...............	.26	-.09	-.42	.25	.21	.29	-.14	-.18	-.47ab	.00	.24	.24	-.05	.07	-.24

a = p<.05 (two tailed test), n = 18 months.

b = No autocorrelation at p>.05.

c = Inconclusive Durbin-Watson at p>.05.

Unemployment produced lagged correlations for the total population (lag 6, .56, $p < .05$), males (lag 6, .56, $p < .05$), the old (lag 6, .64, $p < .05$), and middle-aged (lag 6, .49, $p < .05$). The lagged correlation for the old yielded an inconclusive Durbin-Watson statistic. None of the cross-correlations fits the ideal pattern in that each also showed significant correlations in the lead configuration. These lead correlations were predictable from the fact that unemployment, even after deseasonalizing, showed a nine-month peak to valley cycle.

Absolute economic change yielded no significant cross-correlations and was dropped from the computations for columns 3 and 4 of figure 1.

The relationship between symptoms and inpatient case openings weakens the provocation explanation. As shown in table 3, none of the cross-correlations produces significant lagged relationships. The reduced number of leads and lags in table 3 reflects the fact that only 16 months of survey data were available. The number of cases in the time series analysis therefore varies from 16 in the synchronous configuration to 14 at lag and lead 3.

Table 3
Cross-Correlations between
Symptoms and Inpatient Case Openings

				Dependent Variable			
		Preceding (Months)		Synchro-nous	Following		
	3	2	1	1	1	2	3
All Case Openings	-.11	.25	.01	.05	.26	-.01	-.27
Males	.06	.20	.04	.12	-.07	-.17	-.13
Females	.01	-.31	-.16	.19	.09	.03	.24
Young	.63	-.29	-.42	.03	.30	-.08	.25
Middle-Aged	.10	-.03	-.23	.22	-.07	.03	.00
Old	-.35	.36	.28	.21	-.25	.00	.01

n = 16 in synchronous configuration, and at lag and lead 1, 15 at 2, and 14 at 3.

336

Table 4 shows that the uncovering hypothesis, as opposed to provocation, is supported by the relationship between inpatient case openings and economic change controlling for same month symptoms. The pattern of relationships across the subgroups is similar to that found between economic change and outpatient case openings in table 2. While the magnitude of the correlations is very similar, fewer in table 4 reach significance because of the loss of degrees of freedom incurred by partial correlation techniques.

DISCUSSION

The results described above suggest that in the Kansas City Metropolitan area in the early 1970s, the relationship between economic change and recourse to inpatient mental health facilities was due more to the uncovering than to the provocation of behavioral disorders.

It is a challenge to the uncovering hypothesis to explain the finding that females and the young reacted proportionately to measures of economic well-being, while males, the middle-aged, and the elderly reacted inversely. A plausible explanation of the subgroup differences, compatible with both the uncovering hypothesis and with economic theory, is Barker's (Barker and Schoggen, 1973) concept of over- and under-manning. Barker's model posits that social systems that are under-manned need to be tolerant of participant idiosyncracies to maintain themselves. Over-manned systems, on the other hand, can afford to label their deviants and to exclude them from useful roles because there is a surplus of "normals" to perform necessary functions.

A community with an expanding economy might be considered under-manned and might therefore be willing to provide roles and resources to those with behavioral problems. A shrinking economy could lead to the intolerance of over-manning and less reluctance in labeling deviants. Social sub-systems of the community, ranging from employment settings to schools and families, would all be affected by Barker's concepts. Tolerance for behavioral problems in males and the middle-aged may, for example, decrease as the economy becomes over-manned and

Table 4
Cross-Correlations Between Two Measures of Economic Change and Inpatient Case Openings Controlling for Symptoms

	Dependent Variable														
	Preceding (Months)							Synchronous	Following						
	7	6	5	4	3	2	1		1	2	3	4	5	6	7
All Case Openings															
1 = Unemployment	-.22	.07	-.30	-.23	-.71[a]	-.48	-.14	.02	.03	.05	.07	.18	.06	.60[a]	.34
2 = Weighted Change	.16	.00	-.37	.11	.10	.23	-.38	-.33	.21	-.16	-.33	.05	-.32	.46	-.05
Males															
1	-.03	.14	-.26	-.30	-.75[a]	-.54[a]	-.18	.11	.15	-.10	-.04	.09	.21	.60[a]	.27
2	.23	.00	-.37	.04	.30	.23	-.38	-.48	.10	-.12	.17	.04	-.37	.31	-.06
Females															
1	-.52[a]	-.22	-.31	-.03	-.25	-.22	-.06	-.11	-.33	.35	.36	.19	-.23	.31	.29
2	.13	.03	-.31	.23	-.16	-.20	.00	.01	.48	-.17	.24	.32	.07	.68[a]	.03
Young															
1	-.28	-.05	-.32	.04	-.13	-.18	-.04	-.19	.27	.13	.12	.10	-.36	.08	.01
2	.29	.13	.33	.20	-.24	-.23	-.08	.02	.42	.08	-.25	-.42	-.30	.71[a]	.00
Middle-Aged															
1	-.13	-.07	-.45	-.24	-.59[a]	-.42	-.28	.19	.14	.04	.12	.21	.24	.58[a]	.29
2	.00	.06	-.33	-.08	.27	.10	-.26	-.46	.33	-.26	.22	-.10	-.22	.49	.02
Old															
1	-.11	.26	.03	-.40	-.85[a]	-.57[a]	.06	-.05	.22	.03	-.01	.08	.22	.65[a]	.37
2	.22	-.13	-.43	.40	.23	.24	-.21	-.40	-.26	.01	.01	.26	-.13	-.03	-.17

[a] $p < .05$ (two tailed test), n = 16 months.

therefore more selective. The individual (or his family) may attribute his inability to hold a secure job to a behavioral problem and be driven to professional help that would restore the wage earner to a competitive level of functioning as soon as possible.

The positive relationship of economic conditions to inpatient treatment for women is consistent with the manning model if we adopt the traditional belief that a woman's role is predominantly to supply social support at home, to earn a supplementary income, or both. When the economy turns downward, both roles become increasingly important, and tolerance of idiosyncracies may rise. During times of economic expansion, the perceived need for a strong family unit as a source of consolation and support, or for supplementary income, may decrease. The decision then to seek professional help for behavioral problems may therefore be an easier one for a woman to make.

Barker's manning construct could explain the inverse relationship for the young to the degree that the category included persons still living in the family. Like wives, children can serve as sources of supplementary income and social support, even if slight, during bad economic times. In periods of economic expansion, the primary wage earners may be able to provide enough income to secure care for the marginally disordered. Expansion also means that primary wage earners are not likely to have so much time to provide at-home care or that the family is less in need of mutual support.

The difficulties with the available data discussed above require that conclusions from the results of this study be drawn with great care. Even though these results favor uncovering over provocation, other explanations have not been ruled out. One such explanation is the "private-to-public shift." That is, changed economic conditions may have neither provoked nor uncovered pathology but may only have shifted existing clients from the private to the public sector. Although this possibility was ruled out in Brenner's study in New York (1973), it merits attention in future studies.

Another contending explanation, that case openings may have varied with supply, is not measured in this study. If supply varied with economic change, the observed economic change-case opening relationship would be more apparent than real. Because of the heightened public, political, and mental health professional awareness of Brenner's research, the supply of mental health services may become linked by policy to economic change. If long waiting lists were obtained at mental health centers, fluctuations in supply would then guarantee a strong, if artifactual, relationship between economic change and treated cases. Scholars should watch for evidence of what may be referred to as the "Brenner effect," a special case of the "economic change-supply of services" relationship. Interestingly, even measures of untreated disorder may not be immune to this "Brenner effect." As the popular media sensitize citizens to the links between economic change and disorder, surveyed respondents may be expected to be more conscious of symptoms and to admit to more of them during periods of bad economic news. Additional survey items may have to be developed to check on heightened awareness.

A third explanation of the findings is that the symptom survey may have have reached those persons whose behavioral disorders had been provoked by economic change. It is possible that those who exhibited economically precipitated symptoms were shielded from surveyors by family or professional caretakers.

While the inference that uncovering was at work in Kansas City detracts from Brenner's favored provocation hypothesis, it should be noted that his findings were replicated under conditions specified by his critics. As table 2 indicates, outpatient case openings were related to measures of economic change for each considered subgroup. The hypotheses offered by Pierce (1967) and by Catalano and Dooley (1977) that change per se may be as stressful as directional change was not supported. Absolute change was not related to inpatient case openings or to symptoms. Weighted absolute change, a measure devised to improve on the unemployment rate as an indicator of directional change, produced ideal cross-correlational patterns and should be considered as an alternative to the unemployment rate in future analyses.

IMPLICATIONS

Dooley and Catalano (1977) argue that findings such as those described above have implications for the provision of preventive as well as remedial mental health services. The assumption that economic change provokes disorder has led to the suggestion that primary prevention programs can be devised to meet the needs of those groups most likely to be affected by anticipated economic stressors. The current findings indicate that calls for primary prevention programs based on econometric forecasts may be premature.

The usefulness of measuring the relationship of economic change to the utilization of mental health services remains obvious for planning remedial services. Regardless of whether patients exhibit problems provoked or uncovered by economic change, they will need to be taken care of. To the degree that demand can be anticipated through forecasting based on economic data, the allocation of scarce resources can be made more rational.

It has also been argued that behavioral outcomes of economic change should be included among the costs anticipated by decision makers when conducting cost/benefit calculations for proposed policy shifts (Brenner, 1977). Although these arguments are based on the provocation assumption, they remain valid, with an important exception, if the findings above prove generalizable. The exception is concerned with the human costs of pain and suffering that is assumed to be attributed to economic change by the provocation hypothesis. If economic change provokes disorder, the human costs should be taken into account, along with the cost of serving those victims who request help, and deducted from the anticipated benefits of any policy that encourages change. If economic change uncovers existing disorder, only the costs of servicing new demands should be accounted and deducted. There may, of course, be sub-symptom distress provoked by economic change that should be counted as a cost. The challenge is to measure those beyond the anecdotal level.

CONCLUSION

The application of the logic underlying figure 1 to the Kansas City data was not intended to be the definitive discriminating test between the uncovering and provocation hypotheses. The problems inherent in measuring symptoms and inventorying case openings mean that the reported findings must be considered tentative. This caveat, however, does not detract from the fact that the provocation hypothesis was not supported by state of the art analyses of the best archival data currently available. It seems prudent, therefore, for social scientists to indicate that their support for favored policies springs from moral values rather than from established fact.

REFERENCES

Barker, R. G. and Schoggen, P. *Qualities of Community Life.* San Francisco: Jossey-Bass, 1973.

Brenner, M. H. "Personal Stability and Economic Security." *Social Policy,* 8:2-5, 1977.

Brenner, M. H. *Estimating the Social Costs of Economic Policy: Implications for Mental and Physical Health and Criminal Aggression.* Report to the Congressional Research Service of the Library of Congress and the Joint Economic Committee of Congress. Washington: Government Printing Office, 1976.

Brenner, M. H. *Mental Illness and the Economy.* Cambridge: Harvard University Press, 1973.

Brenner, M. H. "Patterns of Psychiatric Hospitalization Among Different Socio-Economic Groups in Response to Economic Stress." *Journal of Nervous and Mental Diseases,* 148:31-38, 1969.

Catalano, Ralph. *Health, Behavior and the Community.* New York: Pergamon Press, 1979.

Catalano, Ralph and Dooley, David. "Economic Predictors of Depressed Mood and Stressful Life Events in a Metropolitan Community." *Journal of Health and Social Behavior,* 18:292-307, 1977.

Cobb, Sidney. "Social Support as a Moderator of Life Stress." *Psychosomatic Medicine,* 38:300-314, 1976.

Cobb, Sidney and Kasl, S. V. *Termination: The Consequences of Job Loss.* (Report No. 76-1261.) Cincinnati, OH: National Institute for Occupational Safety and Health, Behavioral and Motivational Factors Research, 1977.

deAraujo, G., VanArsdel, P. P., Holmes, T. H., and Dudley, D. L. "Life Change, Coping Ability and Chronic Intrinsic Asthma." *Journal of Psychosomatic Research,* 17:359-363, 1973.

Dohrenwend, B. P. and Crandell, D. L. "Psychiatric Symptoms in Community, Clinic, and Mental Hospital Groups." *American Journal of Psychiatry,* 126:1611-1621, 1970.

Dohrenwend, B. S. and Dohrenwend, B. P. (eds.) *Stressful Life Events: Their Nature and Effects.* New York: Wiley and Sons, 1974.

Dooley, David and Catalano, Ralph. "Economic, Life and Disorder Changes: Time Series Analyses." *American Journal of Community Psychology,* 7:381-396, 1979.

Dooley, David and Catalano, Ralph. "Economic Change as a Cause of Behavioral Disorder." *Psychological Bulletin.* Forthcoming.

Dooley, David and Catalano, Ralph. "Money and Mental Disorder: Toward Behavioral Cost Accounting for Primary Prevention." *American Journal of Community Psychology,* 5:217-227, 1977.

Durbin, J. and Watson, G. S. "Testing for Serial Correlation in Least Squares Regression: Part II." *Biometrika,* 38:159-178, 1951.

Durbin. J. and Watson, G. S. "Testing for Serial Correlation in Least Squares Regression: Part I." *Biometrika,* 37:409-423, 1950.

Durkheim, E. *Suicide.* Paris: Alcan, 1897.

Eyer, J. "Prosperity as a Cause of Death." *International Journal of Health Services,* 7:125-150, 1977.

Ginzberg, E. "The Job Problem." *Scientific American,* 237:43-51, 1977.

Hooker, R. H. "The Correlation of the Marriage Rate with Trade." *Journal of the Royal Statistical Society,* 64:485-492, 1901.

Kaplan, B. H., Cassel, J. L., and Gore, S. "Social Support and Health." *Medical Care 15 Supplement,* 47-58, 1977.

Koutsoyionis, A. *Theory of Econometrics.* London: Macmillan, 1973.

Langner, T. S. "A Twenty-Two Item Screening Score of Psychiatric Symptoms Indicating Impairment." *Journal of Health and Human Behavior,* 3:269-276, 1962.

Lee, S. H. *Cross-Correlogram and the Causal Structure Between Two Time Series,* 1977. Unpublished manuscript. (Available from the author, Department of Psychology, Northwestern University, Evanston, IL 60201.)

Mark, M. "The Causal Analysis of Concomitancies in Two Time Series." Pp. 321-338 in T. D. Cook and O. T. Campbell (eds.) *Quasi-Experimentation.* Chicago: Rand McNally, 1979.

Markush, R. and Favero, R. "Epidemiological Assessment of Stressful Life Events, Depressed Mood, and Physiological Symptoms—A Preliminary Report." Pp. 171-190 in B. S. Dohrenwend and B. P. Dohrenwend (eds.), *Stressful Life Events,* New York: Wiley and Sons, 1974.

Marshall, J. P. and Funch, D. P. "Mental Illness and the Economy: A Critique and Partial Replication." *Journal of Health and Social Behavior,* 20:282-289, 1979.

Mechanic, D. "Illness Behavior, Social Adaptation, and the Management of Illness." *Journal of Nervous and Mental Disease,* 165:79-87, 1977.

Mechanic, D. and Greenley, J. R. "The Prevalence of Psychological Distress and Help-Seeking in a College Student Population." *Social Psychiatry,* 11:1-14, 1976.

Myers, J. K., Lindenthal, J. J., and Pepper, M. P. "Life Events, Social Integration and Psychiatric Symptomatology." *Journal of Health and Social Behavior,* 14:6-23, 1975.

Nuckolls, K. B., Cassel, J., and Kaplan, B. H. "Psychological Assets, Life Crisis, and the Prognosis of Pregnancy." *American Journal of Epidemiology,* 95:431-441, 1972.

Pierce, A. "The Economic Cycle and the Social Suicide Rate." *American Sociological Review,* 32:457-462, 1967.

Rabkin, J. G. and Streuning, E. L. "Life Events, Stress, and Illness." *Science,* 194:1013-1020, 1976.

Roth, A. and Locke, B. *Continuous Community Mental Health Assessment.* Paper presented at the 101st Annual Meeting of the American Public Health Association. Available from NIMH Center for Epidemiologic Studies, 5600 Fisher's Lane, Rockville, MD 20852, 1973.

Sarbin, T. R. "Schizophrenic Thinking: A Role Theoretical Analysis." *Journal of Personality,* 37:190-206, 1969.

Sclar, E. D. and Hoffman, V. *Planning Mental Health Service for a Declining Economy.* (Final Report.) Waltham, MA: Brandeis University, Florence Heller Graduate School of Advanced Studies in Social Welfare, 1978.

346

Scheff, T. J. *Being Mentally Ill: A Sociological Theory.* Chicago: Aldine, 1966.

Segall, A. "The Sick Role Concept: Understanding Illness Behavior." *Journal of Health and Social Behavior,* 17:163-170, 1976.

Seiler, L. H. "The 22-Item Scale used in Field Studies of Mental Illness: A Question of Method, A Question of Substance, and A Question of Theory." *Journal of Health and Social Behavior,* 14:252-264, 1973.

Srole, L., Langner, T. S., Michael, S. T., Opler, M. K., and Rennie, T. A. *Mental Health in the Metropolis.* New York: McGraw-Hill, 1962.

Udell, B. and Hornstra, R. K. "Good Patients and Bad." *Archives of General Psychiatry,* 32:1533-1537, 1975.

U. S. Office of Management and Budget. *Standard Industrial Classification Manual,* Washington: Government Printing Office, 1972.

13
SOCIAL SUPPORT & STRESS: SOME GENERAL ISSUES AND THEIR APPLICATION TO THE PROBLEM OF UNEMPLOYMENT

G. RAMSAY LIEM
JOAN HUSER LIEM

After nearly a decade of seemingly intractable crises in the domestic and international economy, research on the problem of unemployment has expanded rapidly in virtually every area of the social sciences. This work is challenged both by clear and pressing social needs and by conceptual problems in comprehending the manner in which human well-being is affected by a declining economy.

The current interest in the problem of unemployment also represents the revival of a research tradition that originated during the great depression. While the major issues raised by researchers who studied unemployment during the depression focused principally on the economic costs of large-scale job loss and related programs of relief, and only secondarily on social and health consequences, current work has taken the broad human costs of unemployment as its main point of departure. Furthermore, whereas early investigations of unemployment relied heavily on intensive case studies of individual workers and their families, contemporary research has been stimulated by striking findings from longitudinal analyses of aggregate economic and health indices. This shift in methodology and unit of analysis is

*This work is related in part to research supported by the National Institute of Mental Health Grant MH-31316-01.

Many of the issues and ideas discussed in this paper are the product of extensive and ongoing discussions with a number of friends and colleagues. We would like to express our appreciation to Larry Finison, Marc Fried, Susan Gore, Les Howard, Tom Mangione, Steve McElfresh, Elliot Mishler, and Sharon Rosen.

not insignificant, in that it locates the determinants of the social costs of unemployment in the macroeconomy as well as in the personal encounter with job loss. It therefore emphasizes the study of those social structures and processes through which large-scale societal changes in labor force participation relate to social and health consequences for individual workers, rather than simply the dynamics of personal response to unemployment. The conceptual and methodological issues associated with each of these points of view are by no means the same; the former poses a genuinely interdisciplinary problem that cuts across traditional lines of inquiry.

One program of research that has contributed significantly to the creation of this framework for the study of unemployment is the work of Harvey Brenner (1973, 1976), in which several indices of economic change have been demonstrated to co-vary at state and national levels consistently and powerfully with a broad range of health and social indicators. Recent studies by several other investigators (Catalano and Dooley, 1977; Gabarino, 1976; Pierce, 1967; and Sclar, 1978) have followed this tradition and have added to the mounting evidence that such outcomes as mental illness, physical impairment, suicide, and child abuse are closely related to the state of the economy. One long-range challenge to unemployment research posed by these findings is to define the multiple processes and structures through which such effects may occur.

Much of the effort to tackle this problem thus far has focused on the extent to which personally experienced stressors may originate in the economy at large, mediated through intervening levels of the social system (Catalano and Dooley, 1977; Liem and Liem, 1978). It is apparent, however, that the consequences of change in the macroeconomy can differ widely across groups as well as among individuals. This variability may in turn be contingent on the manner in which different economic stressors, or factors that moderate their effects, are distributed within the population. The focus of the present discussion is on the second of these two, and more specifically, on the moderating effects of interpersonal relationships. This particular function of interpersonal relationships, commonly referred to as social support (Cobb, 1978; Cobb and Kasl, 1977; Gore, 1973; and Pinneau, 1975), has received increasing attention in research on stress as well as in medical and psychiatric epidemiology. However, only a minor portion of this work has been devoted to the effects of social support specifically in relation to economic hardship, such as the experience of job loss.

In this discussion we will first draw on contributions from the larger body of work to raise several general issues regarding the conceptualization of social support as a moderator of stress. Then, in light of these comments, we will review some of the research on social support in the context of unemployment stress as a basis for suggesting conceptual and methodological considerations for directing future work in this area. Finally, we will return to the more complex relationship between the macroeconomy and individual well-being and present several preliminary ideas regarding the place of social support in that relationship.

Social Support and Stress

Some of the issues regarding social support as a moderator of stress first came to our attention when we reviewed the literature on stressful life events (Dohrenwend and Dohrenwend, 1974; Holmes and Rahe, 1967; Rabkin and Struening, 1976) to aid in the interpretation of the ecological correlation between psychiatric admissions and employment levels reported by Brenner (1973). We were initially struck by the absence, for the most part, of moderating or contextual variables in the design of early life events studies, implying that the stress of life events is largely invariable across individuals. Life event stressors appeared to be treated as analogs of physical stressors in engineering and mechanical models of stress (Scott and Howard, 1970), where the relatively fixed and delimited properties of physical structures permit the specification of stress limits in categorical terms. One might reasonably assume, however, that, unless life events are defined only as extreme and highly traumatic events (see e.g., Basowitz et al., 1955; Janis, 1954), it would be virtually impossible to define the relevant universe of significant stressful events for different individuals or groups without some consideration of the contexts in which they are experienced. We suspect that the relatively small amount of variance usually accounted for by life events scales in different measures of well-being reflects, in part, the lack of attention to contextual factors.

Recently, life events researchers have given more consideration to those characteristics of the situation and person that may condition the impact of potentially stressful events. Both in efforts to model the process underlying the impact of life events (Cobb, 1974), and in several empirical studies of complications during pregnancy (Nuckolls, Cassel, and Kaplan, 1972) and psychological impairment (Myers, Lindenthal, and Pepper, 1975; Liem and Liem, 1977), social support has been treated as a particularly salient contextual variable for moderating the impact of stress.

The argument for this function of interpersonal relationships has drawn on findings in several other areas of research. In virtually every review of the literature on social support known to us (Gore, 1973; Gore, 1978a; Gore, 1978b; Heller, 1978; Kaplan, Cassel, and Gore, 1977; and Pinneau, 1975), epidemiological research that associates such variables as social isolation and marital status with disorder, experimental studies of affiliation as a response to fear, research on the interpersonal context of work and unemployment stress, and clinical observations of the therapeutic effects of positive interpersonal relationships are cited as offering findings consistent with the hypothesis that interpersonal supports buffer stress.

In spite of the increasing attention given to interpersonal relations as critical contextual factors related to health and social well-being, the proposition that supportive relationships mitigate the effects of stressful experiences still awaits more conclusive tests. As others have observed (Pinneau, 1975; Gore, 1978), the data in regard to this hypothesis are often mixed, and supporting evidence is frequently open to alternative interpretations. Several basic conceptional and methodological issues are suggested by the diverse research bearing on social support and deserve special consideration in future efforts to clarify the stress-reducing functions of interpersonal relations.

The Problem of Categorical Typing

A problem that has perhaps more pervasive significance than any other for research in this area is the tendency, especially at the point of measurement, to treat the functions and qualities of specific relationships as if they were stable over time and situations. The same basic issue was also raised in our discussion of life events research. There we noted that stress levels have often been treated as invariable properties of life events. To some extent, the problem of categorical typing is unavoidable in the construction of any measure of social support for the purposes of prediction. It must be resolved principally in the overall planning of a research strategy, i.e., longitudinal as opposed to cross-sectional designs do not necessitate assignment of absolute characteristics to interpersonal relationships.

Intuitively, the inappropriateness of categorical typing is exemplified by a case in which a relationship (with a close friend, for example) that one defines as source of support may, on some occasions, exacerbate stress by being a source of competing obligations or may simply be irrelevant to the circumstances in which stress is encountered. What determines the particular significance of a relationship at a given moment probably includes a wide range of factors, such as the types of need made salient by the occurrence of a stressor, one's attributions in the situation, and the recent history of the relationship itself. Efforts to assess social support that fail to take into account the importance of circumstancial factors such as these are likely to encounter considerable error variance in analyses of stress/support interaction effects. Furthermore, as noted by Gore (1978a), the absence of attention to factors like these contributes to the difficulties of interpreting such findings as the more favorable health status of married persons vs. those without spouses (Bloom, 1977), or residents of socially integrated vs disintegrated communities (Faris and Dunham, 1934), in terms of the buffering hypothesis. For example, persons with close ties to others may have more and better supportive resources for coping with stress than persons with fewer and weaker ties. It may also be the case, however, that the former have simply been better protected from stressors in the first place. Alternatively, it is possible that persons with few and weak ties may experience greater stress than others as a result of conflict in existing relationships or a recent loss of close ties.

These comments suggest that to evaluate the buffering effects of social support, one needs to ask which relationships moderate stress under what circumstances, rather than which relationships can be categorically defined as supportive or nonsupportive. In the conduct of such investigations, it is also necessary to maintain clear conceptual distinctions among the various ways in which interpersonal relations may influence personal well-being, i.e., through the moderation of stress, the prevention of stressors, or the creation of stress. In addition to these possibilities, we should also consider the role of ties to others in gratifying needs unrelated to the occurrence of stress, e.g., developmental or maturational needs. Because these alternatives may represent important life-enhancing functions of the same human relationship, they can easily be confounded in measures of interpersonal ties designed to assess any one of them.

Support Attributes of Interpersonal Relationships

The critique of categorical typing is relevant not only to the problem of determining the conditions under which relationships are supportive, but also to the identification of the ways in which relationships are supportive. The moderation of stress by a particular relationship theoretically can occur in several ways which may vary across stress situations. Hence, given needs for coping with stress, and precisely how these needs are served by one's relations to others, may be influenced by contextual and historical factors (i.e., needs experienced in the situation, personal attributions, and past experience with ties to others) in much the same manner that the basic functions of different relationships are determined. For example, literature on the job search (Foote, 1973; Sheppard and Belitsky, 1966), indicates that individuals are apt to turn to others who are important to them for varying kinds of help (e.g., emotional and instrumental) as circumstances associated with the job hunt change.

The language used to describe the abstract qualities that have traditionally been associated with supportive relationships differs widely. Nevertheless, there seems to be considerable agreement as to the nature of the attributes themselves. On the most general level, social support includes an instrumental and emotional dimension. The former refers to the direct provision of material resources and services, information, and advice. Emotional support generally includes the expression of positive effects such as liking and caring, affirmation of attitudes and values, and acceptance. Systematic research data indicating that these qualities are crucial is simply unavailable at present. Aside from experimental studies of affiliation during stress (Schachter, 1959), the empirical support for this two-factor classification of supportive attributes comes from observations of helping behavior across a widely diverse body of literature.

Given our assumption, however, that different attributes of supportive relationships are neither consistently descriptive of particular relationships nor relevant in all situations of stress, our inclination is to put aside the development of a comprehensive theory of social support for the moment. Instead, what might be more useful is a somewhat looser conceptual framework that takes into account the situational specificity of needs for support and the potential for change, both in whether or not a relationship provides support and in its particular supportive qualities. It is to this task that we turn next.

The Process of Coping

In light of the general issues we have raised about the contingent nature of social support resources, one way to represent the structure and process underlying the impact of a stressor is a model of coping. This is the strategy we are currently employing in a study of family and individual response to job loss. Our approach to such a model specifies the occurrence of a stressful event, and where relevant a preceding anticipation stage, followed by the experience of stress and a three-part coping process (see figure 1). This structure distinguishes among three moments in the coping process where supportive relations become meaningful in response to specific and, for the most part, unique circumstances, i.e., the stage of anticipation or threat, the initial experience of stress, and the coping process itself. This latter stage of the model is further differentiated into affect maintenance, problem appraisal and definition, and planning and implementation components, each of which makes salient different forms of supportive behavior. This structure incorporates previous work by Cobb (1974), Morley (1970), and Rapoport (1965), and provides a clear set of referents for anticipating the kinds of interpersonal help that may be relevant in the light of a particular stressor.

Two other aspects of the model also help to specify relevant supports. The first is the definition of stressors as the loss of important life-sustaining or life-enhancing resources. Thus, based on the literature on work, one might expect that losses involving financial resources, a source of affirmation and esteem, and a routine that structures time and activities would constitute the potential stress of unemployment. Relevant social supports would be those most responsive to these kinds of losses. A second point of reference for helping behavior lies in the outcome of coping itself. Ineffective coping may generate new stresses that in turn are responsive to particular types of support.

The orientation to process in this model also permits the investigator to attend to changes in the functions and qualities of particular supportive relationships and in the sources of interpersonal supports for particular needs. For example, the process of coping may exhaust some interpersonal resources, create strain in other supportive relationships, or serve to mobilize the help of someone who has previously been indifferent. This kind of change represents the reciprocal relation between stress and support and is an important aspect of our earlier critique of the categorical typing of interpersonal functions and attributes. The model, however, does not provide a formal basis for anticipating changes in relationships that occur outside the coping process.

Figure 1

Interpersonal Supports in the Context of a Process Oriented Model of Coping

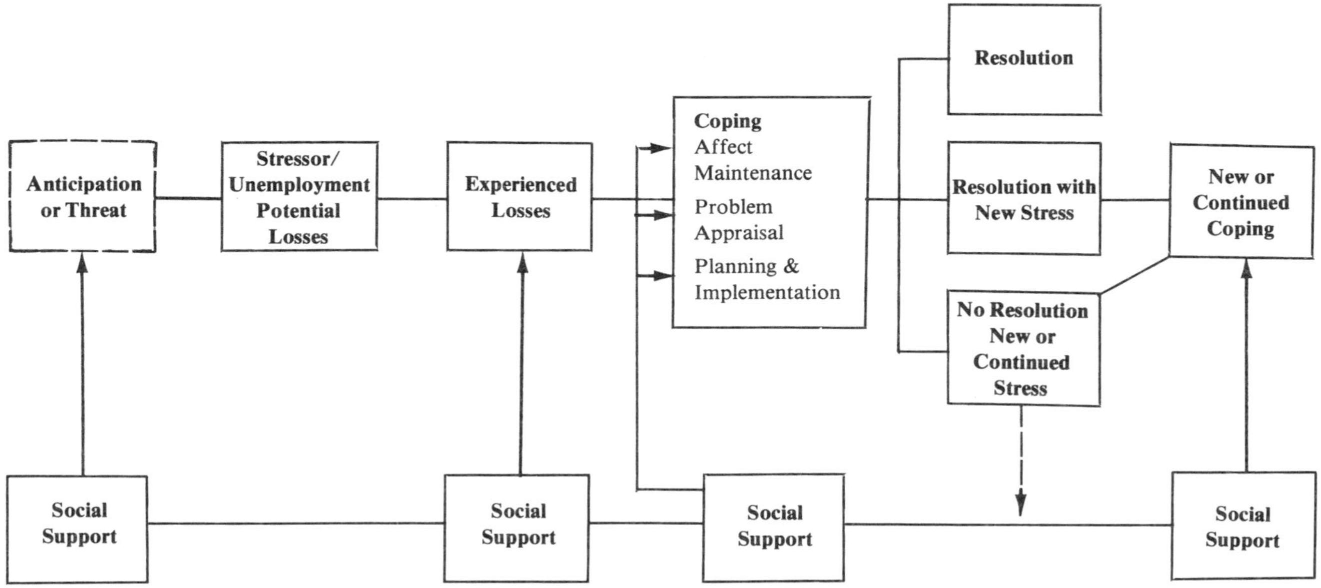

The approach to research on the moderation of stress by interpersonal relations suggested by the coping framework clearly assumes considerable variability in social support resources, and we recognize that this position is largely untested in existing research. It emerged partly as we sought to explain the lack of strong support for the moderating effects of interpersonal relationships in the literature. How necessary a process-oriented approach to social support may be in relation to different stressors remains to be answered by future work.

Alternative Sources of Social Support

Thus far, we have addressed some general conceptual and related methodological issues regarding the moderating influences of interpersonal relationships on stressful life experiences. While the dyadic relationship which has been the implicit focus of these comments may in fact represent the basic unit of social support resources, aggregates of interpersonal relationships may also constitute sources of support. The family, neighborhood, community, and workplace, for example, have all been cited in research on social support, both as locations of significant supportive relationships (Gore, 1978; Ferman, 1975; and Tolsdorf, 1976) and as interpersonal structures that could provide a generalized climate of support (Moos, 1974), a feeling of belonging or of having firm roots (Sarason, 1974), and a protection against exposure to stressors (Gore, 1973). Whether these larger systems of social interaction are most important because of their influence on where one turns for support, because of their role in determining the quality of the dyadic relationships within them, or because of their properties as social systems remains an empirically unresolved question. It can be inferred from some data that persons located in different occupational settings may find co-workers, family and kin, and friends differentially important as sources of instrumental (Foote, 1973) and emotional (Finlayson, 1976) support. Warren and Clifford (1975) and Komarovsky (1940) have provided evidence that structural characteristics of neighborhoods and families are associated with the quality and patterns of the supportive relationships in them. Studies of organizational (Burke and Weir, 1975), family (Moos, 1974), and community climate (Newbrough, 1973) also suggest that dimensions such as exploitative/participatory, cohesive/antagonistic, and autonomous/controlling can be reliably measured and may function in both stress-inducing and reducing capacities. These findings suggest the possibility that social support may be an attribute of systems of interpersonal relationships as well as dyadic relationships.

In view of this possibility, it is important to note that the same cautions regarding the categorical assignment of the function of social support to interpersonal ties apply to other units of analysis as well. Thus, the supportiveness of the family is only one of its many potential functions; it is just as likely that, at times, the family may be a source of significant stress (Croog, 1970). The tendency to conceptualize aggregate interpersonal networks in categorical terms has sometimes been characteristic of the use of the concept of the social network (Tolsdorf, 1976) in the social support literature. The social network is employed in this context principally as a conceptual and measurement tool that summarizes the total array of interpersonal supports available to an individual. Its construction, however, involves the determination of one's direct or indirect ties to close or important persons, the functions of which, as noted earlier, cannot be defined in absolute terms. The notion of a social support network is, in actuality, an abstraction of only one of many qualities from an aggregate of ongoing relationships. These relationships exist within formal and informal structures that embody normative regulations, and hence they reflect a wide range of rights and obligations. The availability of social support from one's network of close relations is therefore dependent both on the substance of these reciprocal expectations and on one's ability to meet his/her obligations.

These comments are not intended to discourage further use of the social network concept. Quite to the contrary, it is one of the few promising approaches to the analysis of human relationships at the macro level in which relational structure and dynamics are not limited to a single institutional or organizational setting. Accordingly it captures linkages across contexts that have hitherto been inaccessible to other theoretical approaches, such as role theory. If pathways to different supportive relationships are constrained by the total nexus of one's relationships, and if the network or particular subsets are important referents for one's feelings of belonging and being supported, the social network can make an important contribution to studies of the moderation of stress. These questions, however, must be approached with the recognition that social networks, by virtue of their highly complex interdependence, contain competition and conflict as well as ties to supportive resources, and that furthermore, these dynamics operate not only between individuals but among aggregates of persons as well.

Process-oriented studies of the use of pathways to resources in one's network, as in Foote (1973) and Granovetter's research (1973) on the job search and Howard's study (1974) of transition from rural to urban life, would seem to represent an effective strategy for exploring network characteristics. They are concerned first with *how* networks are actually used under specific conditions of need and only then with how the choice of pathways to help is constrained by network structure and content. This approach to network analysis seems to us to be an important first step for research on the moderation of unemployment stress which may at some future time permit the construction of network scales with substantial predictive power.

Social Support and Unemployment

We have spent some time in clarifying a number of conceptual issues that bear on social support as a moderator of stress in order to establish a working framework from which to review research on the functions of social support in relation to the particular stressor of unemployment. Our major objectives in this review have been to evaluate the present evidence for a moderating effect by human relationships on stress from job loss, and to suggest a number of directions for future research consistent with these data.

The evidence that interpersonal relationships can moderate the negative effects of unemployment comes basically from two sources. The first consists of a number of in depth case studies of unemployed workers and their families. These studies consistently note the critical role played by family relationships and friends in determining responses to unemployment. By and large, studies of this type were carried out during and immediately following the great depression, although more recently there have been several noteworthy additions. The second source of evidence is a limited number of empirical studies designed specifically to examine the moderating role of interpersonal relationships vis-a-vis unemployment and the strain produced by it.

The early work of such persons as Angell (1936), Bakke (1940), Komarovsky (1940), Jahoda, Lazarsfeld, and Zeisel (1971), and Eisenberg and Lazarsfeld (1938) provides rich descriptions of both the despair, isolation, and resignation accompanying the separation of the individual and the family from the workplace, and the quality of interaction within the family that ameliorates these effects. Komarovsky (1940), for example, noted that the nature of the preunemployment relationship between a worker and his spouse was a critical determinant of the degree of deterioration of family functioning that took place throughout the course of unemployment. Egalitarian marital relationships based on love and respect were more likely to promote a continued family stability in the face of prolonged unemployment than were patriarchal relationships of a utilitarian nature.

Similar attention is drawn to social relationships as important buffers against the stresses of job loss in Bakke's report (1940) of family conditions that foster optimal coping during extended unemployment. Bakke found that the ability and willingness of other family members to assume the provider role following unemployment of the primary breadwinner served to decrease the disruption of family stability. He further observed that extrafamilial relationships were important for sustaining family stability because they provided emotional support and encouragement, financial assistance, job leads, and social pressure to maintain the integrity of the family. Each of these is obviously an example of an emotional or instrumental support. Jahoda, Lazarsfeld, and Zeisel (1971) suggest that differences in family and social relationships, together with differences in financial resources and individual skills and abilities, were responsible for the varied responses to job loss they observed among unemployed workers in Marienthal. Furthermore, they note, as did Bakke, that over time unemployment stress may tax the very relationships that earlier served to moderate its negative effects.

These examples of research carried out during the depression offer richly detailed insights into the potentially moderating roles of family and friends in the face of severe unemployment stress. They imply an appreciation of the experience of job loss and the evolving response to it as a highly complex process in which multiple factors, themselves susceptible to change, determine the outcome. These observations are made largely in reference to family response to unemployment. While it is probably reasonable to assume that the process is similar for the unemployed worker himself, this conclusion rests heavily on inference.

There are also a number of methodological limitations in these studies that suggest caution in relying too heavily on their observations. The data collected were often retrospective, depending on only one or two intensive interviews to capture the broad experience of unemployment. Furthermore, control groups of employed persons were rarely included, leaving to speculation the "main effect" of job loss. Finally, the concept of social support as a particular conditional quality of interpersonal relationships was not addressed directly. Nevertheless, these studies as a group continue to be among our most important resources for a close recording of the experience of unemployment.

A contemporary investigation of a similar nature was carried out by Powell and Driscoll (1973), focusing more directly on the unemployed worker. These researchers outline a four-stage response pattern among unemployed engineers and scientists that includes changes in job-seeking behavior, feelings and attitudes, and relationships with others. Like Komarovsky, Bakke, and Jahoda et al., they observe that support from family and friends is a critical factor in warding off depression and maintaining a consistent job-search effort. At the same time, they emphasize the fact that, over a period of time, unemployment frequently leads to the deterioration of those very same family relations and friendships. In fact, these changes in relationships represent one indicator of the onset of the third stage of unemployment.

A number of other contemporary investigators have noted the negative effects of unemployment on marital relations, and on the family in general (Furstenberg, 1974; Levin, 1975; Rainwater, 1974). Jacobson (1977), however, cautions against blanket acceptance of the proposition that prolonged unemployment per se leads to the deterioration of interpersonal relationships. Working with interview data from a group of middle-class professionals similar to those studied by Powell and Driscoll and looking specifically at the effects of unemployment on friendships, he argues that it is not the quality of particular relationships that changes as a result of unemployment, but rather who is looked upon as a friend. In nonstressful circumstances, persons may identify as friends people who are considered "old" or "close" friends, casual friends, acquaintances, and business associates. When confronted with the stress of unemployment, the criteria become more stringent. What occurs, therefore, is not a loss of friends or a deterioration in friendships, but a recognition that only certain relationships are relevant to the process of coping with unemployment. Jacobson comments further that the availability of financial resources appears to be the leading determinant of mood responses to unemployment as well as of the ability to sustain the job search. It plays a less definitive role in influencing the pattern of relations to others, although it may be more important for the marital relationship. Finally, he takes issue with Powell and Driscoll's concept of fixed stages in the response to unemployment, suggesting that considerable variation in financial resources produces wide variation in the experiences that follow job loss.

Whether unemployment affects important interpersonal relationships by changing one's perceptions and manner of labeling them or by creating circumstances such as a reduction in financial resources that affects relationships, this general body of literature highlights the conditional status of relationships throughout the job loss experience. Consequently, it makes salient the general model we have proposed for research on the stress-support interaction.

Probably the most detailed contemporary report of the role of social supports directly in relation to physical and psychological consequences of job loss is based on a longitudinal study of two groups of blue-collar workers who were terminated from work because of factory closings (Cobb and Kasl, 1977; Gore, 1973; Kasl, Gore, and Cobb, 1975). At each of several data collection points over a two-year period, evidence was obtained that the consequences of job loss were least severe for workers who perceived their spouses, friends, and relatives to be supportive during the course of unemployment. Specifically, Gore (1973) reports that unemployed men with a high perceived level of support had relatively lower and more stable cholesterol levels, reported fewer symptoms of illness and fewer days of not feeling well, and reported less self-condemnation than unemployed men with low levels of perceived support. In addition, unemployed, unsupported men saw themselves as more economically deprived than unemployed, supported men. In fact, while objective measures of economic circumstances indicated that the financial status of both groups of men improved after finding a new job, the inadequately supported men continued to feel economically deprived long after economic stability was reestablished.

These findings make several important contributions to our understanding of the role of social support vis-a-vis unemployment. First, the study provides one of the few empirical tests of the moderating function of interpersonal relationships. Later analyses of more extensive data (Cobb and Kasl, 1977) essentially confirm the earlier findings, although the moderation effect is clearly stronger for psychological than for physiological variables. The longitudinal design in this research also permits observations of the effects of social support at different phases in the experience of unemployment, including reemployment.

The nature of the measures of support employed in this research make it difficult to determine the precise nature of the support provided, as the researchers themselves acknowledge. Gore (1973) suggests that it is likely that the support was of an emotional rather than an instrumental nature, since support did not affect the actual length of unemployment. Finally, the finding that urban men perceived themselves as less adequately supported than rural men is noteworthy and suggests that availability of support may be dependent in part on characteristics of the larger environmental context.

While these data provide the strongest current evidence for a moderating effect of supportive relationships, the findings are in some instances weak and in others difficult to interpret. Cobb and Kasl (1977), for example, find virtually no relationship between measures of perceived social support and their measures of physiological symptoms. Furthermore, there is little evidence that the support variable affects the likelihood of contracting a disease following job loss, except in the case of arthritis. The fact that the measure of support was based heavily on subjective report of the supportiveness of one's spouse and was averaged across the five interview periods suggests two things. First, the test of the effects of social support was conservative, given the global character of the support measure, and second, problems like response bias and social desirability may have confounded the measure of support, making definitive interpretation of the stress/support interaction impossible. We suspect that with finer discrimination in both the measures of stress and support, the overall pattern of results from these data might have been even stronger.

In a recent study of unemployed male and female heads of households, Gore (1977) has begun to examine more directly the kinds of help that an individual needs to cope successfully with unemployment and their influence on one's feelings of being supported. Preliminary analyses indicate that friends are more likely to provide help with the job search than are relatives, while the latter are more apt to provide most other forms of instrumental help (e.g., baby sitting, transportation). These data are unique in their attempt to define more precisely exactly who provides what sort of help during unemployment. An important next step would be to extend this effort by relating these analyses to more differentiated measures of unemployment stress. An interesting related finding is that the amount of help received is not always commensurate with perceptions of being supported. For example, persons who actually receive considerable help from family and friends perceive substantial supportiveness only on the part of kin. While this finding is open to several explanations, its chief significance lies in the need it suggests for the development of social support measures that include more behaviorally oriented indices as well as subjective estimates of social support.

Implications

While the number of studies that bear directly on the issue of the moderation of unemployment stress by interpersonal support is extremely limited, the research as a whole suggests that the moderating effect remains a tenable hypothesis. The moderation of unemployment stress through ties to others can be inferred from early case study observations. Yet, it is apparent that the principal concern of investigators in much of this research was to assess the effects of unemployment on interpersonal relationships rather than to evaluate the effects of relationships on the degree of stress experienced. In the single formal study employing a measure of social support explicitly as a control variable (Cobb and Kasl, 1977; Gore, 1973; Kasl, Gore, and Cobb, 1975), the aftermath of plant closings appears to have had a less detrimental effect on workers who reported high rather than low support. However, the issue of causality in this relation and the nature of the relevant strain responses (physiological and/or psychological) both remain unsettled.

The research strategies for future work that are indicated by this body of literature are to some extent a foregone conclusion for us. The rationale for longitudinal research, based on a model of coping presented at the conclusion of our review of the social support literature, was formulated originally with much of the unemployment research in mind. As we have noted periodically, some evidence exists that the relationships most commonly referenced throughout the literature on social support, i.e., spouses, other family ties, and friends, are often reported as having been affected by the unemployment experience. The fact that potentially supportive relationships are susceptible to change in the face of job loss necessitates process-oriented research strategies for the investigation of the moderation of unemployment stress by one's ties to others. Such an approach is also suitable for an inquiry into which supportive relationships are most resilient in the face of unemployment.

The appropriateness of a research strategy focusing on the process underlying specific responses to job loss is also suggested by some data that indicate significant variation in who it is who provides help for different needs and at different times during unemployment. For example, Gore (1977) reports that for unemployed men, friends or relatives are the major source of help for about half the needs measured. For each need, a large number of persons also receives support from a secondary source. Granovetter (1973) and Foote's (1973) research on the job search also suggests that for different groups of unemployed persons, the most important channels of help may vary. Finally, Jacobson (1977) reports that the designation of a friend changes over the course of unemployment, implying that different needs requiring the support of different relationships develop with prolonged job deprivation. Finlayson (1976), in describing patterns of help for wives of hospitalized spouses, observes a similar pattern that is associated directly with increasingly felt needs for emotional support as stress persists.

Within the framework of the coping process, several more focused considerations for research on social support and unemployment deserve mention. The first pertains to the subjective-objective dimension in the measurement of social support. Short of the use of participant-observers to rate support received on the basis of an independent set of criteria, some attention needs to be paid to the design of self-report, but context specific and behaviorally oriented, measures of social support. Gore's (1977) data, indicating a discrepancy between respondents' recollections of specific forms of help received from others and their overall impressions of being supported, suggest that at least for some respondents and some of their relationships, reported feelings of support cannot be relied upon to capture what may really have transpired. Which component of social support may in fact be most important for moderating unemployment stress is, for the moment, an unresolved issue. But to the extent that concrete help has been received, the measuring of perceived supportiveness alone is inadequate.

Another stronger caution pertaining to the measure of social support is indicated by the work of Finlayson (1976). She asked wives of spouses with heart disease about the kind and amount of help they had received shortly after their husbands were hospitalized. A year later she interviewed the respondents again and asked the same questions about support in reference to the earlier time period. At the second interview, wives consistently underestimated the amount of support they had reported receiving a year earlier. Finlayson interprets this finding as the failure to recall temporary but significant aid by numerous associates at the height of stress and a focusing of attention on the emotional support of a few intimate friends whose support was sustained. The data are especially interesting because they suggest that the observation in some unemployment research (Jacobson, 1977; Komarovsky, 1940) that a few very close relationships are often the most vital sources of support during the job loss period may be partly an artifact of measurement procedures. The well-documented effects of memory loss on retrospective measures obviously constitute a problem for self-report measures of social support that involve recall. The problem is further exacerbated by the fact that unemployment research deals with particularly stressful circumstances. Since stress has a strong effect on memory, some of the strain induced by unemployment may directly influence the measurement of support. While there is no completely satisfactory solution to this problem at present, it reinforces the other arguments for the assessment of social support in as close proximity as possible to specific stresses.

As a concluding reminder, a process approach should be used in future research, not simply to enable one to identify more precisely the significant periods in the experience following job loss where different social supports become relevant. It is also an approach that is compatible with the idea that social support is an endogenous factor in this process, where workers' relationships that are potentially supportive in the face of unemployment stress can also be altered by that stress. The actual moderation of one's stress by the help of another, therefore, represents only one side of a reciprocal relation between stress and support. Furthermore, to the extent that one's social supports are also vulnerable to stresses precipitated by a change in the economy, quite apart from those accompanying one's own loss of work, they may constitute an important element in the larger relationship between the macroeconomy and the individual.

Social Support and the Macroeconomy

We introduced this discussion of the moderation of unemployment stress by noting its potential relevance to the process underlying the relationship between personal well-being and the macroeconomy. Because the literature we have examined focuses principally on the individual or family who faces job loss, we have had few opportunities to address this more encompassing problem. It is important that we return to this issue and establish some initial considerations for locating interpersonal supports in the larger relation.

The most straightforward approach might be to treat social support as a personal resource which, in light of relevant attitudinal and dispositional inclinations, is mobilized in unique ways when coping with unemployment. Interpersonal supports might also be drawn from a variety of sources at different levels of the social organization, e.g., the family, neighborhood, and community. In this framework, social support represents an exogenous variable in the relation between the macroeconomy and the individual. We suspect, however, that the functioning of interpersonal supports here is considerably more complex, if only because of its conditional status vis-a-vis such factors as the attributes of the stressor, the effects of stress on interpersonal relationships, and the structure of the coping process, which we have emphasized repeatedly.

368

The conditional nature of social support may also be related to other factors that are particularly salient in the process linking the macroeconomy to the individual's well-being. For example, the observation has already been made that the availability of a relationship for support may be influenced in several ways by the impact of the stressor itself, especially if the relationship involves reciprocal obligations. Similarly, stress generated by the economy at large can be conceptualized as affecting one's supportive resources through its effects on group-centered supports, e.g., climate or quality of relationships. In our research we are currently examining one critical locus of social support as well as stress experienced by the unemployed person, the family. However, the family itself is of interest to us as an object of economic stress. The mechanism through which stress is introduced into that system is conceptualized as the loss of work by the family breadwinner. The resulting changes in patterns of family activity and relationships are treated as strain. From the perspective of the unemployed person, his/her own unemployment status is therefore a determining influence on the structure and functioning of the family, which in turn determine the availability and quality of family supports. Previous research on unemployment has often treated the family either as a source of potential support or as the object of economic stress. Rarely have family relationships and climate been viewed as dependent measures of family stress *and* potential moderators of individual stress within the same research design. This interdependence between an individual's unemployment and family supports further complicates the process underlying the basic macro/micro relation (see figure 2).

It may also be the case that interpersonal contexts like the family and neighborhood are affected by economic change independently of the employment status of a focal individual. For example, Catalano and Dooley (1977) suggest that one correlate of large-scale unemployment may be an increased frequency of other stressful life events at an intermediate level of social organization like the community. These events, in turn, may negatively influence neighborhood and community climate, so that

369

Figure 2
Interdependency of Family and Individual Responses to Unemployment

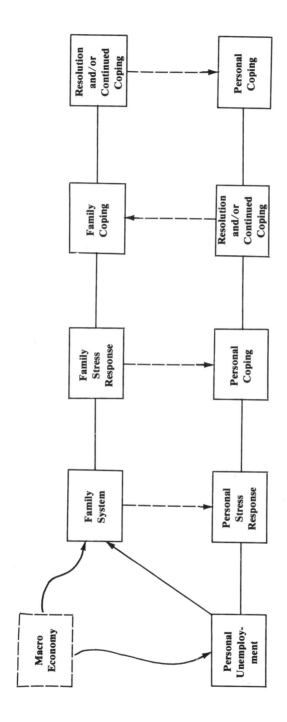

individuals who must cope with their own unemployment also experience the added stress of declining neighborhood morale. Similarly, sectors of one's social network characterized by especially high rates of unemployment (e.g., among work associates or neighbors), may generate nonsupportive climates, and, more directly, may mean that there are fewer persons with the inclination or energy to provide support. Additionally, unemployment, or the fear of it, may create overt competition and tension. Hence the social isolation and withdrawal often taken as evidence of the unemployed person's failure to cope with stress may in fact represent a group rather than individual dynamic. Tolsdorf (1975) has emphasized the importance of one's orientation to the use of the social network for support, e.g., collective vs. individualistic approaches to problem solving, as well as the formal characteristics of the network, for explaining health-related outcomes. Assuming that such dispositions are at least in part situationally determined, they may be responsive to the degree of stress experienced not only by the individual but by his/her network of relationships as well.

Two additional issues deserve some comment. Our ultimate concern is with economic stressors precipitated at the macro level and the ensuing consequences at the micro level. However, the fact that intermediate levels of social organization may constitute important intervening structures makes it relevant to consider the process of coping with economic change at these levels. Without going into an elaborate discussion of this issue, we can simply say that the concept of social support or something akin to it may also be a pertinent factor in, for example, the success of a family as a *social unit* in confronting economic and employment crises. Thus, a second order of social resources, those that aid in the coping of social systems from which individuals in turn draw support, has an indirect bearing on the consequences of stress for the individual. From this point of view the depression studies of supports for *family* coping with unemployment are studies of second-order supportive resources.

This view of intermediate levels of social organization as sources of individual support raises the possibility that the disruption of social relations within communities, neighborhoods, and the like constitutes one of the most important forms of economic change in terms of widespread personal costs. The destruction of socially structured links to others may ultimately prove to be equally, if not more, damaging to the individual than is the direct loss of resources obtained from work. An appropriate analogy is suggested by Fried's observation (1973) of the disintegration of neighborhood life per se during urban renewal as a major loss in the lives of displaced individuals.

A final comment regarding social support resources as a variable in the macro/micro relation pertains to their distribution in the population. When viewed from the perspective of the individual, the determination of particular supportive relationships tends to be located in attitudinal and dispositional characteristics of the interacting parties, and perhaps in the influence of the immediate surroundings. However, as interest shifts to the wider network of social supports, it becomes apparent that potentially supportive relationships are not only situated in varied social systems, but that the latter have in themselves a structured relationship to one another. Thus, a map of one's network of ties to others is shaped by macro social structure as well as the characteristics of more delimited social contexts and one's unique interpersonal preferences. Howard (1977), for example, reports that the characteristics of workers' neighborhood and peer relationships in India are systematically related to workers' locations within the larger system of production, varying especially in relation to the degree of bureaucratization and industrialization in the workplace. To the extent that the pattern of one's associations with others is constrained in important ways by the organization of production, social support resources and economic stressors may have a common locus of social distribution.

A Final Note

The concept of social support as treated in this paper makes most sense in the context of the larger question addressed to each of the contributions in this volume—what bearing does the macroeconomy have on personal health and well-being, and how are its effects generated. As one potential element in this relation, social support deserves consideration at multiple levels of social analysis if its contributions as a moderating variable are to be fully appreciated. Such an approach also has practical implications, given a rapidly developing interest in social support as an attribute of individuals among human service practitioners as well as academic investigators. There is a real danger that a social support bandwagon is in the making that might obscure the central issue of widespread economic and social stressors by focusing attention on the inadequacy of personal supports or of the abilities to mobilize them. Such a development would go hand in hand with acquiescence to national economic policies which define five percent unemployment as a structural necessity for a full employment economy. The irony is that, as the concept of social support gains status among human service providers, this development itself becomes a clear indicator of the existence of widespread social stressors. As we have argued in this paper, social support is not only a personal resource but a socially distributed commodity which can reflect the same degree, if not the same patterns, of those inequalities that presently characterize the distribution of economic resources and stressors.Hence the larger societal issue of structured inequalities is inescapable, whether one's principal concern is with the reduction of social stressors or the enhancement of supportive relationships. The latter cannot be reduced to mere idiosyncratic differences among individuals. The problem of locating social supports in the relation between the macroeconomy and the individual is therefore not simply an interesting academic matter. Its resolution should serve to reveal with greater clarity the extent to which human relationships are societally, as well as interpersonally, structured, and thus the degree to which inadequate access to supportive others is a social as well as an individual problem.

REFERENCES

Angell, Robert. *The Family Encounters the Depression.* New York: Scribners and Sons, 1936.

Bakke, E. W. *Citizens Without Work.* New Haven: Yale University Press, 1940.

Basowitz, Harold, Persky, H., Korchin, Sheldon, and Grinker, R. *Anxiety and Stress.* New York: McGraw Hill, 1955.

Bloom, Bernard. *Community Mental Health: A General Introduction.* Monterey: Brooks/Cole Publications, 1977.

Brenner, M. H. *Estimating the Social Costs of National Economic Policy: Implications for Mental and Physical Health, and Criminal Aggression.* A study prepared for the Joint Economic Committee of Congress. Washington: Government Printing Office, 1976.

Brenner, M. H. *Mental Illness and the Economy.* Cambridge: Harvard University Press, 1973.

Burke, Ronald John and Weir, T. *Organizational Climate and Informal Helping Process in Work Settings.* Unpublished manuscript. York University, 1975.

Catalano, Ralph and Dooley, David. Economic Predictors of Depressed Mood and Stressful Life Events. *Journal of Health and Social Behavior,* 1977.

Cobb, Sidney. A Model for Life Events and Their Consequences in B. S. Dohrenwend and B. P. Dohrenwend, eds. *Stressful Life Events: Their Nature and Effects.* New York: John Wiley and Sons, 1974.

Cobb, Sidney. Social Support as a Moderator of Life Stress. *Psychosomatic Medicine,* 1976, 38:300-314.

Cobb, Sidney and Kasl, Stanislav. *Termination: The Consequences of Job Loss.* National Institute for Occupational Safety and Health. Research Report. Publication No. 77-224, June 1977.

Croog, Sidney H. The Family as a Source of Stress, in S. Levine and N. Scotch, eds. *Social Stress.* Chicago: Aldine, 1970.

Dohrenwend, B. S. and Dohrenwend, B. P., eds. *Stressful Life Events: Their Nature and Effects.* New York: John Wiley and Sons, 1974.

Eisenberg, Phillip and Lazarsfeld, Paul. The Psychological Effects of Unemployment. *Psychological Bulletin,* 1938, 35:358-390.

Faris, R. E. C. and Dunham, H. W. *Mental Disorders in Urban Areas.* Chicago: University of Chicago Press, 1939.

Ferman, L. A. *Family Adjustment to Unemployment in an Urban Setting.* National Institute of Mental Health, Research Proposal, 1975 (Grant #MH-26546).

Finlayson, Angela. Social Networks and Coping Resources: Lay Help and Consultation Patterns Used by Women in Husbands' Post-Infarction Career. *Social Science and Medicine,* 1976, 10:97-103.

Foote, Andrea. *Occupational Mobility and the Job Change: Channels of Job Information in the Detroit Area.* University of Michigan, 1973.

Fried, Marc. *The World of the Urban Working Class.* Cambridge: Harvard University Press, 1973.

Furstenberg, Frank. Work Experience and Family Life. In O'Toole, James, ed. *Work and the Quality of Life Resource Papers for Work in America.* Cambridge: MIT Press, 1974.

Gabarino, James. A Preliminary Study of Some Ecological Correlates of Child Abuse: The Impact of Socioeconomic Stress in Mothers. *Child Development,* 1976, 47:178-184.

Gore, Susan. The Effect of Social Support in Moderating the Health Consequences of Unemployment. *Journal of Health and Social Behavior,* 1978.

Gore, Susan. *The Human Consequences of Unemployment: The Role of Economic and Social Support Resources.* Unpublished manuscript, University of Massachusetts-Boston.

Gore, Susan. *The Social Supports of Urban Unemployed.* Paper presented at the annual meeting of the American Sociological Association, Chicago, 1977.

Granovetter, Mark S. The Strength of Weak Ties. *American Journal of Sociology,* 1973, 78:1360-1380.

Heller, Kenneth. The Effects of Social Support: Prevention and Treatment Implications. To appear in A. P. Goldstein and F. H. Kanfer, eds. *Maximizing Treatment Gains: Transfer Enhancement in Psychotherapy.* New York: Academic Press, in press.

375

Holmes, T. and Rahe, R. H. The Social Readjustment Rating Scale. *Journal of Psychosomatic Research,* 1967, 11:213-218.

Howard, Leslie. *Industrialization and Community in Chotanagpur.* Unpublished Doctoral Dissertation, Harvard University, 1974.

Howard, Leslie. *Workplace and Residence in the Communities of Indian Factory and Non-Factory Workers.* Paper presented at the Annual Meeting of the American Sociological Association, Chicago, September 1977.

Jacobson, D. *Time and Work: Unemployment Among Middle-Class Professionals.* Unpublished manuscript, Brandeis University, 1977.

Jahoda, Marie, Lazarsfeld, Paul, and Zeisel, Hans. *Marienthal, The Sociography of an Unemployed Community.* Chicago: Aldine, Atherton, Inc., 1971.

Janis, I. L. Problems of Theory in the Analysis of Stress Behavior. *Journal of Social Issues,* 1954, 10:12-25.

Kaplan, B. H., Cassel, J. L., and Gore, Susan. Social Support and Health. *Medical Care,* 1977, 15:5, 47-58.

Kasl, Stanislav, Gore, Susan, and Cobb, Sidney. The Experience of Losing a Job: Reported Changes in Health, Symptoms, and Illness Behavior. *Psychosomatic Medicine,* 1975, 37:106-122.

Komarovsky, M. *The Unemployed Man and His Family,* New York: Dryden Press, 1940.

Kroll, A., Dinklage, L., Lee, J., Morley, E., and Wilson, E. *Career Development: Growth and Crisis,* New York: John Wiley and Sons, 1970.

Levin, Hannah. *Work, the Staff of Life.* Paper presented at the Annual Convention of the American Psychological Association, Chicago, September 1975.

Liem, Joan and Liem, G. R. *Life Events, Social Support Resources, and Physical and Psychological Dysfunction.* Submitted for publication, 1977.

Liem, G. R. and Liem, Joan. Social Class and Mental Illness Reconsidered: The Role of Economic Stress and Social Support. *Journal of Health and Social Behavior,* 1978.

Moos, Rudolph and Insel, P. *Combined Preliminary Manual Family, Work, and Group Environment Scales.* Palo Alto, CA: Consulting Psychologists Press, Inc., 1974.

Morley, Eileen. Coping Styles Before the Career Crisis Event: The Anticipatory Phase. In Arthur Kroll, Lillian Dinklage, Jennifer Lee, Eileen Morley, and Eugene Wilson, *Career Development: Growth and Crisis.* New York: John Wiley and Sons, 1970.

Myers, J. K., Lindenthal, J. J., and Pepper, M. P. Life Events, Social Integration, and Psychiatric Symptomatology. *Journal of Health and Social Behavior,* 1975, 16:121-127.

Newbrough, John Robert. *Community Mental Health Epidemiology: Nashville.* A proposal to the Center for Epidemiologic Studies, National Institute of Mental Health, 1973.

Nuckolls, K. B., Cassel, J. L., and Kaplan, B. H. Psychological Assets, Life Crisis, and the Prognosis of Pregnancy. *American Journal of Epidemiology,* 1972, 95:431.

Pierce, A. The Economic Cycle and the Social Suicide Rate. *American Sociological Review,* 1967, 32:475-482.

Pinneau, S. R. *Effects of Social Support on Psychological and Physiological Strains.* Unpublished Doctoral Dissertation, The University of Michigan, 1975.

Powell, Douglas H. and Driscoll, Patrick Joseph. Middle Class Professionals Face Unemployment. *Society,* 1973, 10:18-26.

Rabkin, J. G. and Struening, E. L. Life Events, Stress, and Illness. *Science,* 1976, 194:1013-1020.

Rainwater, Lee. Work, Well-Being, and Family Life. In O'Toole, James, ed. *Work and the Quality of Life Resource Papers for Work in America.* Cambridge: MIT Press, 1974.

Rapoport, Lydia. The State of Crisis: Some Theoretical Implications. In Howard J. Parad, ed. *Crisis Intervention.* New York: Family Service Association, 1965.

Sarason, S. B. *The Psychological Sense of Community: Prospects for a Community Psychology.* San Francisco: Jossey-Bass, 1974.

Schachter, S. *The Psychology of Affiliation.* Stanford: Stanford University Press, 1959.

Sclar, Eliot and Hoffman, F. *Planning Mental Health Service for a Declining Economy.* National Center for Health Services, Research Final Report, Grant #3 R01 HS02266-01, January 1978.

Scott, Ralph Samuel and Howard, Alvin Ray. Models of Stress, in S. Levine and N. Scotch, eds. *Social Stress,* Chicago: Aldine Publishing Co., 1970.

Sheppard, Harold and Belitsky, A. *The Job Hunt.* Baltimore: Johns Hopkins Press, 1966.

Tolsdorf, Christopher C. *Social Networks and the Coping Process.* Unpublished Doctoral Dissertation, University of Massachusetts, June 1975.

Tolsdorf, Christopher C. Social Networks, Support, and Coping: An Exploratory Study. *Family Process,* 1976, 15:407-417.

Warren, Donald and Clifford, David. *Help Seeking Behavior and the Neighborhood Context: Some Preliminary Findings of a Study of Helping Networks in the Urban Community.* Unpublished manuscript, The Institute of Labor and Industrial Relations, The University of Michigan, 1975.

Wechsler, H. and Pugh, T. F. Fit of Individual and Community Characteristics and Rates of Psychiatric Hospitalization. *American Journal of Sociology,* 1967, 73:331-338.

14
UNEMPLOYMENT & MENTAL HEALTH: AN INTERPRETATIVE SUMMARY

S. M. MILLER

To review what occurred at a meeting is a pleasure, for there is the enjoyment of discovering that we did more than we realized at the time. The summarizer role permits one to engage in the near-fantasy of decoding what took place, reconstructing a conference theme that people may not have recognized at the time, and may still not recognize after they have read the summary. I have divided my comments, which do not constitute a comprehensive or true-to-life summary but are my interpretations of themes, into ten parts: 1) the unfolding of research, 2) purposes, 3) the setting, 4) research policy models, 5) economic meanings, 6) the black box, 7) intervention-oriented research, 8) effects of unemployment, 9) methodology, and 10) questions.

1. The Unfolding of Research

This conference should be seen as a middle stage. Metro Center and other organizations have funded a variety of interesting research projects. The conference called together people who have been engaged in this research so that they could construct a common language, become acquainted with each other's work, build a sense of their collective hypotheses and methodologies, and become more broadly acquainted with the data sets that might be available. This conference does not represent the final stage, but rather an intermediate one to be followed by other sessions as research and experimentation continue. This is the end of the beginning: the conclusion of the first stage of commissioning research and conducting studies based on the research findings presently available; a first assessment of what the research is adding up to and a preliminary shaping of what our goals should be.

2. Purposes

Three purposes appeared. Some overlap and some clash; some are broad and others are narrow. One interpretation that can be made of the work on unemployment is that it contributes to the development of a new social-economic paradigm of how the market and economy should function and of what the standards for judging successful economic functioning should be. This emerging paradigm puts productive employment at the center of economic decision making, instead of regarding it as the residue of decisions directed to other goals. The making of that new paradigm in the broadest possible perspective was the aim of this conference.

A second, less ambitious interpretation sees the development of a *challenge perspective,* which questions that easy acceptance of a trade-off between inflation and unemployment. The trade-off approach permits a high level of unemployment as an economically necessary development. The challenge perspective has doubts about the "new wisdom" that unemployment is neither psychologically damaging nor economically disturbing. While it may be difficult to make the attitudinal and policy changes implied in this perspective, it is not so comprehensive as the call for a new paradigm.

The third purpose is to learn how to ameliorate the consequences of unemployment. Explanations of the "black box" or the reality of the connections between unemployment and well-being are not the most important questions, for the point here is to explore what factors would help to make people and communities feel less disturbed and disrupted as a result of unemployment. This is a much more modest outlook than either the challenge or the new paradigm perspectives.

The fact that the conference shifted back and forth among these three perspectives has been a major source of difficulty. People with differing assumptions, issues, and questions learn only late in the day what binds as well as divides them. They learn that others' poetry may have some prose in it, and one's own prose some poetry.

3. *The Setting*

We are discussing the impact of unemployment in an economic-political social climate where this issue is not given a central place; the disturbance is rather concerned with the threat of inflation and the importance of maintaining the economic competitiveness of the United States in the world market. While there has been a loss of faith in economic management, and certainly in the Keynesian paradigm, there are still those who cling to it. The current economic panacea calls for lower taxes on the rich and on large corporations in order to encourage investment; the call is to reduce the public social sector in order to reduce inflationary pressures. This general point of view requires the keeping down of wages and the acceptance of high-level, chronic unemployment as a necessary characteristic of the economy. A special concern is to build-up the competitiveness of manufacturing production in the United States in order to increase exports and decrease imports, thus achieving a more favorable balance of trade. This strategy I have termed "the recapitalization of capitalism."[1] It is an effort to restructure American capitalism for more effective world competition by lowering inflation and growth through reduced taxation and a contraction of the welfare state.

An obvious question then is: Who shall bear the burden of change? Who shall feel the burden of the effort to improve the United States' international position? Who shall suffer from the burden of pro-investment taxation policies and a contracting public sector? Those of us who have been around for some time recognize the profound turn in the ideological and political climate

1. For analysis of this approach, see S. M. Miller, "The Re-Capitalization of Capitalism," *Social Policy,* November-December, 1978.

of the United States. Bold assertions from prestigious people command us to view the sixties as a demonstration of utter failure: nothing works, governments can only fail. Further, it is contended, the important thing in American life today is to reduce expectations, because that would solve most of the difficulties; the problem of the United States is that our expectations of a desirable standard of living, of what the economy can accomplish, are much too high. If only we would lower our expectations, we are told, American society could function effectively. The sixties, then, are viewed as a failure not only in terms of the ineffectiveness of policy and implementation, but as wrong-headed in terms of goals. This interpretation disregards the possibility that the sixties set up high goals and limited means to achieve them from a desire to cope with American difficulties "on the cheap." The attack on the social policy and high aspirations of the sixties questions the very basic goals of greater equality.

I doubt whether the policies involved in the recapitalization of capitalism strategy will be fully carried out, but it is already clear that a significant political-ideological switch has been successfully engineered. We are now faced with the situation of trying to push forward those issues that have been shoved to the rear, particularly the issue of unemployment and its consequences. Consequently, it is important to focus on unemployment and to continue doing so in order to broaden the understanding of this country, its possibilities and its responsibilities, and to move beyond the growing belief that less is more for the vulnerable and that more for the well-to-do is more for all.

One of the gravest dangers in this period is a further split between the marginal working classes in the United States and the organized working classes. If, as I think likely, organized workers do contest the worsening conditions, there may be some loosening of their restraints, and the major brunt of economic change would then be borne by the most vulnerable group, the poor. That is a great danger and it requires that renewed attention be paid to the vulnerables in American society.

4. Research-Policy Models

Let me return now to the issues of research and policy. The direct model presented at the conference is illustrated by worker-organized economic development, particularly as focused on bills proposed in Congress. Research, bill-writing, coalition-building, and lobbying fuse in an effort to produce valuable legislation. This model is built on a direct line between research and action: it requires the ability to capitalize on events and use them for research, promote the understanding of issues, stimulate direct small-scale, local action to solve particular problems, and to move toward legislation that will facilitate the desirable actions. It is a powerful, important, and useful model, one that we should hope to be able to follow.

I think, however, that if we focus on that model alone, we will frequently be disappointed. Occasionally, skillful political-academic entrepreneurs, like those involved in the Whyte-Blasi and the Youngstown-Alperovitz cases, can galvanize legislation and make a fairly direct linkage between research and action. But research and action are seldom connected that directly and suddenly. I emphasize *suddenly*. Sometimes a swift connection occurs, but that is rare. While the model is important and useful, it should not be regarded as the only one possible. I do not oppose it; I simply doubt its widespread applicability.

Personally, and I admit that it is a personality quirk, I am more in favor of a second model, the long term influence of ideas and the basic shaping of the political and social climate. While this model also hopes to influence the current political agenda, it does not see that achievement as the only criterion of success. The quest is to affect consciousness, to identify the issues that are accorded prime attention as well as the ways in which they are defined and talked about. The first model obviously has a similar intent, and the proposing of legislation may be the most feasible educational device. I reiterate that I am not arguing against the first model, which attempts to influence directly and immediately a Congressional or presidential action. Rather, I wish to remind us that such activity requires luck as well as brilliant footwork, that some of us are skillful and dogged at it and most of us are not, and that it is seldom accomplished.

A division of labor has to be accepted in which some are usefully pursuing the second model while others are being encouraged to exert their skills on behalf of the first model. What I fear is that people will feel that nothing worthwhile can be attempted unless supportive legislation can be immediately attained. At its worst, Potomac fever becomes "Washingtonitis," the belief that legislation is exclusively the result of manipulation, idiosyncrasies, and personal networks; this belief rejects the part played by larger economic, cultural, and political forces outside Washington, and ignores the fact that these influences also affect the way in which legislation is implemented. We should regard either model with a high degree of openness, because serendipity—gratuitious and unanticipated favorable events—can have a marked effect on what occurs.

I am skeptical about a tight research agenda, partly because at various times I have tried to organize people into systematic research agendas. Without a sizable amount of money and/or a captive population of researchers, the best that can be done is to get people working in somewhat complementary ways. In my view, a research agenda that we might develop would not be a tight briefing of research issues—someone volunteering for 1-a, sub c, and so on—but, more plausibly, the recognition of the impact that we might have if each one were to take on a particular part of the overall project. This would mean that we were not relying on one another to the extent that if some failed to carry through their assignment, the research agenda would collapse. Thus, we could focus on a limited set of activities in the hope of having a collective impact, a joint effect, without feeling that if we are unable to get a closely aligned set of research data, we will have failed in our endeavor. *Converging work,* rather than a collective piece of work, is our most promising course.

5. *Economic Meanings*

The basic issue of the conference is what we mean by economy and unemployment. There is uncertainty about the extent to which we are exclusively, or, at least, primarily oriented toward the impact of unemployment. Are we equally concerned about other negative economic circumstances, such as low wages or adverse job circumstances? Are we concerned about underemployment, whether of Ph.D.s or high-school dropouts? Is the problem only that of full-scale, direct unemployment, or are we also concerned with underemployment in terms of income and skill? This is an unresolved issue. Obviously we can try to resolve it, but the problem here is that it drives us back to the point where each of us started and to what the purposes of our work may be.

At the policy level, the question becomes: is the goal that everyone should have *a* job adopted because we are so concerned about unemployment, or is it our aim that everyone have a "decent" job? Would we be just as satisfied with a truly full employment economy made up of jobs that people thought were undesirable as with a truly full employment economy made up of jobs that offered much more to the employee? Do we think that the attainment of the second type of full employment economy is too difficult, incurs too great costs, and is too romantic in its view of people's interests and capacities? We divide on such issues, and the tension among us cannot readily be resolved, if at all. It is an issue to which we will return again and again, both in our work and in political discussions.

We now come to recognize that "unemployment" is too gross a label for the processes that concern us. We have discerned different patterns of unemployment—people who are unemployed for a long time with no connection to work at all; people who are unemployed for a certain period but have a parallel involvement in the irregular economy; people who mix together unemployment insurance, welfare, training, and irregular jobs; people who at a particular moment may have regular jobs but who face frequent bouts of unemployment. These are different vectors of experience, and one would expect different consequences to follow. To understand the results of unemployment, we must start with a recognition of various unemployment patterns. We could break up the concept of unemployment into types and patterns and then perhaps trace their respective consequences. We have been concerned here with three major issues: the black box, the intervention-oriented pattern, and the effects of unemployment.

6. *The Black Box*

The black box issue has determined the major orientation of this meeting: if one takes the Brenner data as given, if there is indeed a relationship between unemployment and socially adverse indicators, how should this relationship be explained? What are the connections? What set of intervening processes connect unemployment with the adverse effects experienced by the individual or individuals?

Some of us doubt whether a clarification of the black box should in fact be the core issue in our effort to influence social policy. They believe that research would be much more persuasive and influential if a higher priority were assigned to the unemployment issue; making starkly, unmistakably, and unavoidably obvious the negative consequences of unemployment without any concern with why this is so. A muted reply has been that a depiction of the costs of unemployment would not be convincing. Furthermore, even if we could explain why unemployment has negative effects, that explanation alone would not serve to change people's minds. The implications here are that if one wants to pursue the black box, one should pursue it for its significant consequences in general and not for its influence on public policy. In short, we were offered the black box as a venture because of its potential influence upon public policy; but some of us are questioning the validity of such an outcome.

It may be, however, that in order to make research more useful, we will have to make much more headway in trying to understand the crucial intervening processes. This means that it would be worthwhile to invest in black-box research, even if it should not have a strong pay-off in terms of public influence; this issue is unresolved.

At first, I had the impression that we had not said very much about black-box processes, but, as I thought about our discussions, I discerned a variety of guesses, hypotheses, and possible lines of inquiry about the connections between unemployment and behavior. One such line might be called a set of anomie hypotheses.

Three types of anomie explanations appeared. One was the *destruction of valued economic roles*. What unemployment did was to deprive individuals of economic roles that were significant to them. Second, a derivative to some extent of the first but somewhat independent, was the *destruction of valued social roles*. Difficulties occur not directly from the loss of the job, but from the impact of joblessness upon social living. While similar to the first, it has another nuance. A third anomie hypothesis was the *loss of confidence about the future*. Here it is not so much what is actually happening to the individual as the collapse of expectations that is disturbing. All three of them, in some form or another, are Durkheimian explanations of what is taking place.

Of a different order is number four, *the shock hypothesis:* That it is the rapid, disturbing events that perturb the individual and community; the effect of the shock is the destructive element. In a sense, this too is an anomie hypothesis, which I did not at first realize. The significant factors here are rapid change, the sudden breakdown of norms, and the swift change in life conditions. Perhaps anomie is the only way one can understand the world. (I often wonder what would have happened to Western social science if Durkheim, Weber, and Marx had never lived. Certainly social scientists would have few hypotheses, for the social sciences today are still largely derivatives from the three of them. I would add Freud to the list because the crude psychology that enters into so much current social analysis tends to be Freudian. That doesn't mean that Freudian theorizing was crude, but that much of the application of Freud tends to be so.)

A fifth hypothesis deals with the concept of *loss of meaning*. This refers less to the network of ties that some of us discussed than to all those adverse influences just mentioned—loss of valued economic and social roles, collapse of confidence about the future, the shock of events. Their weakening effect destroys the meaning that individuals have found in their world. The individual, perturbed by what is taking place is his life, lays himself open to a variety of additionally disturbing influences and is forced to seek a new stage of meaning. Until that stage is reached—and this may take some time—a great uneasiness prevails.

A sixth hypothesis, a complementary one that is similar to hypothesis 4, asserts that *any kind of change is disruptive.* Sociologists and psychologists have studied the impact of occupational mobility, both up and down, and geographic mobility. But this hypothesis is broader than that, asserting that the frequency and rapidity of changes are central to the disruption and the negative consequences.

The seventh breaks new ground; it turns to the internal experience of work. Here the unemployed person must face the *loss of the desirable positive aspects of working.* This loss also disrupts the external ties of the individual, but the emphasis is on the job situation itself. The loss of the job situation is, in itself, disruptive to the individual, and it also gives the future a threatening aspect.

A final issue in connection with the black box, one that was not well expressed, is whether it is *change or chronicity* that is crucial. Is the important issue long term unemployment or long term low wages, or is it changed circumstances? Can people or communities be in stable adverse circumstances and yet manage them in ways that are not too disturbing to them, or are such circumstances disturbing to them without their realizing it? Or is change in circumstances the significant force? Recall the de Tocqueville hypothesis that revolutions occur not when things are at their worst, but when they have begun to improve; people's expectations increase more rapidly than improvements can take place, and it is the divergence between expectation and practice that widens and causes unrest. In situations of chronic deprivation, people's expectations are low, and therefore less unrest occurs. The de Tocqueville hypothesis expects unrest to increase in times of slow improvement or of improvement followed by a decline. This is the sort of explanation that was hinted at in some of the discussions, but it never came to the fore.

Another issue that was mentioned at various times but remained unintegrated into our thinking was that of *contextual elements:* to what extent is what is happening to others important in how experience is absorbed by an individual? What effect does a high or low rate of unemployment nationally or locally have on the unemployed individual? Comparative position is important.

A second contextual element, again not well worked out, is to what extent we are concerned about individual reactions or the *reactions of collectivities:* neighborhoods, towns, workers of a particular plant or union? What influences the different feelings and responses of the collectivity and of individuals? For example, individuals may feel that they are coping adequately, but the collectivity may feel that as a group it is failing to do so. This interplay needs consideration, as does the concept of role, and we have not paid sufficient attention to it.

We recognized, though we did not develop the idea, that processes of impact may vary among groups: it may not be the same process, the same black box, for everybody. *Differential response* has to be studied. Further, different patterns of unemployment may have different processes of influence. The challenge was presented that many people may find work unsatisfying, so that its deprivation would not be seen as a threat. The stance that many of us accepted, although we did not always say so, is that while work may be unsatisfying, unemployment is more so. The fact that many people are unhappy at work does not mean that unemployment is a happy condition.

These are some of the issues, hypotheses, guesses, and lines of thought that we had about the black box and the processes by which unemployment affects people.[2]

---

2. Since so much of our thinking about the black box is influenced by Emile Durkheim, we might find it useful to use Melvin Seeman's Durkheimianization of Marx's concept of alienation as a check-list. Seeman distinguishes five dimensions of alienation: powerlessness, meaninglessness, normlessness, isolation, self-estrangement. Melvin Seeman, "On the Meaning of Alienation," *American Sociological Review,* 24:6 (Dec. 1959), 783-91; reprinted (among many other places) in Ada W. Finifter, ed., *Alienation and the Social System* (New York: John Wiley), 1972.

7. Intervention-Oriented Research

Another set of discussions concerned intervention-oriented research, the *amelioratist standpoint* of reducing the impact of unemployment on the individual. I am not clear where those doing social support research intend to move next. What I picked up were some issues that were raised.

One issue is to what extent does social support (network support) contribute to an improvement in people's conditions in the absence of real economic resources? Can the family or neighborhood network be effective even if the larger community does not channel some economic resources to the unemployed? Or does network effectiveness depend on a combination of a social network plus economic resources? Can the social network be effective without economic resources? Conversely, can economic resources be effective without a supportive social network? These are good points that were not probed.

Another issue appeared only once, but it seems worthy of attention. That is the issue of *trust*. To what extent is the network valuable because people feel able to have trust and confidence in others? Does the network engender trust and confidence about what the larger community will do about an individual's situation? In a sense, the concept of trust as it was introduced here was an effort to explain which amelioratist activities might be most effective. The hypothesis might be that without trust, social supports would not be effective.

A different level of interest involved *predispositional problems.* Who was most likely to suffer? The orientation was not primarily toward the identifying of the processes involved in the effects of unemployment; in other words, it bypassed the black box issue. More generally (although more debatably), there is concern about who is most likely to need what kind of help and under what conditions. Many of us conceive of the problem of predisposition in a treatment context. For example, if it were possible to identify those most likely to respond adversely to the stimulus of unemployment, then alleviating measures could be provided early. That thinking led to a broader outlook and to the suggestion that it is worthwhile to study the effectiveness of treatment modalities and programs that have been recommended for those people who suffer the negative consequences of unemployment.

A very different point of view toward social support moved it out of the intervention-oriented perspective and back to the issue of the black box. That idea is to explore the withering of social support and meaning as an integral part of the process by which unemployment adversely affects people. It shifts from the study of social support as an ameliorist activity towards the investigation of such support in terms of understanding anomic processes, i.e., the production of anomie. Those presently involved in social support research do not seem aware of this perspective, and it was suggested as a possible reorientation for social support studies.

A broader contention is that we should consider not only social support but also *income support.* This recommendation returns to an earlier point, which maintains that responses and adaptation to shutdown will differ according to whether there is assurance or uncertainty about future income. Is an unemployment insurance program, which provides strong income guarantees to the community and to the unemployed, responsible for differences in behavior, no matter what the social support situation may be? Does it affect the social support situation? These issues lead to ameliorist questions other than those of social support: how to improve the unemployment insurance system and other income guarantee programs, or, if this is not relevant, how to provide alternative kinds of economic guarantees. This perspective does not look at the issue of intervention narrowly, in terms of social support networks, but takes a more comprehensive view of an *economic support framework,* one of the happier terms arrived at here. The latter perspective was hinted at without being developed.

Intervention-oriented research, then, should be weighed in terms of both social and economic support; ameliorist activities should not be content with only a social support orientation. That is particularly noteworthy because many conference participants, and I certainly include myself in this camp, are quite disturbed about possible abuse of the social support orientation. What might happen—especially in light of the political, economic, social, and attitudinal changes continually taking place in the United States—is that the political palatibility of unemployment might be enhanced by the provision of relatively inexpensive but limited ways of dealing with its adverse effects. Social support would then become a cheap way of dealing with problems of unemployment. The emerging perspective on unemployment focuses on family policy and volunteer activity; not bad ideas in themselves except that they are placed in the context of a belief that social and psychological resources should and can cope with problems. In other words, don't change the economic parameters; don't change economic policy, but persuade people to learn to adapt more readily to the strains we are pressing upon them. Many of us regard this line of argument as a disquieting possibility in the utilization of social supports. This danger is not an inevitable consequence; there may be ways of institutionalizing social support that would limit this possibility, but it is worthwhile to guard against the misapplication of a sound idea.

A final point on intervention-oriented research concerns the issue to which Gar Alperovitz speaks and which came out at various times in the meetings, namely, that we should consider intervention-oriented activity that would facilitate joint efforts of the community or of the plant workers to deal with the issues of unemployment. Some of us talked about whether a disturbing situation might lead to unionization or to other forms of organization supposed to deal with the problem of plant shutdown. Again, we were moving away from the narrow, ameliorative use of social networks and toward economic support and group action. *Intervention is a question not only of treatment, but also of economic and of group action.*

8. Effects of Unemployment

One element of research on the consequences or effects of unemployment is whether we need more research of the kind Harvey Brenner has done, not only to understand the problem better but also to present a more persuasive argument as to the role of unemployment in affecting behavior. I am not sure where our conference people stood on this issue; I now think that we do need more work of Brenner's sort because undoubtedly there will be more and more studies testing, contesting, and applying the Brenner analysis to further methodological issues, as was demonstrated at the conference. Some balance of research will be needed.

A second recommendation is the need for more research on the effects that unemployment has on the community, the neighborhood, and the family. This is also a political question, for people may be much less influenced by national figures on the rate of unemployment that by the experience of unemployment in specific communities. An entity like a town is identifiable and visible, and it has an integrity that people can recognize; it is quite unlike a national percentage. Many Americans may feel that the unemployed or those on welfare do not want to work but at the same time may be concerned about a starving individual. Americans respond to the individualization of problems; therefore community individualization is important. In research, we must understand unemployment in terms of its overall impact on communities and neighborhoods, as well as on individuals.

A third line of study of the consequences of unemployment focuses on those who have not entered the labor market, particularly (but not exclusively) youth. Does widespread unemployment or a low prospect of employment have a real impact upon those who will, or might at some point, be entering the labor market? This applies particularly to women who are thinking of paid employment: will their behavior in the labor market change as they become aware that many are unemployed? The issue here is unemployment's *spread effects* upon those not in the paid labor force.

A fourth consequence is again a broad one. It deals with the effects of unemployment on other parts of the economy: what happens to the local economy, e.g., shopkeepers, when unemployment is widespread? Are those who stay employed likely to have lower incomes and lower wages as a result of the contraction of the local economy? Or does a high rate of unemployment tend to dampen wage increases throughout the nation? The negative consequences of unemployment are visited upon the employed. Similarly, attempts to deal with unemployment may have varied effects on industrial, occupational, and regional sectors. A comprehensive view demands that attention be paid to the diversity of the impacts of unemployment; the immediate situation of the unemployed does not capture the full price of unemployment.

9. *Methodology*

One methodological recommendation is to continue what has been called *descriptive modeling,* that is, the development of typologies, the effort to provide a framework for thinking about specific experiences, the consideration of processes in a consistent and cohesive way, while recognizing that unemployment experiences differ widely. The Ferman work is archetypical in that respect.

A second approach, surprisingly not mentioned, is to study the *reemployed* who had previously been unemployed. Does a positive effect accompany reemployment, or is it limited because of previous job experience or the preceding unemployment? If we are to uncover the impact of unemployment, we might well look at reemployment.

A third suggestion concerning the long term consequences of unemployment upon the community is to investigate the impact on the community of *threats* of unemployment, and not just the fact of unemployment. Threats of unemployment are more frequent than actual plant shutdowns. A fourth suggestion was to study *interventions,* the varying kinds of intervention procedures as outlined above, to discover the conditions that make one or another of these interventions more effective. The fifth recommendation was to study *deviant cases* because the yield from deviant case analysis might be very high.

10. *Questions*

I wish to raise a question specifically for the Metro Center in terms of methodology and the granting process. In some ways, the most provocative and interesting paper at this meeting was that of Peter Marris but I wonder whether an agency like Metro Center can support the sort of research Marris advocates. Metro Center may well be the most open-minded, brave, innovational, and useful of the governmental granting agencies, but even so, it is somewhat captured by the prevailing paradigms and standards in the research that it feels it can and should fund. Should Metro Center be even braver and more imaginative and support the unconventional?

That point leads to the question of what kind of research is useful, which is not a disparaging comment on the research that has been funded, but a question of what activities are useful to engage in, to support, to recognize, and to bring attention to. Why do some questions about economy and unemployment still seem to be unanswered: to what extent are we concerned about change in general or about particular kinds of change; are we concerned about the impact on all groups, or on the most vulnerable groups in society? Most of us seem concerned about the impact on the most vulnerable groups, but there is no full agreement among us. There is no doubt that we must get a sense of where we stand in regard to key questions about the impact of unemployment on the community and on the individual.

It may be my misreading, but I listened to the discussion of physiological indicators with a great deal of disquiet. I gained the impression that they are not reliable indicators to use in measuring the impact of unemployment. They are not, as they first appear, easy and simplified measures, for many supressor effects occur. We should have genuine doubts and questions about using them, and I came away with a critical feeling about relying on them. This reaction may not be realistic, but it is certainly an open question as to what extent these physiological indicators can be used with ease, to what extent with circumspection, to what extent they are useful at all for the kinds of research that we seek.

Another question is: to what extent should we be studying new ways of *community coping* with issues of unemployment? This question includes the new forms of factory ownership that have been suggested and other kinds of community activities. There is the additional question of whether our orientation should be toward studying what actually takes place or toward helping collective or group actions to be more effective. To what extent should we seek an *action research orientation* pointed more toward improvement than toward an analysis of what happened and why? This is the latent, motivating question behind much of the discussion: what kind of researcher do we want to be, what kind of research can be done well and usefully, what makes the greatest contribution in the long run? I am drawn to the action-research approach, partly because of my doubts about much traditional research and, even more, because one learns about history by trying to change it.

Finally, the adequacy of the concept of stress was questioned. A number of people stated their doubts about that term, with all the shades of meanings that it has. I am not clear whether we intend to use it in the future as an organizing concept, or whether it is regarded as a valuable concept in the beginning of research but not later on, or whether it has already outlived its usefulness. Should it be cast aside? If so, what alternatives should come to the fore?

These, then, are some, certainly not all, of the issues and questions of the conference, but this paper is not so much a summary as an interpretation of what is now going on in the United States and where our research might fit in. It also seeks to give some indication of the difficulties and questions that we face in pursuing research. Few studies are directed to unemployment, yet it is and will continue to be a prime, if relatively neglected, issue in the American economy and society. The call is for an effective mobilization of scarce resources to pursue a clear understanding of its consequences and the possibilities of its prevention.

15
FEDERAL LEGISLATION
IN RESPECT TO EMPLOYEE
OWNERSHIP OF FIRMS

JOSEPH R. BLASI

This paper will address the implications of recent Congressional legislation on employee and employee-community ownership of firms that might otherwise be forced to shut down and terminate the employment of their work force. As the Special Assistant for Social Policy for Congressman Peter Kostmayer, I am responsible for the coordination of such legislation, having established the task force that wrote the legislation and served as one of the two major authors of it. William Foote Whyte of Cornell University was instrumental in initiating the project, as a consequence of his research on several firms where employee ownership had grown out of plant shutdowns.

Employee-owned firms are not new, but until now they have been seen simply as a phenomena of little strategic importance in the country's economic and social policy. Whyte has shown that the image of the failing firm that makes local unemployment inevitable is often a myth. Corporations or conglomerates may simply be unwilling to continue operations that yield only moderate profits. This unwillingness to let business enterprises continue to operate which are aimed more at local accommodation and the support of a local work force than at unlimited corporate growth must be recognized as one cause of unemployment. Additionally, the fact that ailing firms can be rejuvenated by community take-overs should suggest that we might look more closely at business shutdowns in general. The need for such examination is justified when we realize that decline in the quality

397

of working life, mistaken steps taken to attain increased worker productivity, denial to workers of participation in management, and a persistent industrial tendency to take operations overseas or to ununionized areas, are all pertinent factors in shutdowns. Economic data in the newspapers cover up social data on the viability of certain organizations.

The legislation referred to above is entitled the Voluntary Job Preservation and Community Stabilization Act. Introduced on 1 March 1978, it provides a fund of $100 million a year for seven years to be loaned to employees out of work because of plant shutdown or relocation, if feasibility studies show that the firm could be run successfully on the basis of employee ownership, perhaps with the help of the community. There are many examples throughout the country of such job-saving mechanisms, and they also have the advantage for the federal government of saving the immense costs of unemployment compensation, welfare and health payments, and job-retraining programs. A recent study by the Department of Commerce, Economic Development Administration praises employee-owned firms for their enhanced profits and points to increased productivity, which has been substantiated by case studies. Robert Strauss, former anti-inflation advisor to the President, told the Senate Finance Committee in July 1978 that employee ownership was an important long term way to combat inflation, particularly since it was connected to increased productivity. The bill is aimed at communities, towns, and neighborhoods where a shutdown means substantial individual, family, and community suffering. It reduces the burden of unemployment on the local business network and avoids a decline in the local tax base. In a sense, it offers a new legislative paradigm for solving national problems.

My own interest in employee ownership stems from research on the Israeli kibbutz. This research was funded by the Center for Metropolitan Studies, as most research in this area has been. The kibbutz was in fact the original inspiration for the legislative criteria emphasized in this bill. In Israel, with its 100,000 members in over 250 full-employment communities that are completely cooperative and employee-owned, the kibbutz is far and away the largest successful example of a voluntary democratic system that takes care of the relationship between mental health and the economy. As our society becomes so fragmented that a centralized federal government can no longer solve our social and economic problems, we must look to modest examples like the kibbutz for a solution based on voluntary citizen cooperation. Strongly embedded in the Israeli union movement and its institutions, the kibbutz is independent of government subsidies for welfare, unemployment, and many other social services. In our current and impending times of social and economic distress and government pull-back, such solutions are likely to assume a crucial importance. The present employee-ownership legislation represents the first appearance on the Congressional agenda of this recognition.

In this conference the issue of justice has never really been raised. Yet, some seventy members of the House of Representatives consider justice a real issue here, and the companion bill in the Senate is supported by Senator Russell Long. I would like to describe this legislation in general terms, and then make clear its connection with the objectives of this conference. First of all, the bill proposes that the Department of Commerce monitor shutdown situations and then, by means of loans to employees or to community groups, help them to purchase the plant. The Economic Development Administration would also provide technical assistance to such groups—explaining the program and outlining the initial steps to its achievement. Justice is an issue here because we spend hundreds of millions of dollars every year so that the Small Business Administration, Farmers Home Administration, and the Department of Commerce can shore up businesses that are, for one reason or another, threatened with a shutdown. On the other hand, we spend very little to help workers and communities deal with a plant's closing once it occurs. So we have a situation of inequity, one that is persuading some of the members of Congress to support this legislation.

Gradually a pattern is emerging. Congressman Breckenridge has pointed out that "it has become clear that we cannot depend on big business for either the preservation or expansion of employment.'' A study made by the House Small Business Committee shows that from 1969 through 1976, our economy produced slightly over 9.5 million jobs, and the one thousand largest corporations contributed less than one percent of them. In this context, conglomerate acquisitions of small businesses may reduce the potential for employment growth. Therefore, part of this proposed legislation will have to do with encouraging those groups that may be willing to support employment growth. There is a current myth that the job loss occurs because the worker is a victim of his or her own inadequacy. In the same way, we might assume that a plant shutdown occurs because the plant has failed in a strictly economic sense. Some research, as we have said, however, indicates that in fact a plant may close its doors because of an unacceptable profit margin. For example, Sperry Rand (which was studied by Whyte), closed their library furniture factory in Herkimer, New York, not because it wasn't making a profit, but because it wasn't making a profit large enough for the conglomerate that Sperry Rand hoped to build. Some of the larger macro-structural features involved in job loss and plant shutdown will merit further discussion.

In this conference an overblown attachment to convention has surfaced, with the assumption that the rules of job loss in this society all follow the same laws. This has led to an overemphasis on the effects of job loss on the individual, and on the subsequent problems to be dealt with. There may, however, be situations in which job loss need not be experienced *at all,* and the loss of social factors associated with work (not the least of which are the support group, involvement in a union, seniority, and so on) cannot be readily assessed statistically. Definitions of various phases of our research may in fact favor the status quo, tending to excuse persons and groups from responsibility for their own actions. Also, as you will see, job loss—and especially in cases of plant closings—should be seen in the larger context of economic and social developments. If we have no wish to be a part of an academic group that is lagging behind Congress in its conservatism, we should be aware of what is happening in Washington. Since this legislation was introduced, there has been considerable excited support from Congress and even some studied expressions of interest from the White House Domestic Policy staff.

When seventy members of Congress, the head of the Senate Finance Committee, and the staff of a major economic committee of the Congress all find themselves interested in the ways in which alternative forms of ownership can help to save jobs, reduce government dependence, and promote employment and community stability, it is not encouraging that our discussions here should center on the status quo. Will the status quo of mounting unemployment, accompanied by the expansion of those long term conditions that cause and feed it, respond to an assumption that it is realistic to hope that unemployment research will lead to new remedial government programs? I think not. The premise that the academic community will define the problem, ascertaining the crucial correlations and areas of intervention, so that the government can create innovative bureaucratic solutions is no longer valid. In a sense, the members of Congress have left the academic community behind, in that they recognize that problems must be defined but that their solutions must be attainable by citizen, local, and cooperative endeavors, thus emphasizing indigenous systems of social support, local self-reliance, and resources released through social and economic cooperation. Such endeavors will increase human motivation and productivity by recognizing that a citizen has a stake in ownership settings and in participation in decision making. True, this is uncharted territory, yet its principles are based on values more in line with our Constitution than are bureaucracies, problem-defining hierarchies, and hand-outs.

It is important that we generate policy recommendations that take into account these new assumptions. The Subcommittee on Economic Stabilization of the House Banking Committee held hearings on this matter on November 20, 1978 and February 27, 1979. Research presented there will prevent the Congress from simply acknowledging a new idea, forgetting that the widespread effects of job loss or mental health, not just on the economy, must be considered when similar hearings are held.

Second, in terms of research, we are in a real dilemma. Because this kind of program lends itself to impressionistic persuasions, you might say that this is one reason why we have obtained so many sponsors in a short period of time. People are searching for new ideas. But the point is that the federal government keeps no record of plant shutdowns. *Dun and Bradstreet* keeps the record, but the actual number of workers affected is the only important variable that is omitted from that record. We need responsible research on the results of plant shutdowns and migration: effects on the family, on the individual, on the community. We believe that individual and community suffering follows, and that suffering can be construed in the social-psychological terms we are considering. But, on the other hand, it can be interpreted in a more structural sense; that is, in terms of a basic injustice, a basic inequality, something that we can't pick up at .001 level of significance but something we can clearly recognize. We don't know how much of the population is being affected by plant shutdowns, because government researchers have not been funded to work in this area. So that an important element of these and further hearings is the presentation of a coherent research agenda to the Congress on this issue. It is crucial that we not remain tied to our old agendas and thus force a situation where new legislative initiatives are begun, defined, and carried through in this area with little benefit from the research method. But you can see that this means a reorientation. It may not have been logical to study so many facets of unemployment for so long without examining the causes of plant closings and the grave cost to the economy of the increased federal dependence—individual and family suffering and multiplied community reactions. Without national statistics, the shutdown problem demands that our research take a more problem-oriented approach. Had we defined the problem of job loss for the members of Congress in light of the obvious lack of government resources for intervention we now expect in the coming decades, our research might now be more in the mainstream of our legislative work. Employee ownership is a new idea in the U.S., and it is grossly understudied. We do not know, for example, what factors make the difference between success and failure in situations of employee ownership. We have not adequately assessed the importance of social participation in management and of the development of a truly democratic organization that will make employee ownership yield a higher quality of working life. Whyte has continually pointed to the fact that employee-owned firms have failed in the United States because economic success has often been accompanied by an inability to cope with the social evolution of the organization.

Third, I think we need to know the effect of economic dislocation, not only on the individual and on the family and on the informal systems of social support, but on formal systems of social service. No matter what our present discussions center on, the Congress is going to be unwilling to foot the bill for comprehensive bureaucratic solutions to the kind of problem that concerns us. We must turn to the consideration of situations in which an alteration in social relations, mutualistic solutions, (what Kenneth Boulding calls unrequited transfers) can present us with a social policy option. It has been pointed out here that it will cost $75 million in the next three years for social services, welfare, unemployment compensation, and so on, if Youngstown Steel Sheet and Tube mill is not rescued. Given the fact that to rescue Youngstown Sheet and Tube may take $500 million with federal loan guarantees of only a fraction of that, the social overhead involved in this situation is sizable and the effect of a mutualistic solution like employee-community ownership, staggering. Youngstown, for complex reasons, may not fully succeed, but it illustrates the need. We should be seeking to establish those economic and social relations that will permit people to solve their own problems through self-reliance and cooperation, while involving the federal government only in an enabling role.[1]

The legislation under discussion is difficult to classify ideologically: it has support from conservative Republicans, from radical Democrats, and from liberals—the sign of a growing consensus on a number of issues not classifiable according to classic criteria. We need research to tell us what happens when you

1. It should be noted here that the Department of Housing and Urban Development has rejected proposals for these loan guarantees. At this time, July 1, 1979, it seems likely that the project to rescue Youngstown will not succeed. *Editors' note.*

404

enhance a social support system and encourage self-reliance and cooperation in solving of unemployment problems. We not only do not know the answer; we do not know how to bring such conditions about. But even as we try to fathom the meaning and effects of job loss, we have a responsibility to identify innovative approaches that may prevent it or, as long term alternatives, may help to reduce it.

16
STRATEGY AND POLICY

GAR ALPEROVITZ

As a preface to this discussion, I should indicate that while professionally I'm an economist, I am also by avocation a lay therapist. So the linkage of issues that is herein proposed is of particularly great concern. . . .

Although the title of this paper seems to stress strategy *and* policy, and although I'll refer to policy, I don't know how to talk about policy in the abstract; what I really think is important is *strategy*. There are a number of policies that one could choose in connection with resolving some of the issues we are considering, but often they are either utopian and illusory, or what I call "crackpot ameliorism." Policies can be good, or bad, or beside the point, unless you have a sense of what is strategic and what is not.

What we choose to work on, either explicitly or implicitly, depends upon all of us having an assumption about the context in which we are living and working, and thus about what is or is not strategic.

My first point is that I think most of us haven't got a clue about how to explicate the context—that we essentially "remember the future." Let me explain. What we think will happen, and therefore what is strategic, is in a very great sense a projection of the last period we lived through. It's so difficult and terribly trying to attempt to deal with the larger, contextual issues that we simply ride with the momentum of *past* intellectual and psychological precepts. We *remember* the future.

In my judgment—and we've been doing a lot of work on this—this is probably the single most inefficient, ineffective, and illusory way to think about the context we're now entering, and therefore to think about strategy, and finally to think about policy. It won't work. I believe that unless we clarify our assessment of where we're going, in explicit terms, we may be doing things that are beside the point, or worse.

I begin such an assessment with the basic judgment that the final quarter of the twentieth century which we and other advanced industrial societies are entering is almost certain to be radically different from what we have come to think of as the normal experience of our society. Now I want to elaborate on that, as it is a major way of breaking with the past.

The post-war boom, if you like, is over. Our particular advanced industrial capitalism is beginning to be encroached upon, first, by the fact that Germany and Japan have rebuilt and recaptured international markets. Our period of substantial hegemony in world markets is over. The trend is for more difficulties imposed by competition in the world economy, and that means dislocation, runaway firms, more imports, disrupted communities, and unemployment.

On another front, there has been a major change in world resource patterns, with accompanying political changes. Energy is the most obvious example: we are now experiencing a period of shortages which is novel in American history. The shortages are compounded by the political capacity of third world nations to organize these resources. What this means for the forecast is that we now must face additional new sources of instability, of shortage, and of changes in real income. The forecast in the final quarter of the century is for more rather than less of this. And this in turn means, given our failures to manage neo-Keynesian economics, inflation. It also means more unemployment because we don't know how to deal with inflation. It means a slowdown of growth and a loss of real income; it means personal insecurity; and finally it means family deterioration, because of the squeeze that inflation, higher taxes, unemployment (and the threat of unemployment) present to the family.

I think that, roughly speaking, on these two fronts—employment and inflation—we're likely to see more problems, of deeper severity, in the coming period and also slower growth, more decay, and the deepening failure of traditional policy mechanisms. Real income will be extracted from the family through the tax system and through higher prices, and the national need for more capital will be experienced in this fashion, by the individual American family directly, as resources are tightened.

Along with this, I would argue that we will see a continued deterioration of the ideology of American progress—both in the larger, societal sense, and in the sense of whether an individual any longer feels in himself or herself the great American dream of upward personal escape and hope. The frontiers of economic, continental, or intercontinental expansionism are being dramatically eroded, and my own assessment is that the final two decades of the century in which we'll live out our active lives will continue to destroy that particular illusion. There will be no way out, even though Jerry Brown and some other people are now looking for space colonies, literally, as a way to get more employment in California. I suspect that illusion, too, will go down—I hope rather quickly.

I'm trying to paint this with broad strokes as a precondition of a serious discussion of strategy. I think we first have to have a sense of context emerging in the wake of the larger economic forces that are moving in on us in the final quarter of this century. I'm an optimist, believe it or not; but I think the context has to be looked directly in the face, or else we will go in the wrong direction.

We are already seeing not only the extraction of resources from the family, but the increasing centralization of power. What this means is that the concept of economic planning, with very large centralized institutions (large public bureaucracies and large corporations) as a nexus, can only increase in the near term. We already have a substantial degree of national economic planning in energy. It is largely done through close cooperation of major energy firms and public bureaucracies, but the system is substantially planned. We also have it now, unproclaimed, in steel, under the new steel plan; it is coming forward now dramatically in transportation; agriculture is a substantially planned economy, as is the medical system—even if the word is not used. But, in fact, the combination of incentives, regulation, directives, administrative control, and qualifications attached to financing, *is* a planning system; and it is a system planned by very large institutions.

The other side of that coin is that it's being done for good reason. Not only is the system increasingly in need of rationalization, but the scarcity of resources forces, politically, the need to cut costs and waste, and this in turn helps put together tight planning systems which regulate more and more. So, too, do unsolved national problems (such as energy) force this issue of planning.

An additional side of the coin, as it were, is the individual as the cog, or as "that which is administered" by the planning system. I think this, too, is a trend which is likely to continue in the near term.

Such are some of the emerging tendencies. Yet tendencies are not the same as inevitabilities. The issue before us is: Is there any way to begin to think through things that matter in our own research which might relate to the emerging context (assuming the picture I have painted is not totally in error), and which, above all, might make a contribution to the solution of our common problems? We need to develop a sense of direction which will allow us to be not totally on the defensive. I think that much of what we do intellectually *is* defensive—it's a response to failures; it's a cleaning up in reaction to "problems." Even the unemployment research is, in a way, reactive to the dislocation phenomenon and the deepening unemployment.

While we *must* seek defensive reactions that contribute to the understanding of the need for defenses, such work does not reach to that part of human activity which bespeaks a positive initiative. I believe we must begin to act in ways which take the initiative for a set of affirmative goals which transcend the immediate reactive phenomenon.

Now that's very difficult. I would say, however, that virtually every advanced industrial country has in the last 15 years gone through a jolting, difficult, uneven process of reaction to inflation, dislocation, and centralization, and also has begun to reconstitute a positive, progressive, or leftward movement, too. The attempts abroad to build both from resistance to problems *and* from positive initiatives, halting as they are, very often have mixed decentralization and issues of conservation with old economic ideas, in ways which have not yet reached to the formal crystallization of a positive vision. Yet, there is a strengthening of groups which are attempting to look progressively beyond reform and amelioration to transformation of the economic system, with perhaps a lag, in this country, of, say, 15 years. It's a very slow and messy business. In other words, the dreary trends and first (conservative) reactions to the emerging context are not necessarily the end of the story; not at all. I would not be surprised (in fact I think it very likely) if, in the wake of failure, we begin slowly to build a new, longer term, positive politics. It is a politics which will be very different, in the final quarter of the century, from the politics of the post-war boom period which was governed by the success and progress of expansion. There is a need, if we are to build, to begin to contribute to a positive vision and positive strategy beyond the purely defensive in the emerging period.

Now what does this all mean to people like us, and how does this relate to the kinds of research issues which have been talked about at this conference?

First, it seems to me that if there is anything to the forecast I've offered, one thing one has to recognize is that the political strategies of the 1950s and 1960s are probably a dead end. For instance, unemployment *per se* is an issue which is, taken by itself, *passe*. This is not to say that we shouldn't be concerned with unemployment, but that in a couple of senses the concept *in general* is no longer a completely useful way to relate what individuals experience in personal life to the larger economic issues. Furthermore, politically, when the issue is posed this way, it is a minority issue of very small importance. This is sad but true. The issue of general unemployment does not relate the concerns of the most disadvantaged to the broader experiences of the vast majority. We are in danger, by focusing on unemployment alone, of over-simplifying and of doing what we did in the 1960s—which was to divide the society between, roughly, the tiny black minority and the vast white majority. That division, now along the lines of employed versus the unemployed, is roughly nine to one, perhaps eight to one. This way of characterizing our difficulties inherently forces those concerned to be strategically defensive. I do not mean that the issue of unemployment does not produce anxiety. It does, as does the *fear* of unemployment (and I don't know how much research work has really been done on *this,* but I know it's endemic: the feeling that you may be next, or your brother, or your uncle, or your neighbor, and "when is it going to hit my family?"). My main point is that unemployment as a *general* intellectual category is, in many ways, at a dead end. What I would substitute for it, and I think it absolutely crucial if we are to get beyond a defensive strategy, is a concept which *unites the vast majority in a common effort,* and *also* helps both those who are hurt the most and those who are hurt, but hurt less.

In this connection, what both our research and our political activity have suggested is that the historic concept of *community* is a terribly powerful intellectual and strategic category; probably the most powerful political category, I would argue, in the coming difficulties. It works in several ways. We've done a lot of work in Youngstown, Ohio, recently, where a New Orleans-based shipping company bought up a steel mill which, for generations, had been owned by people in that community. One day the New Orleans company announced three hours before closing that 5,000 people no longer had jobs. The multiplier minimally is two—the ripple effect moves it up to three. We had 15,000 jobs in Ohio which were probably affected by that decision. Family size minimally is three and a half so that on one day in September, "Black Monday" they call it, at least 50,000 people's lives were affected by a decision made in New Orleans.

Secondly, the small businessmen, the retailers, the school teachers, began to see the implications for their community. Mental health problems, racial tensions, marital problems, alcoholism—all increased. The economic base is sinking, and it will fall dramatically when the supplemental unemployment benefits and trade adjustment allowances run out and the recession strikes home.

That means, too, that the tax base goes down and taxpayer problems go up. The so-called conservatives who worry about taxes—seen not in the narrow blinders of right versus left but as members of the community who are concerned about the larger way in which capital is extracted through taxes—all of a sudden are now members of a community of common concern. The whole community—with one or two major exceptions, primarily the large steel companies governed by Pittsburgh and elsewhere—is a substantially unified group with a common concern transcending the historic divisions of left and right: all are in reality dramatically affected by the pulling of the plug on the local economy. Though there are exceptions, the notion that the community as a whole is in it together inherently unites.

In attempting to set up a community/worker-owned steel mill for 5,000 workers, what people in Youngstown want from Washington is capital and technical assistance, some purchasing of products, and market assistance. All these are part of a planning system. Despite the local decentralization aspect, there is no way out of it—it's a planning system which begins with the criterion of community health first and builds its way up to an aggregate of national full employment.

In this reversal of values, it poses a fundamental alternative to the other planning system, which now, nationally, is to eliminate steel capacity in steel towns like Youngstown. And in this sense, it helps us to begin to think of both strategy and policy in a concrete sense.

Youngstown has probably received much more national attention than other similar communities, but it is not a unique problem. I sometimes say that what has happened there is a dramatic heart attack. But throughout the Northeast, the upper Midwest, and many parts of the southern Midwest, a good part of the Southeast, and even the far West, there is a slower cancer of

412

communities being affected by the pull-out of firms, the shutdowns, the difficulties which hit with trade dislocation and environmental conflicts. The effects of generalized unemployment are seen as they are visited on *specific* communities. You find an economic cancer spreading which people understand destroys very directly the underpinnings of community life.

The great strategic issue before us is, as I have said, how to unify the larger grouping of us all, at least in a beginning way—of the community—of the vast majority, rather than merely the ten percent.

I want to relate this to the contextual issue, and emphasize it. In the coming era of deepening economic difficulties, and in a period when the traditional neo-Keynesian economic solutions cannot work—or as President Kennedy used to say, in a period when the high tide of full employment no longer raises all the boats, because there is no such thing as the high tide of employment (and lots of leaky boats)—*in this context,* the experience of selected communities being wiped out, with no national solutions being offered, some form of Youngstown is likely to become the common day-to-day experience of increasing numbers of citizens. Hence, the experience of the community as "in it together" is bound to grow. And, the possibility of beginning to develop new strategies from this basic experience is thus before us.

Look around the country. It is amazing how quickly people understand. It is not difficult to understand what I'm talking about. It is deep in the experience of ordinary citizens, and not hard to talk about—the feeling that maybe your community will be next, in fact, maybe it's already been hit. In particular, this is clear to religious groupings—for example the ministers, priests, and rabbis who have been involved in Youngstown. Now if you're in a context in which this is likely to be a growing experience, and in which the traditional solution of "full employment" is blocked, then the context sets for us the strategic problem of how to deal with communities. Politically, it also presents the solution to the problem of how to transcend the categories of minorities versus majorities; we are able to reach toward the much more inclusive notion of community—and within that concept, a proportionately expanded support for those most disadvantaged.

Economically, this poses the concrete issues of jobs, of a productive economy, and of the targeting of economic strategies to very specific local communities—and this, in itself, also poses the question of some form of planning. There's no way you can do what is needed without it. However, if you're going to produce *community* full employment rather than simply full employment nationally, it is of strategic importance to note that what the community needs is so obvious that even traditional conservative groups must demand in Youngstown what amounts to national economic planning *based on* the needs of the local community.

So the context forces the very fundamental case for planning, and it reduces it to some very basic local and moral criteria which ought to be part of the understanding of our politics and our general policies in coming years. The fundamental criterion of the kind of planning we need is the health of our communities.

I am also convinced that politically it is very important to speak not simply negatively but of the positive goals of decent communities. Here let me discuss briefly the related issue of positive mental health. Some of you may have read Studs Terkel's book *Working*. It opens with a steelworker who tells you about the degradation of life as a mule, as he calls himself. The book closes with a wonderful discussion by a fireman. He talks about his work as a public servant and as a member of a community of work and a community of service in the most fascinating, unalienated, non-anomic way—in ordinary, day-to-day American prose—about what it means to do something with people who care, of a serving life, of dealing with something a community obviously needs. To read that day-to-day prose is to offer yourself a sense of what positive mental health is all about.

Again, I don't know how much research work can be done here, but I have argued in a prior presentation that one of our major tasks is the elaboration of the elements of what might be incorporated in a *positive* view of what would be required for true mental health. It is enough to have jobs? Jobs which have meaning? Or what does it mean to have a job which makes a contribution? What does it mean not to make napalm but to be a fireman? What is the contribution to mental health when one begins to consider factors that go beyond *how* to make decisions at the workplace to *what* the product is, to whether or not it poisons the air, to whether or not one is contributing in a positive way to the ongoing development of a decent society?

So limited is our vision in America, these days, that these questions come as surprises, or not at all in practice. I beg to remind you that some two-thirds of the world faces such questions constantly when it thinks about economic development. I am convinced that in the next ten years these kinds of issues are likely to deepen in our own discussion. But we need to have a vision so we can begin to direct serious professional work at what it really means to develop a positive concept of mental health in this larger sense.

Ultimately, the issue is both individual and collective: we need to think not merely of how to prevent future Youngstown's, but how to build positively in all our communities. It is terribly important. And I think that it's all very practical. What we found through our Youngstown experience is that the deeper value issues—the issues of community, whether a decent job is there, whether one participates—are also terribly powerful economic and political forces. They are not utopian. There is nothing as practical as unifying a community around a set of values that people share which allows them to act together.

I would say more broadly (here I am being an historian) that unless we are able to piece together what it takes to think intelligently about a new positive direction, we are probably always going to be on the defensive; and in the context we're facing, we will lose. It will be a bleak future. So I think it's terribly practical to begin to develop a concrete vision. I don't think we're going to do what is necessary without this kind of work. So I would divert some intellectual attention, at least, to this task.

I've said enough to give you a feeling for the kind of contribution that I think needs to be worked on. Now I want to give a little warning about some of the difficulties, and then briefly elaborate a series of propositions for discussion.

One difficulty is that politicians seem necessarily to grasp onto every new fad. It is *our* task to let them see the potential dynamic of the community theme. I've spent a lot of time with very high-level people in the White House who "know all the arguments," and will do "what they can." They will use some rhetoric and take a little piece of something, and maybe a couple of secondary actions—and all this is very important. It offers some legitimacy. People sense the need for community, the need for decent responses.

In addition to the concept of community—or community full employment, or community stabilization (as the Kostmayer legislation calls it), or the health of community, or the economy of a community—being strategic, in the emerging context, I would suggest that there are also two critical economic and two political, personal, and institutional questions. Very briefly, the first of these has to do with inflation.

Inflation is indeed a concern of the vast majority. It is an issue which intellectually has been virtually dominated by conservative thought, yet it is an issue which strikes most families, directly, most of the time. Garry Wills' book *Nixon Agonistes* gives a very vivid portrayal of the way inflation undercuts family security and defines the context in which resentment occurs in an amorphous, all-encircling way. We would be guilty of selective disattention were we to think the economy is not doing this steadily all about us right now.

One key pressure which supports a budget-cutting, scapegoating politics is inflation. In rereading the history of the Weimar Republic (and I do not think America is in the Weimar period), it is very instructive to see what inflation does to the psychology of the ordinary citizen. What it does is to open personality structures to insecurity, to demagogic solutions politically, to racism. The intellectual questions which are posed by this phenomenon we hear very little about in the academic world these days; yet I think they are central questions as to whether we can make a serious political response to the coming economic context. So I urge great attention to them, and particularly to inflation in the things that matter most, to the basic necessities of life—food, housing, health care, energy—not *general* inflation, not inflation of private jet airplanes or of the "Phillips curve." The rising cost of things that families experience directly in effect shapes a substantial part of the anxiety patterns of these families, and is an absolutely essential concern.

I think, also, and here I speak politically again, that there are ways to talk about controlling inflation in the basic necessities of life which transcend the Phillips curve, and get you out of the majority-minority bind. Inflation is a uniting issue, and it is an issue of great egalitarian concern if properly posed. A progressive strategy which attempts to control inflation in the necessities of life, in fact, unites the vast majority. The targets of that strategy end up to be energy firms, major agribusiness concerns, the medical complex (and some insurance firms), and interest rates and developers. But a strategy based on controlling inflation in the necessities unites the vast majority, rather than splitting them along the lines of the poor versus the unemployed. Nor does a specific demand that energy prices be controlled lead to budget-cutting as an illusionary answer to generalized inflation. And, by stressing common equity, it builds towards common purpose, hence, community.

The second area is also economic, but it has to do with whether or not the vision of conservation (rather than consumerism) can be seen as a way to organize not only economic phenomena but personal life and attitudes as well. The growing conservation movement, the ecology movement (which I remind you was a conservative movement originally and has now been taken up by people who don't consider themselves conservative), is again a uniting force and terribly important in the period of scarcity in the final quarter of this century. Whether or not people are bombarded constantly by an economy which requires them to satisfy their needs (or thought-to-be needs), or anxieties by consumption and ever more purchases (and thereby squeezes the family budget because of the need to purchase those things as bad proxies for psychological satisfaction); or whether we can begin to look more directly at the phenomenon of limited resources and develop strategies to address it, is the key question. To articulate the psychological issues is a requirement, ultimately, of a serious response.

The final two emerging issues of the new context have to do with the steady expansion of individual responsibility in economic activity, and with democracy itself. We see the possibility of a new role for the individual in the worker self-management, the worker-community movement, the co-ops, the food-buying clubs, etc., in a variety of attempts to get the individual rather than the giant institution more involved in actual decision making in economic affairs. I would urge that more work be done on the positive contribution that this can make in people's lives—self-management, and so forth, not only in the economy but as one aspect of the reconstitution of positive mental health.

Another way to state this is that there is a very great need to extend participation to economic issues. It is more important, more dramatic, as we enter a period of increasing centralization and a potential for repression. The only way to turn the trend around is through a careful extension of democracy to the economy—defining the issues in their widest, majoritarian sense, and carefully articulating in our research the linkages between these purposes.

The last proposition is somewhat more general. Our particular advanced, industrial capitalism is the only one in which the working class is substantially (rather than marginally) divided along racial lines. Let me pose the race issue in its most dramatic form: it isn't just that black people are being dealt with inequitably. Because of the numbers, it is easier in this country than in most others to split the vast majority by accentuating racial differences *in a context when there is dramatic need for scapegoats.*

What we're really saying is that in the context we're entering, one of the absolutely fundamental requirements is to build a vision and a strategy which unite the vast majority. If this is so, then what we call research and programs must relate to that need. A fundamental, not a secondary, question is how to unite the vast majority in a context in which scapegoating is inevitable, and in which the vast majority is racially split. So that inherent in the issue of community and the issue of basic necessities of life is the issue of unifying the vast majority around common positive goals. We must find ways in which to deal *both* with the needs of every day life of the majority *and* the needs of the dispossessed and alienated. A requirement for a program is that it systematically begin to bridge these needs, in an alliance sense and a programmatic sense. To look at only one or the other is to miss the central political problem of the larger context. *Within* the individual, the question of meaning and purpose, I hold, turn on whether what one personally does relates to larger, meaningful, positive goals shared by others.

Those are the basic propositions: the need for community and economic health, and programs that might make this real; the need for dealing with inflation in a way that unites the vast majority around values, around the basic necessities of life; the recognition that conservation is a requirement that we must begin to factor into our economic and psychological research and programs; the need to deepen individual responsibility; and finally, the extension of democracy, both to the politics and to the economic system.

Now, I agree this is a tall order. If the assessment I have offered of the emerging context is at all realistic, and if the assessment of the initial responses of greater conservatism, if not inevitable, at least in the near term, is at all realistic, then one of the primary guidelines for our common activity must be to find a way to unify us further in common purpose. This is another way to say what I've already said: that we must begin to see our research and our politics united along what's important and strategic and what is not. So I urge upon us all as creators of the new ideology—craftsmen, architects, as it were—to look at how indeed we can find ways to work together to construct research and strategies that reach out from the difficult, defensive tasks to build, positively, toward more interpersonal and community relationships.

If it is true that we must hang together or hang separately, then the construction of this community of enterprise is also critical. It is very difficult for all of us, particularly when we do research, because we are used to doing our own thing and not finding ways to link our work.

This conference provides one way to begin. So I'm offering that as a challenge in our *own* lives and not in the abstract: learning to work together must itself be on our general research agenda if we are—to return to my topic—to achieve strategy and, finally, programs which in fact deal with the realities of this new and most difficult period in our economic history.

The alternative is political, moral, and, finally, personal irrelevance to the concerns of the vast majority of our fellow citizens.

CONTRIBUTORS

Gar Alperovitz
Co-Director of the National
Center for Economic Alternatives
Washington, D.C.

Ivar Berg
Professor of Sociology
Chairman, Department of
Sociology
The University of Pennsylvania
Philadelphia, Pennsylvania

Joseph R. Blasi
Lecturer in Education
Harvard University
Cambridge, Massachusetts

M. Harvey Brenner
Associate Professor of Health
Services Administration
The Johns Hopkins University
Baltimore, Maryland

Robert D. Caplan
Associate Research Scientist
Institute for Social Research
The University of Michigan
Ann Arbor, Michigan

Ralph Catalano
Associate Professor of
Social Ecology
Public Policy Research
Organization
The University of California
Irvine, California

Sidney Cobb, M.D.
Professor of Community Health
and of Psychiatry
Brown University Program
in Medicine
Providence, Rhode Island

George C. Curtis, M.D.
Professor of Psychiatry
Research Scientist
Mental Health Research Institute
The University of Michigan
Ann Arbor, Michigan

David Dooley
Associate Professor of
Social Ecology
Public Policy Research
Organization
The University of California
Irvine, California

Louis A. Ferman
Professor of Social Work
and Research Co-Director
Institute of Labor and
Industrial Relations
The University of Michigan-
Wayne State University
Ann Arbor, Michigan

Marc Fried
Professor of Psychology
and Director of the Laboratory
for Psycho-Social Studies
Boston College
Boston, Massachusetts

John Gardner
Instructor of Economics
Dartmouth College
Hanover, New Hampshire

Jeanne Prial Gordus
Assistant Research Scientist
Institute of Labor and
Industrial Relations
The University of Michigan-
Wayne State University
Ann Arbor, Michigan

James S. House
Associate Professor of Sociology
and Associate Research Scientist
Survey Research Center
Institute for Social Research
The University of Michigan
Ann Arbor, Michigan

Michael Hughes
Department of Sociology
Vanderbilt University
Nashville, Tennessee

Robert L. Kahn
Program Director, Institute for
Social Research and Professor
of Psychology
The University of Michigan
Ann Arbor, Michigan

Stanislav V. Kasl
Professor of Epidemiology,
Department of Epidemiology
and Public Health
Yale University School
of Medicine
New Haven, Connecticut

Joan H. Liem
Assistant Professor
of Psychology
The University of
Massachusetts at Boston
Boston, Massachusetts and
Co-Director, Work and
Unemployment Project
Boston College
Boston, Massachusetts

G. Ramsay Liem
Associate Professor
of Psychology and
Co-Director, Work and
Unemployment Project
Boston College
Boston, Massachusetts

Peter Marris
Professor of Social Planning
School of Architecture and
Urban Planning
The University of California,
Los Angeles
Los Angeles, California

S. M. Miller
Professor of Sociology and
of Economics
Boston University
Boston, Massachusetts

CONFERENCE PARTICIPANTS

Saul Blaustein
The W.E. Upjohn Institute
for Employment Research
Kalamazoo, Michigan

Sally Bould
The University of Delaware
Newark, Delaware

David Caplovitz
The City University of
New York Graduate School
New York, New York

John Dixon
Consultant
Washington, D.C.

Robert Foster
Department of Labor
Washington, D.C.

Marcia Freedman
Columbia University
New York, New York

Susan Gore
The University of Massachusetts
Boston, Massachusetts

Gerald Gurin
The University of Michigan
Ann Arbor, Michigan

M. Lieberman
National Institute of
Mental Health
Rockville, Maryland

Elliot Liebow
National Institute of
Mental Health
Rockville, Maryland

Lewis Long
National Institute of
Mental Health
Rockville, Maryland

Joan Schulman
National Institute of
Mental Health
Rockville, Maryland

Eliot Sclar
Columbia University
New York, New York

Elaine Selo
The University of Michigan
Ann Arbor, Michigan

Richard Shore
Department of Labor
Washington, D.C.

Richard Wakefield
National Institute of
Mental Health
Rockville, Maryland

George Weber
National Institute of
Mental Health
Rockville, Maryland

E. Earl Wright
The W.E. Upjohn Institute
for Employment Research
Kalamazoo, Michigan

Barbara Zvirblis
The University of Michigan
Ann Arbor, Michigan